IMAGINING PALESTINE

IMAGINING PALESTINE

Cultures of Exile and National Identity

Tahrir Hamdi

I.B. TAURIS
LONDON • NEW YORK • OXFORD • NEW DELHI • SYDNEY

I.B. TAURIS
Bloomsbury Publishing Plc
50 Bedford Square, London, WC1B 3DP, UK
1385 Broadway, New York, NY 10018, USA
29 Earlsfort Terrace, Dublin 2, Ireland

BLOOMSBURY, I.B. TAURIS and the I.B. Tauris logo are trademarks
of Bloomsbury Publishing Plc

First published in Great Britain 2023
This paperback edition published 2024

Copyright © Tahrir Hamdi, 2023

Tahrir Hamdi has asserted her right under the Copyright, Designs and
Patents Act, 1988, to be identified as Author of this work.

For legal purposes the Acknowledgements on pp. x–xi constitute an
extension of this copyright page.

Series design by Adriana Brioso
Cover image © Majdi Fathi/NurPhoto/Corbis via Getty Images

All rights reserved. No part of this publication may be reproduced or transmitted
in any form or by any means, electronic or mechanical, including photocopying,
recording, or any information storage or retrieval system, without
prior permission in writing from the publishers.

Bloomsbury Publishing Plc does not have any control over, or responsibility for, any
third-party websites referred to or in this book. All internet addresses given in this
book were correct at the time of going to press. The author and publisher regret
any inconvenience caused if addresses have changed or sites have ceased
to exist, but can accept no responsibility for any such changes.

A catalogue record for this book is available from the British Library.

A catalog record for this book is available from the Library of Congress.

ISBN:	HB:	978-1-7883-1340-7
	PB:	978-0-7556-4941-9
	ePDF:	978-0-7556-1784-5
	eBook:	978-0-7556-1783-8

Typeset by Integra Software Services Pvt. Ltd.

To find out more about our authors and books visit www.bloomsbury.com
and sign up for our newsletters.

In memory of

my father, Khalil Hamdi

and
my brother, Hamdi K. Hamdi

If the olive trees knew the hands that planted them, their oil would have become tears

CONTENTS

List of Figures	ix
Acknowledgements	x

INTRODUCTION	1
Imagining Palestine: Defining the concept	1
Beginning with Palestine: The historical context	17

Chapter 1

THE RESTLESS SPIRIT: PALESTINE THEORIZED	27
Said's (Post) catastrophic theoretical oeuvre	27
Theorizing resistance literature: Ghassan Kanafani's contribution	48

Chapter 2

EXILE IS THE WORLD INSIDE: THE POETRY OF RESISTANCE AND SOLIDARITY	55
Exile is the world inside: Darwish, Said and identity in exile	55
On the poetry of besiegement and resistance: Mahmoud Darwish's 'state of siege' and other poems	62
On the poetry of solidarity: June Jordan, Suheir Hammad, Darwish, Adonis, Roger Waters and the Trio Joubran, John Trudell and Lee Maracle	75
On imagining victory: Mourid Barghouti's 'midnight'	103

Chapter 3

WRITING SELF, WRITING NATION IN THE MEMOIR AND THE NOVEL: PALESTINE NARRATED	115
The Palestinian story must be told	115
Said's personal and collective exilic out of placeness	117
The difficulty of representation in the memoir and the novel: Out of place and out of time in the works of Kanafani, Susan Abulhawa, Radwa Ashour and Mourid Barghouti	127

Chapter 4

WRITINGS ON THE WALL	163
Palestine writes on walls and in notebooks: Revolutionary imaginings	163
Olive trees: Uprooting and bitterness: Barghouti and Hamdi K. Hamdi, the intertwining of life, literature and science	166
Drawings on the wall: Naji al-Ali	171
Palestinian song, dance and revolution: From heritage to resistance	179

Conclusion
CONTINUING THE CONVERSATION: PALESTINE, A LIVING CAUSE   197

Notes   212
Bibliography   217
Index   229

FIGURES

4.1	No Reconciliation, No Negotiations, No Recognition – 1948 Refugees[1]	173
4.2	The Cemetery of Exile	175
4.3	The Death of the Artist	176
4.4	Leila Khaled, a Palestinian Icon: Don't Forget the Struggle	177

ACKNOWLEDGEMENTS

Were I not from there, I would have trained my heart to nurture there deer of metaphor ... So carry your homeland wherever you go, and be a narcissist if need be ... .

(Darwish, 2007: 177)

This book was inspired by the bravery and courage of the Palestinian people, who, against all odds, continue to struggle for a free Palestine from the river to the sea. Palestine has always been a very important part of my life. At birth, I was named Tahrir, liberation in Arabic. I have always felt that I need to live up to my name and to carry Palestine with me wherever I go, and so it is and will always be. My father, Khalil Hamdi, never stopped talking about Palestine, even to his last breath, and with this book, I am continuing this conversation.

I am truly grateful to all the great intellectuals, scholars and activists who helped me with their brilliant conversation and advice. My interviews with them in the concluding section have greatly enriched this book, and here I would like to mention Ibrahim Aoude, Leila Khaled, Rami Siklawi, Nur Masalha, Ilan Pappe, Ramzy Baroud, Steven Salaita, Jamal Nassar, Terri Ginsberg and Refaat Alareer. The great Leila Khaled, a remarkable woman and the face of the Palestinian revolution, has been a great inspiration to me during the writing of this book. The valuable advice of Patrick Williams and Lindsey Moore is so greatly appreciated.

I offer my heartfelt gratitude to the wonderful team at *Arab Studies Quarterly*, especially our editor Ibrahim Aoude and assistant editor Rami Siklawi, who have been amazing in giving me advice, support and friendship every step of the way. And to Liana Petranek, associate editor at *Arab Studies Quarterly* and a great intellectual whose voice of solidarity tirelessly echoes across the seas to reach a tortured, but resistant Palestine loud and clear – Palestine hears you, Liana, and echoes back its love.

I would also like to express my sincere gratitude to Suha Ghoul for her constant support, friendship and great humanitarianism.

I am particularly grateful to the wonderful staff at I.B. Tauris and Bloomsbury for their professionalism, especially Rory Gormley and Yasmin Garcha, whose advice has greatly improved this book. Your choice of a cover for this book is immaculate. I also sincerely thank Dharanivel Baskar for his brilliant follow-up.

I wish my brother, Hamdi, had lived long enough to see the publication of this book, but, alas, it was not meant to be. Still, your spirit is here, dear brother – in fact, on every page of this book. I hope this book is as revolutionary as you wanted it to be. So much love and appreciation goes to the people who supported me the most – my mother Naziha, so pure of heart, and like a true Palestinian mother, fiercely committed to the cause; my husband Dirar, who has always been my biggest fan and supporter; my beautiful children, Qais, Hawazen and Zeid, who represent the new generation of Palestinians that will never forget Palestine; my loving siblings, Lama and Yasar, whose friendship, unconditional love and support without which I could never survive and all my wonderful nieces and nephews who give me hope in a more just future that this book represents. To all my students, past and present, I hope you remember to always fight for the oppressed in this world, and to keep talking about and imagining Palestine.

INTRODUCTION

Imagining Palestine: Defining the concept

But, I tell myself, no reality cancels out imagination. Reality waylays us quickly but gives rise in the mind to further imagining. I come close to asking myself if there is a 'truth' outside the human 'imagination' . . . .

(Barghouti, 2011: 91)

We, who have no existence in 'the Promised Land', became the ghost of the murdered who haunted the killer in both wakefulness and sleep, and the realm in-between, leaving him troubled and despondent. The insomniac screams: Have they not died yet? No, because the ghost reaches the age of being weaned, then comes adulthood, resistance and return. Airplanes pursue the ghost in the air. Tanks pursue the ghost on land. Submarines pursue the ghost in the sea. The ghost grows up and occupies the killer's consciousness . . . . .

(Darwish, 2011: 68)

The ghosts of Palestine have already been weaned and have by now reached adulthood. Resistance was born at the very point of rupture, which has been called Nakba or catastrophe and ethnic cleansing,[1] and now the dispossessed are preparing for their return. Palestine and Palestinians will not go away despite the warplanes, tanks, submarines and Mahmoud Darwish might have added a variety of internationally banned weapons such as white phosphorous (Abou Jalal, 2014). All of these weapons of mass *human* destruction are meant to uproot the very idea of Palestine from its people's consciousness. And the harder the killer tries, the more vivid become the imaginings of Palestine and the 'return of the wandering soul as if nothing had happened' (Darwish, 2003: 161). As in the first epigraph above, for Mourid Barghouti, it is the powerful truth of the imagination that can shape a future reality. Palestine is alive and well in the Palestinian psyche, but where is Palestine today?

For the modern myth-makers, as Darwish points out, Palestinians have no existence in the 'Promised Land', which according to the Old Testament was a land promised to the Jews. It is important to point out here that Darwish is not saying that Palestinians do not have a historical presence on the land of Palestine. In fact, Palestinian existence in Palestine goes back thousands of years, a 'four thousand year history' as the title of Nur Masalha's book affirms (Masalha, 2018), and this is a historical and secular fact, not a myth-narrative based on sacred books, as poignantly articulated by Masalha:

> The history of Palestine, unlike the myth-narratives of the Old Testament, has multiple 'beginnings' and the idea of Palestine has evolved over time from these multiple 'beginnings' into a geo-political concept and a distinct territorial polity. The concept of Palestine is often approached in an abstract or ahistorical way, rather than as a contextualized representation of an entity whose (physical, administrative, territorial and cultural) boundaries have evolved and changed across three millennia.
>
> (2018: 8)

The multiple beginnings of which Masalha speaks, similar to Said's beginnings discussed below, are historical, secular and have a concrete existence in reality. These beginnings are also multiple in the sense that they represent *different* political and cultural histories (across time, here millennia) on the land of historic Palestine. Thus, there is no such thing as one pure, essential presence as narrated in the Old Testament of a mythical 'Promised Land', promised to a pristine Jewish people that remains of a pure, uncorrupted blood over thousands of years and who have 'returned' to their uninhabited 'Promised Land' that supposedly has been reserved for them by God under the banner of the European-based imperialist ideology of Zionism. Thus, the words, 'imagining Palestine', which appear in the title of this book do not refer to a Palestine or a Palestinian people who never existed, but to people who indeed existed *historically* and concretely on this land – they are not an abstract idea. This book proposes to imagine Palestine post the 1948 catastrophe, an imagining that means to reconstruct after catastrophe, after rupture, after annihilation, a picking up the pieces and beginning – again.

Palestine does not exist on the world map today. Only small parts of Palestine exist geographically: the occupied and severely decimated (by Israeli settlements) 'West Bank',[2] which is itself a very problematic naming. 'West of what' is a question that Palestinians should contemplate, especially when one considers that this is actually the eastern part of historic Palestine. The term 'West Bank', writes Mourid Barghouti, is an example of 'verbicide' that can lead to 'genocide'. By using a 'single word they redefine an entire nation and delete history' (*New Internationalist*, 2003). Another part of what remains is the 'open-air prison' of Gaza, also known as the Gaza Strip, which has been placed under a devastating siege by Israel, a land, air and sea blockade.

The majority of Palestinians vehemently believe in their *moral* right of return to the lands from which their now dead grandparents and parents were systematically, brutally and immorally expelled by Zionist gangs and terror organizations in order to make room for the establishment of Israel in 1948. This catastrophic event of devastating proportions is known to Palestinians as the Nakba. Thus, the Palestinian people's imagined return is not only to the so-called West Bank or Gaza Strip, which were occupied by Israel in 1967. Return, as represented by the old key on the cover of this book, means a return to all of Palestine, including 1948 Palestine, to Jaffa, Haifa, Acre, Safad, Ramla, Lydd, Beisan, Al-Majdal and others of course, a total of 536 Palestinian towns and villages that were ethnically cleansed of their inhabitants by Zionist militias and from which more than 750,000 Palestinians, about 80 per cent of the population at the time, according to a modest estimate, were forcibly expelled from their homes (Abu-Lughod and Sa'di, 2007: 3).

It seems that interest in Palestine is now picking up pace and energy in the post-millennial postcolonial field, which is definitely a step in the right direction and a moral attempt at redressing postcolonialism's deafening silence on Palestine in the twentieth century. While postcolonial studies has been rather silent on Palestine since its inception in the late 1970s with the exception of Edward Said (who is recognized by many working in the field today as its founding father after Said's publication of *Orientalism* in 1978), there have been some admirable contributions recently, such as Anna Ball's *Palestinian Literature and Film in Postcolonial Feminist Perspective* (2012), Anna Bernard's *Rhetorics of Belonging: Nation, Narration, and Israel/Palestine* (2013) and Lindsey Moore's *Narrating Postcolonial Arab Nations: Egypt, Algeria, Lebanon, Palestine* (2018). These British critics make convincing arguments for placing Palestine at the centre of the postcolonial debate. Ball, Bernard and Moore claim a space for Palestine within postcolonial studies whereby the Palestinian struggle is seen as resisting 'hegemonic colonial narratives by shifting the marginalized voices of the colonized from the peripheries to the centre of cultural consciousness' (Ball, 2012: 3). Bernard makes a poignant argument, which cautions against dismissing ideas on nation as poststructuralist theory (including postcolonial studies) has done, since for the most part the vast majority of anti-colonial liberationist struggles have all but ended in the twentieth century (2013: 7–8).

For contemporary poststructuralist and postcolonial theory, we are now in a post-national era where ideas on national liberation are dismissed, which, as Terry Eagleton insists, 'is to play straight into the hands of the oppressor' (1990: 23). Bernard argues postcolonialism's lack of interest in Palestine could be understood within this context of the general disinterest in the concepts of nation and national liberation in our post-national era (2013: 7–8), and Ball suggests that postcolonialism's disagreement on Israel's colonial status (2012: 4–6) could explain the silence on Palestine. Patrick Williams suggests that this silence on Palestine has much to do with the 'triumphs of the Israeli propaganda machine' (2010: 91) or the Zionist propaganda machine more generally, which has successfully established a harshly restrictive definition of anti-Semitism whereby even any statement that is critical of Israel is labelled anti-Semitic. This also means that any attempt to tell the Palestinian story (which means to expose Israel's consistent and systematic brutal crimes against the Palestinian people and their very existence as a people) will automatically be labelled anti-Semitic. In order to avoid this label, the vast majority of scholars working inside and outside the postcolonial realm have preferred to steer clear from the topic of Palestine. There is more discussion on anti-Semitism and Palestine a little bit later on in this introduction.

Why is it important to imagine/reimagine Palestine? Or perhaps a more basic question is what does it mean to imagine Palestine? First and foremost,

I will contextualize my answers to these questions within the scope of the very important work done on postcolonialism and Palestine by the well-known British critic, Patrick Williams, who I believe has been able to provide a uniquely perceptive understanding of both the aims of postcolonial studies, or perhaps more appropriately decolonial studies and the place of Palestine within it. In his important essay entitled, '"Outlines of a Better World" Rerouting postcolonialism', Williams argues that postcolonial studies needs to reroot and reroute, whereby rerooting means deepening the roots of the concepts of resistance and liberation within the field of postcolonial studies. Any movement away from resistance would mean abandoning 'one of the major justifications for postcolonial studies' (2010: 88). Rerouting, however, entails breaking the silence on Palestine, which Williams describes as the 'worst example of colonialism in the modern world' (2010: 91).

An important concept here, as put forward by Williams, is that postcolonialism must carry within it the impetus of making, imagining and creating a better world, especially the pressing case of Palestine in our modern era, which as Williams believes represents an 'ethical scandal' (92) for postcolonial studies. Williams very effectively quotes the Palestinian poet, Mahmoud Darwish, on the importance of standing with Palestine on this most ethical cause, which postcolonial studies should place at the very centre of inquiry and which would enable the outlines of a better world. For Williams, postcolonialism should be seen not as an 'achieved condition', but as an 'anticipatory discourse' (Williams, 2010: 93). Quoting Darwish, Williams writes, 'From this day on, he who does not become Palestinian in his heart will never understand his true moral identity' (2010: 92). Williams's ideas (and Adorno's before him) enable the true agency of a discipline, in this case postcolonialism and the more recent decolonial studies, to effectively counter what seems to be absolute Israeli power, aggression and brutality. In this way, the '"consummate negativity" of Israeli oppression' (Williams, 2010: 93) is faced by its opposite by means of which 'Palestinians ... begin to imagine a more utopian future' (ibid.).

It is within this context that imagining Palestine, as an anticipatory endeavour, becomes possible where Palestinian defiance and hope in a future, independent Palestine is just as strong, if not stronger, than Israel's brutal aggression and oppression. Thus, I am here proposing a multifaceted approach to Palestine, which combines previous approaches that include belief in the ethicality of the Palestinian cause within the scope of not postcolonial, but *decolonial* study and its anticipatory discourse. The anticipatory nature of the approach that I am introducing here is decolonial (rather than postcolonial) in order to emphasize an ongoing *process*, the not yet done, a revolution in the making, a liberation not yet achieved.

This also entails an emphasis on the necessity of bringing national struggle and national identity back into the discussion and urgent and utopian transnational solidarity with a just Palestinian cause. This endeavour requires combining 'old' and new approaches in order to respond to actual realities and not to merely repeat theoretical and abstract debates. All of these important nuanced approaches to Palestine contribute to not only imagining Palestine, but realizing an actual Palestine, thus bringing to an end one of the most, if not the most, oppressive and brutal regimes of our modern era. Israel is a brutal settler colony that was made possible by British imperialism and further enabled by the greatest state sponsor of terrorism of our times, the US government. The use of the name Israel in this book does not, in any way, serve to bestow legitimacy upon this apartheid settler colonial state, but serves only to facilitate familiarity of expression. Against all odds and superpower support of Zionist settler colonialism, the focus of this book is on imagining Palestine and the ongoing construction of Palestinian identity.

As Rashid Khalidi argues in his book *Palestinian Identity: The Construction of Modern Consciousness* (1997), the construction of Palestinian identity can be understood within the context of Benedict Anderson's concept of imagining a 'political community… imagined as both inherently limited and sovereign' (1983, [2006]: 6). As Anderson clearly argues, this imagining is a form of creation (ibid.). A nation is limited in the sense of it having specified boundaries, regardless of its size or population. Khalidi has perhaps made one of the most important interventions in the examination of Palestinian national identity to date with his book *Palestinian Identity*. In line with Anderson's ideas, Khalidi believes that a national identity is constructed, imagined and dynamic rather than essential and static (xi). Khalidi asks, 'When did a significant proportion of the Arab inhabitants of Palestine begin to think of themselves as Palestinians?' (145). For Khalidi, modern Palestinian consciousness began before the First World War, during the late Ottoman period and continued with great vigour after the First World War (154). An important argument that Khalidi makes is that Palestinian national identity began forming before the establishment of Israel. The historical process, argues Khalidi, is certainly the impetus for the formation or even one's awareness of an identity that would counter the 'other'. Palestinian national identity developed within the context of the colonizing 'other':

> There is a kernel of truth in these assertions: in some measure, as we have already seen, identity develops in response to the encounter with an "other." But for the Palestinians there were always other "others" besides Zionism: among them were the covetous European powers and the country's Turkish rulers before World War I, and the British Mandatory authorities and other Arab peoples after that.
>
> (154)

Colonization, invasion and foreign intervention before the First World War and dispossession and ethnic cleansing after 1948 all had the effect of consolidating Palestinian national identity. After the shock of crises and catastrophe, people are by necessity drawn together by pain and loss and made aware of their collective identity.

However, as Khalidi points out, Palestinian identity was long contested and rejected by much of the West (147), making the acceptance of even the mere existence of Palestinians a controversial issue in countries that accepted the Zionist narrative as the undisputed truth, especially in the United States and the UK (xxvi). Palestinian *national* identity has also been a source of contention even amongst Palestinians themselves with those who believe in a *national* definition of Palestinian identity within the context of Anderson's imagined communities and others who profess an exclusivist and extremist mindset and see identity in terms of an 'Islamic *umma*' (an Arabic word meaning community), such as '*Hizb al-Tahrir al-Islami*, the Islamic Liberation Party' (Khalidi 148) and even groups that are less radical and more mainstream, such as Hamas. However, even these Islamic groups have to contend with the contradiction in their own ideology and make-up. If their definition of identity is aligned with the idea of the wider Islamic *umma*, then why is it that their members are primarily Palestinian, as Khalidi notes? Khalidi writes:

> All subsume Palestinian nationalism within one or another form of Islamic identity, although all are primarily Palestinian organizations in terms of membership, organization, and goals, and it is not clear how they resolve the tension between their universalist Islamic message and the particularist Palestinian reality in which all of them are firmly grounded.
>
> (148–9)

Obviously, a *national* imagining of identities and communities within particular geographic borders is in direct opposition to that of an Islamic *umma*, which in this sense does not comprise an imagined community in Anderson's sense of the word (7). Having said this, however, one should be cognizant of the national Palestinian impulse present even within this Islamic discourse. Theoretically, however, an *umma* of Islam discourse is ironically similar to poststructuralist ideas of a post-national, borderless world, which as Eagleton rightly believes, as stated above, would be doing the colonizer's work.

Emphasizing an exclusivist religious discourse of the type we have seen recently in the Arab world (Iraq and Syria) is dangerous because it is uncompromisingly sectarian, destructive and violent. It also has the effect of de-emphasizing Palestine as a colonized land and emphasizing a paradoxically 'greater' Islamic *umma*/community that excludes certain Islamic sects and other religions as 'infidels' and 'heretics'. This destructive, exclusivist and sectarian discourse rather than an anti-colonial national discourse would, in the end, be doing the colonizer's bidding, separating the people of the region, even from the same country, according to their religions, sects and confessions.

It should be noted, however, that the Palestinian people's weekly Friday prayers at Masjid Al Aqsa (Al Aqsa Mosque) are not only religious acts, but necessary acts of resistance against brutal Zionist colonization. Relentless Israeli attacks against Masjid Al Aqsa and Israel's constant efforts to destroy this mosque and stop Muslims from praying there have united both Palestinian Muslims and Christians in resistance and *sumud* to protect this more than a 1,000-year-old Muslim holy site and the right of Muslims to pray there. *Sumud* is an Arabic word that translates into steadfastness; however, *sumud* has come to take on a particular kind of stoic Palestinian resistance in its diverse forms. Lena Meari defines *sumud* as a 'constant revolutionary becoming, opening up a possibility for an alternative regime of being, for an ethical-political relational selfhood' (549). Thus, the word *sumud* carries with it the ideas of a diversity and constancy of resistance acts and positionings.

In recent years, a new movement of women defenders of Masjid Al Aqsa has arisen and gained the collective support of the Palestinian community inside and outside occupied Palestine. These women call themselves *al murabitat*, an Arabic word meaning those who stay in place in defence of a place and cause. In an article entitled '*Murabata*: The Politics of Staying in Place', Sarah Ihmoud writes:

> I analyze the collective's praxis of *murabata* – the act of staying in place and defending sacred space – as one in a constellation of underexplored and undertheorized strategies of Palestinian feminist resistance, world-making and belonging. In doing so, I center Indigenous women's marginal position as a site of privilege for other kinds of knowing.
>
> (2019: 513–14)

In fact, this *murabata*, this revolutionary 'world-making' that is at once religious, national and feminist becomes a powerful space of resistance. These women's resistance is in staying in place in defence of Masjid Al Aqsa. *Al murabitat* gather at the Masjid everyday where they meet to read, pray and study and defend the holy grounds of Al Aqsa against Israeli incursions and the attacks of Israeli settlers.

As Ihmoud points out, 'the Haram al-Sharif³ became saturated with even more significance as a symbol of the Palestinian nation and its presence in Jerusalem' (514). Thus, protecting Masjid Al Aqsa or the Church of the Holy Sepulchre in Jerusalem/Al Quds is an essential part of the Palestinian national struggle. The Head of the Greek Orthodox Church in Jerusalem, the archbishop, Atallah Hanna, commenting on all those who come to defend Masjid Al Aqsa, said these 'heroes are defending the whole umma as they are standing up against the Israeli occupation, colonialism, oppression, and dictatorship' (*The Palestine Chronicle*, 2021). In fact, some Palestinian Christians, such as Raed Nasrallah from Nazareth, inspired by the *murabitat*, travel to Masjid Al Aqsa to take part in what they consider to be an essential act of resistance. Nasrallah points out, 'Masjid Al Aqsa concerns me as a Palestinian regardless of what my religion is because this is a historical site that represents the *sumud* of the Palestinians on their land' (my translation) (alarab. com, 16 April 2022). With the support of the Muslim and Christian Palestinian community, these women *murabitat* of Jerusalem/Al Quds have literally created, produced their own spaces of resistance, *murabata* and *sumud* against the relentless attacks of Zionist settler colonialism at Masjid Al Aqsa and elsewhere in occupied Palestine.

It is for this reason that an inclusive anti-colonial national discourse must be brought front and centre within the Palestinian context in opposition to a strictly exclusivist discourse that does not see in Palestine a central cause. The sectarian discourses, which were hyped by powerful Arab media outlets in the Gulf, made it possible for a Palestinian living in Gaza, to fight alongside the *Mujaheedeen* in Afghanistan against the former Soviet Union (at the behest of the CIA) in the 1980s or alongside the *Jihadis* in Syria a few years ago rather than fight the colonizer in occupied Palestine. A nation, then, is sovereign in terms of it being limited by specific geographic borders and makes up a community with 'deep, horizontal comradeship' (Anderson, 7). However, this comradeship does not, of course, mean that every member of the community knows every other member of this same community, but all members of this same community know that they share the 'image of their communion' (6). Anderson goes on to quote from different cultural products, such as novels and newspapers to illustrate how a group of people imagine their communion.

In addition to historically significant events that by necessity helped shape Palestinian national identity, Palestinian experience itself brings Palestinian communities in their different cultures of exile together. Khalidi uses the example of borders, airports and checkpoints, what he calls the 'quintessential Palestinian experience' (1). Palestinian identity is realized, writes Khalidi:

> in short, at any one of those many modern barriers where identities are checked and verified. What happens to Palestinians at these crossing points brings home to them how much they share in common as a people. For it is at these borders and barriers that the six million Palestinians are singled out for 'special treatment', and are forcefully reminded of their identity: of who they are, and of why they are different from others.
>
> (1)

Before these words which Khalidi wrote in his 2010 'Introduction' to the reissue of his book, Said poignantly captured this image of communion within the Palestinian context in his book *After the Last Sky* (1993 [1986]). This Palestinian communion and unity are more urgent than the imagined communities of other groups of people precisely because imagining Palestine has been systematically suppressed. The ethnic cleansing of Palestine has been denied, unrecognized and silenced by the dominant narrative, which to this day controls the global imagination, but this narrative is being slowly, but steadily, dismantled. Said captures the essence of an imagined Palestinian community in the following words:

> These intimate mementos of a past irrevocably lost circulate among us, like the genealogies and fables of a wandering singer of tales. Photographs, dresses, objects severed from their original locale, the rituals of speech and custom: Much reproduced, enlarged, thematized, embroidered, and passed around, they are strands in the web of affiliations we Palestinians use to tie ourselves to our identity and to each other.
>
> (14)

This web of affiliations as represented by these mementos, the most important among them for many Palestinian families, as in Said's representative family that occasioned his writing of the above words, are the keys to their homes in Palestine from which they were expelled by Zionist militias in 1948: "'Hold on to the keys and the deed," he told them, pointing to a battered suitcase near his bed …' (ibid.). Of course, whether or not this old rusty key will actually open the door of these Palestinians' old homes is beside the point – it is, most significantly, an emblem of their right to return to their ancestral homes, and this is a memory (or postmemory) that cannot be erased from the collective consciousness of new Palestinian generations. All of these Palestinian families, who are now dispersed all over the world, do not know each other, as Anderson would say, but 'in the minds of each lives the image of their communion' (6).

Anderson argues imagining a nation was made possible only after three 'fundamental cultural conceptions' lost their power and currency in our modern *historical* period. These include, firstly, no longer recognizing one particular language as a sacred bearer of ontological truth, and with this idea, we witness the deterioration of the 'great transcontinental sodalities of Christendom, the Islamic Ummah' …; secondly, the idea of society being organized around a divine leader or monarch and thirdly, antiquity's lack of distinction between cosmology and history (36). For Anderson, the idea of the imagined community was made possible by what he calls 'print-capitalism' (18), which enabled the spread of the concept of this 'new' and 'historical' (11) imagined community. It is interesting that the two examples Anderson gives of this print-capitalism are the proliferation of novels and newspapers, which as Anderson points out, are effective means for '"re-presenting" the *kind* [emphasis in original] of imagined community that is the nation' (25). This kind of re-presenting is possible in this historical (as opposed to divine) order. In a previous age, a universal religious community in Christendom and Islamic *umma* that emphasized a borderless universal community was based on absolute truth and divine power. Thus, this kind of absolutism does not allow for 're-presenting' as discussed by Anderson. 'Re-presenting' entails the idea of constructing and re-constructing, which is the very essence or the core of the whole process of imagining, inventing and constructing a new nation(al) identity/community.

A divine order, in this sense, would not allow for a reconfiguration or reformulation of the 'truth'. This, in fact, is the kind of 'truth' being presented to the world today in the form of Israel, the land divinely promised to the Jews by God. It is also important to point out here that this divine truth which separates the gentile from the Jew is similar to the kind of 'Daesh or ISIS-like' mentality that has recently arisen in Syria and Iraq and elsewhere in the Arab and Islamic world. 'Daesh' (as they are known in the Arab world) and 'ISIS' (as they are known in the rest of the world), Jabhat Al Nusra (the Nusra front), Jaish Al Islam (the army of Islam) and other groups are some of the extremist groups that have sprung up in the Arab region over the past decade. This particular image of the so-called new Islam, which comes with a whole repertoire of jihadi songs, dress and sectarian discourse, is not one that unites and includes, but rather, like Israel, one that excludes the other and can be seen as a replication of the kind of exclusivist ideology of Israel.

These new extremist groups have captured the imagination of thousands of people from all over the Arab and Islamic world over the past few years. These new sectarian groups were very heavily hyped and supported by massive petrodollar-run machinery, especially the most powerful Arab media outlets in the Gulf, such as *Al Jazeera*, based in Qatar and other Gulf media organizations, which function within the *American* sphere of influence (Cockburn, *Independent*, 'We finally know what Hillary Clinton knew all along…', 2016). Alongside this hype for the so-called Islamic state extremists of Iraq and Syria, the ideological state apparatuses (as theoretically described by Gramsci and Althusser) of Arab and Islamic countries in the region, such as mosques, universities, state-run media and others, put their full weight behind the Syrian 'revolution', for example. Divisive, sectarian discourse was (and still is being) systematically and consistently used against Iran and Lebanon's Hezbollah in an attempt to reconstruct a new enemy within the Arab/Islamic psyche (taking the place of Israel) and dividing the Arab region along these deeply exclusivist, sectarian lines 100 years after the Sykes-Picot Agreement between Britain and France in 1916, which divided up the Arab world into several states under either British or French mandates or spheres of influence.

Beyond Anderson's concept of imagined communities, imagining a decolonized, liberated Palestine is based on a specific 74-year-old historical event that saw the violent expulsion of a people from their land. It is for this precise reason that imagining Palestine is a *conscious act* of resistance and defiance, which involves the constant process of reconfigurations and reformulations of Palestinian national and cultural collective identity. This process, of course, involves deep knowledge of the cataclysmic event known as Nakba, but it is not only about recollecting a dead past or trying to tame a past trauma through the process of memory and postmemory as is the usual practice in trauma studies. The Palestinian experience is also not limited to Marianne Hirsch's concept of postmemory, which she describes as:

> the relationship that the 'generation after' bears to the personal, collective, and cultural trauma of those who came before – to experiences they 'remember' only by means of the stories, images, and behaviors among which they grew up. But these experiences were transmitted to them so deeply and affectively as to *seem* to constitute memories in their own right.
>
> (2012: 5)

While the 1948 Nakba or ethnic cleansing is part of the postmemory of the 'generation[s] after', the ethnic cleansing of Palestine is a continuing trauma. The Nakba, as the Palestinian poet Darwish has pointed out, is not a one-time catastrophic event, but a continuing catastrophe: 'The Israelis want to continue the Nakba. They want it to renew and repeat itself, as if the [Nakba] of 1948 and that is what they say had never ended' (Darwish qtd. in Williams, 2012: 30).

Similarly, the Palestinian poet Mourid Barghouti speaks of repeated historical pain (2011: 144). The 1948 Nakba is transformed on the ground into constant daily nakbas. For Palestinians, the Nakba is not merely based on memory or postmemory, but on a catastrophic daily existence of Palestinians living under occupation and in exile. Having said the above, however, does not mean the memory of the first generation of Palestinians is unimportant or useless – far from it. In the absence of 'official' Palestinian history or a simple 'what happened', the reliance on oral history (memory) is crucial to the accurate understanding of the past, what and how it happened in order to make it possible to imagine/reimagine a future Palestine. As very convincingly presented by Pappe in his seminal book, *The Ethnic Cleansing of Palestine* (2006), official history of how Israel was established in 1948 is deeply flawed precisely because this dominant narrative intentionally erased and silenced Arab sources and the oral history of the dispossessed Palestinians who witnessed the 'enormity of the crimes the [Zionist militias] committed' against them (2006: xv).

Almost every Palestinian household the world over has had at least one or two storytellers who have, by necessity almost, narrated to their children what happened in 1948 and after and my family was no different. On a personal level, Palestine existed only in the imagination for me, having visited it only once when I was forty days old as I was told. I heard about its olive and fruit trees, green hills, lazy and carefree lifestyle as vividly and humorously narrated to my siblings and I by my parents who were born in the village of Kharbatha Bani Harith on the outskirts of Ramallah. Palestine was kept alive for us by the many stories that were religiously narrated to us as we were growing up in Chicago in the 1970s and 1980s, thousands of miles away from my parents' beloved Palestine. Although my parents are from 1967 Palestine, the loss of Palestinian lands in 1948 was also their loss, and not long after the establishment of the Jewish state, Palestinian resistance was born.[4]

The beginnings of organized resistance as narrated below refer to the resistance that developed after the 1948 Palestinian dispossession or rupture. My father repeatedly narrated all of the following names and events to us as my siblings and I were growing up in Chicago. My father, Khalil Hamdi (born in 1932), a soft-spoken man who never liked the spotlight and preferred to work in the background, was one of the founders of the Arab Nationalist Movement (ANM), which represented the birth of the Palestinian revolution and active resistance against Israel. My father was positioned in Amman, Jordan in the early 1950s (around 1952); he, like other Arab nationalists at the time, had big dreams – dreams about Arab unity and the liberation (in Arabic *tahrir*, which is the name I was given) of Palestine – all of Palestine, from the river to the sea. As reported to me in a conversation with Khalil Hamdi, the ANM regional command of Jordan and Palestine from the early 1950s to the mid-1960s comprised Khalil Hamdi (Amman), Subhi Ghosheh (Jerusalem), Mohammed Rabee (Ramallah) and Ahmed Al Asis, who was in charge of the military wing of the ANM in Jordan and Palestine. According to the well-known Palestinian writer and political researcher, Saqr Abu Fakhr, the ANM regional command of Jordan and Palestine held their first conference at the beginning of 1965 at Ghor Aljiftlik and voted for the following individuals as their leadership command: 'Subhi Ghosheh, Mohammed Rabee, Hamdi Mattar, Khalil Hamdi, Ghassan Qamhawi, Omar Al Sheikh, Tawfiq Ramadan [and] Amhed Al Asis' (2003: 43).

In the second chapter of his book entitled, 'The Beginning of the Armed Struggle and the Appearance of Combat Organizations', Abu Fakhr points out that it was during this particular conference that the leadership decided to begin *fidayee* operations, officially marking the beginning of the armed struggle for the liberation of Palestine (ibid.), of which Khalil Hamdi was one of the main leaders in Jordan, not only participating in, but also organizing and leading these operations. However, as Khalil Hamdi reported to me, preparations for the armed struggle actually started in the 1950s even before the official statement put out at the above-mentioned conference. These ANM activities landed my father in prison several times in the 1950s and 1960s; in the late 1950s (1957), he was imprisoned and severely tortured at the same time and in the same prison (Mahata prison in Amman) as Wadie Haddad, an ANM member who later became one of the founding members of the Popular Front for the Liberation of Palestine (PFLP).

At another time (1958–9), after a heroic and dangerous escape from two military personnel, Khalil Hamdi hid at the house of another member of the ANM, Rushdie Khatib. Hamdi and Khatib were later taken into custody after Hamdi attempted a second escape by jumping out of a window at Khatib's house, but to no avail as he was slowed down by a spray of bullets with one that narrowly missed his head. In prison, he was so severely beaten and tortured for twenty-three days that he almost died. After this, he was released and forced to go to Kharbatha (my parents' village) where he was placed under house arrest for a whole year. There would also be more imprisonments for his political activism after this episode. And from Amman, Hamdi would go on occasional visits to Damascus and Beirut. In Beirut, he would meet with George Habash (who later went on to become the founding leader of the PFLP after 1967), Wadie Haddad, Ghassan Kanafani, the popular Palestinian novelist and political activist, Nayef Hawatmeh (who later founded the Democratic Front for the Liberation of Palestine, DFLP) and other ANM members in Lebanon. Hamdi's favourite character was Wadie, as he told us, because Wadie was so full of life and energy and definitely the most animated and daring of the group.

Stories of a beautiful, serene pre-1948 childhood and young adulthood in Palestine, to stories of the forced expulsion of Palestinians who became refugees overnight, to stories of massacres, then stories of my father's political activism and repeated imprisonments. All of these stories, never narrated chronologically or linearly, we listened to intently, absorbing every detail – all of them from the serene countryside of Kharbatha with its olive trees and amazing variety of medicinal herbs on the outskirts of Ramallah to the prisons where my father often spent his time for his resistance activities. These events and imaginings were engraved in our memories and became a part of our imagined Palestine, a mystical, magical, but tortured land that exists in our parents' memory, our postmemory and our lived reality of a Nakba that continues wherever Palestinians exist in this world. My father's stories stopped only when his tired, but still defiant eyes closed for the last time on 23 June 2021 before he could see the completion of this book. However, these stories live on through his children and their children, passed down from one generation to the next as is customary in every Palestinian household.

Drawing on Marianne Hirsch's definition of postmemory, Lila Abu-Lughod states that this memory describes the 'experience of having one's everyday reality overshadowed by the memory of a much more significant past that one's parents lived through' (2007: 79). The problematic nature of the concept of 'postmemory' within the Palestinian context, however, has to do with the idea of the trauma involved in living under the shadow of a past traumatic and cataclysmic event that has ended. For Hirsh, while this tragic event has ended, its impact on the present in terms of psychologically affecting the second generation that can only remember this event in terms of a second-hand memory remains. This postmemory, then, is passed down to the second generation by means of storytelling and other strategies. Abu Lughod correctly points out that for Palestinians, the 'past has not yet passed' (ibid.). This, however, is not because the world has not yet recognized or denounced this catastrophic past event (ibid.), or because the Palestinians' trauma has not yet healed (it hasn't), but rather because the Nakba, or more precisely, the repeated nakbas of the Palestinian people under occupation and in exile, have never ended because here the perpetrator of the crimes (Israel) understands that an end to the Palestinian peoples' daily nakbas would also mean the total dismantling of the racist, settler colonial state as it exists today.

Thus, Israel's perpetual strategies of deportation, assassination, war, massacres, transfer in order to limit Palestinian population growth and imprisonment are the ways and means for Israel to continue to exist as such. This is precisely the point made by Judith Butler about Israel in her essay entitled '"What Shall We Do without Exile?": Said and Darwish Address the Future' in which Butler argues that since Israel defines itself as a *Jewish* state and the demographics are not in its favour, the only way that it can maintain a Jewish majority is by keeping the Palestinians expelled from their land: 'Given the shifting demographics of the region, the only way that the project of demographic advantage, the hallmark of contemporary Zionism, can continue is by claiming more land, dispossessing and expelling more people of non-Jewish descent – mainly Palestinians and/including Bedouins' (37). This, of course, entails that when the Palestinians 'become too numerous within the borders' of occupied Palestine, Israel repeats the tactics of the ethnic cleansing of Palestine in the 1948 Catastrophe or Nakba by 'further disenfranchisement, expulsion, and containment' (ibid.). Even before Butler's emphasis on this perpetual expulsion of Palestinians, Pappe similarly argues that in order for Israel to maintain a 'pure ethnic space', in occupied Palestine, the ethnic cleansing of Palestine, which started in 1948 needs to continue and indeed continues to this day (8).

A poignant example of the repetition of the Nakba, which transcends both memory and postmemory, is Abu-Lughod's admission that it was neither her father's (Ibrahim Abu-Lughod's) memory of the Nakba nor even her own postmemory of it, but rather the reality of the life of the Palestinians living under occupation, which for Abu-Lughod is a catastrophe that keeps repeating itself in different forms and ways:

> But they can't capture this particular reality with its growling Hebrew arrogantly proclaiming ownership. With its guns and soldiers everywhere you turn. With its utter separation of Arab and Jew. These experiences, more than my father's

stories, have made me want to write about the Nakba. For the Palestinian catastrophe is not just something of the past. It continues into the present in every house demolished by an Israeli bulldozer, with every firing from an Apache helicopter, with every stillbirth at a military checkpoint, with every village divided from its fields by the 'separation' wall, and with every Palestinian who still longs to return to a home that is no more.

(103)

Abu-Lughod's repetition of the word 'every' accurately captures the repeated daily suffering of the Palestinians living under occupation in the 'West Bank', or rather the Eastern part of occupied Palestine as the poet Mourid Barghouti prefers to say as he told me in an interview in 2016. This suffering is much more pronounced in Gaza, the open-air prison, which is under constant siege from the land, air and sea and is subjected to bombings by Israel every few years.

Thus because the *nakbas* of the Palestinian people are ongoing in the form of a systematic displacement from their homeland, the issue is not really about keeping the catastrophic memory or postmemory alive because the present reality of new generations of Palestinians inside and outside occupied Palestine is just as painful and catastrophic. It is for this reason that imagining Palestine is also an ongoing process. The identity of Palestine and Palestinians is in a constant process of construction and reconstruction, imaginings and reimaginings. Imagin/*ing* Palestine, then, is a conscious, intentional and continuous effort that aims at constructing/re-constructing a collective, inclusive, national and cultural identity that is specifically tied to a certain place or more concretely, a geography upon which the first generation of expelled Palestinians lived before the establishment of Israel in 1948.

It is incumbent upon Arab intellectuals (poets, novelists, artists, cultural theorists and social and political scientists) to provide deep and penetrating analysis and guidance regarding the ongoing Palestinian struggle, which is also deeply intertwined in the dynamics of the region as a whole. How will a future Palestine look? What would be the identity of this new imagined community? What political/ideological form will this future state take? What about the Palestinian diaspora or exile and what about the Palestinian moral right of return? Do the Palestinians form a collective national and cultural identity after more than seventy years of dispersion? The answers to these questions require an ongoing engagement with the Palestinian cause by intellectuals in Said's sense of the word – intellectuals that are willing, under the most difficult conditions, to speak truth to power and to carve out different sites of Thirdspace resistance, which as Edward Soja argues makes up a trialectics of spatiality, historicality and sociality (1996: 71).

Imagining a future decolonized Palestinian community/nation is essentially linked to and is, in fact, conditioned upon negotiating an inclusive identity for the nation to be. In his poem entitled 'From now on you are somebody else', the Palestinian poet Mahmoud Darwish, pondering his identity (both personal and national), states: 'I am not embarrassed about my identity because it is still in the process of being invented' (2009a: 148). Thus, in order to make it possible to imagine a liberated, de-colonized and de-Zionized nation on the geography of historic Palestine, the intellectual must *enable* the imagining of a decolonized identity that envisions victory rather than defeat. Decolonization itself is a complicated concept given the currently ideologically divided atmosphere in the Arab world today. Within the context of this fractious, deeply divided, sectarian and explosive situation, imagining Palestine is important not only to keep the idea of Palestine alive, but also as an essential form of resistance against Israel's brutal and exclusive settler colonialism.

Imagining an inclusive and diverse national community in Palestine is also a direct and defiant response to the exclusivity and racism of Israel's very definition of itself as a Jewish only state as confirmed by the law called 'Israel as the Nation State of the Jewish People' passed in the Israeli Knesset on the 19th of July 2018. In an article entitled 'Israel passes Jewish state law, enshrining "national home of the Jewish people"', Raoul Wootlif states that this 'Basic Law', which functions as a constitution and is immutable, stipulates the following basic principles, which Wootliff published a day earlier on the 18th of July:

A. The land of Israel is the historical homeland of the Jewish people, in which the State of Israel was established.
B. The State of Israel is the national home of the Jewish people, in which it fulfils its natural, cultural, religious and historical right to self-determination.
C. The right to exercise national self-determination in the State of Israel is unique to the Jewish people.

(Wootlif, 18 July 2018)

A careful reading of the above three basic principles of the law clarifies that this conception of identity is not only exclusivist, that is, excluding everyone who is not Jewish, but is also deeply racist and pre-modern – only Jewish people have the 'right to exercise national self-determination in the State of Israel'.

The word 'unique' is very clearly used to emphasize the exclusion of all other non-Jewish people. What about Indigenous[5] Palestinians whose ancestors have lived on this piece of geography for thousands of years, but who in 1948 found themselves living within the borders of this newly established Zionist state? Do these Indigenous inhabitants of the land have the right to exercise their national self-determination on the land of their ancestors? And how exactly does Israel qualify as a democracy? Points five and six of this law concern Jews in 'exile' and 'Diaspora': 'The state will open for Jewish immigration and the ingathering of exiles' (ibid.). This means that any individual who identifies as Jewish from any corner of this earth has a right to exercise his/her national self-determination on this land, a right unique only to anyone who identifies as Jewish regardless of where he/she is from. One wonders what the plight of Arabs within 1948 occupied Palestine is. Will they be expelled, transferred, deported? Doesn't this latest Israeli law qualify as codified ethnic cleansing?

Israel was established in 1948 by means of a systematic ethnic cleansing plan. This plan has now been written into *law*, a law that is as stable as the constitution: 'The law for the first time enshrines Israel as "the national home of the Jewish people." The law becomes one of the so-called Basic Laws, which, like a constitution, guide Israel's legal system and are usually more difficult to repeal than regular laws' (Wootlif, 2018b). Examples of anti-Semitism are provided by the 'International Holocaust Remembrance Alliance' (IHRA). One of these examples, as clearly stated on the IHRA website, is the following: 'Denying the Jewish people their right to self-determination, e.g., by claiming that the existence of a State of Israel is a racist endeavor' is anti-Semitic (holocaustremembrance. com). Accordingly, to argue that Israel is a racist, apartheid state because its very existence as a Jewish-only state (as specifically defined by the 'Israel as the Nation State of the Jewish People' law) is preposterously considered anti-Semitic. Moreover, those who say that Israel is indeed a racist state must suffer the consequences of being continuously attacked and perhaps lose their positions at universities and other institutions. In fact, the British Labour party has recently adopted the complete IHRA definition of anti-Semitism in all its subparts and examples, including the one mentioned above in order to end a 'row that has damaged relations between the party and Jewish community organisations' (Stewart and Elgot in *The Guardian*, 16 August 2018).

It does not take much analysis to comprehend that this conception of identity is neither modern, nor democratic, nor decolonial and is diametrically opposed to Stuart Hall's influential definition of identity as *process*. For Hall, cultural identities in diaspora, such as the Caribbean identities, have undergone changes over centuries, whereby each one has negotiated for itself a unique identity over time and space, and this '"difference", whether we like it or not, is already inscribed in our cultural identities' (2013: 396). It is in this sense that Hall defines identity as a process which is deeply moulded by space and time and not by any 'fixed essence' that is left untouched by culture and history and is by no means a 'fixed origin to which we can make some final and absolute Return' (395). How would the whole Zionist project – that is the establishment of the state of Israel – fare with Hall's theorizations on cultural identity in diaspora? Actually, in this very essay, Hall has this to say about the establishment of Israel:

> diaspora does not refer us to those scattered tribes whose identity can only be secured in relation to some sacred homeland to which they must at all costs return, even if it means pushing other people into the sea. This is the old, the imperializing, the hegemonising, form of 'ethnicity'. We have seen the fate of the people of Palestine at the hands of this backward-looking conception of diaspora – and the complicity of the West with it. The diaspora experience as I intend it here is defined, not by essence or purity, but by the recognition of a necessary heterogeneity and diversity; by a conception of 'identity' which lives with and through, not despite, difference; by *hybridity*.
>
> (401)

Then, according to Hall, the Zionist/Israeli conception of identity is old, imperializing, hegemonizing and backward-looking, and it also meant and still means pushing the Indigenous Palestinians off of their own lands – and the West is complicit in this. Does this make Hall anti-Semitic according to the IHRA definition of anti-Semitism?

The fact that to even discuss publicly what happened in 1948 in Palestine is still off limits or can even be labelled anti-Semitic by mainstream media and various institutions and universities worldwide, especially in the West, is proof that the *Nakba* and the ethnic cleansing of Palestine has not entered mainstream consciousness. On 29 November 2020, a group of 122 Palestinian and Arab intellectuals and journalists put out a statement about the unjust IHRA definition of anti-Semitism that is being forced upon countries and political parties, organizations and educational institutions in Europe and North America. The signatories state:

> To level the charge of antisemitism against anyone who regards the existing state of Israel as racist [....] amounts to granting Israel absolute impunity. [...] The IHRA definition and the way it has been deployed prohibit any discussion of the Israeli state based on ethno-religious discrimination. It thus contravenes elementary justice and basic norms of human rights and international law.
> (*The Guardian*, 29 November 2020)

The IHRA's definition of anti-Semitism intentionally conflates actual anti-Semitism – racism against Jews as Jews with support for the Palestinian cause, which is about the moral right of the Indigenous people of the land of Palestine, the Palestinians, to return to the land from which they were dispossessed in 1948. The intentional conflation of these two ideas is intended to silence the Palestinian narrative and uproot any possible support or solidarity with the Palestinian cause. With the label of anti-Semitism, the aim is to end all discussion even before it begins. This discussion, however, is of the utmost importance in order for there to be a just solution to this ongoing tragedy. It is not a matter of a trauma that needs to be tamed, but rather of an injustice that must be addressed. And for justice to be done, we must begin with Palestine.

Beginning with Palestine: The historical context

> Each brigade commander received a list of the villages or neighbourhoods that had to be occupied, destroyed and their inhabitants expelled, with exact dates. Some of the commanders were over-ambitious in executing their orders, and added additional locations in the momentum their zeal had created.
> (Pappe, 2006: 82)

Beginning with Palestine also entails beginning with a certain time, a specific year, and this inevitably has to be 1948, the year of the *Nakba* or catastrophe. Just a glimpse at the titles of two seminal books on what happened in 1948 begins to tell the long silenced story of Palestine, a sort of, at last – the 'permission to narrate', the title of an essay by Said in 1984 originally published in the *London Review of Books* in February, 1984, and the spring 1984 issue of the *Journal of Palestine Studies*. The first of these books is Nur Masalha's *Expulsion of the Palestinians: The Concept of Transfer in Zionist Political Thought, 1882–1948* (1992). Masalha's title emphasizes that the Palestinians did not leave their lands upon the orders of the Arab armies in 1948 or as a result of the 'exigencies of war' (208), but were expelled from their villages and towns as planned by the Zionist founding fathers of 'Israel'. In fact, Masalha argues that the idea of population transfer is at the very heart of Zionist ideology precisely because it means to establish a homeland for the Jewish people on an already inhabited piece of land; in this case, it was Palestine.

For Zionists, Palestine was a land without a people for a people [the Jews] without a land, the infamous slogan coined by the British Jewish writer, Israel Zangwill (Masalha, 1992: 5). Of course, as Masalha explains, the Zionists knew that there were people living in Palestine, but to their imperialist European mindset, the Palestinians were of no significance as a people and must be at all costs expelled from their native land upon which the Palestinians have lived for thousands of years to make room for the white 'civilized' Jews of Europe. Masalha provides some telling examples of how key figures in the Zionist movement viewed the inhabitants of Palestine (the Palestinians) before the creation of 'Israel' in 1948. Chaim Weizmann, who became Israel's first president, told Arthur Ruppin, the 'head of the colonization department of the Jewish Agency' about the Palestinians: 'The British told us that there are some hundred thousand[] negroes [Kushim] and for those there is no value' (qtd. In Masalha 6). In fact, Zangwill believed that the expulsion of the Palestinians in order to get the land ready for 'Europe's Jewish masses was a precondition for the fulfillment of Zionism' (Masalha 10).

This idea of expulsion or population transfer, born with the beginnings of political Zionism, was put into very effective use in 1948 and then again in 1967 and is still alive and well today. It should not be assumed, argues Masalha, that expulsion strategies are embraced only by right-wing extremists, but are very much a part of mainstream Zionism (208–10). In fact, as Masalha argues in his book (*Expulsion of the Palestinians*), the very concept of the transfer of the Palestinian people from historic Palestine had always been the cornerstone of the Zionist movement's establishment of the Jewish state. Masalha based his information on Israeli and British archival sources. In answer to my question about these archival sources and the general idea of his book, Masalha wrote to me in an email dated 19 August 2021:

> In 1989 I met Dr Walid Khalidi in London and he suggested I should go through Israeli and Hebrew archival sources systematically. The point was: to make a convincing argument about the 'concept of "transfer" in Zionist political thought' (which is what the book is all about) I would need to bring out unpublished sources (located in Israeli Hebrew archives) which the Israeli historians have been reluctant to disclose until then. And indeed, this was the core of the book. But I also use British sources from the Public Record Office

(now called National Archives) in London; in the mid-1980s I had already used British archival sources in my PhD (on the British in Iraq in the 1920s) and I had been familiar with many British archival sources on Palestine. In short: the 'concept of transfer in Zionist political thought' in my book *Expulsion of the Palestinians* is largely based on Israeli Hebrew and British archival sources.

Thus, it was this important book by Masalha that set the stage for other important books that were based on Israel's archival material.

In 1998, fifty years after the establishment of Israel, it released significant archival military documentation that proves that there was indeed an expulsion plan as Masalha's book had already exposed in 1992. Now, Pappe could corroborate Masalha's work: there was indeed a very systematic plan for the expulsion of the Palestinians (*HARDtalk* with Ilan Pappe). The expulsion of the Palestinians involved a systematic plan for the 'ethnic cleansing of Palestine' (as Pappe prefers to refer to what happened in that year) which was put into dramatic effect. It is, according to Pappe in his seminal book, *The Ethnic Cleansing of Palestine* (2006), the Haganah's Plan D or Dalet in Hebrew, which was a detailed and systematic plan whose aim was 'in fact the destruction of both the rural and urban areas of Palestine' (xii). This was the year that hundreds of thousands of native Palestinians were most viciously and barbarically expelled from their land by Zionist terrorist groups (the Haganah, Irgun and Stern Gang), most of whom were immigrants originally from Europe, according to the master plan of the Consultancy (Pappe, 2006: 37), which was made up of the most important political and military figures of what would later become Israel and which Pappe was able to reconstruct. Some members of the Consultancy included the following people: the High Command – David Ben-Gurion, Yigael Yadin, Yohanan Ratner, Yigal Allon, Yitzhak Sadeh, Israel Galili and Zvi Ayalon and field officers such as Moshe Dayan and Yitzhak Rabin were often called to the meetings of the Consultancy (2006: 267).

This Plan D, as Pappe explains, basing his information on Israel's military archives released fifty years after the 1948 ethnic cleansing, effectively produced what Palestinians call the Nakba, a word describing a plethora of events, which included the following crimes against humanity committed by the Zionist militias against the Palestinian people: massive forced expulsions, the destruction and torching of thousands of homes, important buildings and landmarks and agricultural fields, numerous massacres meant to terrorize the people so they can escape and save their lives, biological warfare, which meant infecting the villagers' drinking water with typhoid fever and others (Pappe, 2006: 100–1). The inhabitants of more than half of the Palestinian villages had been expelled between March 1948 and May 1948 before any Arab 'army' had set foot in Palestine, thereby dispelling the myth that the Palestinians were fleeing according to the instructions of the Arab armies (Pappe, 2006: 104). As Masalha makes very clear, one cannot separate the very ideology of Zionism from the concept of expulsion as Theodor Herzl believed that in order to realize the Zionist dream, Zionists needed to 'spirit the penniless population across the border' (qtd. in Masalha, 1992: 207). This was the only way that the Zionists could indeed create a 'purely Jewish Palestine' (Pappe, 2006: 48), 'not only in its socio-political structure but also in its ethnic composition' (ibid.: 15). One can argue that the (continuous) expulsion of the Palestinian population is the basis upon which Zionist ideology is founded. In fact, this is the aim behind the new 'basic' law passed in the Israeli Knesset in July 2018, seventy years after the establishment of the Jewish state.

Thus knowing what happened in 1948 is not only about knowing what happened in the past, but also understanding what is still happening today. One needs to be cognizant that there are close to two million Palestinians living within the borders of 1948 occupied Palestine. Sixty-eight per cent of Israeli Jews believe that these Palestinians should be 'transferred' from their ancestral homes and lands inside 1948 occupied Palestine (Pappe, 2006: 260). It is for this reason Pappe hoped that his book would signal a paradigm shift in discussing the events of 1948. Pappe argues there was no 'war' between Arabs and Jews; he calls this the 'phony war' because the reluctant Arab armies were very late in arriving and were not at all well trained or equipped and were far outnumbered by the Zionist militias. As Pappe explains, what happened in 1948 was a planned and systematic ethnic cleansing of Palestine, which was well underway before the late arrival of Arab armies, not to mention the tacit agreements between Arab leaders and the Zionist movement.

Arab armies stood idly by as the Zionist militias cleansed Palestinian towns and villages, defending only the parts of Palestine (the 'West Bank' and half of Jerusalem) that the Zionists agreed would be a part of Transjordan (the name of Jordan during the British mandate period (Pappe, 43–4). As mentioned above, massacres were an effective method used by the Zionist militias to terrorize the people and quicken the expulsion of the Palestinian population. Although Deir Yassin (Pappe, 40) is the most well-known massacre and created the called-for fear and hysteria (a method more recently known as 'shock and awe', a term used by the United States to describe their initial attack on Iraq in 2003)[6] amongst the unaware Palestinian population, it was not the largest one. That dubious 'honour' goes to the village of Dawaymeh (Pappe, 195), near the town of Hebron where it is believed that hundreds of men, women and children were slaughtered in cold blood. The first massacre in late 1947 was in Tirat Haifa (Pappe, 258).

Pappe very poignantly and painfully points out in *The Ethnic Cleansing of Palestine* that not all of these massacres and their victims have been documented, and that this was still a work in progress even as his own book was still being completed:

> Palestinian sources, combining Israeli military archives with oral histories, list thirty-one confirmed massacres – beginning with the massacre in Tirat Haifa on 11 December 1947 and ending with Khirbat Ilin in the Hebron area on 19 January 1949 – and there may have been at least another six. We still do not have a systematic Nakba memorial archive that would allow one to trace the names of all those who died in the massacres – an act of painful commemoration.
> (258)

Pappe goes on to describe the different massacres in Palestinian towns and villages that he was able to document, such as those in Khisas (57), Balad al-Shaykh (59), Sa'sa (75), Khirbat Nasr al-Din (92), Ayn al Zaytun (111), Tantura (133), Bassa (142) and Khirbat Ilin (258). These expulsion tactics, massacres and ethnic cleansing continued after 1948 as Pappe points out:

> Fifteen minutes by car from Tel-Aviv University lies the village of Kfar Qassim where, on 29 October 1956, Israeli troops massacred forty-nine villagers returning from their fields. Then there was Qibya in the 1950s, Samoa in the 1960s, the villages of the Galilee in 1976, Sabra and Shatila in 1982, Kfar Qana in 1999, Wadi Ara in 2000 and the Jenin Refugee Camp in 2002.
>
> (258)

The ethnic cleansing of Palestine continues to this day (2021) as has been witnessed most recently in the dispossession of Palestinians from their homes in Jerusalem/ Al Quds, especially the neighbourhood of Sheikh Jarrah and the neighbouring town of Silwan and in Nablus, such as the town of Beita.[7] Some of the massacres described by Pappe in *The Ethnic Cleansing of Palestine* have been effectively and dramatically narrated by the Egyptian novelist, Radwa Ashour, the Palestinian American novelist, Susan Abulhawa and other novelists.

Beginning with Palestine, then, means understanding how the Palestinian people were dispossessed from their lands in 1948 by means of Zionist terror tactics meant to achieve the 'shock and awe' of pure, merciless killing, brutality and ethnic cleansing that Zionist militias perpetrated against the Indigenous people of Palestine, whom for the European Zionists and their British allies and co-conspirators, were an uncivilized, non-European (read disposable) population. However, the concept of beginnings in the sense of the word as used by Said (1975: 349–50) is also about endowing Palestinians with agency and power in the face of continuous efforts by Israel and its main supporter, the United States, to break the will of the Palestinian people.

In 2018, the Trump administration halted US aid to UNRWA (the United Nations Relief and Works Agency for Palestine Refugees),[8] which was created in 1949 in order to provide relief for Palestinian refugees who were displaced from their homes after the creation of Israel in 1948. This US action by the Trump administration aimed at putting an end, once and for all, to the Palestinian right of return. In an article in *Foreign Policy* entitled 'Trump and Allies Seek End to Refugee Status for Millions of Palestinians', Colum Lynch points out that internal emails by Jared Kushner, Donald Trump's 'son-in law and senior advisor' show that Kushner 'has quietly been trying to do away with the UN relief agency that has provided food and essential services to millions of Palestinian refugees for decades …' (2018). Kushner wrote, 'It is important to have an honest and sincere effort to disrupt UNRWA … This [agency] perpetuates a status quo, is corrupt, inefficient and doesn't help peace' (Lynch, 2018). Kushner hoped to make the Palestinian refugees disappear, to evaporate into thin air, supposedly by dispersing them all over the world, thereby resolving this 'problem'. This aid was reinstated in 2021 not because the Biden administration supports the Palestinian right of return, but possibly because of their realization that this would not end the Palestinian refugee 'problem'.

By attempting to dismantle or 'disrupt' UNRWA-supported refugee camps and disperse Palestinian refugees, Israel and the United States hope to ensure the Palestinians' *lack* of return to their ancestral homes. Against this background of continued ethnic cleansing supported by the biggest military power on earth (the United States), the Palestinian people need to remain strong in the face of adversity, create beginnings out of what seems to be utter lateness and, most importantly, keep imagining and constructing Palestine. The idea of 'imagin(*ing*)' Palestine is the core of the argument, not only in the sense of Anderson's concept of 'imagined communities' but also in the sense of Palestine being a project under construction, an ongoing process/struggle that is as of yet incomplete. This incompleteness or lack of closure endows the Palestinian intellectual, activist, student and farmer with a sense of restlessness and a refusal to surrender, thus uniting the Palestinian experience whether under occupation or in exile, inside and outside occupied Palestine.

The 'ghosts' of Palestine, so to speak, fuel the psyche of the homeless Palestinian, which can only underscore the idea of a return home, a necessary return that is simultaneously geographical, historical, cultural and emotional. This awaited return, as this book argues, can only be effected by imagining Palestine, and as Said argues, by 'project[ing] ideas of liberation, and to imagine ... a new national community' (*Culture & Imperialism* 241). It is emphasized, as I argue in 'Darwish's geography', that 'imagining a liberated geographical space includes imagining a "decolonized identity"' (2016b: 242), an essential anti-colonial concept, which involves multiple questionings, imaginings and (re)configurations. What is Palestine? Who is the Palestinian? What about the collective right of return? Is return possible? What kind of nation would a future Palestine be? This book grapples with such questions by examining the life, thought and work of Palestinians.

Chapter 1 entitled, 'The Restless Spirit: Palestine Theorized', tackles the theorizations of (post) catastrophic thinking based on the works of well-known thinkers, such as Said and Ghassan Kanafani. The phrase 'resistance literature' was first used by the Palestinian writer and intellectual Kanafani in his work entitled *Resistance Literature in Occupied Palestine 1948–1966* (2013 [1966]). This work marks the beginning of the theorization of Palestine, which Kanafani also narrated in his literary productions, such as *Men in the Sun* (1963), *All That's Left to You* (1966), *Um Sa'ad* (1969) and *Returning to Haifa* (1969).[9] Kanafani's work laid the groundwork for Palestinian resistance literature and enabled different reconfigurations of Palestine. This chapter tackles the theorizations of Said, which as I argue, were inspired by his own imagining of Palestine and its cause. Said's oeuvre is inevitably connected with his 'natal culture' and because of his self-proclaimed exile, he affiliates with Palestine 'through critical consciousness and scholarly work', as Said writes not about himself, but about Auerbach in *The World, the Text and the Critic* (16). This chapter focuses on the restless spirit of the (Palestinian) intellectual, who in Said's case is a humanist 'whose *raison d' etre* is to represent all those people and issues that are routinely forgotten or swept under the rug' as he states in *Representations of the Intellectual* (9). Said's entire corpus (including *Beginnings: Intention and Method* (1975), *Orientalism* (1978), *The Question of Palestine* (1992 [1979]), *The World, the Text and the Critic* (1983), *After the Last Sky* (1993 [1986]), *Representations of the Intellectual* (1994), *Out of Place* (1999) and even the posthumously published *On Late Style* (2007) is charged by the *restless* spirit of Palestine. Many of the ideas presented in these and other works by Said are discussed in relation to their connectedness to Palestine, which enabled Said's groundbreaking theoretical work.

Chapter 2 entitled, '"Exile is the World Inside": the Poetry of Resistance and Solidarity' tackles selected works of poetry by Palestinian, Arab and international poets such as Darwish, Mourid Barghouti, Adonis, June Jordan, Suheir Hammad, Roger Waters, John Trudell and Lee Maracle. Like Said's exiled intellectual, these writers and intellectuals necessarily see exile as the world inside, creating in them and their writings a purposeful anger, restlessness and defiant will that refuses to surrender, thereby keeping Palestine alive in their literary imaginings. Exile is not only a physical state born of catastrophe; it is also a mental state. Exile produces a restless sense of self that speaks to a non-reconciled Palestinian history, which is haunted by the many ghosts of Palestine. Despite the exile, siege and besiegement of the Palestinian people, all of these poets speak of defiance, resistance, and the transnational solidarity of the oppressed, which would lead to the long awaited collective return of Palestinians to Palestine. The theme of return, which is inextricably linked to the Palestinian poet's and (people's) exile, pervades these writers' thinking and work. Darwish poignantly states in an interview with Maya Jaggi in 2002 in *The Guardian*: 'I am writing for the moment when I shall be able to say, "to hell with Palestine" … But this will not come before Palestine is free. I can't achieve my private freedom before the freedom of my country. When it's free, I can curse it' (https://www.theguardian.com). Even the poet's 'private freedom' is conditioned by a *free* Palestine.

Focusing on the memoir and the novel, Chapter 3 entitled, 'Writing Self, Writing Nation in the Memoir and the Novel: Palestine Narrated' tackles the documentation of Palestinian history and the construction of Palestinian national identity, whereby in writing the self, Said and Barghouti in their respective memoirs are also writing the nation. For Said, it is, in fact, the out of placeness of Palestinians the world over that draws them together as a 'nation'. In *Out of Place* (2000), Said describes his journey of becoming Palestinian, a difficult and restless journey that involves a constant process of (re)formulations and (re)configurations – a going back (to a point of origin) in order to move forward. Similarly, Barghouti's journey to Ramallah in *I Saw Ramallah* (2005), which does not represent a 'return' to Palestine, is one of 'multiple displacements'. Barghouti's memoirs describe Ramallah and Palestinian lives and experiences as being out of place and out of time. This chapter also reflects upon the idea of borders, checkpoints, confined spaces and refugee camps. The unconscionable difficulty of the Palestinian experience also makes for a difficulty of representation in the works of Kanafani, Susan Abulhawa and Radwa Ashour.

Like in the previous chapter, the difficulty of the Palestinian experience and the defiant resistance of the Palestinians underscore the urgency of Palestinian return. As Barghouti asserts in his first memoir, *I Saw Ramallah*, return is a *collective* endeavour, not a personal one. However, before the exiled Palestinian can return, there must be a concerted and concentrated effort to imagine a future Palestine as both geography and national community. This chapter and the previous one, then, explore diverse Palestinian spaces, which can indeed be thought of as Thirdspace resistance as theorized by Edward Soja (1996: 97), produced by Palestinian, Arab and international artists. These spaces necessarily become sites of Palestinian cultural production, struggle and *sumud*.

Chapter 4 is entitled 'Writings on the Wall' in the sense that the Palestinian cause, which certainly has gained in recognition and global solidarity recently, has not yet become dominant or won support in 'official' circles, Western governments, powerful institutions, organizations, conferences and mainstream media. In this respect, the Palestinian cause still represents writings and drawings on the wall, specifically refugee camp walls. As Darwish wrote in his long poem 'Mural' (and murals are literally drawings and writings on walls): 'I also have my small notebook./Every time a bird grazes a cloud I write it down./The dream has untied my wings' (2003: 148). These writings in notebooks and on the broken down and peeling walls of refugee camps are fragile. Palestinian writings are not in any way dominant or hegemonic, and they represent the necessary documentation of the Palestinian struggle. Everything, as Darwish says, is being documented in notebooks and on refugee camp walls. This chapter deals with various forms of Palestinian creativity, resistance, resilience and *sumud* as represented by the deeply rooted olive tree in Palestinian literature (specifically in Barghouti's memoir *I Was Born There, I Was Born Here*), science (the Palestinian scientist's Hamdi Khalil Hamdi's work on the olive tree) and everyday life. This chapter also looks at the important political art of Naji al-Ali and his omnipresent character Hanthala. The repurposing of Palestinian heritage, song and dance is also tackled in this chapter by focusing on the dabkeh dance, the singing group Al Ashiqeen and one of the most popular singers of the Palestinian revolution, Abu Arab.

The conclusion continues the conversation Said started with his essay entitled 'On Lost Causes'. In this final section, I engage ten intellectuals (the iconic Palestinian fighter, activist and thinker Leila Khaled, Ibrahim Aoude, Nur Masalha, Ilan Pappe, Ramzy Baroud, Rami Siklawi, Terri Ginsberg, Steven Salaita, Jamal Nassar and Refaat Alareer), who have written about the Palestinian cause, in conversation about their imagined Palestine, resistance strategies, the Palestinian right of return and the vitality of the Palestinian cause today. If there is perhaps one quality that unites the views of these intellectuals, it is the absolute rejection of the defeatist attitude and the true belief that Palestine is certainly a living cause despite the current political divisions within the Palestinian polity itself and the rest of the Arab world, especially certain Gulf countries who have normalized their relations with Israel at the expense of the Palestinian cause. The recent 2021 events in occupied Palestine have reinvigorated the Palestinian cause and have shown the world the deep comradeship and unity of the Palestinian community all over this globe – those under occupation in 1967 Palestine, in 1948 Palestine, in Gaza, in exile, whether in refugee camps inside occupied Palestine or in neighbouring Arab countries or dispersed in different world capitals. The first generation of the *Nakba* have all but died; however, to the dismay of Israel, new generations of Palestinians have continued the struggle for liberation because they continue to live the daily ethnic cleansing and daily '*nakbas*' perpetrated against them by the Zionist settler colonial entity. The conclusion engages intransigent intellectuals who refuse surrender and defeat in the process of imagining and constructing a future Palestine.

The construction of the Palestinian nation and national identity continues because as Darwish asserts in his poem entitled 'You, from now on, are not yourself', identity is our invention, what we construct and not something we inherit from the past:

Oh past! Don't change us as we move away from you.

Oh future! Don't ask us who we are and what we want from you, for we don't know either.

Oh present! Be a little patient with us, for we are only passers-by with heavy shadows.

Identity is what we bequeath, not what we inherit, what we invent, not what we remember.

(2009a: 145)

Palestinian identity and national community are indeed the Palestinian's invention and not merely a matter of inheritance. This is why these concepts are in need of a concentrated intellectual effort of reconfiguration and reconstruction. The process of imagining Palestine is a labour in progress – a task that the intellectuals and poets of Palestine are called upon to undertake. Perhaps Palestine's most renowned intellectual, Said, said it best, commenting on the work and attitude of the (Palestinian) intellectual: 'the intransigence of the individual thinker whose power of expression is a power – however modest and circumscribed in its capacity for action or victory – … enacts a movement of vitality, a gesture of defiance, a statement of hope whose "unhappiness" and meager survival are better than silence or joining in the chorus of defeated activists' ('On Lost Causes', 552–3).

1

THE RESTLESS SPIRIT: PALESTINE THEORIZED

Although ... Auerbach was away from Europe, his work is steeped in the reality of Europe, just as the specific circumstances of his exile enabled a concrete critical recovery of Europe. We have in Auerbach an instance both of filiation with his natal culture and, because of exile, *affiliation* with it through critical consciousness and scholarly work.

(Said, 1991: 16)

I have been working to change the way I speak and write, to incorporate in the manner of telling a sense of place, of not just who I am in the present but where I am coming from, the multiple voices within me. I have confronted silence, inarticulateness. When I say, then, that these words emerge from suffering, I refer to that personal struggle to name that location from which I come to voice – that space of my theorizing.

(Hooks, 1990: 146)

Said's (post) catastrophic theoretical oeuvre

It is perhaps not too much of an exaggeration to say that the Palestinian *Nakba* and the dispossession and exile of the Palestinian people have given rise to the most important anti-colonial and resistance theory of the twentieth and twenty-first centuries. These catastrophic historical events are most certainly the inspiration behind the beginning of what is now known as 'postcolonial' theory with Said being recognized by many working in the field today as its founding father. While it is well known that Said was an active supporter of the Palestinian national cause, which some critics find contradictory to his critical beliefs, given his criticism of nationalist discourses (Said, 1995: 338), it is here argued that Said's theoretical work should actually be seen as corresponding to and complementing his political and humanist vision and activism and not in contradiction to them.

In fact, for Said, the text, any text, is *worldly* – that is, it is inevitably tied to the world of things, not only words; the *Nakba* is an event, not only a word. Bill Ashcroft and Pal Ahluwalia point out that after the 5 June 1967 War between Israel and Arab countries, which resulted in a humiliating defeat for the Arabs, known as the *Naksa*, Said 'began to construct himself as a Palestinian' (3), and it is precisely within the Palestinian context that Said's theoretical work developed and matured: 'It was the colonization of Palestine which compelled Said to examine the imperial discourse of the West, and to weave his cultural analysis with the text of his own identity' (Ashcroft and Ahluwalia, 4). It is Said's *Palestinianness*, then, an identity on the margin and placed under historical erasure by the Zionist occupying power, that shaped his critical consciousness and oppositional thinking, thus enabling his (post) catastrophic theorizations. As bell hooks poignantly points out, 'these words emerge from suffering', and it is specifically this space on the margin that enables the intellectual's theorizing (146). Thus, it is precisely Palestine that has laid siege to Said's theorizing. Theorizing Palestine figured prominently in many of the important ideas that Said contributed to twentieth and twenty-first century critical theory beyond inspiring him to examine the imperial discourse of the West. Said's key ideas on beginnings, secular criticism, the worldliness of the text, speaking truth to power, exile, affiliation and the intellectual and late style, the last being a concept that was delineated in a posthumously published book in 2007, were formed within the context of Said's Palestinian experience.

For Said, theory itself is *worldly* in the sense that it is first and foremost about the real world and not about theoretical abstractions, and the real world is about the oppressed. The well-known postcolonial theorist, Gayatri Spivak had this to say about the Said that she knew: 'I think he often thought I was a fool, to be so persuaded by "theory". His stand ... against pretentious and obscure language was against me as well' (2005: 524). At one point, however, Said came to Spivak's defence, writing simply, 'Gayatri works for the oppressed, stop this', a message for which Spivak 'was immensely grateful that he had somehow drawn me into what was surely his life – working for the oppressed' (Spivak, 2005: 524). Working for the oppressed in Said's mind was first and foremost working for Palestine as Spivak admits in her discussion of her relationship with Said: 'During those early days, it was all about Palestine' (2005: 521) [...] 'And so it went. We did public appearances together, for Palestine' (2005: 523). Thus, Said's public stance for the oppressed and activism for the Palestinian cause cannot be separated from his theoretical oeuvre, which is itself grounded in the world. Said's emphasis on the *worldliness* of the text and the critic is, as Ashcroft and Ahluwalia state, inspired by Palestine, which is the 'key to the prominence of the theme of worldliness in [Said's] thinking and writing. Palestine locates Said's own worldliness in the world' (2001: 117).

As Patrick Williams argues, some of the most important founding principles of postcolonialism revolve around resistance and liberation. Many practitioners of postcolonial studies have moved beyond the colonial and are concerned with matters 'post' the colonial. Excluding Palestine, which is not 'post' the colonial, argues Williams, is to make a travesty of the field (2010: 91–2). Said, who profoundly influenced and some would say whose work helped found postcolonial studies, later disavowed it according to Robert Young (Dar al-Ma'mun Conversations, 2014), possibly thinking that it had become too philosophical, too interested in words rather than things, too 'post' the colonial, a fact that cannot apply to Palestine which inspired Said's initial ideas on the interrogation of colonial discourse. Williams calls out the ethical scandal of postcolonialism that for decades intentionally ignored Palestine, which can be said to be one of the last examples of brutal settler colonialism. The postcolonial field has generally refused to recognize the constant daily suffering of the dispossessed Palestinian people who, to borrow Frantz Fanon's words, are 'the wretched of the earth'. Millions of Palestinians have been living in squalid conditions in UN-run refugee camps for over seventy-four years now. Of course, this is not only a moral scandal for postcolonialism and other disciplines, but for the world in general, a world that for the most part (and with very few exceptions) has turned a blind eye to Palestine and the Palestinians, even labelling the Palestinian narrative and whoever dares to narrate it, anti-Semitic.

Said's theoretical oeuvre is one of 'radical openness' (Soja, 139), which is born out of catastrophic events. His theoretical oeuvre can be seen as being *(post) catastrophic*; however, this is not in the sense that the catastrophic is now post the catastrophe, which within the Palestinian context, has not in any sense passed. The catastrophic is, in fact, continuing and is still very much in the present. My use of the parentheses is to emphasize the parenthetical status of the (post) aspect of the word. However, at the same time, the (post) appears before the word catastrophic in order to acknowledge the initial rupture, the first catastrophe, which has led to many other catastrophes in the Palestinian context. Perhaps the words of the Palestinian poet, Mourid Barghouti can adequately express the role of the (Palestinian) intellectual in what I am calling (post) catastrophic theory or theorizations: 'What can I do with my poetry and my own language here and now, in my part of the world? What happens to a poet in a cataclysmic society, where people live in semi-eternal emergency, and their life is destabilized and exposed to daily horror and endless suffering' (qtd. in Bernard, 71). It is knowing that this is the reality of one's people that forces the intellectual to demand of theory so much more than the abstractions of modernist and post-modernist terminology that can have the effect of numbing the reality of the present, and thus permanently relegating these theorizations to scholarly books and journals. Said's theoretical oeuvre should also be distinguished from trauma theory, for example, because in trauma theory, the traumatic is focused on one past event that has already passed and which the traumatized individual remembers either in memory or postmemory, but not necessarily 'from that space in the margin that is a site of creativity and power', as bell hooks (1990: 152) theorizes in her article aptly entitled, 'Choosing the Margin as a Space of Radical Openness'.

Said's (post) catastrophic theorizations, like those of bell hooks, are written 'from that space in the margin that is a site of creativity and power', an empowering space that Said envisions as late style resistance, which is grounded in the trialectics of spatiality, historicality and sociality, otherwise identified by Soja as Thirdspace resistance (1996: 71). It is in this space in the *margin*, which, for Said, is precisely the space inhabited by the intellectual, a space that is moral, humanist, resistant and *paradoxically* empowering. I say paradoxically, of course, because the margin is the space that the hegemonic or imperialist power reserves for the oppressed and the weak. However, hooks makes the all-important argument that this margin, which is an oppressive, silencing space, can indeed be transformed into one of fierce resistance:

> these statements identify marginality as much more than a site of deprivation; in fact I was saying just the opposite, that it is also the site of radical possibility, a space of resistance. It was this marginality that I was naming a central location for the production of a counter-hegemonic discourse that is not just found in words but in habits of being and the way one lives. As such, I was not speaking of a marginality one wishes to lose – to give up or surrender as part of moving into the center – but rather of a site one stays in, clings to even, because it nourishes one's capacity to resist. It offers to one the possibility of radical perspective from which to see and create, to imagine alternatives, new worlds.
>
> (1990: 150)

People can become radicalized living in marginal spaces precisely because they anticipate better worlds; they imagine alternatives that are the opposite of their oppressive spaces. This is the margin imposed by the white man, not only in the slave-holding era, but also in the ingrained systemic racism of American institutions. This was recently made abundantly clear in the Black Lives Matter movement and police killings of black men and women in the United States, the most prominent of which was the killing of George Floyd on 25 May 2020. It is in the margin of the oppressed that hooks, as an intellectual, *chooses* to exist. The fact that this is her choice is empowering. The Black intellectual, specifically the Black female intellectual, transforms this space into a site of resistance for the imagination and creation of new worlds, new realities.

Leaving the margin would mean leaving the world of the oppressed and joining the centre, thus turning a blind eye to the 'wretched of the earth', to use Fanon's phrase. Interestingly enough, not only does hooks seem to come very close to Said's concept of the intellectual, which is elaborated on below, but she also emphasizes that theory should not be based on abstractions, but on 'habits of being'. Theory must be grounded in the very real suffering of people at the margins of societies, specifically ghettos as in the case of African Americans and refugee camps and occupation as in the case of the dispossessed Palestinian people.

Theorizations such as those by Said and hooks are what I am calling (post) catastrophic in the sense that counter-hegemonic discourses arise from experiences that are catastrophic, but rather than seeing such events as having started and ended in the past, these events continue in the present. The suffering of the oppressed continues. In the case of African Americans, the racism they face in the United States is systemic. Many Black Americans live in ghettos. Palestinians are literally forced into marginal spaces that are enclosed and blockaded spaces. The majority of Palestinians live under occupation, many in Israel's solitary confinement prisons, or under siege in the open-air prison of Gaza; others live in refugee camps inside occupied Palestine or in neighbouring countries. All of these marginal spaces, hooks would argue, become sites of resistance. Of course these marginal spaces exist, as Soja argues, historically and spatially, but also very significantly socially (1996: 11). While these marginal Thirdspaces of resistance were originally spaces of oppression, they are transformed spaces whereby the marginalized, colonized, dispossessed and deprived mount radical creative resistance to this oppression.

These are also (post) catastrophic spaces, as I would argue, precisely because, as hooks explains, they are not 'mythic', but rather come from 'lived experience' (150). In fact, hooks very specifically states that '[w]e come to this space through suffering and pain, through struggle' (153). Hooks cautions against those who would identify themselves as 'radical critical thinkers, feminist thinkers' (151) who speak about the marginalized or dispossessed and who want the marginalized to tell their story and speak about their pain, but not to speak in a 'voice of resistance' (152). For hooks, it is specifically this margin that allows for a space of radical openness. Hooks, however, significantly points out that the margin is not an exclusive space from which only the oppressed can speak. It is rather an inclusive space that allows entry to those who stand in solidarity with the oppressed, but not from their position in the centre, which is the space of the oppressor, the colonizer (151). It is in the margin where different parties can meet as *liberators*:

> This is an intervention. A message from that space in the margin that is a site of creativity and power, that inclusive space where we recover ourselves, where we move in solidarity to erase the category colonized/colonizer. Marginality as site of resistance. Enter that space. Let us meet there. Enter that space. We greet you as liberators.
>
> (152)

Speaking from the centre means speaking from within the ideological and political platform of the hegemonic power and playing by their rules, which inevitably means rejecting the voice of resistance that would lead to the true liberation of the oppressed.

Thus as both hooks and Said believe true resistance and an oppositional counter-discourse can only be constructed in the margin. Hooks is careful to point out that those who stand in solidarity with the oppressed must join the oppressed in the margin because speaking from the centre does not allow the speaker to listen to the 'Other' and experience with them their oppression and their *resistance* to it. This is why it seems to me that British writers who stand in solidarity with Palestine, such as the British critics Patrick Williams, Anna Bernard, Lindsey Moore, Anna Ball and the American geographer/theorist, Edward Soja tend to tread carefully into these marginal spaces.

While Said and hooks emphasize that the lived experience of the oppressed may better position the marginalized individual to choose and speak from the margin, they do not make this a precondition for revolutionary radicalization. An individual who comes from a hegemonizing culture can certainly adopt a marginal position and speak and act with the radical openness of an actual intellectual in exile, such as Said himself. Said states:

> Even if one is not an actual immigrant or expatriate, it is still possible to think as one, to imagine and investigate in spite of barriers, and always to move away from the centralizing authorities towards the margins, where you see things that are usually lost on minds that never traveled beyond the conventional and the comfortable.
>
> (*Representations of the Intellectual*, 1994b: 46–7)

In fact, as we have seen above, hooks 'invites' people from the centre to enter the margin as liberators in her intervention quoted in full earlier. Alternatively, hooks cautions that not all marginalized people are radicalized precisely because they are not aware of the 'nature of power and domination that is confirmed experientially' (1990: 189). To slightly alter Said's words, it can be said that these marginalized people have not consciously travelled into the margin although, ironically, they live there but paradoxically remain in a metaphorical and mental centre of conventionality and supposed comfort.

For Said, the intellectual's true vocation is working for the oppressed, and this work can only be done from the margin, which as hooks affirms is a site of resistance and radical openness. In Said's terminology, the intellectual must maintain a restless spirit lest he/she fall into a state of conventionality, complacency and the comfort of belonging. In this way, the Saidian intellectual's restlessness mirrors the restless spirit of Palestine and Palestinians, the dispossessed population, many of whom have been living in refugee camps for several generations since the *Nakba* of 1948, not only on the margins of societies, but in unlivable and unthinkable conditions. It is this restless spirit of Palestine that motivates the intellectual to stand in solidarity with the Palestinian cause. To speak out for justice in a yet unrealized Palestine is seen as anti-Semitic in many parts and sectors of the hegemonic West that fully supports the brutality of Israel, even describing this aggression and brutality as 'self-defense'.[1] Thus, it is Said's theorizing of Palestine that helped to crystalize much of his theoretical work in exile. Said says of the intellectual exile in *Representations*:

> Exile means that you are always going to be marginal, and that what you do as an intellectual has to be made up because you cannot follow a prescribed path.
>
> (1994b: 45)

> Exile for the intellectual in this metaphysical sense is restlessness, movement, constantly being unsettled, and unsettling others. You cannot go back to some earlier and perhaps more stable condition of being at home; and, alas, you can never fully arrive, be at one with your new home or situation.
>
> (1994b: 39)

Thus for Said, as well as for hooks, the revolutionary intellectual of radical openness chooses the margin as an intentional, ethical and empowering response to all forms of oppression. The comforts of belonging to the hegemonizing or dominant centre are in complete opposition to the vocation of the intellectual whose role is to speak truth to power, to 'raise embarrassing questions, to confront orthodoxy and dogma ... to be someone who cannot easily be co-opted by governments or corporations, and whose *raison d'etre* is to represent all those people and issues that are routinely forgotten or swept under the rug' (*Representations*, 1994b: 9). The restlessness of the intellectual entails that humanist work still needs to be done, and as Patrick Williams states, postcolonial studies is not about what has already been achieved *postcolonially*, but about the injustices and oppression that still remain in our (post) colonial world.

Said's intellectual lives in a metaphorical exile on the margins of society. This margin is an inclusive space that the intellectual enters in solidarity with the oppressed and dispossessed peoples in this world. Rehnuma Sazzad emphasizes the metaphorical context of Said's concept of intellectual exile (2017: 235), which is connected to Said's strong belief that intellectual stances are taken affiliatively rather than filiatively. Political and human stances are chosen, intentional acts that are not bestowed upon someone as a result of the accident of birth. For Said, however, even affiliation can take on the characteristics of filiation, and the intellectual must guard against falling into this filiative trap. This can be avoided only if the criticism offered by the intellectual is *oppositional* with regard to the presumed 'moral' discourses and actions of the hegemonic world order. It is this same world that ensures the enslavement, oppression and dispossession of certain populations while it secures the power, dominance, affluence and prosperity of the 'first' (white) world. The title of Gauri Viswanathan's book *Masks of Conquest* (1989) fittingly describes these discourses and strategies of colonization whether they be missionary work or English literary study in the not too distant past or the more recent 'wars on terrorism' and 'wars for the freedom' of peoples in nations not within the American/Western sphere of influence.[2]

The argument in favour of the metaphorical exile of the intellectual put forward by Sazzad in her book *Edward Said's Concept of Exile* (2017), which I wholeheartedly support, is nuanced, especially in the following quotation where she states: 'Therefore, the exilic framework could be tested with respect to contemporary intellectuals who endure colonial and imperial domination and yet retain their faith in a humanistic world through their creativity, that correlates conflicting identities' (237). Many of the critics and intellectuals of postcolonial theory originate from the previously colonized world, or, as in Said's case, the colonized world. Since Palestine is still a colonized land, this adds a certain *urgency* to Said's (post) catastrophic formulations and strong stances of speaking truth to power, upholding a secular and critical consciousness and speaking from marginal spaces.

In fact, Said felt the loss of his people, a loss the ramifications of which continue to be felt to this day. In a documentary produced by the BBC entitled 'In Search of Palestine – Edward Said's Return Home', documenting his visit to occupied Palestine after his leukaemia diagnosis, Said becomes quite emotional at a certain point as he describes the constant uprooting of the Palestinian people, in this particular case, the Jahaleen Bedouin who were uprooted from the Negev desert in 1948. The Jahaleen settled in several places in the 'West Bank', and at the time of this documentary, they were settled near Jerusalem. The Zionist occupation has constantly expelled the Jahaleen Bedouin from every place they ever settled, including their most recent place of settlement where their tents and belongings were very barbarically taken down and scattered. Said, who is shown witnessing this latest expulsion, has this to say as he fights back tears:

> For the last several days, they've been living without shelter, and their plight is … well, I think the only word for it is tragic, it's disastrous. And this in essence is the Palestinian tragedy, the daily uprootings, daily evictions, daily destruction of property and homes takes place and people are powerless to do anything about it. The world has taken very little notice of this, and I must say that it's very, very hard for me to stand here talking about it when I see my own people going through this. It's endless cavalry without any relief, without any sympathy or support from the so-called civilized world, which backs Israel and these barbaric, inhuman practices.

Said, here, is speaking from a space of great pain and loss that can be said to be based on the experience of 'my own people' as he very specifically says in a broken and tearful voice. Being born a Palestinian, however, is not enough to create an oppositional, resistant and exilic identity – this transformation is inevitably *metaphorical* as Sazzad insists in her overall argument of Said's concept of exile and the intellectual.

In this sense, Said was not merely born a Palestinian, but more importantly *became* a Palestinian when he constructed himself as one after the 1967 Arab defeat or *Naksa*. This event is what effected his transformation into a Palestinian, meaning one with a resistant, exilic mindset. However, the nuance here is important – can one really affirm that Said's pre-1967 exilic existence in the United States was totally and utterly (non) Palestinian. I strongly believe that it would be fair to say that regardless of the significance of this year (1967) for many Arab intellectuals, and especially for Said himself, Said's Palestinian identity and sense of belonging to an oppressed and dispossessed people must have always been brewing deep inside this American ivy-league professor and only surfaced at this particular point due to the urgency of that particular moment in time. Although, as mentioned a little earlier that after 1967, Said 'began constructing himself as Palestinian', I think that the building blocks for this construction process were already there pre-1967 – it was very much a process of *becoming* or in the making. Said told Tariq Ali in conversation that before 1967:

> I had taken in a few things along the way. I was obsessed with the fact that many of my cultural heroes – Edmund Wilson, Isaiah Berlin, Reinhold Niebuhrwere fanatical Zionists. Not just pro-Israeli: they said the most awful things about the Arabs, in print. But all I could do was note it. Politically, there was no place for me to go.

(2006: 71–2)

Thus, one could say that pre-1967, Said was observing, noting and possibly already imaginatively constructing his own space, a sort of beginning. This sense of being a part of a dispossessed community underscores that Said's identity as a Palestinian or his journey of becoming Palestinian inevitably means that his personal identity is also a national one. However, Said's emphasis on a Palestinian national identity is at the same time to resist the extinction of a people, culture and their way of life. It is in this sense, then, that Said differentiates between the identity politics, for example, of the white nationalistic supremacy of the Western hegemonic world, which can only be destructive, bringing 'trouble', 'suffering' and 'killing rather than living', and the identity politics of the dispossessed and oppressed Palestinian people, for example, due to the fact that their identity is constantly under the threat of extinction: 'I speak only of aggressive identity politics, not the defense of identity when threatened by extinction, as in the Palestinian case' (*Humanism and Democratic Criticism*, 2004: 77).

This is precisely why it took a Said to initiate the interrogation of colonial discourse and theorize the culture of imperialism and inevitably the culture of resistance. Having said this much, however, it should be emphasized here that the point being made is not an argument based on the importance of a filiative order or a nativist position, which Said himself very much despised and spent much of his intellectual career railing against, but rather one based on *experience*. In the 'Afterword to the 1995 Printing' of *Orientalism*, Said, commenting on Basim Musallam's critique of *Orientalism* as being a book that could only be written by a an individual 'with a particular background and experience' (338), and 'not just any "Arab"' (ibid.), admits that his book (and I would add, his whole theoretical oeuvre) did indeed arise out of a very deep and painful feeling of national and personal loss not felt by other Arabs:

> Musallam correctly notes that an Algerian would not have written the same kind of generally pessimistic book.... So while I would accept the overall impression that *Orientalism* is written out of an extremely concrete history of personal loss and national disintegration – only a few years before I wrote *Orientalism* Golda Meir made her notorious and deeply Orientalist comment about there being no Palestinian people – I would like to add that neither in this book nor in the two that immediately followed it, *The Question of Palestine* (1980) and *Covering Islam* (1981), did I want only to suggest a political program of restored identity and resurgent nationalism.
>
> (338)

Thus, Said is careful to point out that he is not interested in, nor did he aim to write, a book to suggest any kind of narrow political programme or a nativist position or attitude, but rather to examine how dominant narratives and discourses, such as Western Orientalism and Zionism construct themselves as modern, Western and civilized and are pitted against backward-looking, Eastern or Oriental and uncivilized discourses and societies.

Said's three topics, the Orient or the East, Palestine and Islam in his trilogy of *Orientalism*, *The Question of Palestine* and *Covering Islam* respectively are to be seen in the same context of the Orientalism and racism of the West against the cultures, histories and religions of the Arab region. Palestine and Islam, from the perspective of the liberal West and Zionism, are to be seen within the context of Orientalism. Constructed as such by Western and Zionist discourses, these 'primitive' and 'barbaric' societies and causes are silenced and do not have the 'permission to narrate', which is the title of Said's 1984 essay. Thus, it is within this discourse of Orientalism that Palestine is textualized and contextualized by Western Zionism for the world. Identified and defined in this way, Palestine and the Palestinians are easily effaced for the sake of a '"higher" … interest, cause, or mission' (Said, 1992 [1979]: 15):

> These 'higher' things entitle their proponents not only to claim that the natives of Palestine, such as they are, are not worth considering and therefore nonexistent; they also feel entitled to claim that the natives of Palestine, and Palestine itself, have been superseded definitively, transformed completely and beyond recall …. Here again the Arab Palestinian has been pitted against an undeniably superior antagonist whose consciousness of himself and of the Palestinian is exactly, *positionally*, superior.
>
> (Said, 1979: 15)

This is indeed the same positional superiority that Said addressed a year earlier in the first part of his trilogy, *Orientalism* where he writes: 'Orientalism depends for its strategy on this flexible *positional* superiority, which puts the Westerner in a whole series of possible relationships with the Orient without ever losing him the relative upper hand' (1978: 7). The Palestinian, then, is constructed as the primitive Oriental without a just cause unlike the Jewish Israeli who has a higher cause and represents Western civilization.

Not only were the founding fathers of Israel Western Zionists, but even today, Israel considers itself, and Europe considers it, a European country (it won the song contest 'Eurovision' in 2018). It is a Western state, regardless of its geographical Easterness. It is civilizationally and culturally a Western state and rightfully so, since, it is after all, an unnatural presence on this geographically, historically and culturally, Eastern space. The paradox of Israel's Western identity in this Eastern space is especially pronounced in this speech by the Russian born (born in Leningrad, the Soviet Union in 1975) Israeli Knesset member, Anastasia Michaeli, who had this to say about the Muslim call to prayer in Jerusalem:

> Muslim clerics must find another way to call to prayer or send religious and national messages, not through defiance and demonstration of ownership [at the expense of] life quality as they do today, but in a way that doesn't disrupt the lives of citizens, and takes into consideration that we live in a Western and civilized country.
>
> (qtd. in Schwarz, 2013: 2034)

Thus, Palestinian Muslims, who have been living in Jerusalem for over 1,000 continuous years and where the Muslim call to prayer, the *athan*, has been heard throughout the city for an equal number of years, are now being told by this Russian born Israeli Knesset member that the *athan* is not allowed in the 'Western and civilized' city of Jerusalem. Western and civilized aside, it is obvious that the main aim behind this kind of Zionist discourse is to erase Arab Islamic culture from the soundscape of Jerusalem. In a similar gesture, the Israeli Culture and Sports Minister, Miri Regev, introduced legislation in the Israeli Knesset that would demand loyalty to/with (Israeli) culture (Lis et al., 2016). Again, the aim behind such legislation is to criminalize Palestinian Arab culture and at the same time force loyalty to Israeli culture upon Palestinians. Here again, we see a slow, steady process of the ethnic and cultural cleansing of Palestine and Palestinians.

Before Said published his trilogy mentioned above, he published an expanded version of his doctoral dissertation, entitled *Joseph Conrad and the Fiction of Autobiography* in 1966 and then after the 1967 Six Day War, or *Naksa* (setback) as it is known in Palestinian terminology, Said reinvented himself as a Palestinian as mentioned earlier. After this catastrophic event, Said published his 1975 book *Beginnings: Intention and Method*, which introduced to the world Said's theoretical framework. Said based his concepts of origins and beginnings on the work of the seventeenth-century Italian philosopher, Giambattista Vico. Said's secular ideas with regard to history and the historical process were definitely taking root and forming the core of his early theoretical ideas at this early point in his career, and this is obvious by his emphasis on the very idea of beginnings and human intention, which he differentiates from origins or any given form of sacred knowledge. Said writes:

> For the searching modern mind, as for our savage first fathers, a principle of 'divinity' arrived at through fear and not reason 'reduces a liberty gone wild'. Only by imagining (divining=inventing) a force anterior to our origin, a force for Vico capable of preventing further regress into irremediable savagery, can we begin to be human ... for according to Vico, most history is a human and *gentile* affliction, whereas for the Jews there is life 'founded by the true God' .... The crucial distinction is between the gentiles who divine or imagine divinity, on the one hand, and the Hebrews whose true God prohibits divination, on the other. To be a gentile is to be denied access to the true God, to have recourse for thought to divination, to live permanently in history, in an order other than God's, to be able genetically to produce that order of history. Vico's concerns are everywhere with this other order, the [world] of history made by men.
>
> (1975: 349–50)

It is my firm belief that Said's deep thought about the Palestinian *Nakba*, the dispossession of the Palestinians, the ethnic cleansing of Palestine and the constructed Western/Zionist narratives to justify the establishment of Israel had much to do with the development of his theoretical oeuvre. Said's distinction (and

Vico's before him) between the gentile and the Hebrew world concerning history is pivotal to understanding secular man-made history (Said, 1975: 349–50).

Said, in fact, does not leave this idea without explanation in his trilogy, a few years after the publication of *Beginnings*. The idea of the 'Promised Land', a sacred land promised by God to the Jews is a narrative that would play out well in the Christian West, and it did indeed because Israel, as an 'advanced Western state', naturally became an integral part of the Judeo-Christian Western tradition and an extension of the West and how the West saw itself as opposed to a 'dumb, essentially repellent population of uncivilized Arab natives' (Said, 1979: 8), as Zionists were able to successfully represent to the West. This narrative has been very widely diffused in the 'civilized' world for decades to the total exclusion and silencing of a counter Palestinian narrative. Said well understood that the 'Promised Land' idea and the slogan popularized by Israel Zangwill of 'a land without a people, for a people without a land' (Masalha, 1992: 50) were used specifically to erase the actual *historical* presence of the Palestinians as a people. The Palestinians were unworthy of consideration since they were irrelevant in the greater scheme of things as clearly spelled out by Arthur Balfour, the British Prime Minister from 1902 to 1905 and later Foreign Secretary from 1916 to 1919. In a memorandum, Balfour wrote:

> *For in Palestine we do not propose even to go through the form of consulting the wishes of the present inhabitants of the country* .... The four great powers are committed to Zionism and Zionism, be it right or wrong, good or bad, is rooted in age-long tradition, in present needs, in future hopes, *of far profounder import than the desire and prejudices of the 700,000 Arabs who now inhabit that ancient land.*
>
> (qtd. in Said, 1979: 16–7)

Thus, proponents of Western imperialism and Zionism were well aware of the existence of the inhabitants of this ancient land. It is just that these people were of no importance and did not even have to be asked about their impending dispossession and eradication since they would be removed or transferred for a 'far profounder' cause. This cause was rooted in 'age-long tradition', which is an obvious reference to the Judeo-Christian tradition that is based on the idea of God's promise to the Jews the land of Palestine.

Here, gentile human history has been replaced by the sacred decree of the one true God to whom only the Hebrews have access. Within the context of the law of the Hebrew God, the Palestinians actual historical existence on the land of Palestine is totally wiped out. Said's understanding of history is a gentile, secular one based on human intention or agency to invent, divine, imagine the truth, a truth based on human effort. This kind of divination or imagination is rooted in human history, and grants humankind the ability to begin and begin again, especially after catastrophe. This is precisely what Said's own people experienced in 1948, a catastrophe that was enabled by all the world powers at that time, but especially by the British who were directly responsible for the establishment of

Israel, which was promised to the Jewish people by God and Britain as detailed in the 1917 Balfour Declaration. Britain promised the Jewish people a national home in the land of Palestine. The arrogance of the British colonial master was such that he saw fit to do whatever he wanted with a territory under his mandate without even a consideration for the actual inhabitants of this land as Said points out in *The Question of Palestine*:

> Balfour's statements in the declaration take for granted the higher right of the colonial power to dispose of a territory as it saw fit. As Balfour himself averred, this was especially true when dealing with such a significant territory as Palestine and with such a momentous idea as the Zionist idea, which saw itself as doing no less than reclaiming a territory promised originally by God to the Jewish people.
> (1992 [1979]: 16)

Considering the divinity of the sacred Hebrew God, Said proposes a secular divinity, the power to divine and imagine, which bestows upon the human being the power to act, to resist, to begin. Beginning, then, is to be seen as a form of resistance that allows the oppressed to reject the status quo, the 'sacred' givens in any society. This is a point that Said repeatedly underscores in his theoretical oeuvre. In one of his posthumous publications, Said states that '[h]umanism is, to some extent, a resistance to *idees recues*, and it offers opposition to every kind of cliché and unthinking language' (*Humanism and Democratic Criticism*, 2004: 43).

The very idea of resistance seems to occupy Said's imagination whether it is resistance to received ideas, oppressive hegemonic discourses, colonizing powers or systemic racism ... wherever the humanist intellectual encounters power, he/she must speak truth. Said finds these humanist qualities in the likes of (I list them here in the order that Said does in his book *Humanism and Democratic Criticism*): John Pilger, Alexander Cockburn, Chomsky, Zinn, Eqbal Ahmad, Germaine Greer, Mohammed Sid Ahmad, bell hooks, Angela Davis, Cornel West, Serge Halimi, Miyoshi, Ranajit Guha, Partha Chatterjee, Seamus Deane, Luke Gibbons, Declan Kiberd (2004:126). I would add, Roger Waters amongst others. So for Said, it is not enough to 'define the situation, but also to discern the possibilities for active intervention' (*Humanism and Democratic Criticism*, 2004: 140).

This intervention is the very act of resistance that would help bring forth, to quote Patrick Williams, who was quoting Ernst Bloch, the 'outlines of a better world' (2010: 93), which, for Said, should be the goal of the humanist intellectual (that is one who works in the humanities) and not the petty '[p]rovincialism of the old kind – for example, a literary specialist whose field is early-seventeenth-century England – rules itself out and quite frankly, seems uninteresting and needlessly neutered' (*Humanism and Democratic Criticism*, 2004: 140). This provincialism, unfortunately and quite ironically, is still alive and well at universities in the Arab world, where there is a very strong resistance to allowing the 'intellectual' outside the narrow field of his/her area of specialization, which Said correctly describes as being 'neutered'. In complete opposition to the 'safe' non-political scholar and expert of a specific field of literary study, a type very prominent at Arab universities' humanities' departments, Said proposes the intellectual's critical consciousness, a concept adopted and adapted by Said from Luckacs's idea of the proletariat class consciousness that has insurrectionary potential. In the same way, the Saidian intellectual's critical consciousness has a similar revolutionary potential to create a 'better situation from the known historical and social facts' (ibid.).

Perhaps the Saidian idea of resistance is best encapsulated in his concept of late style, which is a form of (post) catastrophic resistance that is both simultaneously personal and national/collective. Said elaborates on late style, borrowing important concepts from Theodor Adorno's discussion of Beethoven's late works, in a posthumously published book entitled *On Late Style: Music and Literature Against the Grain* (2007):

> But what of artistic lateness not as harmony and resolution but as intransigence, difficulty, and unresolved contradiction? What if age and ill health don't produce the serenity of 'ripeness is all'? .... Beethoven's late compositions are in fact about 'lost totality', and are therefore catastrophic .... For Adorno, lateness is the idea of surviving beyond what is acceptable and normal .... Lateness ... is a kind of self-imposed exile from what is generally acceptable, coming after it, and surviving beyond it.
>
> (7–16)

Said's response to his ill health, specifically to his leukaemia diagnosis, is one of defiance and intransigence, a late style resistance that does not 'admit the definitive cadences of death; instead, death appears in a refracted mode, as irony' (2007: 24). It is his impending death that seems to have reinvigorated Said's attachment to his homeland in the form of introducing his children, Wadie and Najla, to his personal and of course collective 'lost totality', and which he documented in his memoir *Out of Place* (2000) and his documentary *In Search of Palestine: Edward Said's Return Home* (1998). After his diagnosis, Said admitted that his immediate reaction was that he 'had been thinking regressively about finding a place to die in. I gave up the idea' (2000: 215). Said had decided that he would not 'admit the definitive cadences of death', but rather that death (which 'appears in refracted mode') had ironically brought out in Said a defiant will to live and not to surrender to this catastrophic situation. Said, the person, like Beethoven and Adorno, became the living embodiment of late style. This survival 'beyond what is acceptable and normal' requires an artistic and actual (as in surviving difficult situations) repertoire or survival kit, so to speak, and this most aptly describes the Palestinian situation as Micheal Wood points out in his introduction to *On Late Style*. Quoting an unpublished note by Said, Wood writes: '"We are a people of message and signals," he says of the Palestinians, "of allusions and indirect expression"' (Said qtd. in Wood, 2007: xix).

In fact, in describing the style of his book *After the Last Sky*, Said comes very close to what he means by late style, which, unlike Adorno, Said puts to cultural and political use. In this book of text and photos, Said describes the aesthetics of his book, which as he says, also describes the Palestinian people's difficult existence and struggle:

> The whole point of this book is to engage this difficulty ... [to capture] the complex reality of [Palestinian] experience. Its style and method – the interplay of text and photos, the mixture of genres, modes, styles – do not tell a consecutive story .... Since the main features of our present existence are dispossession, dispersion, and yet also a kind of power incommensurate with our stateless exile, I believe that essentially unconventional, hybrid, and fragmentary forms of expression should be used to represent us.
>
> (6)

The artistic and aesthetic difficulty of late style then mirrors the (post) catastrophic existence of the Palestinian people who are indeed living daily catastrophes, tragedies and dispossessions as discussed earlier in this chapter. This national/collective and political connection of Saidian late style is even more pronounced in his article entitled, 'On Lost Causes' from his book *Reflections on Exile and Other Literary and Cultural Essays* (2001) where Said speaks not only personally, but also collectively, often referring to the Palestinian people as 'we', in his response to what he considers to be the utter defeat of the Palestinian leadership after signing the Oslo Accords with Israel. Here Said writes both personally and nationally: 'To me and every Palestinian I know these agreements [Oslo Accords] signify defeat, not only militarily and territorially but more important, morally' (2001: 550). For Said, these Accords meant that the Palestinian leadership had surrendered its right to struggle for self-determination and the liberation of historic Palestine. He felt that the Palestinian leadership, led by Yasser Arafat, had accepted defeat instead of the refusal to surrender, which had been a principle of the Palestinian revolution. 'Now', Said writes, 'we had conceded that we were prepared to exist not as a sovereign people on our land but as a scattered, dispossessed people ...' (2001: 550–1). But to Said's mind, this is not the spirit of a people who refuse to surrender or accept defeat, and here again Said remembers Adorno who 'posits as an alternative to resigned capitulation of the lost cause the intransigence of the individual thinker whose power of expression is a power ... that enacts a movement of vitality, a gesture of defiance' (2001: 552–3) and, for Said, whatever form this survival takes, it is better than 'silence or joining in the chorus of defeated activists' (ibid.).

Within the context of the above conceptualizations of Saidian late style, I find Khaled Mattawa's representation of late style in Palestinian literature generally and in Darwish's work specifically to be not very accurately (re)presented. Late style does not mean that Palestinian literature needs to leave the discussion on Palestine behind and concern itself with the aesthetics of poetry separately from any consideration of Palestine in order to make headways into the Palestinian contribution to the modernization of Arabic literature. Saidian late style is not only an aesthetic style, but also a way of life for Said, and as I would argue, for the Palestinian struggle in the post-millennial era in general. Mattawa seems to imply that Darwish could only show his aesthetic skill when he separates himself from Palestine, quoting the Bahrani poet Qassim Haddad about the seeming Palestinianlessness of Darwish's long poem, 'Mural', in compliance with the rules of postmodernism and post-nationalism:

> He [Darwish] longed for an opportunity to demonstrate his skills in the daylight of artistic judgement alone. With *Mural*, Darwish appeared to do that, and he received the acclaim he needed. For the acclaimed Bahraini poet Qassim Haddad, *Mural* was the first time he was able to 'read Darwish without his Palestinianness and I must say that that feeling pleased me'.
> (Mattawa, 2014: 146)

One wonders how poets and critics, such as Mattawa and Haddad, believe that a poet like Darwish can separate his artistic skill from his experience and identity or put them on hold in order to emphasize his aesthetic skill as if the two are not intertwined. Mattawa and Haddad should have concentrated more deeply on Darwish's line 'The martyr teaches me: no aesthetic outside my freedom' from his poem 'State of Siege' (2007: 163), which is discussed in Chapter 2 of this book. Mattawa seems to relate Saidian late style with postmodernism's disinterest in 'grand narratives' and Palestinian literature's late style interest in what he calls 'normalization … in keeping with contemporary global aesthetic standards and historical paradigms' (2014: 139).

While I totally agree with Mattawa that aesthetic skill is indeed of the utmost importance, I believe that he is totally off the mark to argue that Palestinian culture, as a crises culture, should follow in the footsteps of postmodern standards. Summarizing Ghassan Kanafani's position on the aesthetics versus politics debate, Bashir Abu Manneh rightly points out that inside post-1948 occupied Palestine, which was put under a cultural siege by Israel in the years after the creation of the Jewish state, 'traditional cultural forms' were used in Palestinian poetry 'for more urgent and immediate political purposes: those of defending and maintaining Arab cultural identity under threat of extinction' (2016: 76). How Mattawa is able to make this particular point about the separation of aesthetics from the Palestinian cause in the context of Saidian late style is, at the very least, extremely ironic when Said himself makes the absolute opposite observation in his *Representations of the Intellectual* in which he argues:

> The purpose of the intellectual's activity is to advance human freedom and knowledge. This is still true, I believe, despite the often repeated charge that 'grand narratives of emancipation and enlightenment', as the contemporary French philosopher Lyotard calls such heroic ambitions associated with the previous 'modern' age, are pronounced as no longer having any currency in the era of postmodernism. According to this view grand narratives have been replaced by local situations and language games; postmodern intellectuals now prize competence, not universal values like truth or freedom.
> (1994b: 13–14)

Thus, in Said's mind, late style, which constitutes a 'form of exile' (2007: 8) is the attitude the secular intellectual adopts and whose significance is not merely in the professionalism involved in 'local situations and language games' and 'priz[ing] competence' in a particular field of study. For Said, late style resistance is the work of the intellectual amateur whose distinguishing characteristic is restlessness and 'constantly being unsettled, and unsettling others' (*Representations*, 1994b: 39) and most importantly, taking a principled stance of 'speak[ing] the truth to power' (*Representations*, 1994b: 71).

The intellectual, then, will always be on the uncomfortable margin and speak the truth that would unsettle others. One of the most urgent examples of this unsettling truth that today's intellectuals must tell involves the truth of Palestinian dispossession, which is narrated in varying degrees of truth and untruth by experts and politicians on both the right and left of the global political spectrum. Some of these experts and politicians do not know the truth due to a very powerful Zionist propaganda machine; others know the truth and wish to conceal it for ideological reasons and still others who know the truth, but continue to practice self-censorship, fearing they may be labelled anti-Semitic. Very few intellectuals can truly speak the truth to a worldwide hegemonic power apparatus, which can crush all who dissent, oppose or resist this unjust colonial machinery of thought and control. This is why the truly principled intellectual's space must always be an oppositional and resistant one, and in our times, Palestine has become the most silenced of discursive spaces.

After I completed the writing of a major part of this book, I read the latest book by the well-known critic Hamid Dabashi entitled *On Edward Said: Remembrance of Things Past* (2020) in which Dabashi writes about how Palestine inspired Said's theory, which corroborates what I am arguing in this chapter. Dabashi's words are worth quoting here:

> Said's eminent contemporaries like Jean-Paul Sartre or Michel Foucault or Noam Chomsky have cared a little bit about everything. Said, on the contrary, cared for Palestine as if it was the very first and the very last reason for justice on planet Earth. Everything else he cared for and articulated came out and flowered theoretically from that singular cause of his moral outrage.
>
> (14)

Dabashi goes on to say that 'Palestine remains an open wound and an open-ended metaphor' (15). It is indeed the literal and metaphorical 'open wound' of Palestine, this grave historical injustice of our present time that has caused the restlessness of the Palestinian imagination, and which has, I believe, allowed for the development of Said's most important theoretical ideas. These ideas have become for many working inside and outside the postcolonial and the more recent and perhaps more radical field of decolonial studies, the maxims of critical and oppositional thinking and anti-colonial discourse in the twentieth and twenty first centuries. Said's groundbreaking and revolutionary ideas (secular criticism and the critical consciousness, worldliness, beginnings, late style and speaking truth to power) were most essentially enabled by, what I am calling, the *theorization of Palestine*. The intellectual, who stands with the oppressed in that marginal space, is by definition, dealing with catastrophic situations and peoples; however, the catastrophic, instead of creating the pessimism of loss, which translates into defeat and a defeatist mentality, on the contrary, engenders defiance and the intransigent will to survive and resist.

Thus, to choose the margin, as bell hooks would say, is to choose to resist, which is in itself an intentional act of empowerment, a concept that can indeed be placed alongside Said's emphasis on beginnings, which are chosen (again, note the intentional act of choosing) rather than origins, which are given. Thus, Palestine, which fuelled Said's critical and theoretical ideas, and enabled a massive interrogation of colonial discourse in what came to be known as postcolonial studies, is bringing the postcolonial debate back to where it started, Palestine, where the wound still bleeds and the injustice remains. This is indeed a wake-up call to all principled intellectuals in the humanities and other fields, but specifically, the postcolonial field, where a postmodern smugness and love of abstract terminology have set in and have conveniently bypassed the unfashionable lateness of a still colonized and traumatized Palestine. This postmodern smugness infiltrating the postcolonial field has led those thinkers who are uncomfortable with this development to establish the more radical field of decolonial studies mentioned earlier.

What many postcolonial practitioners seem to overlook is that Said's intellectual is very much the revolutionary whether this entails an intellectual and cultural resistance or actual bodily resistance whereby the use of violence, or more specifically and appropriately termed, armed struggle, becomes an utter necessity. In fact, it is natural to come to this conclusion when we combine Said's ideas on the intellectual, the restless spirit, who chooses the margin, which is the space of the oppressed, with the late style thinker with the intransigent mind whose power is 'a gesture of defiance, a statement of hope' (2001: 552–3) against all odds. Said delineates his idea of resistance in *Culture and Imperialism* (1994a) where he clearly writes:

> Just as culture may predispose and actively prepare one society for the overseas domination of another, it may also prepare that society to relinquish or modify the idea of overseas domination. These changes cannot occur without the willingness of men and women to resist the pressures of colonial rule, to take up arms, to project ideas of liberation, and to imagine (as Benedict Anderson has it) a new national community.
>
> (241)

Thus Said's ideas on resistance involve intellectual, cultural and imaginative resistance, which means projecting ideas of liberation and imagining Palestine, as I am arguing here, but this form of resistant thinking also involves taking up arms in order to fight the colonizer.

Said's ideas on resistance came as a surprise to the host of *HARDtalk*, Tim Sebastian, in 2002 when a then terminally ill, late style defiant Said made his views abundantly clear in this exchange:

> Edward Said: I think the Palestinians need protection. Absolutely. The problem is that the last time there was an international peace force run by the US was in Lebanon in 1982, we had the massacres of Sabra and Shatila, they left too early.
> Tim Sebastian: Palestinians don't need protection if they stay in their houses and don't riot on the streets, do they?
> ES: Oh you mean eat grass and stones.
> TS: No, I mean don't attack Israeli border positions.
> ES: Look, it's not Israeli border positions, it's Israeli occupation forces who are deep in Palestinian territory, that is the problem ...
> TS: One was attacked actually as an agreement was being signed in Sharm Al Sheikh.
> ES: Good, I think it's important to attack occupation forces, wouldn't you attack an occupation force in your country, of course you would.
> TS: You've changed.
> ES: I haven't changed at all.
> ....
> TS: You're asking people to attack border posts?
> ES: I'm asking people to attack occupation forces, absolutely, I'm not a pacifist. I deeply believe that occupation, apartheid have to be resisted. And this is what we've been given from the Israelis ....
> TS: But you are openly advocating violence.
> ES: No, I'm not openly advocating violence, I'm simply saying that it is one's duty as a citizen to resist occupation; it may be non-violent resistance, certainly, I'm for that if it can be done. I'm for any kind of violence that would resist occupation and apartheid. It was the ANC position ....
> I'm simply saying that occupation and apartheid have to be resisted by whatever means bring about their end.

Said's stance on resistance, that is to resist colonization, occupation, apartheid and all forms of oppression by 'whatever means bring about their end', echoes, in fact, Fanon's and other 'Third World' revolutionary thinkers' positions on resistance and liberation, such as Aime Cesaire, Amilcar Cabral and the great Palestinian novelist and activist Kanafani. Fanon, like Said, spoke of using 'all means to turn the scale, including, of course, that of violence' (1963: 37). A bit later in his book *The Wretched of the Earth*, Fanon is even more adamant, saying that the colonized must liberate themselves by the 'use of all means, and that of force first and foremost' (61).

Said also lauds the military victories of the Lebanese resistance Hezbollah and their leader, 'Sheikh [Hassan] Nasrallah, [...] [whom] I found to be a remarkably impressive man. A very simple man, quite young, absolutely no bullshit' (*Power, Politics and Culture: interviews with Edward Said*, 2004: 445). Although as a secular intellectual, Said does not support any religious ideology, whether this be Hamas's or Hezbollah's or any other ideology per se, he wholeheartedly supports all forms of resistance against the (Zionist) colonizer. In this particular case, Said speaks of the euphoria of victory after twenty-two years of Israeli occupation of Lebanese land as shown in the following exchange with a *Ha'aretz* interviewer who mentions Said's now iconic image of his stone throwing at Fatma Gate at the Lebanese border with occupied Palestine:

> *Throwing stones at Fatma Gate when Israel had just ended its occupation of southern Lebanon seems to be not only a celebration of liberation, but a very basic rejection of something. Of what?*
>
> (Italics in original)

> A rejection of Israelis. The feeling is that after twenty-two years of occupying our land, they left. And there is also a sense of dismissal. Not only are you leaving, but good riddance to you. We don't want you to come back. So the atmosphere is rather 'carnivalesque', a sense of healthy anarchy, a triumphant feeling. For the first time in my life, and in the lives of the people gathering at Fatma Gate, we won. We won one.
>
> (*Power, Politics and Culture*, 2004: 446)

In these two interviews that Said made late in his life and career, he clearly spells out his position on resistance and liberation in what could be called his own, personal late style. These late style interviews serve as examples of his triumphant and 'carnivalesque' defiance, a defiance that shows how this public intellectual is able to put his theory into practice.

Without using complex theoretical abstractions, Said shows how theory is not about words and abstractions, but about things, real events that directly affect people's lives. This catastrophic reality of Palestine enabled Said to theorize and more importantly humanize Palestine, which in essence meant theorizing a revolutionary form of opposition and resistance based on humanizing the oppressed other or 'wretched of the earth', in the academy and outside it and endowing the oppressed with the power to resist.

Said's theoretical oeuvre revolves around the power of culture to create reality: 'Most importantly, such texts [imperialist or orientalist texts] can *create* not only knowledge but also the very reality they appear to describe' (*Orientalism*, 1978: 94). This Saidian perspective on culture is also obvious from the title of his book *Culture and Imperialism* (1994a) in which he argues that the imperialist project could not have been possible without culture, here specifically, the English and French novel. Said also believes that in the same way that culture enabled imperialism, it can essentially be used to resist colonialism by means of constructing a strong culture of resistance.

This same argument appears in Said's oeuvre in different guises and wordings in most, if not all, of his books. In *Covering Islam: How the Media and the Experts*

Determine How We See the Rest of the World (1997 [1981]), Said examines how the media is utilized not only to represent Islam in a certain way (basically the demonization of Muslims), but also to prepare the American public for war in a specific country, which could be any Arab or Muslim country depending on American economic, political and ideological interests at the time. The demonization of Arabs and Muslims is effectively achieved by manipulating the media apparatus,[3] thus manufacturing the required consent of the public as argued by Edward Herman and Noam Chomsky in their book entitled, *Manufacturing Consent: the Political Economy of the Mass Media* (1988).

The mass media and religious apparatuses in the Arab world over the last decade have played a major role in spreading toxic sectarian discourses meant to destroy these multi-ethnic and multi-religious societies that have lived together for hundreds of years. The well-known and highly respected Lebanese journalist, Talal Salman who was the editor-in-chief of the *Safir* newspaper for many years, had this assessment of the Arab situation:

> One must recall that maps of the region were hastily established in the 1920s at the whim of the colonialists and according to their calculations. The region was divided into political entities in accordance with their interests, and through open bargains between the British and the French, openly agreeing to clear a future place for the Israeli entity. All this is now being threatened by the possibility of a [popular] reevaluation of a status quo that has enabled international powers supporting the myth of a 'Shiite Crescent' to carry on implementing their plans in accordance with the principle of a new partition along confessional and sectarian lines.
>
> (qtd. in Hamdi, 2019: 60)

This new partitioning of the region based on confessional and sectarian lines would of course keep Arab populations fighting each other and would have the effect (as it has already) of inventing a new enemy for the majority *Sunni* Arab population, an intentionally emphasized term that is needed in the formation of new realignments.

Based on these realignments, Iran is the 'new enemy', taking the place of Israel, which for the supposedly 'moderate' Arab regimes has become an important ally. Also, please note the popular use of the word 'moderate' before Arab regime or country. The question to be asked is moderate in terms of what? Moderate here means US-backed or propped-up regime even if this regime imprisons its own people for the mere expression of a political opinion on social media that is seen to be problematic for this regime. The term 'Shiite Crescent' was first used in the year 2004, one year after the American 'shock and awe' invasion of Iraq. This newly invented term (the Shiite Crescent) first used by the leader of an Arab country (but perhaps designed in Western intelligence centres) historically allied to the UK and United States, signalled the formal beginning of this new partitioning of the Arab region, which would be disseminated by the ideological state apparatuses (ISAs) of US-backed Arab regimes, namely mass media and the religious apparatus. I would like to draw attention to Salman's use of the word '[popular]' in brackets, which I believe can have two possible meanings: firstly, this 'reevaluation of a status quo', which entails a realignment of Arab states based on sectarian lines, is popular in the sense that the majority of the Arab populace supports such a confessional realignment and secondly, it is a manufactured popularity. It was made popular by means of the direct involvement of these regimes' state apparatuses, a manufactured consent as theorized by Antonio Gramsci, Louis Althusser and more recently by Said and Chomsky.

Two years later in 2006 during Israel's invasion of Lebanon specifically to root out Hezbollah, the US Secretary of State, Condoleeza Rice, announced that this Israeli aggression represents the birth of a new Middle East, which would of course come with the necessary pain of massacring thousands of people: 'What we're seeing here, in a sense, is ... the birth pangs of a new Middle East and whatever we do, we have to be certain we're pushing forward to the new Middle East, not going back to the old one' (Condoleeza Rice qtd. in *International Socialist Review*, 2006). Of course, this new Middle East would be one realigned according to American and Israeli interests, a Middle East totally devoid of any resistance to these imperialist and Zionist interests. The United States and Israel failed miserably to crush the Lebanese resistance; however, the birth pangs described by Rice were indeed 'experienced after "creative chaos", the strategy envisioned by the Bush administration to create havoc in the Arab world in order to restructure a "new Middle East" whose necessary pain has been catastrophic for key Arab states, especially Iraq and Syria' (Hamdi, 2016a: 36). However, this new Western realignment of the Middle East may not be as successful as Western and Zionist interests hoped for due to a strong culturally charged counter-discourse that is making its effects felt around the region. This is elaborated on in the upcoming chapters.

Theorizing resistance literature: Ghassan Kanafani's contribution

Said was not the first Palestinian intellectual to theorize Palestine. At least a decade before Said, Kanafani, a firm believer in the effective use of culture and armed struggle, wrote some important essays on resistance literature. Once referred to as the 'commando who never fired a gun' (Harlow, 1986: 9), Kanafani began his own quest to theorize Palestine. Kanafani, who was assassinated (along with his seventeen-year-old niece, Lamees) by the Israeli Mossad in 1972, first coined the phrase 'resistance literature' as pointed out by Barbara Harlow in her seminal book *Resistance Literature* (1987: 2). It is interesting to note that Harlow, agreeing with Kanafani, saw resistance literature to be a cultural and historical production that is 'no less crucial than the armed struggle' (7). This is a view that corresponds with the formulations of Fanon, Cabral, Said and Kanafani himself.

Culturalism, for 'Third World' intellectuals, plays a pivotal role in the liberation struggle, especially in organizing and mobilizing the masses. Fanon clearly acknowledges the essential role of violence not only for the purposes of liberating the colonized land from the colonizer, but also as a form of psychotherapy whereby the dehumanized, colonized individual is rehumanized by using violence against the colonizer. He, however, posits the precondition of constructing a strong national culture without which there could be no successful revolution. This culture of resistance, for Fanon, most importantly revolves around what he calls a 'fighting literature', a 'revolutionary literature', a 'national literature', whereby the native intellectual becomes an 'awakener of the people' (1963: 223). It is perhaps worth mentioning here that, for Fanon, a national culture is a *unifying* culture that is inclusive of all its citizens and here Fanon distinguishes between custom and culture. This inclusivity of culture is a necessity for a people that 'undertakes an armed struggle or even a political struggle against a relentless colonialism' (1963: 224). Custom has an exclusive quality that is stuck in the past and is not dynamic, inclusive and progressive; in other words, its traditional and perhaps nativist character does not acknowledge the change brought about by the historical process.

Similarly, Amilcar Cabral, the Bissau-Guinean revolutionary and anti-colonial leader, sees national liberation as 'necessarily an act of *culture*' (Emphasis in the original, 1994: 56). A strong national culture is a unifying mechanism that must precede the necessary armed struggle on the path to liberation: 'The need for such an analysis of cultural values becomes more acute when, in order to face colonial violence, the liberation movement must mobilize and organize people, under the direction of strong and disciplined political organization, in order to resort to violence in the cause of freedom – *the armed struggle for the national liberation*' (Emphasis in the original, 1994: 62–3).

In line with this kind of revolutionary thinking, the Palestinian revolutionary thinker, activist and novelist, Kanafani also argues for the dominant role of culture, and specifically what he called 'resistance literature', in educating and mobilizing people, something which needs to precede the armed struggle and which would lead to national liberation. For Kanafani, the armed struggle for liberation cannot be separated from political and cultural work, and it is precisely cultural resistance that strengthens the armed struggle and enables its eventual success (1968: 9).

It should be noted that these thinkers emphasize an inclusive culture that cuts across ethnicities, religions and social classes. The essentialization of the character of the struggle is dangerously destructive precisely because essences, such as 'negritude, Irishness, Islam, or Catholicism', as Said explains, means to 'accept nativism' and this inevitably translates into accepting the 'consequences of imperialism, the racial, religious, and political divisions imposed by imperialism itself' (*Culture and Imperialism*, 1994a: 276). By accepting such essentializations, we are abandoning the historical, secular world and embracing a deadly sectarianism, such as we have seen in the Arab world recently, where we are literally witnessing the destruction of Arab and Islamic societies from within as a result of the divisive incitement of Sunni/Shia divisions[4] designed and encouraged by Western imperialism, Zionist interests and Arab states allied to the West through their so-called wars of freedom in several Arab countries, such as Iraq, Syria and Yemen.

Bashir Abu Manneh points out that unlike previous generations of Arab writers, such as Jabra Ibrahim Jabra, and I would add Naguib Mahfouz, Kanafani 'comes to embrace' the entanglement of culture in 'this broad struggle for humanist articulation', which literally translates into the direct use of politics in literature, creating a revolutionary and humanist cultural production (2016: 71). This theorizing of a revolutionary, humanist cultural production is, for Kanafani, based on the ongoing Palestinian revolutionary struggle, a cause that has come to take on universal significance (ibid.). In fact, Kanafani was indeed directly involved in the Palestinian revolutionary struggle from the very beginning, writing revolutionary 'political journalism for the Arab Nationalist Movement ANM' in the 1950s even before he became a member of the Popular Front for the Liberation of Palestine (PFLP) into which the ANM developed after the 1967 Arab defeat, known as the *Naksa* or setback (Abu Manneh, 2016: 72).

Theorizing Palestine, for Kanafani, came naturally. He did not follow any methods or particular theoretical ideas – it was literature and his own experience as a Palestinian that led Kanafani to write about the cause and not any particular political organization that led him to literature as he points out in the following quotation:

My political position springs from my being a novelist. In so far as I am concerned, politics and the novel are an indivisible case and I categorically state that I became politically committed because I am a novelist, not the opposite. I started writing the story of my Palestinian life before I found a clear position or joined any organization.

(qtd. in Abu Manneh, 2016: 72)

Kanafani's point above, I think, is very important in understanding any intellectual's role in standing on the margin with the silenced and oppressed, the wretched of the earth, so to speak. Palestine is very much the test for an intellectual's humanity, solidarity and commitment.

It is the very fact of the Palestinian people's dispossession, something that Kanafani experienced first-hand, that led to his committed literature, and I would add to his theorization of Palestine and specifically 'resistance literature', which is a revolutionary literature of hope, especially, in Kanafani's case after 1967 when in response to defeat, he 'radically overturned' Arab politics and culture (2016: 75) singlehandedly, re-creating and transforming Arabic literature from one of despondency and despair to one of radical and revolutionary potential. This, as Abu Manneh points out, is because '[i]f ... politics was about act and organization, culture was its condition of possibility. Culture was the foundation from which politics would emerge' (2016: 73). Thus by transforming culture, Kanafani hoped to transform Arab politics in general from one that relied on defeatist discourses to revolutionary discourses that made it possible to imagine liberation in various forms of cultural production. As Kanafani writes in *Resistance Literature in Occupied Palestine 1948–1968*, culture is just as important as the armed struggle for liberation: 'Cultural resistance is essential and is no less important than the armed resistance itself' (2013 [1968]: 9–10). In fact, Kanafani goes on to say that successful armed struggle has deep roots in the 'fertile ground' of cultural resistance; there is no separating the two (ibid.).

In a work by Kanafani entitled 'Resistance Literature in Occupied Palestine', which appeared in *Afro-Asian Writings* (1968) and translated into English, Kanafani introduces some essential elements of resistance literature. In this long essay, Kanafani fleshed out the characteristics of Palestinian resistance literature or the literature of combat, which he identifies with the literature of Occupied Palestine, a few years after the establishment of Israel. Kanafani points out that it took about five years after the catastrophe or *Nakba* for Palestinians to realize that 'they had lost not only their families and friends but their country as well' (69). In 'Resistance Literature' (1968), Kanafani, basing his observations on the 'new poetry' coming out of Occupied Palestine, such as that of Darwish, Samih Al Qassim and Tewfiq Ziad, makes two initial observations: the poetry of Occupied Palestine, unlike the 'poetry of exile' at the time, 'is not characterized by a note of lamentation, or despair, but reflects an admirable hope and a constant revolutionary fervor' and the second observation revolves around how enmeshed this resistance literature is in the political events of the Arab world (70), especially those Arab battles fought against colonization, which for Kanafani form a 'natural fusion' (72) with the Palestinian cause. In fact, the second observation is later expanded when Kanafani points out that Darwish's first poetry collection entitled, *Birds Without Wings* or *Wingless Birds* (1960), valorized the African liberation struggle, thus exhibiting solidarity with other liberation struggles worldwide (71).

Singling out the three Palestinian poets, Darwish, Samih Al Qassim and Tewfiq Ziad, Kanafani delineates the main features of the poetry of resistance, written by the 'fighting writer', the 'militant and committed Arab writer, struggling against all atrocities and oppression' (Kanafani, 'Resistance Literature', 1968: 77). The main characteristics of this combative literature include biting sarcasm, challenge and defiance. Within the context of an impending confrontation, the literature of resistance turns to decisive attack (ibid.). This literature 'remains above desperate tears, laments and complaints'; it is rather always on the offensive, in anticipation of an impending victory (ibid.). Its defiance is a key feature in the sense that it never surrenders or despairs because this literature is self-aware and has full comprehension of the situation and '[i]ts vision' is 'deeply conscious ... of the aspects of the battle in which it found itself involved' (78). The strong relationship between the social and political situation is clear in the literature of resistance. This is to be seen within the context of the 'organic link between the issue of resisting Israeli occupation and the liberation causes in Arab countries and throughout the world' (77). A clear commitment to all revolutionary movements in the world is pronounced (78). Three main organic links of resistance literature (in Occupied Palestine) are outlined by Kanafani: the social aspect, especially the 'toiling class' who are the rank and file of the resistance movement, the greater Arab dimension and a genuine commitment to world revolutionary movements (ibid.).

It is interesting to note that much of what Kanafani outlines as part and parcel of resistance literature strongly resonates with the 'Third World' intellectual Fanon's third phase in the development of the native intellectual in his seminal book *The Wretched of the Earth*. This last stage of decolonization is what Fanon calls the 'fighting phase' (1963: 243); compare this with Kanafani's fighting writer:

> Finally in the third phase, which is called the fighting phase, the native, after having tried to lose himself in the people and with the people, will on the contrary shake the people. Instead of according the people's lethargy an honored place in his esteem, he turns himself into an awakener of the people; hence comes a fighting literature, a revolutionary literature, and a national literature.
>
> (222–3)

In his work 'Resistance Literature' (1968), Kanafani was able to outline some key elements of resistance literature, which he extended in his literary work. In his emphasis on the organic link between the Palestinian revolution, revolutionary struggles in the Arab world and the rest of the world, Kanafani underscores the importance of *affiliation* as a social and political stance against the filiations of blood and tribal ties. This stance of affiliation can be very clearly seen in his novella *Returning to Haifa* (2000). Said's emphasis on intention, human effort and choice through an affiliative stance as opposed to a filiative one based on blood, religious and tribal ties as detailed in his two books, *Beginnings: Intention and Method* (1975) and *The World, the Text and the Critic* (1983) is the theory put into practice in Kanafani's novella, *Returning to Haifa* (2000).

Kanafani's novella begins in the aftermath of the 1967 Arab defeat. Israel occupied the 'West Bank', or the Eastern part of Palestine and allowed Palestinians who were from 1948 Palestine to see (read, only *see*) their former homes. This is how we meet the husband and wife, Said and Saffiya, as they make their journey to their old home in Haifa, which they abandoned in 1948. However, they are also 'returning' (but not really returning) to Haifa to see what happened to their abandoned five-month-old baby Khaldoun, whom Saffiya left behind when she was forced to flee along with the masses of people who headed for the port in hysteria and panic and who were helped (to leave) by the British army. Here Kanafani offers his lesson for the Palestinian people and all Arabs by means of the character of Khaldoun who is now Dov, a twenty-year-old Israeli soldier, who tells his biological parents that 'man is a cause' (181) and not flesh and blood. Kanafani is here foreshadowing Said's concept of secular criticism and emphasizing an antisectarian discourse, which unfortunately is currently dominating the discourse of the Arab world nowadays. Kanafani's emphasis on defiance and a refusal to surrender even in the darkest hour resonates strongly with Said's description of late style.

In an important essay by Kanafani entitled 'Thoughts on Change and the "Blind Language"', the novelist focuses on the importance of the "younger generations" in the Arab world and the possibilities for social and political renewal that they represent' (trans. by Harlow and Yaziji, 1990: 133). This is very clearly expressed in Kanafani's novella, *Returning to Haifa* when Said tells Safiyya that it is now up to the new generation to set their parents' past mistakes right, a new generation that represents a defiance that the previous age did not seem to possess because they saw Palestine only nostalgically, a sentimental memory. It is their son, Khalid, who understands the true Palestine, and here I will quote this important passage in its entirety:

> Nothing. Nothing at all. I was just asking. I'm looking for the true Palestine, the Palestine that's more than memories, more than peacock feathers, more than a son, more than scars written by bullets on the stairs. I was just saying to myself: What's Palestine with respect to Khalid? He doesn't know the vase or the picture or the stairs or Halisa or Khaldun. And yet for him, Palestine is something worthy of a man bearing arms for, dying for. For us, for you and me, it's only a search for something buried beneath the dust of memories. And look what we found beneath the dust. Yet more dust. We were mistaken when we thought the homeland was only the past. For Khalid, the homeland is the future. That's how we differed and that's why Khalid wants to carry arms. Tens of thousands like Khalid won't be stopped by the tears of men searching in the depths of their defeat for scraps of armor and broken flowers. Men like Khalid are looking toward the future, so they can put right our mistakes and the mistakes of the whole world. Dov is our shame, but Khalid is our enduring honor. Didn't I tell you from the beginning that we shouldn't come – because that was something requiring a war? Let's go!
>
> (2000: 187)

Kanafani's Khalid, who represents an unsentimentalized future Palestine, finds his more recent counterparts inside Occupied Palestine tens of years later.

Occupied Palestine's new generation, like Kanafani's Khalid exude hope, defiance and a deep belief in an impending victory, and this is clearly seen in the many acts of bravery and power, such as the brave, young Gaza medic, Razan Al Najjar, the defiant fighter Ahmed Jarrar of Jenin and the double amputee activist, Ibrahim Abu Thurayah of Gaza; such brave young people are the leaders of the 'Great March of Return',[5] which on its first Friday (30 March, 2018) saw at least eighteen young martyrs and about 1,500 injured. On the second Friday (6 April, 2018), which has been dubbed 'Black Tire Friday', these defiant young people hoped that the burning of black tires would create enough smoke to make it difficult for Israeli snipers to kill them. The largest death toll in a single day in the 'Great March of Return', was at least sixty martyrs. The defiant creativity of young Gazans is observed in what has come to be known as Gaza's 'fire kites', which young Gazans direct against Israel. Occupied Palestine has proven that its *creative resistance* has yet again preceded the theory of resistance in terms of action and articulation. New Palestinian generations possess self-knowledge and an unsentimentalized and non-nostalgic understanding of history. The nostalgia for Palestine of previous ages proved to be a defeatist formula because nostalgia suggests passivity rather than agency, a feeling of helplessness and an inability to change the present. Kanafani rejects this attitude in *Returning to Haifa*: 'Tens of thousands like

Khalid won't be stopped by the tears of men searching in the depths of their defeat for scraps of armor and broken flowers' (187).

Said's (post) catastrophic writings and Kanafani's theorizing of resistance literature represent writings that spring from within the context of a crisis culture, both theoretically and practically, or rather the two together with one feeding into the other alternately, signalling a paradigm shift in twentieth and twentieth-first century anti-colonial thought. Within the context of Palestinian literature, this essential shift is from the *nostalgia* of the older generation to the *restlessness* of the newer generations who are empowering themselves from their spaces in the margin and are literally fighting back, using all means possible. This restlessness of the refugee and the exile mirrors the restlessness of Said's intellectual who may live in a real physical exile, but by necessity, resides in a metaphorical one, on the margins of society with the oppressed. However, it is important to point out here that the world of the refugee and the exile, that space on the margins of society, becomes a space of resistance and 'radical openness' in the words of bell hooks. This is the space wherein radical change is imagined and made possible, leaving open the possibility of constructing the 'outlines of a better world' (Willaims, 2010: 86).

2

EXILE IS THE WORLD INSIDE: THE POETRY OF RESISTANCE AND SOLIDARITY

Exile is the world inside: Darwish, Said and identity in exile

It is not at all strange to discover that in both theorizing and narrating Palestine, we come up against the same terminology; it is as if the theorizing and the narrating come together, coalesce and refuse separation. Thus in the narration, there is theorization and in the theorization, there is narration. Like Said, Darwish speaks of catastrophe, dispossession, exile, siege and hope. And in the writings of these two intellectuals, the catastrophic, exile and siege are real and metaphorical. Exile is the world outside, but even more essentially and urgently, exile is the world inside, as Darwish writes in 'Counterpoint', his tribute to Said after his death in 2003. This poem was translated by Mohammad Shaheen as 'Counterpoint', which appears in *almond blossoms and beyond* (2009b) and by Mona Anis as 'Edward Said: A Contrapuntal Reading' (2007). Both are excellent translations, but the one I use here is the Anis translation. In the imagined dialogue between the theorist/critic and the poet, Darwish asks Said about his identity to which the late theorist/critic responds in the words below:

> What about identity? I asked.
> He said: It's self-defense ...
> Identity is the child of birth, but
> at the end, it's self-invention, and not
> an inheritance of the past. I am multiple ...
> Within me an ever new exterior. And
> I belong to the question of the victim. Were I not
> from there, I would have trained my heart
> to nurture there deer of metaphor ...
> So carry your homeland wherever you go, and be
> a narcissist if need be/
> The outside world is exile,
> exile is the world inside.
> And what are you between the two?
>   (Trans. Mona Anis in *Cultural Critique*, 177)

Darwish's imagined definition of Saidian identity seems to belong to both Said and Darwish himself: both men are Palestinian, about the same age, both live in exile, both are suffering in terms of their health (Darwish from heart disease and Said from leukaemia) and both have theorized and narrated Palestine's pain, which they have transformed into a universal pain, with the personal not only coalescing into the collective, but also into the human and the global.

Identity for both Said and Darwish is a complicated matter made up of a multiplicity of elements that include one's birth identity, but more essentially identity as one's own invention and legacy, and this, of course, is further transformed by exile, which is for Said and Darwish, an outside world but more significantly, an inner world. For Said, this is the inner world of the exiled intellectual. This individual 'belong[s] to the question of the victim', the oppressed whom the intellectual represents, and even if he was not from *there*, his trained heart must nurture the 'deer of metaphor', which is the occupation of Said's intellectual. The trained heart affiliates with the cause of the oppressed, but paradoxically just as Said and Darwish try to dis-attach themselves from a physical place, they are pulled even stronger to their homeland, which they carry wherever they go, narcissistically, 'if need be', adds the poet. The intellectual is to enter that place in the margin (even if they '[w]ere ... not from there') in solidarity with the oppressed, and the reader here is quickly reminded that the place and cause most urgently in need of the voice of the intellectual is Palestine.

If Said's is the theory of (post) catastrophe as discussed in the previous chapter, then Darwish's is the poetry of (post) catastrophe. In fact, in Darwish's imagined conversation with Said in 'Counterpoint' or 'A Contrapuntal Reading', the poet makes specific reference to the ongoing catastrophe of Palestine and Palestinians and the role of poetry in this. Darwish grieves for the fallen, the countless martyrs, the Palestinian blood that Israel has spilled, blood that has now out-spaced the land itself. To emphasize the omnipresence of spilled Palestinian blood, the poet uses the language rules of Arabic whereby the word blood changes its form based on its grammatical context: 'dam*o*n' with the 'o' sound here pronounced as one would pronounce the 'o' in the word 'hope' when it appears as the subject of the sentence; 'dam*a*n' the 'a' in the second syllable pronounced like the 'e' sound in the word 'men' when it is the result of an action – here the shooting of the snipers and 'dam*i*n' with the 'i' pronounced as the 'i' in the word 'in' when the word comes after a preposition.

Thus, the listener in Arabic hears three versions of the word 'blood' – 'damon', 'daman' and 'damin', which has the effect of emphasizing, in the consciousness of the reader, the fact that blood is found everywhere – in all contexts, spaces and places, spilling out of the old and young alike. The form of the poem (grammatical context) is indeed mimicking the real as the poet says in the same poem (see the lines below these). Below the poet ponders what the poetry of catastrophe can possibly do:

What can poetry say in a time of catastrophe?
***

Blood
and blood,
blood
in your country,
in my name and in yours, in
the almond flower, in the banana skin,
in the baby's milk, in light and shadow,
in the grain of wheat, in salt/
***
Adept snipers, hitting their target
with maximum proficiency.
Blood
and blood
and blood.
This land is smaller than the blood of its children
standing on the threshold of doomsday like
sacrificial offerings. Is this land truly
blessed, or is it baptized
in blood
and blood
and blood

(2007: 181)

Darwish is describing the catastrophic, its omnipresence in places where one would least expect it – in the almond flower, in the baby's milk. Everyone is fair game for the adept Israeli snipers. The Zionist regime has turned Palestinian children into sacrificial offerings, their blood baptizing the land.

The poet dwells on the question of what poetry can do at the time of catastrophe a few lines later. Darwish's answer is significant in that the poet endows poetry with the power to inspire hope and immortality. In fact, the poet says that the aesthetic cannot be separated from the real – the poem speaks of the depth of the wound, a truth that cannot be captured by the camera or the journalist. The poet refuses to surrender to the catastrophic. In the lines below, Darwish hands his friend Said the honour of speaking on what a poem can indeed do because this is precisely what Said was able to do in his theorizations, especially on late style whereby in the face of catastrophe, the writer/intellectual defies the catastrophic and indeed death itself and refuses to surrender:

He says: The poem could host
loss, a thread of light shining
at the heart of a guitar; [...]
the aesthetic is but the presence of the real
in form/
[....]
Invent a hope for speech,

> invent a direction, a mirage to extend hope.
> And sing, for the aesthetic is freedom/
> ***
> I say: The life which cannot be defined
> except by death is not a life.
> ***
> He says: We shall live.
> So let us be masters of words which
> make their readers immortal
>
> (2007: 187)

Thus, Darwish is endowing the poetry of pain with the power to invent hope, to sing the 'aesthetic of freedom'. The pain of loss can be transformed in the light which shines 'at the heart of a guitar', which of course here represents the aesthetic. This does not mean that art does not recognize the painful and the catastrophic, but rather can transform it into hope, to anticipate a better world because life cannot be defined by death; even when death seems so near, one must still choose life as Said says in the poem, 'We shall live.'

The final part of Darwish's tribute to his friend Said is perhaps the most beautifully touching of the whole poem. The closing words of this poem also resonate with the late style theme of the refusal to surrender. Here the two men converse about their impending deaths and Said urges Darwish to do the impossible as the narrative voice of Palestine, the master of words:

> He also said: If I die before you,
> my will is the impossible.
> I asked: Is the impossible far off?
> He said: A generation away.
> I asked: And if I die before you?
> He said: I shall pay my condolences to Mount Galilee,
> and write, 'The aesthetic is to reach
> poise.' And now, don't forget:
> If I die before you, my will is the impossible.
> ***
> When I visited him in New Sodom,
> in the year Two Thousand and Two, he was battling off
> the war of Sodom on the people of Babel ...
> and cancer. He was like the last epic hero
> defending the right of Troy
> to share the narrative.
>
> (2007: 182)

Whether or not this was a real conversation between the two men is beyond the point – the message is clear: Said is asking of (post) catastrophic poetry or what in the final line of this poem the poet calls, the poetry of pain – the impossible. While

Said asks the impossible from Darwish should he die before the poet, Darwish asks Said what he would do if Darwish dies before him to which Said replies, I will pay my condolences to the mountains of Galilee, the birthplace of the poet. I think here the reference to the *Galilee* can suggest two things: firstly, Darwish emphasizes that the very nature of Palestine mourns for its children, thus underscoring the inseparability of the Palestinian from his/her land. Secondly, the poet creates an imagined narrative that allows for the idea of making the impossible *possible* by aligning this idea with the very specific mention of the mountains of the Galilee (part of 1948 Palestine from which the Palestinians were dispossessed). This suggests the very possible return of both the land and Palestinian exiles to their homeland, all of Palestine from the river to the sea.

Darwish, in writing about Said, is also writing about himself; this represents a marriage between poetry and theory. Impending death cannot stop Said because the Trojan thinker (Darwish called himself the 'Trojan poet')[1] was fighting terminal cancer at the same time he was fighting and resisting America's (New Sodom) build-up for the invasion of Iraq (Babel) in 2002 (the actual US invasion of Iraq started in 2003). Said, like Darwish, was defending the right of Troy because Troy never had a chance to share its narrative with the world. The Trojan thinker/ theorist and the Trojan poet speak on behalf of the oppressed, the silenced, those in the margin who were not allowed to sing their song. Thus, the Trojan/Palestinian poet/theorist is imagining the very real notion of the return to the homeland, here represented by the mention of the Galilee, the birthplace of the poet. It is in this sense that 'Counterpoint' or 'A Contrapuntal Reading', a poem of tribute from Darwish to Said represents the Trojan narrative, whether that is the Iraqi one, which Said was fighting for in 2002 or the Palestinian one, which is now over seventy-four years old as of this writing. The last message seems to be the return of the exile to his home. This, the poet says, before he bids farewell to the poetry of pain at the end of his tribute to the great Palestinian thinker.

Said, like Darwish, is not under the false impression that exile is a modernist and elitist position or state to be glorified, but is rather a most tragic and painful reality that individuals and collectivities experience, as he writes in his important essay 'Reflections on Exile'. Said argues that one should never mistake exile for a modern, romantic and humanist endeavour that is relegated to the realms of literature, but should see it for what it truly is – a terminal loss that lacks the mercy of death:

> On the twentieth-century scale, exile is neither aesthetically nor humanistically comprehensible: at most the literature about exile objectifies an anguish and a predicament most people rarely experience first hand; but to think of the exile informing this literature as beneficially humanistic is to banalize its mutilations, the losses it inflicts on those who suffer them, the muteness with which it responds to any attempt to understand it as 'good for us'. Is it not true that the views of exile in literature and, moreover, in religion obscure what is truly horrendous: that exile is irremediably secular and unbearably historical; that it is produced by human beings for other human beings; and that, like

death but without death's ultimate mercy, it has torn millions of people from the nourishment of tradition, family, and geography?

(2001: 174)

Said wants to impress upon us that literature and religion cannot make exile 'aesthetically and humanistically comprehensible' to those who are not exiles for the pain and loss of forced exile seem to be insurmountable. Rootedness, states Said in 'Reflections of Exile', quoting Simone Weil 'is perhaps the most important and least recognized need of the human soul' (2001: 183). Exile means being uprooted, out of place and restless. The uprooted exile envies the non-exile's rootedness and sense of belonging. Because the exile's identity has been shattered by the uprooting, it is inevitable, as Said states, for exiles to be in a constant process of reassembling their identities 'out of the refractions and discontinuities of exile' (2001: 179).

In fact, this reassembling of identity can be seen as the link between the many cultures of Palestinian exile and national identity, which are two terms that appear in the title of this book and which are two concepts (exile and nationalism) that Said discusses in the above-mentioned essay. At first glance, the two terms, exile and nationalism, appear to be at utterly opposite poles: exiles are uprooted individuals and populations that suffer from a lack of belonging to any place whereas nationalism, as Said writes, 'is an assertion of belonging in and to a place, a people, a heritage' (2001: 176). However, as Said argues, there is a deep affinity between these two opposite states of existence: 'Indeed, the interplay between nationalism and exile is like Hegel's dialectic of servant and master, opposites informing and constituting each other. All nationalisms in their early stages develop from a condition of estrangement' (ibid.). It is precisely this estrangement, this loss, this uprootedness that 'unites' Palestinians in different cultures of exile in a kind of 'horizontal comradeship' that involves a constant reassembling of national identity: '... Palestinians also know that their own sense of national identity has been nourished in the exile milieu ....' (2001: 178). This is made possible by these different cultures of Palestinians, living in exile, under occupation and siege or within the confines of the Israeli apartheid state. All of these Palestinian groupings participate in imagining and constructing Palestine, thus enabling the outlines of a better world, so to speak.

Exile is by its very definition about painful separation, a break from all forms of rootedness, an unnatural separation from one's home, soil and earth, and for the violently uprooted Palestinian, exile underscores the necessity of return. As Said points out in 'Reflections on Exile', the exiled individual is in search of what has been lost and stolen and needs to be restored. In quoting from Darwish's poem below, Said emphasizes the importance of remnants and a desire for wholeness. These are ideas that Said finds most clearly expressed in Darwish's early poetry from which he quotes the following lines:

Restore to me the colour of face
And the warmth of body

> The light of heart and eye,
> The salt of bread and rhythm,
> The taste of Earth ... the Motherland.
> Shield me with your eyes.
> Take me as a relic from the mansion of sorrow.
> Take me as a verse from my tragedy;
> Take me as a toy, a brick from the house
> So that our children will remember to return.
>
> (qtd. in Said, 2001: 179)

Said emphasizes the incompleteness of exilic existence, which is especially pronounced in the Palestinian context. While modernist theory and literature have now conveniently moved beyond the national in what have come to be known as post-national and transnational spaces, this cannot be said to be true of the Palestinian experience where the national is a state of existence that has not yet been achieved. It is an unfinished project that is in process, or as Darwish himself puts it, 'I am not ashamed of my identity because it is still in the process of being written' (http://hebaalbeity.wordpress.com).

The Palestinian national liberation struggle continues and to intentionally overlook one of the last remaining examples of settler colonialism in our world today (Israel) is to perpetuate the suffering of the Palestinian people and help maintain their oppression. Thus, it is impossible, in the case of Palestine, to move beyond the national when Palestinians are still without a homeland. For Palestinians living under occupation and under siege, in exile – many in refugee camps that are now seventy-four years old, the struggle must, by necessity, continue. Like all people, Palestinians desire to belong, to be rooted to a land. Imagining Palestine enables the ongoing construction of national identity and the moral right of return to the homeland. As Said argues above, human beings have an instinctual sense to belong, to be rooted to a land. Speaking of the Palestinian experience of exile, Darwish writes in *In the Presence of Absence* (2011):

> You wondered: How many nails have you hammered into the walls of other houses? How many paintings have you hung? How many beds have you abandoned for others to sleep afterward? How many drafts and beginnings have you forgotten in other drawers?
>
> (83)

Darwish, like other Palestinian exiles, is haunted by this feeling of temporariness caused by that initial rupture, the originary moment of separation, the 1948 *Nakba* that took away from the Palestinians their land and livelihood – in fact, their very existence as a people and turned their present into a struggle between the past and the future.

On the poetry of besiegement and resistance: Mahmoud Darwish's 'state of siege' and other poems

For the Palestinian intellectual, geographical and psychological exile means to be constantly besieged by the plight of the oppressed and their suffering, especially if the oppressed are one's own people. In Darwish's mind (and Said's), exile and siege become synonymous, with one word (and state) flowing into the other. The exiled mind is a besieged and restless one; it is paradoxically always on the move, but is incessantly being besieged by the pain of the oppressed. Indeed, Darwish, the poet/philosopher, creates from the very essence of his oppression and his people's oppression, the spirit of resistance. In fact, Darwish experienced different states of actual siege. As a young man, he was imprisoned by Israel several times for writing rebellious poetry. This, then, led to the poet's exile that took him to Moscow after which he went to Beirut, which became the capital of the Palestinian revolution. Then in 1982, Beirut came under siege as a result of the brutal Israeli bombardment of Beirut, which also became the site of the horrifying Sabra and Shatila massacres that were carried out under the cover, protection, support (both military and logistical) and some would say, the actual involvement of the Israeli army.[2] Probably the most controversial of Darwish's poems, which came out of the Beirut period of Darwish's exile is 'Praise of the High Shadow', a long poem which has not been translated in full. It exhibits intense anger with the world and the Arab regimes that betrayed the Palestinians in Beirut, a betrayal for which Darwish cannot forgive the world and especially the Arabs, not only for turning their backs to the unfolding tragedy, but also for conspiring against the Palestinians, a betrayal that enabled the unforgivable tragedy that awaited helpless Palestinians and Lebanese at the Sabra and Shatila refugee camps in 1982.

It is important to emphasize here that siege is not only forced upon Palestinians under occupation in the 'West Bank' and besieged Gaza, but also to Palestinians in exile, especially in refugee camps. In fact, Israel's policy has always been to destroy any significant Palestinian presence that could represent some resistance anywhere in this world and Beirut in 1982 was no different. Darwish documented these events in many of his poems from the 1980s, such as 'Earth Presses Against Us', a poem which inspired the title to Said's 1986 book *After the Last Sky*, his (Darwish's) important prose reflection on the 1982 siege of Beirut, entitled *Memory for Forgetfulness: August, Beirut, 1982* (2013) and in other works where he briefly revisited these events as he did in his later work, *In the Presence of Absence* (2011). In 'Earth Presses Against Us', the continuous Israeli besiegement of Palestinians does not leave any space for them to exist on this earth. Like the poet himself, Palestinians are always having to travel from one border to another, from one piece of land to the next, from one massacre to the next, always on the move, in a constant state of instability and restlessness. The poet writes:

> Earth is pressing against us, trapping us in the final passage.
> To pass through, we pull off our limbs.
> Earth is squeezing us.
>
> (2003: 9)

What is significant here is that Darwish's words above address not only the squeezing out of Palestinians from Beirut in 1982, which he calls the 'final passage', but also the historical dispossession of Palestinians from several spaces and places across time. In other words, the word 'final' paradoxically reflects a *continuity* of historical events. This dispossession is obviously not the first and nor will it be the last despite Darwish's use of the word 'final'.

If we apply Soja's idea of Thirdspace resistance to Darwish's perspective on these events, I think that this would help facilitate a better understanding of much of Darwish's work. The poet writes from a trialectics of historicality, spatiality and sociality that underscores a historical and geographical continuity of lived events, which encompass the original context of dispossession, the 1948 *Nakba*, the 1967 *Naksa*, the Black September events of 1970–1 in Jordan between the Palestinians and the Jordanian army and what Darwish refers to above as the final passage or dispossession in Beirut in 1982 simultaneously. The target of Israel's invasion of Lebanon in 1982 was the Palestinian resistance, which at that time was represented by the PLO, the Palestine Liberation Organization. The Palestinian presence in Beirut in 1982, which of course was a direct result of the original catastrophic event of 1948, had to be, from the standpoint of Israel, historically, geographically, culturally and socially erased from the last border with occupied Palestine – that is from Lebanon's southern border. Space is very much an essential part of this equation. Without the actual presence of the Palestinian resistance (here, the PLO in Lebanon), there was the real danger of massacres in the refugee camps.

Darwish references the mutilation of bodies in the lines quoted a little earlier, 'we pull off our limbs'. To pass through this final passage, Palestinians are forced to pull off their limbs. Palestinians are once again dispossessed of land, home and their very bodies – their bodies literally being mutilated in the massacres of Sabra and Shatila with no armed fighters to protect the refugee camps. The bitterness of the poet's voice is clear in the lines of this short poem:

We glimpse faces in their final battle for the soul, of those who will be killed
by the last living among us. We mourn their children's feast.
We saw the faces of those who would throw our children out of the windows
of this last space.

(2003: 9)

Lebanon, which for Darwish is the last space and where he himself lived at the time of the Israeli invasion and siege of Beirut, was also the space where 'our children' would be thrown out of the windows in this 'final battle for the soul', where those who conspired with Israel celebrated the mutilation of Palestinian children. This is what leads to Darwish's line that was commemorated by Said: 'Where should we go after the last border? Where should birds fly *after the last sky*?' (My emphasis, ibid.). With the words 'the last sky', Darwish is here obviously alluding to the Quranic verses concerning the seven skies, which in religious interpretation means the celestial sphere or the heavens. Darwish here, however, is rereading the traditional concept of the last sky in Islamic teachings to underscore the catastrophic situation of the Palestinians in Beirut and the refugee camps. The people of the camps were betrayed by Arab regimes.

The last sky here, instead of the promised heavens, becomes an actual hell on earth, which makes the poet wonder where the birds should fly to now, what new destination, what new skies? The poet, perhaps seeing the desolate situation on the ground, which is also reflected in his verse, finishes off his poem in a uniquely Darwishian manner – that is by nurturing a defiant hope:

> We write our names in crimson mist!
> We end the hymn with our flesh.
> Here we will die. Here, in the final passage.
> Here or there, our blood will plant olive trees.
>
> (2003: 9)

In a voice that is angry, defiant and resistant, the poet underscores the utter importance of the sacrifice and the inevitable shedding of blood. Palestinians have no choice. They were given no other choice – history itself has betrayed the Palestinians, and this is the point being made here by Darwish, which forces Palestinians to 'end the hymn with our flesh' where 'we will die ... in the final passage' or elsewhere on this earth that keeps squeezing them out of place, space and time. It is the necessary sacrifice that will enable Palestinians to 'plant olive trees', which are deeply embedded in Palestinian culture and sustenance as can be seen in Barghouti's work as well (see Chapter 3 for more on the olive tree and its significance in Palestinian life in general). It is Darwish's refusal to surrender, his Thirdspace resistance that is based on the trialectics of historicality, spatiality and sociality, which is here written in 'crimson mist' that allows for hope as represented by the olive tree, a symbol of Palestinian survival.

One of the most painful tragedies that is still engraved in Palestinian memory is the Sabra and Shatila refugee camp massacres that many Arab and other artists have documented in their literary productions, including Darwish himself in his short poem, 'Sabra and Shatila' in which Darwish not only details the horror of the massacres, but also lays the blame on many sides. These include the killers (the Israeli army under the leadership of Ariel Sharon and the Lebanese Maronite Christian militias allied with Israel), the Arabs and the Palestinian leadership itself for leaving behind defenseless Palestinians and confiding in the false promises of the United States to ensure the safety of the Palestinian refugee camps. Accordingly, the Palestinian resistance (the PLO) left West Beirut. The 'evacuation was carried out from 21 August to 1 September 1982. By 10 September, the US, French, and Italian troops that had overseen the operation had left the country' (Shahid, 2002: 37). The stage was set for the Israeli army's complete siege of the Palestinian refugee camps on Wednesday, 16 September before the mass slaughter began on Thursday, 17 September:

> *Sharon arrived at 9:00 A.M. to oversee operations. By noon, while the IDF push into West Beirut continued, the IDF had completely surrounded the camps, setting*

up checkpoints and roadblocks that controlled all entrances and exists. It also occupied a number of multistoried buildings on the perimeter as observation posts and established its forward command post in a seven-story building at the Kuwait embassy traffic circle, which according to Time *magazine, enjoyed 'an unobstructed and panoramic view' of the Shatila camp 200 meters away.*

(Shahid, 38–9, Italics in original)

The difficulty of even comprehending the ruthless massacres and dispossession represented by Sabra and Shatila revolves around the incomprehensible joy the monstrous killers felt, not only by the killing of Palestinian civilians in cold blood, but also by dismembering the victims' bodies. These refugee camps were completely surrounded by those who celebrated the slaughter – the Israeli Occupation Army. This documented fact is here narrated by Darwish in his poem, 'Sabra and Shatila', from the early eighties at about the same time of the tragedy:

> the fascist cuts her breasts – the night reduced
> he then dances around his knife and licks it.
> Singing an ode to a victory of the cedars,
> And erases
> Quietly … Her flesh from her bones
> and spreads her organs over the table
> and the fascist continues dancing and laughs
> for the tilted eyes
> and goes crazy for joy, Sabra is no longer a body ….
>
> (medium.com, The Palestine Project)

Sabra, in Darwish's poem, becomes a defenseless 'sleeping girl' whose men have left her. This is a clear reference to the Palestinian leadership and fighters who evacuated Beirut, leaving behind them unprotected old people, women and children in refugee camps. The reader feels that Sabra, who the fascist dismembered and whose organs he spread over the table, represents not only the refugee camps themselves, but also Palestine.

The drunken euphoria these killers felt by committing unspeakable horrors, such as dismembering the bodies of innocent Palestinian children, has been documented by many journalists. David Hirst, a British journalist, wrote the following account in his book, *Beware of Small States* (2010):

> Journalists descended on Sabra and Shatila to find the hundreds of bodies which the Phalangists had not had time to bury, the limbs which protruded from the hastily dug graves of those they had, the naked women with 'hands and feet tied behind their backs, the victims of car-dragging, one of them with his genitals cut off, piled in a garage, the baby whose limbs had been carefully laid out in a circle, head crowning the whole …'
>
> (159)

Perhaps neither poetry nor prose possesses the narrative power to fully express the unspeakable horrors of Sabra and Shatila, which are a direct result of the 1948 ethnic cleansing of Palestine. Why exactly the Palestinian leadership left these innocent civilians to the hungry wolves, Darwish cannot understand.

The Palestinian fighters left Sabra in the same way Palestinians, escaping their impending massacre by Zionist terror gangs in 1948 left Palestine, thinking that they would soon return. One is reminded of the title of Darwish's poetry anthology, *Why Did You Leave the Horse Alone?* (1995). Darwish rages against the multiple exiles of the revolution, especially as we have already learned from 'Earth Presses Against Us', the Palestinian revolution left the last border with occupied Palestine:

> Why do you go?
> And hang your night
> Over the camp and the national anthem?
> Sabra – covering her naked breasts with a
> farewell song
> Counts her palms and gets it wrong
> While she can't find the arm:
> How many times will you travel?
> And for how long?
> And for what dream?
> If you return one day
> [to] which exile shall you return,
> which exile brought you back?
> Sabra – tearing open her chest:
> How many times
> does the flower bloom?
> How many times
> will the revolution travel?
>
> (ibid.)

Darwish calls out the Palestinian 'revolution', as he names it, for its repeated exiles, leaving Palestinian refugees to fend for themselves. What good are empty, bombastic nationalist songs to the naked breasted Sabra? Is this all the Palestinian revolution has to offer – songs? The poet asks in the lines above, not why did you leave, but why *do* you leave because ever since the first dispossession in 1948, Palestinians keep getting pushed out, squeezed out of their place. But in this poem, the poet aims his questions or rather questionings towards the protectors of the defenseless refugees, the Palestinian resistance organizations. With every exile, which takes the Palestinian revolution farther and farther away from the borders of occupied Palestine, the more Sabra is mutilated both physically (geographically) and psychologically (ideationally). The poet interrogates the Palestinian revolution, but here more specifically, the leadership of the resistance: how many times will the revolution travel and for how long? This makes one wonder: can a revolution be conducted from outside occupied Palestine and from places thousands of miles away from Palestine?

Even the word 'return' becomes ambiguous in the poet's mind – if the revolution were to return, which return would that be, a return to the previous exile, the exile before the current exile, making the return to Palestine seem almost impossible and unreachable? This distance in both space and time from Sabra/Palestine enrages her, making her tear open her chest as she asks, 'How many times will the revolution travel?' In fact, in speaking about his own experience to an interviewer, Darwish expressed this criticism of the Palestinian leadership that was exiled to Tunis in 1982 where the poet also found himself after Beirut: 'I saw the Palestinian revolution staying at a hotel on the shore of the sea. The scene was very painful, and required writing a novel about this fate' (Mahmoud Darwish Foundation). The sorry state of the Palestinian revolution in Tunis by which, of course, Darwish means the PLO and its fighters, staying at hotels in Tunis, underscores the absolute absurdity of the situation. What good is a revolution if not in or near occupied Palestine? What good is a revolution if it does not protect its base, the hundreds of thousands in refugee camps?

The memory of Sabra and Shatila was so strong in the poet's mind that he revisits it in his later work, such as *In the Presence of Absence* (2011), in which, as Sinan Antoon writes, the 'poet reflects on his own existence, intertwined with that of his exiled people ...' (6). In this work, however, Darwish makes use of Jean Genet's compelling literary representation of what he (Genet) personally witnessed in Shatila in 1982 as he was one of the first people who were able to enter the camp after the horrendous massacre. For Said, Genet's affinity and 'enraptured identification' with the Palestinian cause is a 'vital act of Genet's solidarity' with the oppressed, especially in the late 1960s when Genet fell in love with the Palestinian cause and specifically the Palestinian fighters called the *fidayeen* at a time when the Palestinian struggle was 'strenuously contested' (n.p. grandstreet.com). Genet's brave act of solidarity with the Palestinians is noted by both Said and Darwish, who writes in *In the Presence of Absence*:

> You will know from radio stations that the night of Sabra and Shatila was lit up so that the killers could peer into the eyes of their victims and not miss a moment of ecstasy on the slaughtering table. You will read what Jean Genet wrote:
>
> *What partying, what feasting went on there as death seemed to take part in the pranks of soldiers drunk on wine, on hatred, and probably drunk on the joy of entertaining the Israeli army, which was listening, looking, giving encouragement, egging them on. I did not see the Israeli army listening and watching. I saw what it did. Killers carried out the operation, but numerous torture squads were probably the ones who split skulls, slashed thighs, cut off arms, hands and fingers, and dragged the dying and disabled by ropes, men and women who were still alive. A barbaric party had taken place there: rage, drunkenness, dancing, singing, curses, laments, moans, in honor of the voyeurs who were laughing as they sat on the top floor of the Akka hospital.*
>
> (76–7)

Why does Darwish, the master of words, quote another master of words, Genet, to say what he wants to say about Sabra and Shatila, other than, of course, that Genet was one of the first people who were there to see the aftermath of the massacres? After all, Darwish in this 'poetography' (Antoon, 'Translator's Preface', 6), or this autobiography of his soul and the soul of his people could have said in prose and poetry together what has already been said and reported. Other than the essential importance of Genet's eyewitness account, I believe that like Said, Darwish understands the supreme importance of *repetition* with a difference, lest the memory fall into oblivion and disappear. In his book, *The Politics of Dispossession* (1995), Said writes, 'the interesting thing is that there seems to be nothing in the world which sustains the story; unless you go on telling it, it will just drop and disappear …' (118).

It is to create this effect of a living memory that Darwish retells the story with the help of Genet. There are details that Darwish wishes to relay that he himself has not previously expressed in his poetry. Darwish does not usually use the name of Israel as the perpetrator of the grave injustices it caused the Palestinian people in his poetry. However, sometimes, the details must be made clear for the sake of history, justice and humanity. Genet does not leave much to the imagination in his memorable piece 'Four Hours in Shatila' (1983) as to who the maestro was that orchestrated this feast of butchery at Sabra and Shatila. The Israeli maestros were voyeurs with their panoramic view, enjoying the show from their residence atop Akka Hospital, which was only forty yards from one of the entrances to the Shatila refugee camp (18).

As previously discussed, Sabra, in Darwish's short poem about the massacres, is a metaphor for Palestine. Thus, if one were to consider why such a bestial feast had been planned in the first place, what could be some possible answers? Genet does ponder this question in his piece, and his simultaneous response as he finds himself standing inside the killing fields of Shatila is:

> What did Israel gain in the Shatila massacre? Answer: what did it gain by entering Lebanon? What did it gain by bombing the civilian population for two months; by hunting down and destroying Palestinians? What did it want to gain in Shatila: the destruction of Palestinians. It kills men, it kills corpses. It razes Shatila.
>
> (15)

As Genet points out, with such actions, Israel wants 'the destruction of the Palestinians'; however, I think that what Israel wants even more than the bodily destruction of Palestinians is the destruction of the Palestinian cause and the very idea of a future Palestine. In other words, Israel hopes to make the imagining of Palestine impossible. Thus, Israel is trying to create a 'shock and awe' effect so strong within the Palestinian imaginary, that by 'kill[ing] corpses', to use Genet's term, it is also killing the Palestinian cause once and forever. By carrying out such massacres, Israel hopes to break the will of the Palestinian people to resist. Ever since the 1948 *Nakba*, any geography with a sizable Palestinian population bordering occupied Palestine has been placed under siege, either directly or indirectly by Israel. Beirut and especially the Palestinian refugee camps were placed under a stranglehold siege as was the 'West Bank'. Gaza is, up to this day, very much an open-air prison, blockaded by Israel and Egypt from every direction. Siege and besiegement best describe Palestinian daily existence in places and spaces heavily populated by homeless Palestinians, and this, of course, allows for the atrocities committed at the whim of the colonizer/occupier.

Although the siege of Beirut and the ensuing massacres captured the attention of many Palestinian, Arab and international artists, it was not the only siege in recent memory. Darwish, in fact, was able to reflect more deeply on the very idea of siege and besiegement in his long poem entitled 'A State of Siege', written in 2002 when the poet was in Ramallah, which Israel at the time had placed under a very brutal siege and bombardment that also saw the infamous Jenin Camp massacre. Darwish examines the concept of siege itself whereby siege becomes both time and place, real and metaphorical, the waiting, the exile, the tension, the material for poetry and prose and the haunting absent presence of the martyr, and then the martyr's lesson to the poet of humanity. In fact, in this poem, the siege itself becomes that place in the margin of which Said, hooks and Soja speak, the 'Thirdspace', which comprises the trialectics of historicality, spatiality and sociality – that lived space from which resistance springs.

Finding his own Beirut home under the siege of Israeli tanks and practically looking down the muzzle of Israeli guns, the poet was sent into a more distant exile that finally brought him to Paris where he spent about ten years. Several years later, the poet found himself closer to home in Ramallah trapped under yet another siege, and it is at this very point where 'A State of Siege' begins:

> Here, by the downslope of hills, facing the sunset
> and time's muzzle,
> near gardens with severed shadows,
> we do what the prisoners do,
> and what the unemployed do:
> we nurture hope.
>
> (121)

Despite the siege or 'time's muzzle' (as in the muzzle of the gun) and 'severed shadows', a stark image of mutilation, the poet declares defiantly that like prisoners and the unemployed, we nurture hope. The poet's response is to nurture hope precisely because the colonizer's/occupier's aim is to break the will of the Palestinian population. Unlike normal siege warfare whereby one army hopes to starve the opposing army by forcing them to fight a war of attrition, here there is no opposing army or weapons.

So what other reason does Israel have other than to break the will of the Palestinians, to make them surrender life itself. Since the enemy's aim is to practice this kind of psychological warfare, not against an opposing army, but against civilians, the poet practices his own kind of reverse warfare, the wisdom of the poet:

> (To a killer:) If you'd contemplated the victim's face and thought, you would have remembered your mother in the gas chamber, you would have liberated yourself from the rifle's wisdom and changed your mind: this isn't how identity is reclaimed!
>
> (131)

Here Darwish is giving the enemy the chance to ponder his past by looking into his Palestinian victim's face and perhaps see his own mother's face in Germany's gas chambers. Israel uses barbaric violence, the 'rifle's wisdom', to savagely 'reclaim', or more appropriately, falsely 'claim' an identity on a land already populated by its Indigenous Palestinian population. Perhaps, the enemy hopes to make the Palestinians disappear by practicing the most modern techniques of warfare, torture, violence, collective punishment and ethnic and cultural cleansing. A reclamation of identity that means the destruction of another people and their culture can be nothing but barbaric as poignantly elucidated by Stuart Hall in his conception of cultural identity, where he rejects an Israeli identity based on destruction and annihilation and which inevitably 'means pushing other people into the sea. This is the old, the imperializing, the hegemonising, form of "ethnicity". We have seen the fate of the people of Palestine at the hands of this backward-looking conception of diaspora – and the complicity of the West with it' (235).

Darwish intentionally uses the title 'A State of Siege' (حالة حصار) to mean a physical, social and psychological state of siege; in fact, this triad tension is at the heart of this poem. This siege is the cause of all kinds of pain, but at the same time, creativity and hope are born out of pain. Siege, says the poet, 'is the waiting/the waiting on a ladder leaning amid the storm' (135), the waiting for the end of the siege, the waiting for liberation, the waiting for the return of a loved one from prison, the waiting in the exile of nonbelonging – it is, most of all, a waiting in tension and restlessness, a restlessness that afflicts the young and old, the intellectual and the farmer, the man and the woman. It is also the siege of the poet/intellectual who by necessity lives inside a 'metaphorical siege' that 'will extend/until I teach myself the ascetics of meditation' (147). The poet orders his poetry to 'Besiege your siege' (149) lest the siege lead to mental and physical paralysis.

In fact, the poet urges prose to '[d]rag the evidence/out of the scholar's encyclopedia to a present/that the evidence destroyed. And explain your dust' (149). Darwish, like Said, loathed dogmas and 'facts' concretized in scholarly encyclopaedias that totally dismiss the lived present, the unfolding present that prose's supposed evidence cannot explain; thus, Darwish's angry rebuke is seen in the poet's command to prose to 'explain your dust' (ibid.). In Arabic, the word for prose is نثر, which literally means to spread out, as in spreading out sand or ashes, thus becoming dust. It seems that Darwish's solution for exposing the dust of prose is for both poetry and prose to work together: '(To poetry and prose:) Fly together/

as the wings of a swallow carry the blessed spring' (ibid.). This again reminds us of the intimate relationship between theory and poetry, revolutionary theory and the actual struggle of the oppressed, scholarship and the unfolding present, siege and hope. The poet's words strive against separation and are in a constant struggle for wholeness, but at the same time there is a realization that there will always be incompleteness. Darwish, in fact, shows how prose and poetry can fly together, which he represents here with a stanza that begins journalistically and closes it poetically:

> Our losses: from two martyrs to eight
> every day,
> and ten wounded
> and twenty homes
> and fifty olive trees,
> in addition to the structural defect
> that will afflict the poem and the play and the incomplete painting.
>
> (137)

The poet begins prosaically, counting the daily losses of the siege, from people, to homes, to the olive trees, which, of course, represent the livelihood of the Palestinian people – and as if the next two lines are innately connected to the above-recounted losses, the poet pauses and says 'in addition to', the 'structural defect that will afflict the poem and the play and the incomplete painting'. This underscores the impossibility of the separation of art and the everyday life and tragic suffering of the Palestinian people, a suffering that started in the early part of the twentieth century with the British mandate/colonization of Palestine and culminated in the catastrophic 1948 *Nakba* and then continued with (post) catastrophic *nakbas*, punctuating the months and years of the twentieth and twenty-first centuries.

This (post) catastrophic tension afflicts the art of Palestine, and this 'structural defect' and 'incompleteness' are at the core of the very nature of Palestinian cultural production. Thus, Palestinian art is not of harmony and completeness, but as Said sees it, 'Adorno's "fractured landscape" [that] is only one of the ways in which late works quarrel with time and manage to represent death, as he puts it, "in a refracted mode, as allegory"' (Wood, 2006: xii). When the poet is representing death, specifically unnatural, violent death, the structural defect afflicting the fractured landscape of the work is the most prominent feature of such works, which for Said and Darwish are late style works. Late style, for Said, represents those works that are 'in fact about "lost totality," and are therefore catastrophic' (Said, 2006: 13). And it is precisely at this point that theory and cultural production flow into each other, supplying each other with both the ideas and the terminology that would try to explain or make sense of the difficulty (and tragedy) of human experience.

Such theory is born out of necessity, pain, suffering, what Said would probably say, is a kind of lateness and the reason for his admonitions to the theorists of abstraction is that the key to theory and criticism is worldliness, the lived reality of critics, intellectuals and their texts in the world. It is this worldliness, precisely the tragic worldliness of the Palestinian people under siege, in what seems to be a continuous siege, that is both real and metaphorical. This feeling of besiegement is what controls the fragmented narration of Darwish's 'A State of Siege', a poem translated by Fady Joudah in the book, *The Butterfly's Burden* (2007), where the most powerful image is that of the martyr. In fact, it is a repeated theme, and the *repetition* here is, I think, very significant:

> The martyr is the daughter of a martyr who is the daughter of a martyr
> and her brother is a martyr and her sister is a martyr and a daughter-in-law
> of a martyr's mother who's the grandchild of a martyr's grandfather
> and a martyr's uncle's neighbor etc., etc.
> And nothing happens in this civilized world,
> the age of barbarism is over,
> and the victim is nameless, ordinary
> and the victim ... like truth ... is relative
> etc., etc.
>
> (167)

The repetition of the word 'martyr' is for all purpose and effect to focus on the very ordinary nature of this happening within Palestinian society, and I think this is also the reason that the poet here chooses to keep the martyrs nameless (unlike W. B. Yeats in 'Easter 1916', where the poet specifically chooses to name the martyrs as a mother would name her child: 'our part/To murmur name upon name, / As a mother names her child.'). I believe that the effect Darwish wants to create is to emphasize that anyone can become a martyr in Palestine. School children going to their schools in the morning can be martyred by Israeli soldiers for taking the wrong turn on the road; a girl can be martyred sitting next her house; an old man can be martyred for watering his olive trees; an autistic man can be martyred for not responding quickly to the screams of a fully armed Israeli soldier in the same way that a brave young man or woman can be martyred for attacking Israeli soldiers.

Thus, the repetition of the word martyr, the intentional namelessness of each of these martyrs and even the abbreviation of the word etcetera are to emphasize its all too common occurrence in Palestinian society. There is no response to this continuing human tragedy in the 'civilized world' by which Darwish means the West because this (intentionally) ignorant and arrogant world has declared, it seems, that the 'age of barbarism is over'. After all, to the 'civilized' West, Israel is a Western, democratic nation, and Palestinian victims are not even recognized as victims because 'the victim ... like truth ... is relative etc., etc.'. The use of this second 'etc., etc.' at the end of the stanza, unlike the first use of 'etc., etc.', is to shift emphasis to the nonsensical illogic of Western discourse, which for Darwish, does not deserve the completion of the (un)poetic line.

Darwish is very careful to allow the Palestinian martyr, who has been silenced and demonized in Zionist and Western discourse, to speak, to clarify his narrative that has been intentionally distorted by the enemy. Darwish writes:

> The martyr clarifies for me: I didn't search beyond the expanse
> for immortal virgins, because I love life
> on earth, among the pines and figs, but
> I couldn't find a way to it,
> so I looked for it with the last thing I owned:
> blood in the lapis body.
>
> (163)

The Palestinian martyr as Darwish clarifies in the persona of the martyr is a human being who wants to live a dignified life on his land among the pines and figs, which the expansionism of the apartheid state does not allow because, like cancer, it keeps growing, stealing and annexing more and more Palestinian land. The Palestinian martyr, Darwish clarifies, is not a Western defined fanatic who wants to die so he can go meet the virgins in heaven. The martyr is a lover of the land, here, on earth, a land that he was deprived of so he gave it the last thing he owned on this earth, his blood. This is a narrative that is intentionally distorted by the pro-Israel West in order to turn the Palestinians and their cause into something unfathomable and mysterious and their martyrdom, an irrational desire to be with immortal, virgins rather than the moral and humanitarian right to live in their homeland in dignity.

The most fascinating part of 'Siege', however, is perhaps what the martyr can teach the poet himself, a poetic line so essential to the poet and the poem that Darwish presents it as a separate stanza, standing on its own to enable the reader to absorb the weightiness of the 'lesson': 'The martyr teaches me: no aesthetic outside my freedom' (163). This is a pivotal line on two main levels. The first level, of course, is the inevitable link between the lived experience and literature. Literature cannot be separated from the social, cultural and political reality of, in this case, Palestinian experience and the construction of Palestinian spaces in the literature of Palestine, both under occupation and in exile. Darwish's aesthetic cannot ever be 'free' of Palestine. In fact, this poem, 'A State of Siege' is in a sense autotelic with many of its stanzas being besieged by the concept of the martyr, occupying the space of several stanzas. The martyr asks of the already physically besieged poet in his home in Ramallah to consider the plight of the martyr who represents the blood of Palestine and its people. The martyr's open wound haunts the poet to the point of not allowing him, a creator and master of words, to find the appropriate words to answer the martyr's questions/questionings:

> The martyr besieges me whenever I live a new day
> and asks: Where were you?
> Give back to the dictionaries all the talk
>
> (161)
>
> ....

> The martyr besieges me: Don't walk in my funeral
> unless you had known me.
> I need courtesy from no one
>
> (165)

These questions, questionings and interrogations are obviously internal forms of exile, the intellectual's restless mind being besieged by the death of so many martyrs. Where were you? the poet asks himself – no words can clarify or explain the lack of action on the part of poets, intellectuals and so-called leaders of the 'free' world and beyond. All that talk can be given back to dictionaries as it does not do the martyrs any good, and there is no need to walk in the martyrs' funerals just to clear one's conscience or show them courtesy.

Darwish's poetry is one of besiegement. It is the exile inside and perhaps the best example of what I am calling Said's (post) catastrophic theorizations that are based on the world, the lived reality of the oppressed, and this is the second level to which Darwish's poem speaks, the inevitable link between this lived reality and theory, thus merging Palestine theorized with Palestine narrated. The parenthesized (post) in (post) catastrophic is to emphasize that the catastrophic continues and has not passed or become a part of the past. Both Said and Darwish want their theory, literature and criticism to do, to act, not simply to speak.

The poet cautions that this siege will not weaken, but rather intensify, because its aim, as was mentioned previously, is to break the will of the people, to tighten the chains of mental slavery like nooses upon their necks and give them the freedom to choose to be enslaved:

> This siege will intensify
> to convince us
> to choose a harmless slavery,
> but with total freedom of choice
>
> (165)

Choosing slavery 'with total freedom of choice' reminds one of Gramsci's ideas on hegemony and consent. The state, through its institutions, 'convinces' the people that their consent has been taken in the same way the imperial power gains the consent of the indigenous population to be ruled by the colonial power. Most essentially, within the Palestinian context, this happens by convincing the colonized, the occupied that they have been defeated. In other words, there remains absolutely no hope – no hope of victory, no hope of liberation, no hope of a future Palestine; thus, imagining Palestine becomes something impossible, an unreachable and unrealizable fantasy.

Drawing on Ernst Bloch's idea of utopia in his essay, '"Outlines of a Better World": Rerouting Postcolonialism', Patrick Williams argues that postcolonialism should be directed toward an:

> engaged pursuit of those elements acting towards the creation of a genuinely utopian future ... a practical project: 'concrete utopia' – as opposed to the abstract

utopia of the day dream – is something which has to be built. 'Expectation, hope, intention towards possibility that has still not become'.

(93)

It is this utopian future, I believe, that Darwish is constructing in 'Siege' and in his poetic oeuvre in general, especially his later, more mature work. While the main themes in this long poem are siege and besiegement, both actual and metaphorical, and the haunting, ghostlike presence of the martyr, Darwish's resolution is in hope with which he begins his poem and ends it. This belief in a utopian hope is the function, motivation and inspiration of the poet/intellectual who declares, 'no aesthetic outside my freedom'. The poet, ever more and more resolved in his resistance, which he calls his 'chronic illness' continues 'to resist, to live, to love, to procreate, to always 'be certain of the well-being of the heart and testicles' and to suffer from the 'illness of hope' (165), not only to continue to be a producer of art, but to become art itself. This siege will not break the poet of Palestine, but will transform him 'from a singer into ... / a sixth string on the violin' (165) for the poet can certainly see the 'outlines of a better world'.

If the aim of siege and besiegement is to silence, exterminate and break the will of a people to resist as we have seen in Israel's siege of Beirut in 1982, its siege of the 'West Bank' in 2002 and its ongoing siege and total blockade of Gaza, then international solidarity is of the utmost importance to break the silence and expose the brutal apartheid tactics of Israel. The work of activists in this regard and especially that of intellectuals, writers, artists and poets who have an impact on their own societies can and has brought about, to a certain extent, the necessary and urgent awareness of the tragic plight of the Palestinian people.

On the poetry of solidarity: June Jordan, Suheir Hammad, Darwish, Adonis, Roger Waters and the Trio Joubran, John Trudell and Lee Maracle

Genet's solidarity with the Palestinian cause has been repeated elsewhere by artists and poets, writing and creating from that space in the margin, which according to bell hooks, is 'a site of creativity and power' (1990: 152) and 'where we move in solidarity to erase the category colonized/colonizer' (ibid.). An African American poet who entered that space as a liberator is June Jordan who, like her French counterpart Genet, visited the camps after the horrific massacres in 1982 and bore witness to the horror in her literary work and essays. Jordan came to love the Palestinian cause, and for her, it seems that her awakening came as a result of the siege of Beirut and the Sabra and Shatila massacres, which she records in many of her poems. Two of these poems are 'Apologies to All the People in Lebanon', which she dedicates to the '600,000 Palestinian men, women, and children who lived in Lebanon from 1948–1983' (poetryfoundation.org) and 'Moving Towards Home', which interestingly enough appears on a website called 'Al Awda: The Palestine Right of Return Coalition'. Jordan writes:

> I do not wish to speak about the bulldozer and the
> red dirt
> not quite covering all of the arms and legs
> Nor do I wish to speak about the nightlong screams
> that reached
> the observation posts where soldiers lounged about
> ....
> Nor do I wish to speak about the father whose sons
> were shot
> through the head while they slit his own throat before
> the eyes
> of his wife
> Nor do I wish to speak about the army that lit
> continuous
> flares into the darkness so that others could see
> ....
> Nor do I wish to speak about the piled up bodies and
> the stench
> that will not float
> ....
> because I do not wish to speak about unspeakable
> events
> that must follow from those who dare
> 'to purify' a people
> those who dare
> 'to exterminate' a people
> those who dare
> to describe human beings as 'beasts with two legs'
> those who dare
> 'to mop up'
> ....
> to kill the elected representatives
> of the people who refuse to be purified
> those are the ones from whom we must redeem
> the words of our beginning
> because I need to speak about home
> I need to speak about living room
> where the land is not bullied and beaten into
> a tombstone
> ....
> I need to talk about living room
> because I need to talk about home

> I was born a Black woman
> and now
> I am become a Palestinian
> against the relentless laughter of evil
> there is less and less living room
> and where are my loved ones?
> It is time to make our way home.

In the lines quoted above (some lines from the poem were left out), Jordan intentionally does exactly what she tells us she is not going to do – 'I do not wish to speak' and 'Nor do I wish to speak', but speak she does. She speaks the unspeakable, detailing the atrocities of the Israeli army and their puppet allies the Lebanese Christian *Kataeb* or Phalangists. As Therese Saliba points out, Jordan's use of a 'negative construct' in this poem has the effect of exposing the media's and academia's silencing techniques by employing a 'sanitized discourse' and abstract terminology, thereby 'cover[ing] over the horrific violence that assaults our collective humanity' (the feministwire.com).

Thus, by detailing all of these crimes against humanity, Jordan is breaking the silence of those who have been silenced, mutilated, raped, tortured, purified, exterminated, mopped up, thrown in the red dirt, piled one on top of the other, those 'beasts with two legs' who were not dignified with a proper burial. This is one dimension of her poem. The other involves the idea of home, or more specifically, '*moving* towards home' (my emphasis) where there is 'living room'. It is obvious that Jordan is juxtaposing the comfort of the living room, a safe family space with the fact that Palestinians do not have homes and no *living* room, no living space, no homeland. In the last stanza of the poem, Jordan declares her complete solidarity with the Palestinian cause: 'I was born a Black woman/and now/I am become a Palestinian/against the relentless laughter of evil/there is less and less living room/ and where are my loved ones? /It is time to make our way home.' Jordan's use of the words 'I am become a Palestinian' rather than just 'I am a Palestinian' is significant in that her identification is a *becoming*, a revolutionary becoming.

Using hooks's words, Jordan has chosen that space in the margin, which is a space of radical openness. The poet's solidarity with the Palestinians is a revolutionary and defiant act by means of which she is rejecting the oppressive power structure in the United States and other imperial centres in this world. Jordan's act of radical openness and defiance is the very definition of Said's and hooks' intellectual, a relentless fighter for the oppressed who speaks truth to power. Jordan may also be suggesting that it is time for Palestinians to return to their homeland. Now that Jordan is in the process of becoming a Palestinian, she says '[i]t is time to make *our* way home' (my emphasis). The word 'our' represents a collective cry of the oppressed who are moving towards home, whereby home, here, is Palestine and more – it is the home for all the oppressed around the world 'where the land is not bullied and beaten into a tombstone'.

In answer to Jordan's solidarity with the Palestinian people, the daughter of Palestinian refugees who has become a highly respected Palestinian American poet,

Suheir Hammad published her first poetry collection entitled *Born Palestinian, Born Black & The Gaza Suite* (2010) about twenty-five years ago and an updated edition in 2010. In her 'author's preface' from 1996, Hammad writes: 'The last stanza in June Jordan's "Moving Towards Home" changed my life. I remember feeling validated by her statement. She dared speak of transformation, of re-birth, of a deep understanding of humanity' (13). In his 'afterword' to Hammad's book, Kazim Ali underscores the affinity between Mahmoud Darwish, June Jordan and Suheir Hammad not only in the three poets' politics in standing up for the oppressed around the world, but also in their aesthetic style, which Ali says is not subject to artifice as much as it is 'grounded in orality' and the reality of this life, mimicking the immediacy, humanism and earthiness of their subject matter. Ali calls this style, commenting on Jordan's poem 'Moving Towards Home', 'circular prosody', which he describes as a:

> prosody that works not line by line but by sense entire throughout the poem as a whole – a poetry not unlike Hammad's, grounded in orality, in the immediacy both emotional and verbal of spoken communication. You can't fake it – its art is not from artifice but from the actual given world.
>
> (93)

It is the real world in which Hammad lives and moves that animates her poetry and endows it with its performative power. Hammad's oeuvre, as are Jordan's and Darwish's, is a poetic history from below. In the same way that the Palestinian cause became for Jordan the symbol of universal suffering and a 'litmus test for morality' (Solidarity for Palestinian Human Rights-McMaster), Hammad, likewise, enters an African American space in her poetry aesthetically, socially and politically.

For Hammad, blackness and Palestinianness merge into the colour black, which she defines in her 'author's preface (1996)' to *Born Palestinian, Born Black* as something valuable, mysterious, massacred, shamed, othered, colonized, dirty, ingenious, pure, magnificent and beautiful:

> Black like the coal diamonds are birthed from
> like the dark matter of the universe
> the Black September massacre of Palestinians
> the Arabic expression 'to blacken your face'
>   meaning to shame
>
> Black like opposite of white
> the other ....
>
> Black like the genius of Stevie, Zora and Abdel-Haleem
> relative purity
> like the face of God
> the face of your grandmother
>
> (12)

For Hammad, words matter. She rejects the stability of words and believes in the ability of words to transform meanings and reality through performance as in the above lines where black transforms from being shamed and othered to becoming powerful and beautiful. In Hammad's poetry, the othered and colonized are empowered and energized with the African American and Arab cultural creativity and genius of Stevie Wonder, Zora Neale Hurston and Abdel-Haleem Hafez. From her exile in New York, Hammad lives in black and Palestinian spaces, spaces that 'carry history and emotion', poetic spaces that awaken awareness and the solidarity of Hammad's audiences with the Palestinian cause because these spaces are 'real and breathing' and allow the poet to 'make [her] own way home' (13).

Weaving African American poetic and musical styles, such as rap and hip hop with revolutionary Palestinian songs and themes, Hammad creates a distinctive style that is not only popular with African American and Palestinian American audiences, but also with white American audiences, especially women. As bell hooks argues, one can and should enter the margin in solidarity with many oppressed communities as the poets discussed here have done, and it is no different for Hammad. Anna Ball writes, '[f]or Suheir Hammad, ... it is possible to belong to many communities, and different potentials for agency, opposition and solidarity are to be found in each' (147).

In her poem entitled 'silence', Hammad weaves together short lines suggesting danger, urgency and immediacy with a haunting song entitled 'Bear witness world to us and to Beirut' originally sung by the Palestinian music band, *Al Ashiqeen*. By repeating the words 'American bullets', Hammad is emphasizing the United States' destructive role in the Arab world as we have seen over the past several decades;[3] however, the specific place and time in this poem as in the poems by Darwish and Jordan above, is Beirut in 1982. Hammad, from her place of exile in the United States, is speaking truth to power by directly implicating the US government in the genocide of the Palestinian people. Breaking the silence, Hammad writes:

> i wonder what he
> heard as he ran
> wonder what he
> thought as the
>   american bullets
> flew from
>   israeli hands
> through
>   god's air
> to murder another
> one of freedom's sons
>
> (48)

Hammad's short, unpunctuated lines create the atmosphere that it is describing. These lines seem to be running, breathless along with the boy who is running, trying to dodge the American made and Israeli handled bullets that are going to kill Palestine's sons of freedom. It is interesting to note that the three lines that are indented more than the other lines are 'american bullets', 'israeli hands' and 'god's air' to emphasize who the perpetrators are – the Americans and Israelis, committing their war crimes in god's air and in places and spaces that do not belong to them, murdering people for wanting to be free.

Hammad wants the world to know the truth of Palestinian life:

he had lived with his eyes

seen so much
palestine occupied   freedom denied   my people's genocide
seen with his eyes
felt with his heart
struggle of life under
army boots
palestine alive
(singing) *Wa men ma shaf bil ghorban ya Beirut*
Aman ayoon Amreeciya
(And those who don't see through the sieve
Are blinded by American eyes)

(49)

For Hammad, Palestine *lives*, despite being occupied, denied freedom and massacred, struggling under the siege of the colonizing and occupying Israeli army. Not only does Palestine live, it also *sings* the truth in the face of brutal power. Hammad's stanzas, each revealing the instability of Palestinian life, which is always on the run, 'so used to running / we are it seems / we palestinians are always running' (49), end with song, asking the world to bear witness to the unfolding tragedy, which is a clear reference to the massacres of Sabra and Shatila, '*Ishad ya alam alene wa a Beirut* / (Bear witness world to us and to Beirut)' (ibid.), and not to pretend not to see the genocide as the Americans would have it. Hammad is asking the world to bear witness and to enter that space in the margin in solidarity where the oppressed are relentlessly besieged by unspeakable horrors as Genet and Jordan significantly did in their life and work.

Jordan's solidarity with the Palestinian cause predates and presages the deep affinity that would soon develop between Black American and Palestinian activists in their struggle for human rights in the twenty-first century. Even before the popularity of the Black Lives Matter movement in 2020 with the killing of the unarmed African American man George Floyd by a white police officer,[4] the solidarity of Black and Palestinian activists had already been firmly planted decades before this event. This solidarity began developing after the 1967 Arab-Israeli war (2015: 1017) as pointed out by Kristian Davis Bailey in his article entitled 'Black-Palestinian Solidarity in the Ferguson-Gaza Era'.[5] This relationship specifically started with the meetings between the Black Panther party and the PLO in Algiers whereby the two sides strategized together 'under a project of revolutionary internationalism and anti-imperialism' (Bailey, 1017). The Black American activist Angela Davis affirmed that a letter of solidarity that she received from Palestinian prisoners in Israeli jails is what sustained and empowered her during her own time in prison (ibid.). It was perhaps the American Ambassador to the UN, Andrew Young's meeting with PLO representative at the UN in 1979 that refocused attention on the Black-Palestinian relationship in the United States with many Black American activists and leaders examining the similarities between the Black and Palestinian struggles for justice. Jesse Jackson, a well-known black American leader from Chicago, was quite vocal in making this comparison as I recall growing up in Chicago in the 1970s and 1980s.

It is, however, during the Ferguson-Gaza moment that Black-Palestinian solidarity received some widespread exposure, particularly on social media. In fact, it was a young Palestinian American man by the name of Bassem Masri who participated in and live-streamed the Ferguson Uprising for the world to witness in 2014. This brave young Palestinian American activist established a strong basis for Black-Palestinian solidarity for a new generation of activists in both communities. The Black American filmmaker Sabaah Folayan wrote on Twitter after the passing of Masri in 2018: 'Rest in Power #Bassem ... He is the reason many of us learned about #Ferguson. He grounded us in awareness of our shared struggle with #Palestine. We lost a real one today' (@sabaahfolayan, 2018). Further solidifying these ties, American Congresswoman Cori Bush praised the bravery of Masri in a speech to the American House of Representatives in May 2021. After Bush's speech, the Palestinian American human rights attorney and activist wrote on Twitter in a post, dated 14 May 2021: '@CoriBush gave a whole sermon on militarism, imperialism, & #BlackPalestinianSolidarity forged in the crucible of the #Ferguson#Gaza moment in the most moving tribute to Bassem Masri, a warrior gone too soon.' Sadly, it was only in 2021 that I learned that Masri's mother is my first cousin – such is the plight of the Palestinian dispossession.

The degree of the solidarity between members of the Black Lives Matter movement in the United States and Palestinian activists in Gaza and the rest of historic Palestine reached a point whereby Palestinian activists undergoing heavy Israeli bombardment in Gaza and other parts of occupied Palestine sent Black American protesters in Ferguson and other American cities not only messages of support and solidarity, but also messages of advice on how to deal with police brutality and gas inhalation with Palestinian activists writing the following on social media:

Solidarity with #Ferguson. Remember to not touch your face when teargassed or put water on it. Instead use milk or coke! – مريم البرغوثي (@MariamBarghouti) August 14, 2014.

Don't [k]eep much distance from the Police, if you're close to them they can't tear Gas. To #Ferguson from #Palestine – Rajai abuKhalil (@Rajaiabukhalil) August 14, 2014.

Always make sure to run against the wind / to keep calm when you're teargassed, the pain will pass, don't rub your eyes! #Ferguson Solidarity – مريم البرغوثي (@MariamBarghouti) August 14, 2014.

(Goldstein, yesmagazine.org)

The connection between the Black and Palestinian (under occupation and in exile) communities was made even more apparent when it was revealed that the American police underwent training in Israel with one of the police chiefs who was trained in Israel being a past 'chief of the St. Louis County Police Department [who] was one of many US police officials to travel to Israel for joint "security" training' (Bailey, 1019). This proves that the tactics being used by the American police against Black people are similar to the tactics employed by the Israeli army against Palestinian protesters in the occupied 'West Bank' and the rest of historic Palestine. However, one needs to keep in mind the essential difference that Israel is a settler colonial state acting against a colonized people. Black Americans are Americans who face systemic racism that is deeply entrenched in America's slave past and the post-slavery Jim Crow era,[6] and this racism continues to our present era of white nationalism (Trumpism).[7]

Hammad's poem 'A Prayer Band' written in 2005 for the mostly Black American victims of hurricane Katrina tackles systemic racism against Black Americans while at the same time merging the suffering of Black Americans and Palestinians in a prayer band of transnational solidarity that emphasizes the mobility of affiliations:

> i have known of displacement
> and the tides pulling every thing
> that could not be carried within
> and some of that too
> ....
>
> i have known of promises to return
> to where you come from
> but first any bus going any where
>
> tonight the tigris and the mississippi moan
> for each other as sisters
> full of unnatural things
> flooded with predators and prayers
> ....
>
> who says this is not the america they know?
>
> what america do they know?
>
> were the poor people so poor they could not
> be seen?
>
> were the black people so many they could not
> be counted?
>
> this is not a charge
> this is a conviction

if death levels us all
then life plays favorites

(electronicintifada.net)

In the above lines, Hammad's solidarity, or as Hind El Hajj and Sirene Harb term it, the poet's 'mobility' that is deployed by Hammad to 'destabilize racialized structures and definitions' (2015: 224) emphasizes the suffering of Black Americans and Palestinians in terms of displacement and their refugee status. For the Palestinians, this is a result of the 1948 *Nakba* and for Black Americans, on this particular occasion that inspired the writing of this poem, it is a result of the devastation of hurricane Katrina and the intentional neglect of the American government of the plight of New Orleans' Black population.

The poet asks in biting sarcasm, are Black Americans so poor they cannot be seen or too many that they cannot be counted? Hammad, however, makes it clear that the US government's racist handling of this catastrophe harks back to America's slave past and its deeply entrenched, institutionalized systemic racism in her line 'who says this is not the america they know?' The poet is adamant – this has always been America's truth. America, like Israel, was founded upon the enslavement and massacres of other peoples, and 'this is not a charge / this is a conviction', writes Hammad, and she has human history and nature to back her up for the Mississippi and Tigris rivers have spoken as they 'moan for each other as sisters full of unnatural things flooded with predators and prayers'. These two great rivers have witnessed the suffering of Black Americans and Palestinians.

The unnatural separation of these people from their homes has unleashed not only flood waters, but also predators and the anguished prayers of the preyed upon. If it could sensibly be said that death is the great leveller, postulates Hammad in this poem, then life is not so for 'the wretched of the earth', to use Fanon's words. Hammad's use of the Mississippi and Tigris rivers that have stored the silenced histories of Black Americans and Palestinians respectively alludes to the great Black American poet Langston Hughes' poem entitled, 'The Negro Speaks of Rivers' where Hughes lists several great rivers, such as the Euphrates, Congo, Nile and Mississippi that have borne witness to the long history of Black people who built all the great civilizations that sprung up around these rivers, which silently recorded the histories of Black peoples over many centuries (1990: 4). Black Americans and Palestinians have undergone catastrophic experiences that have enabled the emergence of an 'organic solidarity ... from the ground up between communities bearing the brunt of state repression' (Bailey, 1019).

Another space in the margin that Palestinians have entered in global solidarity is reflected in Darwish's poem 'The Speech of the Red Indian'.[8] Darwish introduced this poem in front of a live audience before reciting it in the following way (my translation):

The year 1992 marked the 500th year anniversary of the biggest and most well-known mistake in the history of humankind – Christopher Columbus set sail from Barcelona [Darwish's audience is heard laughing and clapping] in search of India, but he discovered America by mistake. This poem was written on this occasion, and it is based on a tradition of 'Red Indian' leaders, who, when they were defeated and then surrendered, would give a rhetorical speech about their philosophy on nature and life in front of the white man. This is the penultimate speech of the 'Red Indian' to the white man.

(YouTube)

The first part of Darwish's statement above is spoken in a half jesting manner – that the biggest mistake in history is the discovery of America. However, in reality, Darwish actually did mean it. The United States is the biggest imperializing power in this world, and it certainly has not been a friend to the dispossessed, colonized and marginalized in this world. In fact, the United States is the cause of the wretchedness on this earth, intones Darwish.

Darwish's poem seems to have been little analysed and perhaps little understood. There have been several attempts to analyse this poem, such as those by Steven Salaita, Ramzy Baroud and Ben White.[9] These critics' contributions, while interesting and certainly provocative, are in need of further elaboration and clarification. In addition to the obvious drawing attention to the strong parallels between the Native American and Palestinian struggles, that of the ethnic and cultural cleansing of both peoples by the white man, I believe that Darwish also wants to draw attention to the concept of the *indigeneity* of the two peoples – the Native Americans and the Palestinians – and especially the Palestinians. Darwish knows that his interest in the Native American struggle as a Palestinian poet of his great stature, a poet who represents Palestine or more specifically Palestine's cultural life, will immediately conjure up comparisons between the two peoples, the two nations and the two struggles. It is also commonly accepted that the Native Americans are indeed the Indigenous people of the Americas, North, Central and South.

However, the Zionist propaganda machine has been and still is so strong that the indigeneity of the Palestinians in Palestine has not become a global commonplace as America has for the remaining Native American population. This is due to a very misleading but popular Zionist argument that asserts that all Palestinians came from the country of 'Arabia' or any other Arab country a couple of hundred years ago. The reason, I think, Darwish is focusing on the concept of indigeneity within the Palestinian context can be found in 'The Speech of the Red Indian'. Zionist ideology has used the concept of the 'Promised Land' quite successfully to argue that world Jewry has been in diaspora for over 3,000 years and that Jews were finally able to 'return' to their homeland and re-establish the 'Kingdom of Israel' in 1948. This inevitably meant that the Jewish people, who were supposedly made up of scattered tribes roaming this earth, had a God-given right to take possession of historic Palestine, thereby dispossessing the Indigenous population who were actually living on the land in 1948, the year of the Palestinian *Nakba*.

The Zionist narrative does not recognize the natural right of the Palestinian people to live on the land of their ancestors who lived in Palestine for thousands of years. The Zionist version of the narrative is the accepted one for many in the West, especially the religiously inclined and even those who are not religiously committed. To this, Darwish writes in the voice of his Native American narrator,

Chief Seattle who is, of course, warning the white man against using religious myth to lay claim to the Americas, the land of the Indigenous Native American inhabitants. Of course, the reader should read into this the idea of the 'Promised Land', which according to the Old and New Testaments God promised to the Jews. The narrative of the reimagined 'Promised Land' does not hold any credence for Darwish or Said and Hall, for that matter. Darwish came back to the idea of the 'Promised Land' in other poems, especially in *In the Presence of Absence* (2011). In the following lines from *In the Presence of Absence*, Darwish emphasizes the indigeneity of the Palestinians and how they lost their past and present in a moment to foreigners who cultivated the myth of the 'Promised Land':

> We take water from the neighbors' wells and borrow bread from the rock's bounty. We live, if we are able to live, in an infant past, planted in fields that were ours for hundreds of years until a moment ago, before the dough rose and the coffeepots cooled. In one ill-fated hour, history entered like a bold thief through a door as the present flew out through a window. With a massacre or two, the country's name, our country, became another. Reality became an idea and history became memory. The myth invades and the invasion attributes everything to the will of the Lord who promised and did not renege on his promise. They wrote their narrative: We have returned. They wrote our narrative: They have returned to the desert. They put us on trial: Why were you born here? We said: Why was Adam born in paradise?
> (46)

In these lines, Darwish very elegantly narrates the Palestinian narrative by underscoring the Palestinians' natural ties to this land (water from wells and bread from rock's bounty) by juxtaposing two important elements, the very *real*, personal loss of Palestinians that is based on lived experience as opposed to the abstract Zionist myth of the 'Promised Land'.

Darwish is able to effectively personalize the national by using diction such as 'before the dough rose and the coffeepots cooled', thus allowing the story to enter the reader's home, a personal space. Darwish emphasizes the suddenness of the change with concrete reality becoming an abstract idea and actual history turning into a hazy memory in 'one ill-fated hour'. The poet here is underscoring the fact that religious myth was used (and is still being used) to destroy a whole people and 'attribute [] everything to the will of the Lord'. Then, the colonizers wrote the narrative of the victors and the defeated. The colonizers controlled the narrative, which Darwish is deconstructing in his own history from below. Although Darwish wrote these words in Arabic, it is obvious that the poet is also directing his message to the outside world and means for his poetry to travel, crossing borders and breaking the silence on the American Indian and Palestinian narratives. Like his Chief Seattle in 'The Speech of the Red Indian' who addresses the white man, Darwish is also addressing the white man who is the Zionist colonizer of Palestine. Darwish's Arab audience understands this very point, and the crossover from America to Palestine is easily traversed for the poet's audience. The causes of these two Indigenous peoples are brought together in the poet's consciousness.

Ramzy Baroud argues that Darwish wants to underscore this very concept of indigeneity in 'The Speech of the Red Indian': 'Our pastures are sacred, our spirits inspired, / the stars are luminous words where our fable / is legible from beginning to end …' (*The Adam of Two Edens*, 2000: 129). Baroud perceptively points out that Darwish wrote these lines about the Native Americans, but he also meant the Palestinians (gulfnews.com, 2016). In fact, if one were to compare two of Darwish's poems, one about the Native Americans and the other about Palestinians, the striking similarities between the two peoples and their struggles in Darwish's imagination become clear to the reader. Even the diction used by Darwish to describe the two peoples is strikingly similar. In 'The Speech of the Red Indian', Darwish writes:

Don't kill the grass any more,
It possesses a soul in us that could
shelter the soul of the earth.

Tamer of horses, teach your horse
to ask forgiveness of nature's soul
for the way you've treated our trees:
O Sister tree,
look how they've tortured you:
the way they've tortured me;
never ask forgiveness
for the woodcutter whose axe felled
both your mother and mine …
….

All told,
you killed over seventy million hearts,
more than enough for you to return from slaughter
as a king on the throne of a new age.

(*The Adam of Two Edens*, 2000: 129–31)

In 'On a Canaanite Stone at the Dead Sea', Darwish writes:

A war rages against me, a war rages inside me.
Stranger, hang your weapons in our palm tree
and let me plant my wheat in Canaan's sacred soil.
….

Leave Jericho under her palm tree
But don't steal my dream, ….

Have you come, then murdered, then inherited,
Only to increase the saltiness of the sea?

I'm growing greener with the passing of years
    on the oak's trunk.
....
The sea descends below sea level
so my bones float like trees over the water.
Trees are my absence.
The moon is the shadow of my door.

(The Adam of Two Edens, 2000: 75–7)

Several aspects come to light when comparing the above lines from these two Darwishian poems, one of course about Native Americans and the other about Palestinians. Both of these peoples are inherently tied to the land, which they consider to be sacred. The Canaanites, the ancestors of the Palestinians (again this emphasis on indigeneity), are so deeply rooted in this land that they have become the very nature of Palestine itself unlike the invader who came from afar to murder the Palestinian and inherit the land of Palestine. Thus, these two points are interrelated – the Palestinians' inseparability from the nature of Palestine is deeply intertwined with their indigeneity because historic Palestine is the real, lived space/place of the Palestinians, with which they have an intimate relationship.

The Palestinians are basically an agricultural people who are descendants of the ancient Canaanites, who as Munir Akash explains are a matriarchal people 'who lived in agricultural communities and worshipped the Moon Mother Astarte [another name of Anat]' (2000: 37). The story of the Canaanites, the Indigenous people of Canaan/Palestine, is re-interpreted by Robert Allen Warrior, an American Indian scholar, in his important article entitled, 'Canaanites, Cowboys and Indians' (1989). Warrior urges American Indians and other Indigenous peoples in the world to reconsider/re-examine the Exodus story *not* as a discourse of liberation precisely because here God delivers Jews from their oppression by promising them the land of Canaan, and commands them 'to mercilessly annihilate the indigenous population' (22). Warrior warns American Indians that they (the American Indians) are actually the Canaanites in this story and not the Jews.

As Warrior argues, in the Exodus narrative, Indigenous communities, such as the people of Canaan/Palestine and America (the land of the American Indians), god is a conqueror and not a saviour. The Exodus narrative is a poignant story for Warrior because, as he argues, the extermination of Indigenous communities is seen to be the religious right of 'god's chosen people', the Jews in Israel and the white Puritans who 'were fond of referring to Native Americans as Amelkites and Canaanites' and themselves 'as a "chosen people"' (25). Thus, instead of Exodus being a story of liberation, it is actually the story of the colonization, dispossession and extermination of Indigenous people. To this Warrior asks, 'Is there a god, a spirit, who will hear us and stand with us in the Amazon, Osage County, and Wounded Knee? Is there a god, a spirit, able to move among the pain and anger of Nablus, Gaza, and Soweto?' (26)

It is only fitting, then, that Darwish stands in solidarity with the Indigenous American Indians whose land is sacred soil, which the white man, who came from across the sea, has tortured and devastated. The white man who 'killed over seventy million hearts' 'will never understand the ancient words/here in spirits roaming free/between sky and trees' ('Speech of the Red Indian', 2000: 130). The intermingling of the experiences of these two peoples is made clear in some lines which appear in 'The Speech of the Red Indian' rather than in 'On a Canaanite Stone at the Red Sea', lines that urgently apply to both Palestinians and American Indians:

> You have your god and we have ours,
> you have your religion and we have ours,
> Don't bury your God
> in books that back up your claim of
>   your land over our land,
> don't appoint your God to be a mere
> courtier in the palace of the King.
>
> <div align="right">(<i>ATE</i>, 2000: 132–3)</div>

In the above lines, the Red Indian/Darwish tells the White Man not to bury his God in books (religious books, the Torah, the Bible) that support the colonizer's claim to 'our land', the land of the Deer people/the land of Palestine. The Red Indian/Darwish then warns the colonizer not to appoint God as a courtier in the palace of the King – that is not to politicize religion, which, here, is a reference to the use of the Torah and Bible as political tracts to prove that twentieth and twenty-first century Jews from different parts of the world have a right to the land of Palestine.

The Syrian poet Adonis, like Darwish, criticizes the Promised Land argument that has violently dispossessed Indigenous peoples by means of the most brutal kind of settler colonialism in his book length poem called *Concerto al-Quds* (Jerusalem) (2017). Like Darwish, Adonis also rejects the myth of the Promised Land and God's 'Chosen People' argument, which was used by the Zionist movement to dislodge the Indigenous Palestinians from their ancestral home. In his late style poem *Concerto al-Quds* (2017), Adonis, creating a metaphorical 'concerto' of sounds, voices, histories and images of Jerusalem, shows his displeasure with the colonizer's use of divine prophecy as pointed out by Khaled Mattawa, who also translated this poem into English (Mattawa, 'On Adonis's *Concerto al-Quds*').

Adonis's *Concerto*, which re-enacts the disruptions it narrates, in Saidian-like late style, alternates between poetry and prose and presents different voices and religious texts in fragmented fashion over many chapters, sections and subsections. As in an actual concerto with the orchestra playing against the soloist, in Adonis's *Concerto*, the secular, solo voice of the poet is heard in opposition to the orchestra of voices from the colonial and Zionist interpreters of religious texts and dogmas. In the section of this poem entitled 'Afflictions', the speaker begins with questions about Palestine and its continuing tragedy:

> *Why is every atom of Palestine's ash an open wound?
> *How does this wound create life with the implements of death?
> *Is Palestine's history an autumn that has migrated beyond the seasons?
>
> ('Afflictions', kenyonreview.org)

The first two questions address Palestine's still open wound, out of which the bleeding nation, resiliently and steadfastly, creates life. But the third question is of a more critical nature, why is Palestine's history only an autumn? What about the other three seasons, the poet critically ponders? Adonis, always critical of any form of dogma, religious or otherwise, is here disrupting arguments that would only recognize Jerusalem as a *sacred* city, awaiting the fulfilment of divine prophecy. Jerusalem obviously has an earthly existence, a history of colonization and occupation, a history of culture and exquisite architecture, which represent the other missing seasons that seem to have 'migrated beyond the seasons', and that lack any form of existence in our earthly world – the *worldliness* of Jerusalem, to use Said's term.

Extending the biblical metaphor allows Adonis to question the wisdom of the colonizer's interpretation of divine prophecy, which seems to have a destructive effect on humanity. In the subsection of 'Afflictions' entitled 'B. Letter to Ezekiel', the speaker interrogates the prophet Ezekiel, who prophesized the destruction of Jerusalem and the establishment of the Kingdom of Israel (britannica.com):

> Ezekiel, visionary and seer,
> look again and again,
> Ruin is still the daily bread of God's earth. Will the prophecies also turn into a siege?
> Will tunnels be burrowed into their words? Will their visions splinter into missiles and
> bombs, into volcanos of gas and phosphor? Is it true, dear Ezekiel, that you have befriended this dragon?
>
> ('Afflictions', kenyonreview.org)

Biblical allusions abound in Adonis's prolonged interrogation of the colonialist/Zionist interpreters of sacred books as the poet asks Ezekiel to examine the ruin of Jerusalem and to consider how these biblical interpretations have turned life on earth into a siege and how humanity has become beholden to weapons of mass destruction, such as missiles, bombs, gas and phosphor. The speaker asks Ezekiel if he has met Salome, a biblical symbol of female evil. The poet goes on to further interrogate the prophet, 'And we, the concubine's children, what must we do when the earth itself is a / concubine in the grip of divine prophecies?' Of course, here, the reference to 'we' being the 'concubine's children' is an allusion to Hajar or Hagar, the concubine wife of Abraham and the mother of Ishmael, who is said to be the forefather of modern day Arabs.

Thus, here the poet is asking in an angry tone the politician/prophet, what is to become of the 'concubine's children' – the Arabs generally and Palestinians specifically who have been excluded from living on the only land they call home and for whom the earth itself has become a concubine placed under the siege of the Zionist interpreters of divine prophecy? These interpretations, writes the poet, lack any form of humanity, which makes the speaker in the poem scream out in anger:

> 'Salome,
> blood is spilling on thresholds, walls, and windows.

You know the hearts of these masters, these prophets and politicians. Tell me, what do their hearts actually pump?'

....

Why do the books deceive?
       Why is every letter of the alphabet chained,
              every human mouth bridled?
Why can the sky not be seen except as
       owned, branded, tattooed, guarded, and walled?
Is it a stockyard for language?
Is it a storage room for the gold of prophecies?
Salome-Herodias-Hero-shima!

('Afflictions', kenyonreview.org)

Adonis's attack on the settler colonialist's interpretation of divine prophecies becomes stronger with every line. Here, the poet criticizes how politicians use sacred books and questions what these politicians/prophets' hearts actually pump. He decries the besiegement of language, humanity and the limitless sky that has been 'owned, branded, tattooed, guarded, and walled' to politicized divinations, thus creating 'Hero-shima'. The poet forms this name from the names of Salome's parents: her mother, Herodias and her stepfather, Herod, but before the poet completes the letter 'd' in Herod's name, he re-writes it, or perhaps, reinterprets it as 'Hero-shima'. The allusion here is, of course, to Hiroshima, the Japanese city devastated by the dropping of the atomic bomb by the United States in 1945. Adonis is emphasizing the devastation caused to humanity and earth by the settler colonialist's interpretation of divine prophecy, which instead of bringing people together in harmony, has emphasized the discourse of exclusivity and destruction.

In fact, this is precisely what the 'Basic Law: Israel as the Nation State of the Jewish People' passed in July, 2018 does. Part C of the '1- Basic principles' clause specifically states that '[t]he right to exercise national self-determination in the State of Israel is unique to the Jewish people' (Wootliff, 2018). Thus, Palestinians and their ancestors who lived on this land for thousands of years have no right to 'exercise [their] national self-determination' in historic Palestine. Yet, Jews from anywhere in the world, as stipulated by the fifth part of the clause, '5-Ingathering of the exiles', '[t]he state will be open for Jewish immigration and the ingathering of exiles' (ibid.) who have a right to 'return' from their 'exile' to the 'Kingdom of Israel'. Even with this kind of exclusion of the Arab population living inside the boundaries of 1948 Palestine that modern day Palestinians and their ancestors have inhabited for thousands of years, Israel as a Jewish only state is still seen as a 'democratic' state by the world's hegemonic powers and the most powerful metropolitan centres. To criticize any aspect of Israeli policy or its exclusivist and racist laws is considered anti-Semitic,[10] according to the definition of anti-Semitism published by the International Holocaust Remembrance Alliance (IHRA). In this definition of anti-Semitism on the IHRA website, it states that it is anti-Semitic to consider Israel and its racist laws, racist.

Racist is not strong enough a term to describe Israeli laws that are put in place to continue the ethnic cleansing of the Palestinian people from the lands of historic Palestine, literally lands that these people have been continuously living on for thousands of years, in the same villages, towns and cities. It is quite ironic that the IHRA's definition of anti-Semitism can be found online under the title 'The Working Definition of Anti-Semitism', published by the American Jewish Committee (AJC): Global Jewish Advocacy, which states as its mission 'To enhance the well-being of the Jewish people and Israel, and to advance human rights and democratic values in the United States and around the world' (ajc.org). One wonders how the project of the ethnic cleansing of Palestine in order to make room for the establishment of Israel fits into the equation of human rights and democratic values that the AJC is promoting. According to Darwish in his 'Speech of the Red Indian', the white man's, and of course, Zionist claims to this land (America and Palestine) are buried in religious books that put the 'superior' white man's god against the other's god. These are essentialist claims of racial purity and an identity of the return of 'scattered tribes' that Hall calls 'imperializing' and 'hegemonising' 'form[s] of "ethnicity"' (401) as mentioned earlier in this book.

Darwish, who calls himself the 'Trojan poet' (Antoon, 2008), is not only standing in solidarity with Native Americans, but he is significantly breaking the silence and allowing history from below to be told – here the history of the Native Americans and the Palestinians. Darwish explains '[t]he Trojans would have expressed a different narrative than that of Homer, but their voices are forever lost. I am in search of those voices' (qtd. in Antoon, 2008). White Americans from European descent have told the world their history from the perspective of the victors, the powerful whose narrative has become 'official history'. We have often heard about the 'Founding Fathers', most of whom were slave holders of course, and about their 'great achievements'. However, the Native Americans exist only as others, if they exist at all, in American history books. Darwish's commentary on Native Americans in 'The Speech of the Red Indian' can also be said of the Palestinians. In fact, the two struggles, histories and landscapes coalesce and become one. According to Munir Akash, Darwish's encounter with Native American literature 'enabled the exiled poet's imagination to respiritualize the Palestinian universe in a healing way, with a repatriated attachment to Mother Nature' (2000: 40). In the poem, Darwish identifies 'himself with the legendary Chief Seattle' (Akash, 2000: 40), and the Palestinian people become the Deer people while Gaza coalesces with Channon County, 'Deir Yasin with Wounded Knee, Trail of *Nakba* ... with the Trail of Tears and refugee camps with Indian reservations' (ibid.).

Thus, as Akash explains in the 'Introduction' to *Mahmoud Darwish: Adam of Two Edens*, these '"two tragedies" become "one grief"' (ibid.). Akash places Native Indian tragedies, some of which are mentioned in Darwish's poem, alongside Palestinian tragedies in order to underscore how Darwish himself sees the similarities between the histories of these Indigenous peoples. The essential similarity that Darwish sees between these two peoples is the precariousness of their survival, but as the Native American activist, Russel Means, states: 'It is ... the role of all natural beings to survive. A part of our survival is to resist' (qtd. in Akash, 2000: 43). Both Native Americans and Palestinians, then, resist the 'threat of total extermination with the deepest will to survive' (Akash, 2000: 42). In fact, this resistance and defiance can be discerned in this poem despite the precariousness of Native American, and by comparison, Palestinian survival. In fact, when Darwish recited the lines below in Arabic in front of an Arab, but mostly Palestinian audience, he received enthusiastic applause because his audience noted the defiance of the poet's words and tone (Darwish's recitation of the 'Speech of the Red Indian' on YouTube):

Take my motherland by the sword!

I refuse to sign a treaty between victim and killer.

I refuse to sign a bill of sale

that takes possession
of so much as one inch of my weed patch,
of so much as one inch of my cornfield
even if it's my last salutation to the sun!

(*ATE*, 2000: 140–1)

While these words are Chief Seattle's speech to the white man, they are also Darwish's words to several parties, including Israel, the Palestinian Authority (PA), especially signing a 'treaty between victim and killer', Arab nations (that have signed and are now signing treaties of surrender with Israel) and to the rest of the world who have turned a blind eye to Palestinian suffering. These are certainly words of defiance and a refusal to surrender 'even if it's my last salutation to the sun!' declares the poet to applause.

While I do agree with most of Salaita's analysis of Darwish's 'The Speech of the Red Indian', especially that Darwish is aware that for Native Americans 'colonization exists in totality' (2016: 129), I do not think it is fair to say that Darwish's Native American offers only a 'compromise born of desperation' (ibid.). It is true that Darwish's Native American does offer the white man 'the earth and the sun' and asks him to 'leave the land of our names', but Darwish is very direct and forceful later on in the speech as shown above. I think that Darwish is emphasizing the American Indian's philosophy of life, which is based on their peaceful and sharing nature. Right before Chief Seattle refuses to sign a peace treaty with the white killers of his people, he says: 'We brought you tidings of the Spring. / *(Don't point your guns at us!)* / We can exchange gifts, we can sing' (*ATE*, 2000: 140). The point that Darwish is making here is that the Native American made the ultimate sacrifice and refused 'to sign the treaty between the victim and the killer'.

Darwish's Native American, like his Canaanite Palestinian, chooses death over enslavement as the poet declares in 'On a Canaanite Stone at the Dead Sea': 'One tribe became extinct. One told the new Hulagu, / "We're yours." / I say: *We're not a slave nation, / with all due respects to Ibn Khaldoun. / I am myself, despite being shattered on metallic air*' (*ATE*, 2000: 80). Palestinians, like the Native Americans, will fight and defend their right to the land until death, refusing to surrender as

Ibn Khaldoun did in centuries past. The Palestinian will not surrender to 'new Hulagu', and here Darwish is taking a swipe at Ibn Khaldoun,[11] a very important fourteenth-century Arab thinker and historian, who signed a treaty of surrender with the Mongol leader as a result of the Mongols' siege of Damascus in 1400. Of course, the new Hulagu, to which Darwish refers, is the current colonizer of the land of Canaan, the Zionist rulers and their Western allies. The Palestinians, declares Darwish, are not a slave nation.

One of the most powerful sections of Darwish's 'The Speech of the Red Indian' is produced by the technique of repetition, the repetition of the word death in all its variations in order to emphasize the death and destruction caused by the white man/master/colonizer, the ancestors of the founding fathers of the United States of America. Darwish focuses on the brutal death and destruction the white man with the white Lord (*ATE*, 136) and the 'new steel god' (*ATE*, 139) and the 'iron crosses' (*ATE*, 141) caused:

> There are dead and there are colonies.
> There are dead and there are bulldozers.
> There are dead and there are hospitals.
> There are dead and there are radar screens
> to observe the dead
> as they die more than once in this life,
> screens to observe the dead who live on after death,
> the dead who feed the beast of civilization on death
> as well as those who die
> to lift the earth above all that has died.
>
> O white master, where are you taking my people
>   and yours?
>
> (*ATE*, 143)

The white master has built up his civilization upon the death and destruction, the ethnocide and memoricide of the Native Americans. The left side of the stanza describes the Native American, the dead upon which the white man with the steel god has built his colonies with bulldozers, thus destroying the sacred relationship between the 'red Indian' and nature and feeding the 'beast of civilization on death'. The parallel with the massacres and ethnic cleansing of Palestine is unmistakable, bringing to mind Deir Yassin, Saliha, Tantoura, Al-Dawayima, Kibbyeh, Sabra and Shatila and the Jenin Camp massacre among many others.

This section of the poem has been recently performed by Roger Waters, co-founder of the rock band Pink Floyd who teamed up with the Palestinian music group, the Trio Joubran who provided the musical background to Waters solemn recitation of half of section 6 of the poem, looking straight into the camera in a black and white video entitled 'Supremacy'. The translation shown below is the one that appears in the actual video by Waters and the Trio Joubran and which was translated by Fady Joudah with the help of Waters. This translation differs slightly from that of Sargon Boulos, which is the version that appears in *The Adam of Two Edens*.

The more faithful translation is the one provided by Boulos; for example, what Darwish says in Arabic is 'سنَمْضي إلى حتْفنا، أوّلاً، سنُدافع عن شَجرٍ نَرْتَديه' which Boulos translates as 'We will face our death, but first/we'll defend the trees we wear' (*ATE*, 142). Fady Joudah's original translation of this line in *Harvard Review* reads, 'But first, we will march to our doom, we will defend the trees we wear' (2009c: 158). The 2018 Joudah/Waters dramatic video version reads 'We will face the long march, but first we will defend the trees we wear.' Boulos's more literal translation can here be said to be the more accurate one because it captures the full impact of Darwish's line, which emphasizes the defiance of the Native American who understands the *imminence* of his death, but dauntlessly and fearlessly defends his way of life and his intimate relationship with nature.

Below is a reworked version of Joudah's original translation that appears in the very powerfully presented Waters/Joubran video entitled 'Supremacy'. The breaks between the lines are as they are spoken by Waters in the video:

A long time must go by
before our present becomes history
just like us.
We will face the long march
but first
we will defend the trees we wear.

We will defend the bell of night and the hanging moon
over our huts.

We will defend the leaping deer
and the clay of our pots
and the eagle feathers in the wings of our final songs.

But soon you will erect your world on our remains.
You will pave over the sacred places
to open a road to the satellite moon.

This is the age of industry.
The age of coal
fossils to fuel your thirst for fine wine.

('Supremacy': 2018, YouTube)

For Darwish, the self-styled 'Trojan poet', the telling of the narrative of the Native Americans, who faced the effects of colonization in its totality and all of its savagery, so that the white man can build his 'age of industry' (translated as 'Iron Age' by the poet Boulos in *ATW*, 142), upon the corpses of the Indigenous inhabitants of the land is a story that Darwish feels needs to be urgently told. It is interesting to note that the Trio Joubran and Waters felt it imperative to perform this section of the poem as a response to 'Trump's recognition of Jerusalem as the capital of Israel last December [2017] [which] gave the track new relevance' (Parry, 2018).

The Trio Joubran and Waters reimagined Darwish's poem about the 'red Indian' within the Palestinian context whereby the ruthless, forward movement of the colonial project from America to the 'Middle East', more adequately referred to as West Asia, is based on the destruction and erasure of the other, their land and culture. The symbolism here is quite stark: the white man/god as represented by the arrogant, white supremacist President of the United States, Donald Trump, declares Jerusalem, a city that Palestinians have inhabited for thousands of years and where the Muslim call to prayer has been sounding and resounding from Masqid Al Aqsa and the Dome of the Rock for over 1,500 years, the 'official' capital of Israel. With one stroke of a pen, the white man hopes to erase a whole history and culture of a people in favour of what 'Salish and Cree writer and activist Lee Maracle' (Salaita, 105) calls 'the newest colonizing settler state in the world' (qtd. in Salaita, 105).

A similar theme is struck by the Native American poet, John Trudell whose poem/song 'Rich Man's War' presents what Salaita fittingly calls 'geographies of pain' (2016: 111) that the white man perpetually creates to satisfy his unquenchable thirst for continuously enriching himself. Trudell mentions several geographies of pain, the people that have been historically preyed upon by the rich man. These people's narratives represent histories from below, which makes them marginal spaces that all Trojan poets, to use Darwish's term, must enter in solidarity, agency and mobility, so that their causes do not die in silence. Without dwelling on any one of these geographies of pain, Trudell uses the strategy of listing to speak about these geographies collectively in order to address their collective suffering at the hands of the rich, white man who is constantly starting wars from which he would benefit. To the hauntingly sad Native American vocals in the background, Trudell solemnly and boldly speaks his truth to power:

> Rich man's war
> industrial streets, class lines
> money talks, turning language to paper pieces
> rich man's war free man's society.
> Raging violent insecurity
> nuclear man, nuclear woman
> unclear how to act.
> ....
> Rich man's war
> Central America bleeding
> wounds same as Palestine and Harlem
> Three Mile Island in El Salvador
> Pine Ridge in Belfast
>
> Rich man's war
> the poor, starving for food

starving for land, starving for peace
starving for real.

rich man's war
attacking human, attacking being
attacking earth, attacking tomorrow

Rich man's war
thinking of always war
thinking of always war.

(antiwarsongs.org)

Like Darwish's reference to the white man with the steel god, constructing his iron/industrial age upon the lands of the dead and dying and their tortured earth, Trudell's rich man with his destructive 'always war' and his 'raging violent insecurity' is bent on destroying the Indigenous peoples of this earth in Central America, Palestine, Harlem, El Salvador and Ireland, where these besieged peoples are starving for food, land and peace – 'starving for real', emphasizes Trudell, underscoring the harsh reality of these 'expendable' peoples.

These peoples are expendable because the 'rich (white) man' needs black, brown, yellow and red men and women from all over the globe as fodder to feed their war industries of which the top three firms in the '$398 billion global arms industry' are American with Lockhead Martin topping the list, followed by Boeing and Raytheon (Macias, 2019). These companies and others thrive on the 'always war' policy of the world capitalist system, which gave birth to slavery and the colonialist enterprise. Despite the massive accumulation of wealth as a result of colonialism and endless wars, the rich man is never satisfied, ravaging this earth, its inhabitants and its nature with more and more destruction, 'attacking human, attacking being/attacking earth, attacking tomorrow'. This is a brutally destructive colonial race and class war that pits the nuclearized white north against the suffering global south. This 'always war' attacks not only human life, but also earth, the environment, the effects of which we are seeing today with the very destructive effects of climate change, such as the wildfires that devoured vast areas of different parts of the world in 2020–1, which are continuing as of this writing. With this kind of devastation, the rich man's 'always war' will leave nothing for tomorrow's children, children even of his own kind. While the future threat to tomorrow embraces all people, especially in terms of environmental genocide and its devastating impact on humanity, historically silenced peoples, such as Native Americans, Black Americans, Palestinians and other peoples, especially from the global south, suffer the most under the constant siege and bombardment of the white man's 'always war' and their causes and injuries are still open wounds.

As pointed out earlier, one of Darwish's aims in reaching out to the American Indian is to underscore the indigeneity of the two peoples. Similarly, the conversation between Palestinians and American Indians is a transnational dialogue that Salaita adeptly describes as 'inter/nationalism' in his book of the same name. Salaita describes inter/nationalism as a transnational performative solidarity between 'nations', which are in Salaita's mind 'Indigenous nations', such as the American Indian nation and the Palestinian nation, and these should be distinguished from the colonial 'nation states', such as the United States and Israel (xv). Salaita goes on to say that 'inter/nationalism' with a hard slash should be differentiated from 'internationalism' without the slash precisely because the hard break of the slash places emphasis on the word 'nationalism' or nation building that needs to be brought into dialogue between 'Indigenous nations', as opposed to 'internationalism', which 'connotes cosmopolitan modernity' (xv).

Salaita offers several possible reasons for the interest of American Indian studies in Palestine and the Palestinian cause. These reasons include the 'Holy Land ethos' (7) and 'messianism' (12) that the United States and Israel share whereby the extermination or dispossession of the Indigenous population of the land is justified. This 'justification' is based on Israel's neoliberal policies 'at the expense of indigenes' (10), Israel's claim that it is a 'modern incarnation and proud conserver of American manifest destiny' (15–16) and their belief in their own exceptionalism (17), thus denying that the United States and Israel are colonizing nation-states. However, it is Salaita's last point that most closely speaks to my interpretation of why American Indian studies has shown greater interest in Palestine and the Palestinian cause over the past several years, and this can be gleaned from their poetry.

The most important point that Salaita makes concerns the semantic baggage that comes with the term 'indigenous', which 'simultaneously appropriates Natives into an extraneous debate whose conduct invalidates their agency' (19). Salaita's words here are very relevant not only to my analysis of the American Indian poems below, but I think to the overall argument of this book, which is emphasized in its title, *Imagining Palestine*:

> The debate [extraneous debate] invalidates Indian agency because rarely does it visualize Natives as living communities engaged in the work of repatriation – or even in the work of survival. When a person says 'Jews are the Indians of the Holy Land', the statement affixes Indians into a specific historical posture that renders them rhetorical but is so because the claim is fundamentally statist, referencing a particular history to support an argument of the present. The referenced history does not make it into the present. The argument it informs already occupies that space .... Further evidence that this sort of move invalidates Indian agency is available in the language of the rhetoric itself.
>
> (19)

So here is the main point. American Indian solidarity with the Palestinian cause will have the effect of pulling the American Indian cause out of the rhetoric of a dead and static past to a very living present where a cause is still being fought. It is a work in progress, very much a part of the *imagining* process.

It is also the difference between Jewish claims to indigeneity in the land of Palestine and Palestinian claims. Jewish claims are tied to the messianic 'Holy Land' ethos of scattered tribes that have 'returned' to a land of origins 3,000 years later after roaming the earth (something that Hall attacks as hegemonizing and imperializing), while the Indigeneity of the Palestinians is historical, as opposed to mythical. It is of a continuous past and present, an ongoing struggle that is, in fact, gaining mass support in many areas of the world, especially in areas that have suffered from slavery, dispossession and colonialism. Those who have been tragically impacted by the neoliberal and militarized policies of the hegemonic powers, areas in the world today known as the 'global south' find common cause with the Palestinians. More and more younger generations are standing in solidarity with the oppressed as a result of the strong and clear messaging from organizations and movements, such as the Palestinian campaign of Boycott, Divest and Sanctions (BDS) founded by Omar Barghouti and Ramy Shaat,[12] especially on college campuses.

Thus, Palestine, for American Indian studies and activists, is not, by any means, an 'extraneous debate', but is rather 'contemporaneous' and its claim against the colonization of land is not only moral and rhetorical, but also real, political, present and *urgent*. By standing in solidarity with the Palestinians, Indigenous nations, such as the American Indians and the First Nations of Canada, transform their cause from being relegated to the permanent status of 'displacement and disenfranchisement' to one that is dynamic by means of imagining the very real possibility of victory and rejecting the 'permanence' of defeat (Salaita, 22). So it is here that I would like to pick up the argument, and refer again to Williams's important ideas detailed in his influential article, 'Outlines of a Better World': Rerouting Postcolonialism', in which he calls for an 'engaged pursuit' (93) of a better future for all the disenfranchised in our world, a concrete goal and not an abstract utopia, argues Williams (ibid.). It is then not only the theorizing and narrating that is important, but also their performativity. The crossing of borders on the part of American Indian poets and intellectuals in their solidarity with the Palestinian cause is, as I believe, to practice this performativity and to obtain real hope from the vitality of the Palestinian struggle against the so-called permanence of the Zionist's state's setter colonialism.

Salaita believes that the alliance between the United States and Israel is 'military, economic, diplomatic, cultural, historical, religious', but is most profoundly ideological (22). Salaita quotes Tim Giago who compares the American and Israeli 'Holy Land' ethos that emphasizes the sacred right of white Christians and European Jews to dispossess Indigenous peoples from their ancestral homelands:

> The early settlers believed it was God's will (Manifest Destiny) that the heathens be driven from the land. It was God's will that the land be settled and populated by white Christians. They looked upon the indigenous population as a mere obstacle to be slaughtered or removed.
>
> (Giago qtd. in Salaita, 22)

Based on this line of argument, the United States is perceived through the narrative myth of the 'ancient Israel of the Old Testament' (Salaita, 22) and twentieth-century Zionism and the creation of Israel in 1948 is 'justified' by the same ethos that justified the creation of the United States. According to the myth of 'Manifest Destiny', white Christians would replace 'heathen' Indians in America and based on the myth of the 'Promised Land', European Jews would replace Arab Muslims and Christians in Palestine – this, then, is the messianic exceptionalism of the 'Manifest Destiny' and the 'Promised Land' ethos.

However, to historicize the American Indian and Palestinian causes and to place them in the context of secular history, using the argumentation of Said, is to endow the dispossessed with agency. Said, in fact, disavows the use of sacred texts as political tracts and believes intellectuals 'must be involved in a lifelong dispute with all the guardians of sacred vision or text, whose depredations are legion and whose heavy hand brooks no disagreement and certainly no diversity' (*Representations*, 1994b: 65). American Indian solidarity with the Palestinian cause stems from the desire to endow the American Indian cause with the kind of agency that a living cause of the present, based on secular human history, possesses.

Thus, it is in this light that many of the Indigenous Indian poems of solidarity should be read. One such poet is Lee Maracle, an Indigenous First Nation Canadian poet, writer and activist who has often written and spoken about Palestine, which has become a touchstone of symbolism in Indigenous poetry, offering 'wonderful symbolic possibilities for the Native poet' (Salaita, 132). The resilience of Palestinian resistance has had the effect of deterritorializing Palestine, and making it a global symbol of defiance for all dispossessed, Indigenous people in this world (Salaita, 119). I would also add that it is the 'presentness' of the Palestinian cause and the Palestinian refusal to surrender that spark a light of hope for all Indigenous causes that have been spoken about rhetorically with a strong emphasis on their 'pastness' and the impossibility of their contemporaneity in the rich, white man's capitalist, neoliberal era of technology.

In her poem, 'Song to a Palestinian Child' from her poetry collection called *Bent Box* (2000), Maracle imagines a young Palestinian girl, very much like her own daughter, whose home has just been levelled to the ground. However, instead of the helplessness that usually envelopes such a situation, Maracle describes the great defiance of the girl, a defiance which springs from a deep attachment to home and the willingness to sacrifice one's own life for a cause: 'Bombs crash about her levelling her home/Clutching an olive branch she raises a defiant fist' (33). While the 'olive branch' in a 'defiant fist', clearly points to the refusal of Palestinian surrender, in the second stanza, Maracle makes it clear that the struggle is more than planting or caring for olive trees, which are indeed very important to the survival of Palestinians. Maracle actually points to the necessity of an armed struggle: 'I see a child rising from a place far away / In one hand an olive branch in the other a gun' / which Maracle significantly follows up with 'of much sweat and red blood is Palestine' (ibid.). In the last three lines of this stanza, Maracle deploys two strategies to underscore the final message of her short poem, one aesthetic and the other thematic: her switch from visual imagery (green grass, olive branch, copper sun, red blood) to audial imagery also sounds the poet's deep and impassioned solidarity with the Palestinian cause. In a very touching metaphorical embrace of the Palestinian child and cause from the other side of the world, the

Indigenous Canadian poet calls out in transnational affiliation: 'I hear you calling me. Raise my banner high / (Victory), victory to Palestine I answer in kind / of humble tears my salute to Palestine' (33). To the Palestinian child's scream across the ocean as indicated by the parenthesized word '(Victory)', the tearful poet shouts back 'victory to Palestine', saluting the defiant resistance of the Palestinians. It is then this hope of victory that is transferred to all other Indigenous movements the world over.

In a longer poem entitled 'Remembering Mahmoud, 1986' (2012), Maracle sends a very powerful message of solidarity aimed at building bridges between Indigenous communities, thereby strengthening the purpose and resolve of their causes and emphasizing their contemporaneity and the forward movement of their struggles. In this poem dedicated to Darwish, Maracle emphasizes forward movement and return and endows her solidarity with performative power as she takes actual part in the actions of the Palestinian boy in the picture at which the poet is looking. The histories of the Palestinian and Indigenous peoples merge and coalesce and their present is deeply entwined in a brutal struggle for their freedom and a return to their lands:

> It's December
>   Toronto
> Gaza is on fire
>   Again
> Another Wounded Knee
> Another massacre
> No muskets this time
> Tanks, monster machines
> Bombs and missiles pummel the children
> How brave is that?
>
> -40 C in Winnipeg
> Palestinians and Indigenous children wave placards
> *Stop killing children in Palestine*
> ....
>
> In between the rubble
> Darwish's last words look at the world
> Say good bye to Edward Said
> Peer past the camps, the bombs, and the hypocrisy
> Stubborn,
> Resistant
> Eternal: *There is no tomorrow in yesterday, so let us advance*

The great interest of indigenous poets and intellectuals in Palestine as a global symbol of resistance for the dispossessed in this world is made crystal clear in Maracle's poem where 'inter/national' solidarity, to use Salaita's term, is the main theme in the poet's essential and strategic remembering of Darwish's words. Maracle is not only speaking of an abstract solidarity, but a strategic one that is social, cultural, ideological and political – it involves words welded into action. She endows her poetry with agency, activism and engagement with the world.

While globalizing and deterritorializing Palestine can become fraught with certain dangers, Maracle does not fall into this trap. Maracle's 'deterritorialization' of Palestine, so to speak, does not lose it its specificity and its attachment to a certain place and history nor does her engagement with Palestine limit it to the realm of symbology and rhetoric. Maracle is very careful to emphasize the rootedness and 'placeness' of the Palestinian cause and her solidarity is presented in terms of building bridges. While the poet obviously means metaphorical bridges, the possibility of real, logistical support bridges are also left to the readers' imaginations to contemplate. Maracle registers the differences between the Palestinian cause and other Indigenous causes, which is reflected in her phrase 'Gaza is on fire', to emphasize Gaza's actual, current plight on the one hand and its symbolic fire, continuously searing the world's conscience on the other. The poet first draws on the similarity, then notes the difference between the experiences of Indigenous peoples, the Palestinians and the Indigenous communities of North America, here specifically in Toronto and Winnipeg, where, as the poet notes, the temperature is –40 degrees Celsius (to be contrasted with Gaza being on fire). If heat is a determinant of the volatility of the cause, then Gaza's fire speaks volumes here. While the geographies, cultures, environments and climates are radically different, the similarity of experience of Indigenous communities is quite telling in terms of a history of human suffering.

In besieged Gaza that is on fire, frequent and heavy Israeli bombardment has turned Gaza into repeated Wounded Knees, a reference to the Wounded Knee Massacre in which about 300 people from the Lakota tribe were killed in cold blood in an area called the Lakota Pine Ridge Indian Reservation (in the US state of South Dakota) on 29 December 1890. The massacres of the Indigenous peoples, from Wounded Knee to Sabra and Shatila merge into a long, painful tale of the many voices of human suffering, voices silenced forever unable to narrate the horror that befell them. However, the muskets used in Wounded Knee become much more lethal 'tanks' and 'monster machines' and 'bombs' and 'missiles [that] pummel children' from afar. This is not bravery, Maracle angrily declares. The –40 degrees Celsius in Winnipeg does not stop Palestinians and Indigenous children waving placards that say '*Stop killing children in Palestine*'. Maracle insists that, like the phoenix, Darwish's words rise out of the rubble, defiantly speaking truth to power directed at the militarized, capitalist monsters of this world, words that Darwish spoke to his dear friend Said, words that spring from the bombed out camps of Palestine, words that are 'Stubborn, / Resistant/Eternal: *There is no tomorrow in yesterday, so let us advance*'. Darwish's words become Maracle's rallying cry for all Indigenous peoples.

After introducing the reader to the present reality of Palestine, Maracle zeroes in on the specific in the second part of her poem. Here the poet is able to enter the world of the picture of the little boy that she is staring at and from his place in Palestine, this little boy's stubborn resolve becomes the global tenacity of all Indigenous peoples. Below Maracle describes how the stones that the little boy gleans from the rubble of his bombed out home in Gaza are utterly transformed:

He looks to advance
The stones are no longer simply rubble
They cradle a story
They cradle his memory
They cradle his hope
They cradle Darwish's last testament:
There is no tomorrow in yesterday, so let us advance

His face is set
His eyes see past this rubble
They see forward to his return
Forward to the restoration of his homeland
Forward to the right of return
In his eyes I see Indigenous global tenacity
I touch the stones in the photo
Caress his face
Commit to building a bridge
An arc of light
Under this wind of war
Of dispossession
I want to build a pathway
and blow us all toward freedom and justice
I want the wind of freedom to echo
The resonance of Mahmoud's breath tracks of being
Let us pick up this stone of justice
Build this bridge
That will lead us to the laughter of belonging
Of being where we belong
Of being who we are and always will be

This light shines back at me from his eyes
The light illuminates his stones
Bound as these stones are to his resolve
To traverse across the abyss
Between his refuge and the tanks
My commitment to Palestine
Floats on the light emanating from his eyes and captures my heart
I whisper Palestine, Palestine – Free Palestine
Wounded Knee, Wounded Knee, no more Wounded Knees
I imagine him listening, hearing me

Nearly smiling
Just before he throws his stones

Maracle's repetition of words and phrases such as 'advance', 'see past', 'see forward', 'forward', 'right of return', 'build this bridge' placed alongside Darwish's line *'There is no tomorrow in yesterday, so let us advance'* underscores the poet's determination to dismantle the discourse of defeat by rejecting the 'permanence' of the defeat of the Indigenous peoples' causes in the past and placing them in static extraneous spaces by all segments of the ideological spectrum. To this, Maracle delivers a resounding refusal and insists on moving forward that is reminiscent of Jordan's previously discussed poem, 'Moving Forward', about her solidarity with the Palestinian cause. Maracle reaches into the picture of the little Palestinian boy who is cradling the stones and touches the stones and caresses his face, extending her solidarity and receiving from him his tenacity and resolve, which becomes the resolve of all Indigenous peoples who are building bridges of solidarity and commitment, bringing the two causes together, Palestine and Wounded Knee. The boy, imagines the poet, can hear her 'Just before he throws his stones'.

Like the gun in the girl's hand in the previous poem, this boy's stones are transformed in this poem and carry with them the weapons of his people's struggle – their 'story', 'memory' and 'hope', suggesting in Fanonian and Saidian fashion, that colonization and occupation must be fought by all means possible and most essentially by means of cultural resistance and the armed struggle in parallel. Through this kind of empowering Indigenous peoples' solidarity, causes are pulled out of the silence of the past to the vitality of a *living* present, a stubborn present that comes with a deep understanding of the past, but refuses to dwell in its throes of defeat, so it is only fitting to repeat the poets' words (both Darwish's and Maracle's, who has appropriated the Palestinian's poet's words into her own poem), '[t]here is no tomorrow in yesterday, so let us advance.'

On imagining victory: Mourid Barghouti's 'midnight'

Mourid Barghouti has also chosen to advance by imagining victory over defeat and the discourse of defeatism, which has dangerously become the discourse of many in the Arab region. To use Darwish's words, the 'chronic illness' of resistance also runs through Barghouti's poetic veins, drowning out the voices of defeat, which for Barghouti is the persistent echo of the so-called moderate Arab regimes and their destructive credo of surrender and defeat as evidenced by their signing of treaties of surrender of not only normalization, but also treaties of *alliance* with Israel. Most, if not all the intellectuals, critics and poets I have dealt with in this book emphasize the absolute necessity of imagining and working towards constructing a better world by believing in the very real possibility of the victory/liberation of the oppressed, colonized, silenced and marginalized peoples of this world. Fanon heralded the inevitable arrival of a new order when 'the last shall be first' (1963: 37), Bloch spoke about the principle of hope, Said created beginnings and insisted that no cause is a lost cause, Williams described the outlines of a better world, Darwish nurtured hope, and in his long poem aptly titled 'Midnight', Barghouti implores his people to '[b]e a little angry but don't die! /Remember that we have a lot of work to do' (2008: 110).

Barghouti's admonition is more of a warning than a rebuke to his readers, instructing them not to die, not to surrender while at the same time acknowledging the unspeakable tragedy of Palestinian life under occupation where:

> No special gods
> have been assigned by the ancient Greeks
> to come to your rescue
> whenever abject despair overcomes you.
> History has offered you no pair of shoes
> with which to traverse this wilderness.
>
> (2008: 108)

Barghouti is cognizant of the fact that without a powerful myth to support the Palestinian narrative ('No special gods') and with the almost complete silencing of Palestinian history by the dominant Zionist narrative ('History has offered you no pair of shoes'), the onus is on the poet who must necessarily create the myth and write the history of Palestine (without ever mentioning the word Palestine) for his people 'with which to traverse this wilderness', even if it means to stand on the threshold of danger.

In 'Midnight', Barghouti constructs a powerful and often critically sharp and intense poetic narrative, one that I would call (post) catastrophic, empowering his people (and other oppressed peoples) and inspiring them to look for 'that single shining button, lying there, / after all the rubble had finally been cleared' (2008: 92) and rebuild after total destruction. In his 'Introduction' to Barghouti's *Midnight and other poems*, Guy Mannes-Abbott calls the poet the 'Brink-Man' (9) alluding to Walter Benjamin's statement 'I gather flowers on the brink of subsistence' (qtd.in Mannes-Abbot, 10). Mannes-Abbot appropriately concludes his 'Introduction' by underscoring what I believe is Barghouti's late style in *Midnight*: 'Mourid Barghouti's poetry is a writing against all conceivable odds: brinkmanship of the highest aesthetic order' (28). The 'brink-man', to use Mannes-Abbott's term, underscores Barghouti's style of taking his reader to the edge of danger, often visiting gravesites with stoic women, Palestinian mothers in their embroidered Palestinian *thobs*, then flying away to another realm with butterflies, all as the poet/brink-man looks out his window on New Year's eve, reflecting, creating and imagining the coming triumph of the oppressed as he speaks his difficult truth to arrogant power, exposing the brutality of the Occupation, the suffering of Palestinians under occupation and casting serious doubt on the enemy's temporary victory over the oppressed who refuse to be defeated.

Barghouti's late style is suggested in the very title of this long poem, 'Midnight', and almost specifically stated in the poem itself: 'I wait for you. / What does it matter if you're late? / Waiting is like a gazelle in the woods; it surfaces and recedes in the shadows' (124). The poet has learned the lesson and strategy of waiting, which can also be interpreted to mean the art of survival and resistance – it involves both knowing when and how to surface and when to recede, depending on the danger of the situation. However, the poet here who lives in a deeply catastrophic situation does not surrender to it as he waits for his tomorrow and closes his 'ears to the roaring, / and resume[s] play' (126) while at the same time being totally conscious of the drawing near of the 'open jaw' (ibid.). Death in these lines appears, as Said says in *Late Style*, in refracted mode (24). However, as Patrick Williams states, commenting on Darwish's poem written in 1982 during the siege of Beirut, 'Praise of the High Shadow', sometimes the writer/poet needs to be raw to be able to capture the genuine horror of the situation.

In Barghouti's 'Midnight', death in all its rawness takes centre stage. It is true that Barghouti, as he says in the introduction to the book *Midnight and other poems*, opens windows and asks his reader to look, without commenting, without directing: 'I don't ask you to feel this way or that way, or to direct the emotions of the reader. I just open a window' (14). However, the images of death are so clear, stark and potent and the brutality of the occupier is so unconscionable that they haunt the reader during his reading and after. I am reminded here of the grieving mothers, who are described only by their clothes, who are seen at their sons' tombstones. This is a potent strategy often used by Barghouti in this poem:

> You, whose mother gave birth to you
> in the homestead of the Orient,
> where everything began,
> you will see embroidered dresses
> stooping over tombstones,
> you will see the ones you love lining up to meet their deaths
> like the buttons of a shirt
> lining up with their buttonholes.
>
> (60)

I think here in Barghouti's *Midnight*, as with Darwish's 'State of Siege', the lack of naming and personifying of the martyrs, is to underscore that the death of young people under brutal Israeli occupation is a *normal* happening. These young people are simply like buttons, 'lining up to meet their deaths', a happening that should never be normal and should never numb the world's conscience to unnatural, brutal death. These mothers are attired in 'embroidered dresses', translated from the poet's Arabic words 'الثياب المطرزة', which literally means the embroidered Palestinian *thob*.

Thus, the poet is certainly clear about this – while these mothers can, of course, represent all such suffering mothers, it is clear that Barghouti is referring to Palestinian mothers. Sometimes, the poet seems to doubt his own confidence in overcoming such vulgar brutality and endless violence, writing:

> Can you oppose the muscles of this world
> with an army of metaphors?

> Can you, with the eloquence of porcelain,
> plead against their discourse of iron?
>
> The scene is choked with smoke.
> Bodies coloured with fiery red,
> sudden stains upon the windows of the ambulance.
> Your friend will never go anywhere ...
>
> (60)

This occasional doubt, however based on reality (Israel, armed to the teeth, has behind it the 'muscles of this world' as represented by the United States and the West in general), does not overpower the poet who declares that the surviving butterfly already represents half the victory over the pounding iron of Israel and its American protector.

However, Barghouti is obviously also saying that one cannot fight steel and iron with porcelain and metaphors. Violence begets violence. One should not forget Fanon's highly influential statement that 'decolonization is always a violent phenomenon' (1963: 35). For Barghouti, the brink-man who is an intellectual *fidayee*, the worst of crimes is the broken will – this is something that the poet will never surrender to the worshipper of steel, and that is his will to survive, which Barghouti has written about often in his poetry and two memoirs. The Palestinian people have learned the art of survival, better, perhaps, than most people because necessity has taught them how to survive under the most oppressive circumstances. In fact, this is what any Palestinian story will inevitably be about – the creativity of survival and resistance. In 'Midnight', this spirit of resistance is there – against all odds, and the odds are indeed tremendously set against any form of Palestinian life, even as it attempts to take its first few gasps of life or perhaps, one should say, even before new life is allowed to enter into this world of steel, iron, tanks and checkpoints under occupation.

Two of the most potently disturbing and harrowing images involve a child and two newborns, and the stories they tell are heart wrenching and utterly unforgettable:

> I, who saw a boy the size of a bouquet of jasmine
> chasing a tank
> the size of history.
>
> A bouquet of jasmine
> lying on the asphalt.
> Where did its red come from?
>
> (162)

It is obvious that Barghouti is narrating another story of young martyrdom, something that has become so much a part of 'normal' Palestinian life, something that the poet warns against in much of his work. Barghouti distinguishes between survival and resistance to the Occupation and becoming complacent about it and accepting it as normal. The poet states in his memoir, *I Was Born There, I Was Born Here*, 'I don't want my verse to get used to living in graves' (2011: 191). Barghouti does not want his people to get used to living under occupation. That would mean to accept the status quo. Thus, it is important to remind his readers that it is not normal for a tank to mutilate the body of a little boy as in the above image. The poet's representation of the total imbalance of the two sides above – the colonizer/colonized, occupier/occupied as represented by the 'boy the size of a bouquet of jasmine' and the 'tank the size of history' underscores the utter abnormality, inequality and brutality of the Occupation. The Occupation can never be accepted as normal as argued previously in this chapter.

Another common theme shared by Darwish and Barghouti is the omnipresence of the martyr that haunts/besieges the poets in their waking and sleeping hours, again emphasizing the psychological truth of Darwish's line that 'exile is the world inside':

> His picture appears,
> his picture persists,
> his picture knocks on the window.
> How did he reach you,
> you secure in your confusion,
> you, hiding in words?
> He does not know you,
> he does not ask for your pity,
> he does not even ask for your embarrassment.
>
> (162)

The knocking of the martyr as the poet is looking out of the window on New Year's eve is a reminder that the past has not passed nor are we (post) the catastrophe, especially at the very moment when the poet is turning a new page of the calendar, awaiting a new day, a new year. Barghouti's martyr knocks, Darwish's interrogates. Barghouti's martyr appears and persists while Darwish's besieges. Barghouti's martyr does not want the mourner's pity, and Darwish's martyr 'need[s] courtesy from no one' (2007: 165). The martyrs of Palestine can never be forgotten because they and their cause do not only belong to the past.

Baby martyrs are also waiting to be born just seconds before they die at birth as can be seen in the horrifying images in Barghouti's 'Midnight'. It is as if their role on this earth is to become a martyr at birth for the crime of being born Palestinian:

> The way to the maternity hospital is blocked.
> The baby girl born first on the asphalt
> died first;
> her twin, born second,
> died second
> (there was no time to give them names).
> The age of the first baby:
> zero.

> Her sister's age: one day.
> The two new-borns managed to die
> at a military checkpoint.
> How's that for an achievement?
>
> (136–8)

The heartbreaking truth is that the situation described above is not simply a figment of the poet's imagination or a poetic re-telling of an isolated incident. This is the truth of the brutal Israeli Occupation of the 'West Bank' or the Eastern part of Palestine, as Barghouti would prefer to call it. In fact, there have been United Nations' reports, medical journals and newspaper articles describing the brutality of Israeli military checkpoints and the unnecessary and cruel death of newborns and their mothers at these checkpoints. The titles of some articles need no further explanation: 'Checkpoints Compound the Risks of Childbirth for Palestinian Women' (United Nations Population Fund, UNFPA, 15 May 2007); 'Childbirth at checkpoints in the occupied Palestinian territory' (Shoaibi, 2011); 'Israeli checkpoints kill women in childbirth, says new study' (*The Electronic Intifada*, 6 July 2011); 'Palestinian Newborns Are Dying at Checkpoints' (Powell, *New Internationalist*, 13 July 2011) and 'Palestinian pregnant women giving birth at Israeli checkpoints – HRC seventh session – UNHCHR report' (United Nations, 11 March 2019).

According to an article published in the respected medical journal *Lancet*, Halla Shoaibi writes that delays at Israeli checkpoints from the years 2000–7 'resulted in 69 births, and 35 infant and five maternal deaths at the checkpoints' (5 July 2011). The simplicity of Barghouti's style above in reporting the deaths of the newborns at the age of zero and one day is powerful as an image of innocent death. No embellishments and no metaphors are needed. It is as if poetry is simply paralyzed in the face of truth and reality so raw that all figurative language falls silent.

Other unforgettable scenes in 'Midnight' are the recurring images of the poet's grandfather and his amputated arm and the several references to rubble and ruin. It is indeed hard to fathom how a long piece such as this, haunted by the many images of death, amputation and ruin, can also be about hope, construction and an imagined victory over defeat. However, this is what Said's late style is all about – this tenacious spirit to not only survive, but to do so stubbornly and ironically even joyously. A defiant Barghouti declares, 'you were born for joy' (34). Barghouti proceeds to give several examples where joy as a form resistance can be called forth to conquer pain, 'even the gods of ancient epics, / haunted by the curses of oracles/and the deaths of heroes, / leave their temples / to steal away / and have some fun' (74–6).

However, perhaps a more complex image in this long poem is the poet's grandfather's amputated arm, which, is, as I believe, the imaginative principle that helps guide the poet's tremendous capacity for imagining victory. In fact, the story of the poet's grandfather is used to envision the beginning of the narrative when his grandfather supports the poet, then a little boy, with his arm when the scent of flowers made him dizzy, a happy and harmless memory, but one that makes the poet reflect in parentheses '(there's always an arm without whose help we die)' (70). We are told about the grandfather's arm in a later visitation that comes to the poet through an open window, which is also a metaphorical window, of course, as all these images come floating in as episodic memories, one after another. After an Israeli bulldozer turns the family home into rubble, the poet recalls the resolute tenacity of his grandfather, who standing among the rubble, 'hugs me and maintains a silent gaze, / as if his look/could order the rubble to become a house' (90):

> He slowly clenches his fist,
> recapturing a boxer's resolve in his right hand,
> his coarse bronze hand,
> the hand that tames the thorny slope,
> ...
> the hand which, with a single blow,
> splits a tree stump in half,
> the hand that opens in forgiveness,
> the hand that closes on the candy
> with which he surprises his grandchildren,
> the hand that was amputated
> many years ago.
>
> (88–90)

The above lines, as I believe, represent Barghouti's concept of imagining victory, if I may term it as such, both syntactically and semantically. While the reader is busy envisioning what the grandfather's hand *can* do from clenching into a fist like a boxer, taming the thorny slope, splitting trees with a single blow, asking for forgiveness to closing on candy to surprise his grandchildren – descriptors presented to us in the present tense: clenches, tames, splits, opens, closes – we are surprised at the end of this stanza to learn that this hand that still possesses such strength and resolve to perform all the mentioned activities was actually amputated (note the past tense) many years ago. All these present tense verbs, some of which I deleted to save space, are lined up like an army to overpower the lone past participle verb 'was amputated' to underscore the will to live and resist, to imagine the amputated arm still there, to imagine victory rather than loss and despair, 'against all odds, [Palestinians] manage [...] to survive' (142), and like Barghouti's grandfather, to order the rubble to become a house.

In addition to writing against all odds, Barghouti, like his friend Darwish, exposes the false narrative of the invincibility of Israel, a strategy similarly used by Arab resistance movements, such as the Lebanese and Palestinian resistance. Darwish, in the epigraph of the introduction to this book, speaks about how '[a]irplanes pursue the ghost in the air. Tanks pursue the ghost on land. Submarines pursue the ghost in the sea. The ghost grows up and occupies the killer's consciousness' (Darwish, 2011: 68). Darwish's ghost being pursued by warplanes, tanks and submarines reminds the reader of Barghouti's butterfly who evades the enemy's iron and steel. Against the enemy's high-tech weaponry, the butterfly is 'armed with nothing but its beauty and the thrust of its wings'; unafraid, the butterfly 'enters the contest, sure of death' (46), knowing 'that it will die', but gleans from a future window that 'it will return, / flapping its wings in the room of fancy' for the 'soul retains its passion even on the cross, / even on the ropes, the body has its dance' (48).

The invincibility of Israel is likewise disarmed in Southern Lebanon in 2000, which led to Israel's withdrawal. A heavily armed and US-supported Israel was defeated by the much less armed, but tenacious Lebanese resistance, Hezbollah, whose leader Sayyid Hassan Nasrallah forcefully declared from the town of Bint Jbeil in Southern Lebanon on 26 May 2000 that Israel is weaker than a spider's web:

> Indeed the road to Palestine ... O people of Palestine, indeed, your path to freedom is through resistance and uprising, serious resistance and a real uprising ... O' our dear, beloved brethren in Palestine, I tell you O' our people in Palestine: Indeed this Israel, which [has] nuclear weapons and the strongest air force in the region, by God, it is weaker than a spider's web. By God, it is weaker than a spider's web.

Any resistance movement needs to be able to see that the enemy is not invincible as Nasrallah says above, '[b]y God, [Israel] is weaker than a spider's web'. It is the determination of the resistance, the faith of individuals in their just cause that empowers them. Nasrallah perhaps intentionally used the line 'weaker than a spider's web' to allude to a verse from the *Holy Quran*[13] in which this phrase appears to describe the weakness of those who do not put their trust in Allah, but hide in the weakness of their protective shields like the spider that hides in its web, the weakest of houses.

Likewise, Barghouti's imagined power also means to be able to perceive the enemy's weakness and to realize that there are no absolutes, no absolute power, no absolute silence, no absolute strength and where the defeated are not quite defeated and the victorious not totally victorious. These are some of the reflections that the poet has – significantly at midnight. It is literally in the middle of the night, late in the day, but it is at the same time, the beginning of a new day and not any new day but the first day in the New Year. The placing of Barghouti's closing lines in 'Midnight' is not only important, but also strategic. Barghouti begins the concluding lines of his long poem by addressing the enemy:

> To the victorious
> I will send an unsettling message
> and these simple questions:
>   ....
>
> Enemies,
> victory has become your daily routine
> like your morning toast.

Why, then, this hysteria?

....

Enemies,
something makes me suspicious.
What, at the climax of your victory, is it
that makes you so scared?

(167)

Barghouti, like Nasrallah of the Lebanese Resistance, emphasizes Israel's weakness and fear. Despite Israel's victories, nuclear weapons and the most advanced warplanes and submarines, Israel remains unhinged. It is always standing on its tiptoes, so to speak, waiting, listening for the slightest noise as described by Barghouti:

In your intimate madness,
you'll keep listening
to the rustle of leaves though the window:
March, February, August, January, June
...

Perhaps the months, appearing as they do above in such a chaotic and disordered way, are meant to reflect the mental state of Israel. It is obvious that Barghouti's message is to deconstruct the false notion that many in the Arab world seem to hold – that is Israel cannot be defeated – it can and has been defeated, argues the poet.

'Midnight' is not the only place that Barghouti has addressed the danger of the defeatist mentality of the so-called moderate Arab regimes, which the poet abhors. In his second memoir, *I Was Born There, I Was Born Here*, Barghouti lashes out against all the defeatist 'moderate' Arab regimes and the Palestinian Authority. I will quote this passage from the memoir at length:

The Authority has decided to sit on its throne waiting for the Israeli tank to smile.

The tank doesn't smile. The Arab rulers behave as though their countries are in a dilemma that can be resolved only by making concessions to their enemy ....

The Palestinian people, on whose disappearance it based all its calculations, haven't disappeared and are still here, in its singular hell known as "the Occupied Homeland." .... Arab leaders have yet to lose their fear of victory. Indeed they rejected victory when they clearly achieved it in 2006 in southern Lebanon and claimed defeat, so attached were they to the latter.

(212–13)

In his stinging criticism above, Barghouti repudiates the so-called moderate Arab position. The word moderate, as used by world media and specifically

Western media, means that these states are allied to the West and specifically to the United States, acting at the beck and call of the US government. So, it is in this sense that these states are 'moderate' and not in the sense of upholding the human rights of their populations as some may mistakenly believe. These are the same states that are currently rushing to make treaties of surrender with Israel, overlooking (as they always have) the basic human rights of the Palestinian people. These are the same 'moderate' Arab states that Barghouti says prefer defeatism and aligning themselves with Israel. The poet argues that these Arab regimes reject victory even when it is handed to them on a silver platter. However, I think the issue is more complicated than that of which I am sure the poet himself is aware. The poet is speaking of Hezbollah's victory over Israel in 2006, which many 'moderate' Arab regimes rejected because they operate within the US sphere of influence.

It is clear that the poet is an ardent supporter of the resistance (to Israel). Barghouti rejects a defeatist mentality that obsequiously awaits a smile from the occupier's tanks, which does not know how to smile, writes the poet. The poet rejects this humiliating subservience and refuses to live by its rules for as the poet writes in the closing lines of 'Midnight':

In such a night,
when some stars die and others are born,
when neither the dead are dead
nor the new-born born,
when neither the master is completely a master
nor the slave completely a slave,
when the bells have their silence
and silence has its bells,
what can you do?

These thoughts come to the poet on 'such a night', the midnight of New Year's Eve, on the cusp of the New Year. The poet is reminded that while some stars die, others are born and the presence of the dead feels so real that they cannot possibly be dead – the presence of their absence is powerfully felt. We are also reminded of the newborns at the Israeli military checkpoint who were not allowed to be born. Perhaps, the poet's most poignant lines in this stanza is 'when neither the master is completely a master/nor the slave completely a slave' by which he means that there is always hope for the oppressed to fight back and dislodge the master, a Fanonian thought whereby the poet can imagine the slave in the place of the master and where everything can be reversed – the bells go silent and silence is broken.

For Barghouti, victory, like the future Palestine, must be constructed imaginatively, and the role of the poet, the writer, the intellectual is to make it possible to imagine victory, to imagine and work towards the 'outlines of a better world'. Barghouti is a firm believer in the power of the human imagination to inspire change, a power so strong that it can help shape a future reality. Barghouti writes in *I Was Born There, I Was Born Here*:

> But, I tell myself, no reality cancels out imagination. Reality waylays us quickly
>   but gives rise in the mind to further imagining. I come close to asking myself
> if
>   there is a 'truth' outside the human 'imagination', and am at loss for an answer.
> (91)

I understand Barghouti's lines above through Williams's application of Theodor Adorno's concept of the 'consummate negativity' to the Palestinian situation (93) whereby the reality of the brutal Israeli occupation and the colonization of Palestine in its extreme negativity can only by necessity give rise to 'further imagining'. Williams, quoting Adorno, writes that this 'consummate negativity, once squarely faced, delineates the mirror-image of its opposite' (qtd. In Williams, 93). Thus, it follows that Barghouti's further imaginings are the absolute opposite of the colonizer's negativity – brutal occupation breeds voracious resistance, making the imagining of Palestine the intellectual paradigm that would herald the arrival of a better, moral world.

To summarize, the closing lines of Barghouti's 'Midnight', then, present three main movements: the first is to expose the fear the enemy has of the people they oppress that cannot be remedied by its tremendous military might and the full support of the sole superpower in this world, the United States. The second movement deconstructs the idea of absolutism. As Barghouti emphasizes, in this world, the master is neither completely a master nor the slave completely a slave. The final lines (the third movement) of 'Midnight', based on the above two givens, significantly announce the coming of a new day, a new year, against all odds. The brink man's last touches are succinctly felt as he leaves his readers, imagining a better world: 'On the same nail, / from the same wall, / hang the new calendar; / that's all you can do' (168). The spirit exhibited in these lines is that of Saidian late style, which despite the catastrophic, the destruction and the lateness of the day, the strong-willed refuse to surrender and with the last bit of energy summoned out of their fractured existence, they defy defeat and hang the new calendar, thus welcoming the arrival of a new beginning that is waiting to be born at *midnight*.

3

WRITING SELF, WRITING NATION IN THE MEMOIR AND THE NOVEL: PALESTINE NARRATED

They uprooted indigenous songs, and planted lies in the ground to grow a new story.

(Abulhawa, *The Blue Between Sky and Water*: 59)

The Palestinian story must be told

Palestinian narratives, whether memoirs or novels, are writings that preserve the memory of personal and national identity against the natural process of forgetting. Within the Palestinian context, however, this form of writing becomes necessarily *urgent* for the sake of preserving memory against forgetfulness, especially when this memory is of the history, culture and the very existence (past and present) of Palestine that is being placed under erasure or what Pappe has called 'memoricide' in his seminal book *The Ethnic Cleansing of Palestine* (2006). Memoricide describes the whole process that involves the 'erasure of the history of one people in order to write that of another people over it', writes Pappe (231). Haifa Rashed, Damien Short and John Docker (2014) argue that this memoricide and the massacres that Zionist terror groups perpetrated against the inhabitants of many Palestinian villages in 1948 amount to genocide and should be seriously considered within the field of genocide studies (6).

The actual and cultural genocide of Palestine, then, is what led intellectuals, such as Said to lament that the Palestinian story must continue to be told because it, unlike other narratives, does not have an 'institutional existence'[1] (1986). The titles of Darwish's greatest works testify to this fear of the Palestinian narrative slipping away. Thus, the poet ensures its preservation in poetic murals, such as in his long poem 'Mural', which tackles his personal and national fight against the dying of his own body and Palestine. In 'Mural', Darwish, realizing the fragility of Palestinian existence, orders his poetic voice to '*Write to be. Read to find. If you wish to speak, you must take action*' (2003: emphasis in original, 126). The poet emphasizes the importance of documentation: 'I also have my small notebook. / Every time a bird grazes a cloud I write it down. / The dream has untied my wings' (148). The notebook, rather than the more stable book, represents the Palestinian people's tenuous existence. However, the poet promises to document every detail, every crime done to his people. Other Darwish works that underscore the fear of erasure and absence, such as his great prose poem *Memory for Forgetfulness: August, Beirut, 1982* (2013) and his poetic memoir *The Presence of Absence* (2011) document both personal and national narratives by constructing various Palestinian spaces of the past and present to 'remember [...] towards the future' (Moore, 252).

This section examines Said's memoir *Out of Place* (1999) in tandem with his reflections on Palestinian lives in his book *After the Last Sky: Palestinian Lives* (1993 [1986]), Mourid Barghouti's *I Saw Ramallah* (2005) and *I Was Born There, I Was Born Here* (2012), Ghassan Kanafani's *Men in the Sun* (1999; originally published in 1962) and *Returning to Haifa*, Radwa Ashour's *The Woman from Tantoura* (2014) and Susan Abulhawa's *Mornings in Jenin* (2011). The memoirs and novels discussed here not only reconstruct the past and present, but also reclaim and reconfigure a future Palestine (Moore, 2018: 251). As Lindsey Moore very effectively argues in her book *Narrating Postcolonial Arab Nations* (2017), Palestinian narratives 'privilege ways of remembering towards the future' (252). Moore's descriptor of Palestinian narratives – 'remembering towards the future' – very perceptively and succinctly encapsulates the intended performativity of these narratives. In all of these narratives, whether they describe the lives of the authors or their characters, the *Nakba* is represented as shaping the lives and futures of millions of Palestinians under occupation and in exile, both personally and collectively. Anderson's idea of 'horizontal comradeship' is a fitting description for these texts in dialogue with each other, sharing historical knowledge, appropriating narratives and incorporating ideas and poetic lines from other Palestinian texts.

Abulhawa, answering Said's call for the institutionalization of the Palestinian narrative (*Mornings in Jenin*, 327), appropriates some plot elements from Kanafani's *Returning to Haifa* in her two novels, *Mornings in Jenin* and *The Blue Between Sky and Water*, continuing the telling of the Palestinian narrative from where Kanafani left off. Whereas Kanafani's seminal *Returning to Haifa* ends with the 1967 *Naksa*, Abulhawa ends her earlier novel *Mornings in Jenin*, narrating, reflecting upon and picking up the pieces after the Jenin refugee camp massacre in 2002. Abulhawa's novel *The Blue Between Sky and Water* tackles the continuing siege of Gaza to which her Palestinian American character, the 'out of place' Nur returns. Barghouti, like Abulhawa, continues the conversation with his good friend Kanafani who narrates the 'return' of his characters (Said and Safiyya) to Haifa, which we are told is no return at all. To that, Barghouti describes his own 'return' to Ramallah after three decades of forced exile as merely 'seeing' Ramallah in *I Saw Ramallah* because a genuine return could only be a collective one, which is the return of the Palestinian masses from their exile as he writes in *I Saw Ramallah* (38). This is what the poet told me in an interview in 2016, explaining the title of his first memoir, and why he disagreed with his publisher on the title: 'My publisher wanted to say Return to Ramallah; he started to beautify [by using] alliteration. I told him No! I did not return; I am trying to be precise – I saw Ramallah' (662). In dialogue with Darwish, Said uses one of the poet's lines from the poem entitled 'Earth Presses

Against Us' as the title of his book about Palestinian lives, 'after the last sky' to describe the continuous displacements of the Palestinian people, both physically and psychologically.

Said's personal and collective exilic out of placeness

Edward Said's life seems to be divided up into different beginnings, whether those beginnings are academic, political, social, cultural or personal and most of the time, they were all of these together. Ruptures usually create beginnings, and so it was with Said. In an article entitled 'Ibrahim and Edward' in *Arab Studies Quarterly*, Elaine Hagopian states that it was the 1967 June war between Israel and some Arab states, otherwise known as the *Naksa* or Setback that jolted Said out of the Western literary scene and into the causes of the Arab world and specifically, Palestine. This led to his 1968 essay 'The Arab Portrayed', which was a precursor to *Orientalism* (6). Hagopian underscores the influence of Ibrahim Abu-Lughod, the dynamic Northwestern University professor originally from Jaffa, a city in 1948 occupied Palestine, upon Said: 'Not only did Ibrahim introduce and nurture Edward's engagement with the tragedy that was Palestine and the struggles of non-western peoples, but he also introduced Edward to worldly Eqbal Ahmed, himself one of the most analytically brilliant political activists in recent history' (6).

Said called Abu-Lughod his guru in an article he penned in 2001 as an elegy to his close friend:

> Ibrahim believed in scholarly, intellectual standards, whether in Arab culture or in the West. He was elated when he found someone in whom he discerned promise or talent, because that would give him an opportunity to bring out what was hidden and make it shine. There are many people – I am one – who feel that they were discovered, appreciated and subsequently enlisted in the ranks, by Ibrahim. He was the greatest of encouragers, protectors, sponsors.
> (*London Review of Books*, 2001)

To what extent it can be said that Said was 'discovered' by Abu-Lughod is debatable, but it is obvious that Abu-Lughod was indeed the force behind some very important political, social and academic accomplishments in the Arab American community. Said points out that Abu-Lughod was one of the main founders of the Association of Arab-American University Graduates (AAUG). Abu-Lughod also founded the journal *Arab Studies Quarterly* (*ASQ*) with Said in 1979, one year after the publication of *Orientalism*. This journal continues to this day in the spirit of its original founders with Ibrahim Aoude, a Palestinian American scholar and professor of political science at the University of Hawai'i at Manoa, now as its Editor. Liana Patranek serves as Associate Editor, and I serve as an Assistant Editor along with Rami Siklawi and Yousef Baker. Salam Mir is the Book Editor of *ASQ*. Thus, this journal continues the mission of its original founders, but has of course, effectively responded to the new developments in the Arab world, especially and most urgently, in Palestine.

For all his writings on exile and being out of place, one feels that Said was most in place, and in fact, felt great pride when he was talking about Palestinians as a collectivity despite the diversity of their experiences. It was indeed the very 'placelessness' of the Palestinians or what Said calls their 'itinerant' status (*The Pen and the Sword*, 36) that draws them together as a community in comradeship wherever their geographical location may be on this earth. One particular statement that is eye-catching, and I feel one said with great pride comes from *After the Last Sky* where Said, commenting on the global Palestinian community, states: '*We are at once too recently formed and too variously experienced to be a population of articulate exiles with a completely systematic vision, and too voluble and troublemaking to be simply a pathetic mass of refugees*' (My emphasis, 6). It is precisely because of their mass exile and their awareness of it that Palestinians have constructed their 'palestines' in exile and sometimes to the displeasure of hosting countries, such as in Jordan in the 1960s and early 1970s and in Lebanon in the 1970s and early 1980s. Said juxtaposes the word 'troublemaking' with 'pathetic', which is in line with Said's distinction between intellectuals who speak truth to power and professionals who speak in the name of power. The Palestinians' troublemaking status, according to Said, underscores their refusal to accept defeat. The Palestinian people in their different cultures of exile continue their struggle and *sumud* against all odds.

Being/Feeling out of place, both personally and collectively, is, for Said, an empowering and enabling stance. In fact, in his memoir *Out of Place*, Said describes himself as a troublemaker (192). I would argue that it is, in fact, this troublemaking status, this personal and collective crisis, the lack of a homeland, the collective exile, the continuous catastrophes befalling one's people, the very precariousness of the Palestinian nation and national identity that binds the personal to the collective ever more closely. It is in the very act of writing the self that one is also writing the nation, which is an essential act of resistance against erasure and death. Moore states that after 1967, Said began his journey of becoming Palestinian. As argued earlier in the book, the building blocks, the seeds for this becoming, however, were already in place before 1967. The actual rupture, though, that signalled the official beginning was, as Moore and other critics have described, the 1967 *Naksa*. Moore, describing the necessary relationship between origins and beginnings as defined by Said in his book *Beginnings: Intention and Method*, writes:

> If 1967 is the catalyst that 'sets' the author 'back' in the sense both of a rupture with his prior conception of the past and a reorientation – turning back in order to keep going, [...] – then the significance of Palestine must also be retroactively constructed. Its significance is translated *from* an origin – 'a place I took for granted [...] the country I was from, where family and friends existed (it seems so retrospectively) with unreflecting ease' and which lends itself to 'unremarkable' memories – into a more intentional beginning.
>
> (262)

Thus, as Moore explains above, in order for Said to be able to affiliatively connect with Palestine, he needed to go back filiatively to that place of origin where everything began in order to be able to move forward. Said then begins, in terms of a chosen beginning, his journey of becoming Palestine.

Supporting this interpretation, Ahmed Qabaha (2018) writes that 'Said's filiation to Palestine reinforced his affiliation to it as a cause' (136). Thus, Said's becoming Palestinian after the 1967 rupture is very much a chosen affiliative stance. This is not a stance that Said had to take or took because of the mere chance of being born Palestinian. Said *chose* this marginal space, which was very controversial in the late 1960s and is to this day. It is indeed through the seminal work of Said, one of the most important intellectuals in the twentieth- and twenty-first centuries, that Palestine has indeed become a more recognized and understood cause in academia and beyond. However, paradoxically, it was Said's actual exile in the United States, away from his family, that Said was able to become Palestinian. This reconstruction or reconfiguration of Said's (national) identity was enabled by the placelessness of his exile in the United States that also meant that Said could free himself of the restrictions placed upon him by his parents who wanted a more English atmosphere and identity for the Said children. This Said makes very clear at the beginning of his memoir:

> All families invent their parents and children, give each of them a story, a character, fate, and even a language. There was always something with how I was invented and meant to fit in with the world of my parents and four sisters.
>
> (3)

> And thus I became 'Edward,' a creation of my parents whose daily travails a quite different but quite dormant inner self was able to observe, though most of the time was powerless to help.
>
> (19)

The words above show that even the two words filiation and affiliation are relative terms and are in themselves very nuanced with one running into the other and back again. First of all, we are filiatively born in a given country and into a family or tribe with a particular religion and culture; however, we are already being ideologically invented, so in a sense we are given specific affiliations in a world not of our choosing. We are given a story in which to believe. For Said, this story was that he was 'Edward', a 'foolishly English name' (3), chosen by his mother who named him after Edward, the 'Prince of Wales, who cut so fine a figure in 1935' (3).

The fact that Said was named Edward after the Prince of Wales has nothing to do with him being born a Palestinian, thus we already have several layers of filiations and affiliations. Thus, even at the level of filiations, affiliations have already been created for us by our parents. In fact, in *The World, the Text and the World*, Said states that over time, affiliations in a society function in the same way as natural filiations (19–20). This entangled web of filiations and affiliations is what has probably led to these vastly opposing perspectives on Said's concept of exile and its relationship to the filiation/affiliation debate. Critics, such as Aijaz Ahmad and Bryan S. Turner, as Qabaha (2018) points out, believe that Said's concept of exile is in line with that of Euro-American modernist writers, which means that exile for Said is a 'condition of the soul', marked by 'detachment (or being out of place)' (140). Anna Bernard seems to agree with this perspective as discussed earlier in this book, arguing that Said's concept of exile involves a western style of modernist detachment, which she argues, Said superimposes upon Palestinian experience in general.

Perhaps, it is statements such as the one below from *Out of Place* that may lend credence to arguments made by Ahmad, Turner and Bernard. It should be pointed out that the passage below is the last paragraph in Said's memoir, which can be taken to be Said's concluding thoughts on how he understands his own existence in exile and his personal/national identity:

> I occasionally experience myself as a cluster of flowing currents. I prefer this to the idea of a solid self, the identity to which so many attach so much significance. These currents, like the themes of one's life, flow along during the waking hours, and at their best, they require no reconciling, no harmonizing. They are "off" and may be out of place, but at least they are in motion, in time, in place, in the form of all kinds of strange combinations moving about, not necessarily forward, sometimes against each other, contrapuntally yet without one central theme. A form of freedom, I'd like to think, even if I am far from being totally convinced that it is. That skepticism too is one of the themes I particularly want to hold on to. With so many dissonances in my life I have learned actually to prefer being not quite right and out of place.
>
> (295)

It is reflections on identity and exilic existence, such as a 'cluster of flowing currents', rather than a 'solid self', 'no reconciling, no harmonizing', 'out of place', 'in motion, in time, in place' and 'dissonances' that make some critics refer to Said's supposed exilic elitism, western style modernism and exile of the soul as opposed to the actual material aspects of exile.

Qabaha forcefully and poignantly makes this very point when he argues that Said warned against seeing 'exile or being out of place merely as an emblem of the intellectual and a condition of the soul unrelated to the facts of material life' (141). In fact, Said makes this point repeatedly – exile in the case of Palestinians is both a condition of the soul and a real, material condition and in terms of the materiality of this condition, it is not one made out of choice. One does not choose exile and displacement. In fact, at the beginning of his essay 'Reflections on Exile', Said describes exile as 'terrible to experience' and states that the 'unhealable rift forced between a human being and a native place ... can never be surmounted' (173). It is precisely because of this being out of place that exiles who are 'cut off from their roots, their land, their past' (177) are in a constant search for and urgent need to re-construct their nation/al identities despite their diverse experiences in exile.

Thus when Said speaks of himself in *Out of Place* as a 'cluster of flowing currents' that are unreconciled and dissonant, he is speaking about both a personal and a collective condition. I would add that this condition is both of the soul and material – that is exile is both the world inside and the world outside. Internal and external exile is a general Palestinian condition despite the diversity of experiences whether under occupation, in refugee camps, under siege, or even in Arab and world capitals. This, of course, does not mean that we should equate the suffering of Palestinians in exile in Amman or New York to that of Palestinians living under siege in Gaza or in refugee camps inside and outside occupied Palestine.

To clarify that Said did actually see his own personal identity as part and parcel of the greater Palestinian national identity, all one has to do is compare the concluding passage of *Out of Place* with the 1999 'Preface' that Said wrote about Palestinian lives in *After the Last Sky*, which was published at about the same time. In this 1999 'Preface' to *After the Last Sky*, Said writes:

> Looking at *After the Last Sky* as objectively as possible, I find that it may be something of a source book for the Palestinian condition [...]. It is an unreconciled book, in which the contradictions and antinomies of our lives and experiences remain as they are, assembled neither (I hope) into neat wholes nor into sentimental ruminations about the past. Fragments, memories, disjointed scenes, intimate particulars.
>
> (xi)

The unreconciled, contradictory, disjointed, fragmentary memories, identities that cannot be assembled into a solid self or neat wholes are descriptors that Said uses to talk about his own personal identity and the common condition of the Palestinian people in *Out of Place* and *After the Last Sky*.

In *After the Last Sky*, Said, in fact, speaks of Palestinians as forming a 'community, if at heart a community built on suffering and exile' (5). Said understood the difficulty of representing this community's diverse experiences, their different cultures of exile – he asks 'How, though, to convey it?' (5) Questions such as who, how and what to represent are pertinent as Palestinian lives in exile are indeed disparate and diverse and do not tell one linear tale, but are rather disjointed and fragmentary narratives. Thus, I do not think it is either fair or accurate to speak of Said's concept of exile as being western style modernism. In fact, exile is the actual condition of the Palestinian community both inside and outside occupied Palestine. Occupation is itself an exile from what is normal. Living under occupation can never be seen as normal and should never be viewed as an accepted way of living. This kind of acceptance and normalization would mean to surrender to mental and physical enslavement. There is always this disconnect between the land and the people under occupation because the law of the land does not serve the occupied people's interest or their livelihoods.

Said's stance is an intricate web of filiations and affiliations to Palestine, and again this is very clear in both *Out of Place* and *After the Last Sky*. When people feel the closeness of death, an impending death whether that is the death of the self, people or nation, the urge is to fight against the dying of the body, the soul or the idea – to fight against extinction. No one wants to fade into nothingness, to disappear without a trace. It is Said's impending death after his leukaemia diagnosis that suddenly awakens the urge in him to narrate as he says in *Out of Place*: 'A vague narrative impulse seemed to be stirring inside of me ...' (215). His mother's death and his leukaemia diagnosis, especially the latter, led to this strong narrative impulse to 'return' to the place of origin – Palestine, where Said was born: 'In 1992 I went with my wife and children to Palestine [read, not Israel], for my first visit in forty-five years; it was their first visit ever' (215). This filiative positioning is also deeply linked to his affiliative stance, but ironically, Said needed to deconstruct, or perhaps to destroy, the 'Edward' that his parents invented in order to be able to construct the Edward that was lurking inside but was too timid to come out: 'The underlying motifs for me have been the emergence of a second self buried for a very long time beneath a surface of very expertly acquired and wielded social characteristics belonging to the self my parents tried to construct, the "Edward" I speak of intermittently ...' (217). These two personas or Edwards are mentioned much earlier in Said's memoir (19).

Thus, *Out of Place* represents the emergence of this Palestinian self that is very much a part of the greater Palestinian community of which he speaks in his earlier book, *After the Last Sky*. Of course, by the time Said started writing his books (with the exception perhaps of his doctoral dissertation), he had already gone through this transformation, which was ignited by the rupture of 1967 and the overwhelming Arab defeat and loss of more Arab land to Israel. This rupture had a profound effect on many Arab writers and thinkers and spawned many important literary works, such as Kanafani's *Returning to Haifa* and the Iraqi dramatist, Yusuf Al Ani's plays, especially *The Key*. In addition to bringing about a significant transformation and a newly emergent sense of purpose and cause for Arab American intellectuals, such as Said and Abu-Lughod, the poets of the Arab world, such as the great Syrian poet Nizar Qabbani, underwent changes and new commitments as a result of the dramatic loss of 1967.

The 1967 *Naksa* resulted in the additional loss of Arab land to Israel: the Golan Heights in Syria, the Gaza Strip and the Sinai Peninsula, which were under Egyptian control and the 'West Bank' and East Jerusalem, which were under Jordanian control. According to AJ Naddaff, writing for arablit.org, it was after the 1967 *Naksa* that Qabbani committed himself to writing political poetry, which was inaugurated with his poem 'Margins on the Notebook of Al-Naksa', from which I quote these lines as they appear in Naddaff's article:

O my sad homeland
You have changed me
In a single moment
From the poet writing of love and longing
To a poet writing with a knife.

(Qabbani qtd. in Naddaff)

Thus, 1967 can be said to have been a watershed moment for many Arab intellectuals living inside and outside the Arab world. As Said himself said in a conversation with Tariq Ali, 1967 transformed him into an Arab even before he 'became' Palestinian:

> TA: The 1967 war radicalized you, pushed you in the direction of becoming a Palestinian spokesperson?
> ES: Arab, at first, before Palestinian.
>
> (2006: 9)

Said's transformation, then, should be seen within the greater context of changes, transformations and beginnings that swept the collective Arab consciousness.

Because 1967 also marked the 'official' end of the Arab nationalist dream of Arab unity, Palestinians realized that the liberation of Palestine mostly fell upon their own shoulders. With this new sense of purpose, Palestinians realized that they would have to take on the main (if not the sole) responsibility for fighting and sacrificing for their homeland, preserving its memory and imagining and constructing it. Saying this, however, does not at all exclude Arab, Muslim and foreign nations, groups, institutions, organizations, writers and intellectuals from their very necessary and *urgent* solidarity with the Palestinian cause, but it does signal the end of Arab officialdom's solidarity with what was once said to be the cause of all the Arabs. Official Arab withdrawal from the Palestinian cause and the beginning of 'peace' with Israel were inaugurated with Egypt's treaty (of surrender), otherwise known as the Camp David Accords, with Israel under Anwar Sadat in 1978 and continues in 2020–21 with Arab-Israeli *alliance* treaties. This has led some Arab states to help Israel further oppress Palestinians by assisting Israel in modernizing its military checkpoints,[2] ensuring the 'permanence' of the Occupation.

Although Said did not live to see to what degree the Arab abandonment of the Palestinians and their cause would reach, he was able to witness the direction in which the Palestinian leadership and Arab regimes were moving. Said had very harsh words for Yasser Arafat and the catastrophic Oslo Accords, which Arafat signed with Israel in 1993. These statements are from the 'Preface to the 1999 Edition' of *After the Last Sky*: 'The Oslo process regularized the Israeli occupation and had turned Arafat [...] into an enforcer for the occupation' (ix) 'I regard him [Arafat] as [...] a total catastrophe for his people, corrupt, short-sighted, incompetent, and dictatorial' (x). Thus, at the same time that Said was becoming more affiliated with Arab issues on a greater scale, he was simultaneously looking inward into his own Palestinianness, his own voyage in, so to speak, especially as the Palestinian situation seemed to be entering a late style stage, thus demanding of him more defiance, resistance and *sumud*. In *After the Last Sky*, Said uses the pronouns 'we' and 'us' often, signalling his deep sense of belonging to a people and a cause. This memoir of Palestinian people in exile underscores how these people, many destitute, live on the hope of return and memory, which Said describes as adding 'to the unrelieved intensity of Palestinian exile' (12). The old die, says

Said, and pass on to their descendants not only their memories of Palestine, but actual mementos, such as the keys and deeds to their former homes (*After the last Sky*, 14). These mementos obviously do not perform their past function, but they significantly represent the Palestinians' moral right of return to their homes and lands. They also represent the web of filiations and affiliations that brings the Palestinian community together imaginatively despite the thousands of miles that separate them in their different exiles.

Although this is a passage I have quoted earlier in this book, it is worth repeating here to underscore the importance of preserving some aspects of the Palestinian past in order to keep/construct a collective Palestinian consciousness. Said writes:

> These intimate mementos [....] [p]hotographs, dresses, objects severed from their original locale, the rituals of speech and custom: Much reproduced, enlarged, thematized, embroidered, and passed around, they are strands in the web of affiliations we Palestinians use to tie ourselves to our identity and to each other.
>
> (14)

A point that Qabaha makes clearly about filiations and affiliations and that Moore strongly suggests with her idea of going back in order to move forward as previously discussed is also echoed in the above-quoted lines. However, the point that I am making here is that the sharp cut between Said's own concepts of origins and beginnings is not that well defined, and I think that this is why we have works, such as *Out of Place* and *After the Last Sky* where there is a sliding of one into the other, especially within the Palestinian context.

Moore's careful analysis of the last two narrative movements in *Out of Place*, I think, underscores this paradox or contradiction in Said's presentation. Moore rightly argues that Said's final chapter brings together the origins versus beginnings argument that Said made in his book *Beginnings: Intention and Method* (1975) in which he argues that origins are given and beginnings are intentionally chosen and are invented by the individual (261). Moore points out that near the end of the book, Said's statement, 'I was no longer the same person after 1967; the shock of that war drove me back to where it had all started, the struggle over Palestine' (293) seems to suggest the importance of going back to a point of origin. This, however, as Moore argues, is reframed with the concluding paragraph re-establishing Said's belief in one's identity being more like 'flowing currents' that 'may be out of place', forming 'all kinds of strange combinations' rather than a 'solid self' (295). Again, I would emphasize that it is not easy to disentangle filiations from affiliations, and as Said himself makes clear in *The World, the Text and the Critic*, affiliations in society can and do mimic filiations over time, and this we see in Said's parents whose 'affiliations' are *given* to Said filiatively. They certainly were not of his choosing.

Here, I think it is important to point out that within the Palestinian context, where the tragedy is of such great magnitude, the suffering so extreme, and the dehumanization of the Palestinians so systematic that returning to an origin, to where it all began is *necessary*. It is to say that we, the Palestinians, were a people and we are a people now – not only that we exist now, but also that we existed before Israel was established. By this very important gesture, the Palestinians are writing themselves back into history – Palestine was never a land without a people. This point needs to be well recognized by western (and Arab) critics writing about Palestine. The Palestinian cause does not need to fit neatly into any theoretical construct, but is rather at the forefront, creating its own theoretical constructs, a sort of theory in the making. Thus, Said's gesture of going back to where it all began in Palestine is a form of establishing Palestinian existence in the present, but also in the past. This is a kind of rehumanization of the oppressed after a very painful process of dehumanization. In this sense, it can be said that Said was not only becoming Palestinian, but also becoming *human*, and this is the ultimate affiliative position and positioning with the oppressed in our world. To repeat Darwish's statement, 'From this day on, he who does not become Palestinian in his heart will never understand his true moral identity' (Darwish qtd. in Williams, 2010: 92).

Coming back to Said's modernist definition of exile, which some critics (Aijaz Ahmad and Bryan Turner) have called 'Euro-American' modernism, a few words are in order here. In fact, Said's modernist description of the condition of exile, both personal and collective, is quintessentially Palestinian. In his book on collective Palestinian exile, *After the Last Sky*, Said writes, and I will quote at length here in order to render the full meaning of what he is presenting about the condition of Palestinian exile:

> There [Arab and other countries where there are large Palestinian communities] too we are in dispersed camps, regions, quarters, zones; but unlike their Israeli counterparts, these places are not the scientific product of 'pure planning' or 'political planning'. The Baqa'a camp in Amman, the Palestinian quarter of Hawaly in Kuwait, are simply there. [....] Since our history is forbidden, narratives are rare; the story of origins, of home, of nation is underground. When it appears it is broken, often wayward and meandering in the extreme, always coded, usually in outrageous forms – mock-epics, satires, sardonic parables, absurd rituals – that make little sense to an outsider. Thus Palestinian life is scattered, discontinuous, marked by the artificial and imposed arrangements of interrupted or confined space, by the dislocations and unsynchronized rhythms of disturbed time. Across our children's lives, in the open fields in which they play, lie the ruins of war, [...] of cast-off or abandoned forms. How odd the conjuncture, and yet for Palestinians, how fitting. [...] We linger in nondescript places, neither here nor there; we peer through windows without glass, ride conveyances without movement or power.
>
> (20–1)

It is quite obvious here that Said's description of the Palestinian condition is quite similar indeed to his description of his own exilic identity in the last paragraph of *Out of Place*. This is indeed the Palestinian condition, which is best expressed using modernist techniques and strategies as Said states at the beginning of *After the Last Sky*. Because the Palestinian condition is one of dispossession and dispersion, the modernist style of expression, the 'interplay of text and photos, the mixture of genres, modes, styles [...]' (6) are most appropriate to Palestinian existence. Thus, Said's modernist representation of exile is more commensurate with the Palestinian reality rather than the 'Euro-American' modernist one of which Aijaz Ahmad speaks.

Palestinian existence is scattered, broken, discontinuous, fragmented, disjointed and yes, artificially imposed upon a confined space. All one has to do is visit any Palestinian refugee camp, for example, the Baqa'a camp in Amman as mentioned in Said's passage above. The Baqa'a camp is the largest refugee camp in Jordan, and its residents number about 119,000 (Alduraidi and Waters, 2017: 437), but people living in the camp say that the actual number is double this figure (Maqusi, 2016). According to Samar Maqusi, whose work revolves around Palestinian refugee camps and spaces of refuge, people now residing in the Baqa'a camp are mostly '"second-time" refugees' who were forcibly displaced to Jordan after the 1967 *Naksa* 'from the refugee camps that had been established in Jericho in 1948' after their forced displacement from their 1948 towns and villages in historic Palestine (Maqusi, 2016). Refugees in this camp and other Palestinian camps in Jordan and the Arab world live in squalid conditions, sometimes in rat-infested, confined spaces underground where children play in meandering alleyways with open gutters. In refugee camps in Lebanon, the situation is even worse as Palestinian children live and play in spaces cluttered with ruins of war.

These are all fractured spaces that house refugees whose lives have been interrupted, confined to the most degrading and dehumanizing living conditions. Because of Palestinian dispossession and dispersion, 'all residence is exile' (*After the Last Sky*, 21), whether this residence is inside or outside occupied Palestine. Despite what seems to be an utterly hopeless situation of being 'neither here nor there' (ibid.), Palestinians have to inevitably fall back on their resourcefulness to maintain their existence through their creative resistance, knowing that they possess what Richard Falk (2013) calls the 'moral imagination' (85) of a just cause. Although entangled in a web of filiations and affiliations, Said's final stance concerning Palestine is a humanist one. This is a stance that is *positional*, affiliated with a just cause of an oppressed people that is gaining more and more support, not only among peoples and nations that would naturally stand in solidarity with Palestine, but also in western academic circles in the UK and the United States.

Said's stance on Palestine is, in fact, at the heart of his global humanist vision. Solidarity with the oppressed was always at the top of Said's intellectual agenda. He was not unaware of the necessary act of linking causes together. On his last trip to South Africa in 2001, Said visited the District Six Museum located in an 'area in Cape Town [...] where over 60,000 of its inhabitants were forcibly removed during the 1970s by the apartheid regime [...]. Said signed his name and wrote a simple yet profound one-word message on the museum's memorial cloth in Arabic: "Return"' (Vally, 2017: 4). The Palestinians, like the South Africans, with the strength of their moral imagination and resourcefulness, will inevitably and in due course, return to their home as Darwish asserts in his poem 'I Belong

There': 'To break the rules, [...]/I have learned and dismantled all the words in order to draw from them a/single word: Home' (2003: 7).

The difficulty of representation in the memoir and the novel:
Out of place and out of time in the works of Kanafani,
Susan Abulhawa, Radwa Ashour and Mourid Barghouti.

Darwish has 'dismantled all the words' to enable him to write about 'Home' because this kind of dismantling of previous discourses, narratives and forms is essential for the necessary act of representing the Palestinian cause. The question of how to represent the ongoing Palestinian *Nakba* or catastrophe is an often-debated topic within Palestinian, Arab and international political, literary and cultural circles, whether these concern politics, literature, film, art, dance or song. In *After the Last Sky*, Said equates the difficulty of the Palestinian experience with the difficulty of representing that experience, which for him, must be represented. Drawing on Said's comments about representation and form, Karim Mattar points out that the *Nakba* is a 'trauma too vast to be encompassed within coherent aesthetic form' (2014: 176). The difficulty of the representation of the Palestinian cause does not only revolve around the narrative or aesthetic form used. This difficulty involves dismantling theoretical discourses and terminologies, such as postcolonialism, trauma studies or even terms such as 'diaspora', which is rejected by Said himself. As Patrick Williams points out, the bases for such a rejection include this term's close historical relationship with the 'Jewish diaspora'. The apolitical nature of this term does not enable it to account for the 74-year-old refugee crisis (as of this writing).

There are certainly better words that would more accurately describe the Palestinian experience, such as '*shatat* [dispersion], *ghurba* or *manfa* [exile]' (2009: 84). Said told Salman Rushdie in an interview on the occasion of the publication of his book *After the Last Sky* that he does not like the 'sacred' connotations that are attached to the word diaspora. The more appropriate word is dispossession. In his poignantly entitled essay, '"Naturally, I reject the word "diaspora"': Said and Palestinian Dispossession', Williams explains his own difficulty as an essayist to render the full impact of the 'sheer awfulness of the human misery involved [which] is beyond the scope of an essay such as this to encompass' (2009: 84). Said rejected the word 'diaspora' to speak about the Palestinian dispossession, precisely because in the world imaginary, it has long been associated with the 'Jewish diaspora', which presumably ended when Zionists claimed to have 'returned' to the land of Palestine after three thousand years of 'diaspora'. Exactly how after 3,000 years of diaspora, living in disparate parts of the world and belonging to different cultures and races, the Israelites remained one people and one nation that 'returned' to reconstruct the Kingdom of Israel has never really been explained or proven. As a result of this extreme form of settler colonialism, the Palestinian people have been dispossessed, many of them living to this day in sub-human conditions in refugee camps inside 1967 occupied Palestine and neighbouring Arab countries. This is the *reality* (as opposed to myth) and the historical consequence of the establishment of Israel. Thus, it is based on this clear, historical fact in the real world that one cannot compare 'diasporas'.

Williams speaks of different types of Palestinian dispossession – these include 'the territorial, the ontological, the narrative, the historiographical, the ethical and the dialogic' (2009: 85). Williams argues that the territorial dispossession of land (the 1948 *Nakba*) is the centre from which all the other dispossessions are effected. Ontological dispossession revolves around Zionist denials that Palestine and the Palestinians exist or ever existed. This brings to mind Israel's first woman prime minister, Golda Meir who infamously declared in 1969 '[t]here was no such thing as the Palestinians, they never existed' (qtd. in Williams, 85). So not only does Palestine not exist now, but it never existed – it is made to be, according to the notorious and often quoted Zionist slogan, 'a land without a people for a people without a land'. Narrative dispossession refers to the fact that up to the last couple of decades, no Palestinian narrative accounting for the Palestinian catastrophe pre and post 1948 has ever been told.

Related to narrative dispossession is the historiographical – the actual historical narrative of Palestine is not only distorted, as Fanon asserts with regard to the history of colonized people (169), but is also erased and Palestinian historical archives destroyed. This happened in 1948 when the Zionist Haganah stole and destroyed Palestinian manuscripts and 'tens of thousands of Palestinian books' (Mattar, 2014: 177). This was repeated in 1982 when the invading Israeli army again pillaged the 'Palestine Research Centre's "Beirut Archive" of 25,000 bound volumes and subsequently bombed the Centre itself' (ibid.). Yet again in 2001, the Israelis continued their erasure of Palestinian historical archives when they attacked the Orient House in East Jerusalem, confiscating hundreds of thousands of books and documents (ibid.). It is indeed very ironic why the Israelis would be so keen on destroying, looting, literally erasing every trace of Palestinian heritage, history and culture when, as they claim in the words of Golda Meir, 'they [Palestinians] never existed'. Williams explains that ethical dispossession involves not recognizing the human rights of Palestinians. In fact, any mention of Palestinians would literally not be allowed (87) and the final dispossession of which Williams speaks is dialogic (87–8). For Said, as Williams points out, all these multi-layered dispossessions on the global stage do not allow for an accepted narrative that could then pave the way for a Palestinian homeland (86). Said's actual words on this topic are indeed essential for the purpose of this section concerning the narration of the Palestinian experience and a future homeland: '... the "idea" of a Palestinian homeland would have to be enabled by the prior acceptance of a narrative entailing a homeland. And this has been resisted as strenuously on the imaginative and ideological level as it has been politically' (*The Politics of Dispossession*, 1995: 256).

The imaginative and ideological resistance to an imagined Palestine *must* be countered precisely by imagining Palestine, the most basic and at the same time the most difficult mode of resistance. It is basic in the sense that it is the most natural and instinctual response to the intentional silencing of the story and the most difficult precisely because the Palestinian cause has been subjected to multiple and diverse levels of systematic erasure. All these modes of dispossession, as detailed by Williams, compound the difficulty of the representation of the Palestinian experience. The difficulty of representing the Palestinian experience, then, is inevitably linked to what we have all along been describing as being out of place in addition to being out of time, which are the two descriptors that are here being used to contextualize and thematize the Palestinian narrative as represented in Ghassan Kanafani's novels *Men in the Sun* and *Returning to Haifa*, Susan Abulhawa's *Mornings in Jenin*, Radwa Ashour's *The Woman from Tantoura* and Mourid Barghouti's two memoirs, *I Saw Ramallah* and *I Was Born There, I Was Born Here*.

In her chapter entitled '"Who would Dare to Make It into an Abstraction": Mourid Barghouti's *I Saw Ramallah* (2013)',[3] Anna Bernard argues that Said attempts to establish a unified Palestinian existence based on the 'experience of exile', something which she believes Barghouti refuses to accept in *I Saw Ramallah* (*ISR*) (2005) as the poet's memoir is based on the 'materialist aesthetic' (2013: 15) of occupation that 'emphasizes both the circumstantial diversity of Palestinian lives and Barghouti's sense of his own responsibility, as a poet' (2013: 69). In this sense, Bernard believes that Said's description of Barghouti's memoir as 'one of the finest existential accounts of Palestinian displacement that we now have' (Said's 'Foreword' to *ISR*, vii) and his declaration in *The Question of Palestine* (1992 [1979], xxxi) that 'exile is the "fundamental condition of Palestinian life"' (Said qtd. in Bernard, 69) are essentialist statements that impose Said's own exilic experience from his place of comfort in the United States onto the lives of the Palestinian people as a whole, both inside and outside occupied Palestine. The point that, I think, Bernard seems to overlook here in particular is that, for Said, exile does not have *only* a physical and material existence, but also a metaphorical and psychological one. This exilic existence or Darwish's description of exile as being the world inside (as we saw in the previous chapter) is something that Palestinians living inside occupied Palestine feel as do those living in the 'bourgeois diaspora', as Bernard calls Palestinians living in exile, quoting Glenn Bowman (70).

In fairness, however, it should be pointed out here that the majority of Palestinians living outside occupied Palestine do not live in a 'bourgeois diaspora'. In fact, many of them are refugees who live in bordering countries, such as Jordan, Syria and Lebanon. In Jordan alone, there are 'more than 4.3 million Palestinian refugees and their [descendants] displaced in 1948 [who] are registered for humanitarian assistance with the United Nations' (al-awda.org). In further support of Said's statement that 'exile is the fundamental condition of Palestinian life', Karim Mattar quotes from the *Survey of Palestinian Refugees and Internally Displaced Persons* (2012):

> The percentage of refugees in the oPt [the Occupied Palestine Territories of Gaza and the West Bank] is about 42 per cent of the total population … the *Survey* estimates that, at the end of 2011, 'there were at least 7.4 million displaced

Palestinians representing 66 per cent of the entire Palestinian population (11.2 million) worldwide'.

(qtd. in Mattar, 106)

Thus, displacement or exile does seem to be the overwhelming *physical* condition of the Palestinian population. However, my argument here is that exile is also the psychological or mental condition of the vast majority of Palestinians, whether they are living in exile or under occupation.

Exile, for Said, as I understand the term, is an inclusive descriptor, composed of a structure of feelings that incorporates displacement and the restlessness and unbelonging of both exile and occupation. It, at the same time, nurtures the hope of return. I asked Barghouti in an interview I conducted with him in 2016 about this critical debate regarding Said's possible misrepresentation of exile and occupation in his first memoir *ISR* to which the poet responded:

> ... I don't think Edward Said wanted to use my book to endorse his feeling/ understanding of exile. By 'displacement,' Said is referring to my Arabic term 'ghurba' .... One of the essential themes in my book is the broken will. A person with a broken will. My will is broken by the occupation, exile, worth, waiting, hope, despair; everything is governed by my will that is not my will. Anything I want to do is juxtaposed with what the occupation allows or does not allow .... I don't want to make this dividing line between occupation and exile. There is no concrete wall between the two ideas.
>
> (Hamdi, 2016c, 664–5)

As can be seen from above, Barghouti, like Said, seems to see Palestinians as sharing in a 'deep horizontal comradeship', to use Anderson's terminology, whereby the *diversity* of Palestinian experience, which Bernard rightly emphasizes, is by no means cancelled out or essentialized. In fact, it cannot be overemphasized that Palestinians do not share the *same* experience.

In fact, I would even argue that not only should we distinguish between the experiences of Palestinians in exile from those living under occupation, but I would go further and say that Palestinians living outside occupied Palestine experience diverse cultures of exile, ranging from the most underprivileged living circumstances in Lebanon's refugee camps to what Bernard and Bowman call the 'bourgeois diaspora'. It should also be pointed out that some Palestinians living under occupation in Ramallah in the Rawabi district, for example, live much more affluent lives than those Palestinians living in refugee camps in bordering countries, such as Ain Al Helwa or Sabra and Shatila in Lebanon or Al Baqaa and Al Wehdaat in Jordan. Thus, I would again emphasize that lived Palestinian experience, whether under occupation or in exile, should not be generalized and lumped into one category; however, at the same time, one should not overlook the fact that for many Palestinians, if not for the majority, Palestine is still their cause, their nation and national identity in the making. One can indeed say that there is a 'deep horizontal comradeship' across time and space that enables the imagining of Palestine, and thus keeps the idea of Palestine alive.

Bernard argues that in Said's reading of *ISR*, the '"Palestinian experience" becomes identified with a permanent state of detachment, and Barghouti's personal experience becomes metonymic for the experience of all Palestinians, the relative material comfort of his exile and the specificity of his work as a poet notwithstanding' (69). Bernard's use of the word 'detachment' to describe Said's analysis of exile and *ISR* is peculiar and explains her choice of the word 'abstraction' in the title of her chapter/article on Barghouti's memoir. If by detachment, Bernard means that Said's relationship to Palestine and the Palestinian cause or even his concept of exile is one of estrangement, distance or neutrality (towards the Palestinian cause), then I do not think that this is a fair assessment. In fact, Said's whole project of worldliness, affiliation, engagement and the role of the intellectual is enough proof that Said's concept of exile by no means translates into modernist detachment. In fact, detachment is exactly what Said stood against. Mattar is right to point out that Barghouti's 'flexible' understanding of exile, 'based on lived experience, redefines occupation as a particular form of displacement and why not – of exile, and thus establishes continuities between disparate Palestinians on the basis of similarities underlying, rather than cooperation despite, difference' (104).

In fact, Said's statement in the 'Foreword' to *ISR* about this memoir being more about exile than repatriation ('... this narrative return at bottom reenacts exile rather than repatriation', xi) underscores the idea of occupation as displacement. In Barghouti's 'return' to Ramallah, there is no real return: 'What does my return, or the return of any other individual mean? It is their return, the return of the millions, that is the true return. Our dead are still in the cemeteries of others. Our living are clinging to foreign borders' (*ISR*, 38). In a conversation with the poet before my formal interview in 2016, the poet explained to me why he chose the title 'I Saw Ramallah' rather than 'I returned to Ramallah'. Barghouti said that his visit did not mean an actual return; Palestine has not yet been liberated, and its people, in their millions, have not returned.

Barghouti's physical return or even Darwish's residence in Ramallah did not end their exile. Exile is not only a geographical term. It is also a mental state as described by Darwish's line that appears in the title of the previous chapter: 'Exile is the world inside'. Even, and perhaps, especially, Palestinians living under occupation are also exiled from their homes and lives, especially when their home does not feel like home, when they are not allowed to move from one place to another without passing through a checkpoint and when going to the hospital means having to pass through a military checkpoint and a long wait even for the seriously ill.

An interesting point brought up by Mattar negates Bernard's argument that Barghouti does not 'thematize exile'. Mattar argues that even Bernard's example of Palestinians living under occupation who are able to acclimatize to the strangeness of their cities and towns, rather than feeling exiled from them, is inaccurate. Barghouti goes on to say that this acclimatization is a '"bribe" proffered by "Life" to ward off against the relentless discontent and suffering of exile' (Mattar, 107). In fact, I would argue that for Barghouti, as for Said and Darwish, the exilic structure of feelings is foundational within the context of the Palestinian experience. While the will to live and survive is natural, the occupation can never become an acceptable way of life – this would mean to accept defeat. It is the uprootedness and restlessness of exiles that does not allow them to accept this unnatural existence. The mind of the exile is one of constant besiegement, and this is what compels poets and intellectuals or ordinary individuals to besiege their siege.

In his thought-provoking article entitled 'Mourid Barghouti's 'multiple displacements': exile and the national checkpoint in Palestinian Literature', Mattar uses Williams's ideas on the multiple dispossessions of the Palestinian experience, dispossessions that are based on Said's own scattered ideas, to discuss what both Williams and Mattar call a 'post-Saidian theory of Palestinian exile' (Mattar, 2014: 103). However, this post-Saidian theory is not really 'post' in the sense of leaving Said's ideas on Palestinian exile behind as much as it is a concretization of Said's ideas on Palestinian exile, a sort of materialization of what some critics refer to as an abstract rendering of exile and the Palestinian experience, especially Bernard's interpretation of Said's concept of exile in her article/chapter '"Who would dare to make it into an abstraction": Mourid Barghouti's *I Saw Ramallah*' (2007). In the same way that Bernard uses Barghouti's question about the 'Occupied Territory', 'Who would dare make it into an abstraction?' as a title and theme for her chapter on *I Saw Ramallah* in which she critiques Said's interpretation, Mattar counters with another line from the same memoir, '[d]isplacements are always multiple' (131) as a title and theme to his own article in response to Bernard, which would actually help to clarify Said's interpretation of the Palestinian experience as one of 'multiple displacements'.

It is important to point out here that for Palestinians generally the idea of not having arrived or waiting for something to come and not being in place is more than just a geographical characterization. In fact, one can be displaced in his/her place, especially for people now living under occupation – displacement is indeed multiple, as described by Barghouti. An overarching theme in the novels and memoirs considered here is the difficulty of representation, especially as the characters and their worlds tend to be out of place and out of time. For Barghouti, for example, his multiple (physical) displacements or exiles – from his home in Deir Ghassanah, outside of Ramallah to Cairo, Kuwait, Beirut, Budapest and Amman – represent his experience of being forced out of his place, especially after the 1967 *Naksa*, which meant that Barghouti could never really return. He was a student at the time, studying in Cairo and could not return to Deir Ghassanah. This lack of return is the actual result not of the 1967 *Naksa*, but the original crime of 1948, which is the cause of Palestinian suffering, as Barghouti points out in *I Saw Ramallah*: 'But this truth does not absolve the enemy of his original crime that is the beginning and the end of this evil' (41).

Displacement describes the life of Palestinians not only outside the borders of occupied Palestine, but also inside its borders, those from the 'coastal cities and villages in 1948' (40–1) who now reside in refugee camps on the 'West Bank', or what Barghouti likes to call, 'Eastern Palestine'. So it is the great rupture, the *Nakba*, the ethnic cleansing of 1948 that had, and of course still has, the greatest impact on Palestinian life. Palestinians continue to live a fragmented existence where members of one family can be living in three, four or five different countries all over the world. The natural life of Palestine came to a stop in 1948, something that Barghouti describes in relation to time. In order to understand Palestinian life, writes Barghouti, one needs to distinguish between the facts of the journalist and the reality of the poet, which 'includes all the emotions of people and their positions ... [a]nd which includes also triangular time (the past of moments, their present, and their future)' (43). What Barghouti calls 'triangular time' can also be explained through Soja's, not quite similar, but related 'Thirdspace' or trialectics of spatiality, historicality and sociality. In order to truly understand the reality, then, of Palestinian life, one needs to consider the history of the catastrophe and its effects, which are ongoing and have resulted in the utter fragmentation of Palestinian life, the destruction of the space, place and time of the Palestinian, underscoring the great difficulty of representing the Palestinian experience in a definitive historical or narrative account.

The wound of Palestine is still open, still raw and very painful, and Israel is responsible for Palestinian pain and dispossession, responsible for 'our being in Sabra, Shatila and Burj al-Burajneh, for our being in the camps at all, for our being despite ourselves in the countries of others, for the shape of our fate, whether in Palestine or in the Diaspora' (*ISR*, 2004: 156). Like Hall, Said, Darwish and Adonis, Barghouti does not accept the mythical story of Israel as the 'Promised Land' for all the Jews in the world. Again, it is about time and time is historical, and history is man-made, not God-made. Barghouti speaks very clearly and unambiguously about where he stands on this issue of who has rights to this land and God's promise:

> But I cannot accept any talk of two equal rights to the land, for I do not accept a divinity in the heights running political life on this earth. Despite all this, I was never particularly interested in the theoretical discussions around who has the right to Palestine, because we did not lose Palestine in a debate, we lost it by force.
>
> (*ISR*, 2004: 157)

This theme of rejecting the religious (Jewish) claim to historic Palestine is repeated again in *I Was Born There, I Was Born Here* (2011) in Barghouti's discussion of Jerusalem of the sky, which of course he asserts is not sky, but occupied land. Barghouti goes on to concretize the reality of the occupation of Jerusalem with its military police, electric fences, military checkpoints and more police than holy sites (74–5). Occupied Jerusalem is of this world with the 'Israeli policeman [who's] now the master of the city ... [i]t is the armed policeman who organizes and decides, not the heavens or amulets' (74). It was not God who built all the machinery of occupation to torture the Indigenous people of the land. It is the occupier, the colonizer, writes Barghouti. Jerusalem is an occupied city with 'government centers, police goons, surveillance cameras on electricity poles, nationality laws, police stations, army camps, torture sessions, and conquerors' (75). This is the concrete reality of Jerusalem that was constructed by the colonizer/occupier, and this was not ordained by God. Palestinian lives, then, inside and outside occupied Palestine are controlled by the violent and genocidal establishment of Israel, a reality in both place and time.

Barghouti, despite the difficulty of representing the Palestinian experience, is very *clear* about the cause of Palestinian suffering, and this is clearly stated in *I Was Born There, I Was Born Here*. At the end of this memoir, Barghouti ends with the beginning, again emphasizing the idea of the original crime and underscoring his dislike for theoretical debates that often resort to sacred and mythological books to prove this or that argument. He searchingly and urgently asks in the last chapter of *I Was Born There, I Was Born Here*, a chapter significantly entitled 'An Ending Leading to the Beginning?': 'Wasn't the beginning that a land was occupied and has to be reclaimed? And that a people was expelled from its land and has to return? Is the end that we have come to today anything other than that beginning?' (214) As Barghouti is saying here at the end of his second memoir, the Palestinian narrative began with Palestinian dispossession, and this can only be rectified with the return of the homeless to their homeland. This is the fact, and this is the beginning that brought the Palestinians to this end.

In *The Ethnic Cleansing of Palestine*, Pappe speaks movingly of Palestinian return in the 'Acknowledgements' section of the book:

> And finally, this book is not formally dedicated to anyone, but it is written first and foremost for the Palestinian victims of the 1948 ethnic cleansing. Many of them are friends and comrades, many others are nameless to me, and yet ever since I learned about the Nakba I have carried with me their suffering, their loss and their hopes. Only when they return will I feel that this chapter of the catastrophe has finally reached the closure we all covet, enabling all of us to live in peace and harmony in Palestine.
>
> (x)

Acknowledging this incontrovertible fact means one must address the very root of the cause of Palestinian suffering. This, as Barghouti asserts, means 'starting over again from the beginning' (*I Was Born There*, 214), which Pappe above is also positing as the only logical solution, which is the return of all the Palestinians and their descendants to Palestine.

The Oslo Accords, which gave birth to the Palestinian Authority is rejected by all Palestinians with the exception of those who are benefitting from the inflow of cash, those who spend their evenings in the 'most luxurious hotels and restaurants' (*I Was Born There*, 211). The PA does not represent Palestinians nor can it speak on their behalf, which brings the argument back to the original crime of Palestinian dispossession and multiple displacements. The 1948 *Nakba* and ethnic cleansing of Palestine effectively resulted in the out-of-place and out-of-time status of the Palestinian population, a description of Palestinians in exile as well as those living under occupation and inside the apartheid state. This does not, of course, mean that all Palestinians share the same experience by any means, but they can indeed be united under the common experience of multiple displacements, which is a prominent theme in the work of Palestinian artists and intellectuals.

However, as this section shows the difficult existence of the Palestinians and the difficulty of representing Palestinian experience is not met with defeat and surrender, but as narrated by Palestinian intellectuals, is countered with resilience and ingenuity. In *I Was Born There, I Was Born Here*, the most prominent example of this resilience is Chapter 1 entitled 'The Driver Mahmoud', Mahmoud being Barghouti's driver in Ramallah. Barghouti admits that Palestinians living under occupation seem to have a peculiar stoicism that is not possessed by those, like the poet himself, who have been distanced from their homeland (3). This stoicism of course can only be honed under the harsh conditions of occupation, which keeps coming up with endless ways to stop the continuation of Palestinian life by imposing checkpoints, obstacles, chasms in roads travelled by Palestinians – anything that would make life difficult, unbearable and unlivable. Acknowledging that this so-called conflict is uneven, Barghouti goes on to wonder whether or not it is a strength or weakness for the oppressed to become accustomed to the oppression in the sense that they 'no longer complain to one another about the prisons, the curfews, the repeated closures and invasions' (8). However, Barghouti affirms in the next lines that this stoicism should not be interpreted as an acceptance of their own oppression, but rather 'stoking the elements of a hidden strength' that awaits a certain time of 'unspoken readiness to respond ... however distant that time may be' (8).

Out of difficulty, obstacles and death, Palestinians create life. Barghouti describes a particular incident that becomes symbolic of the creativity of Palestinian resistance and resilience. Barghouti narrates how once he and a group of foreign writers wanted to travel to Birzeit University from their Ramallah hotel and came upon a trench in the road, a 500-meter trench created by the Occupation army that had previously destroyed this road, effectively cutting them off from their destination. The taxi driven by Mahmoud carried a carful of the most eloquent international artists: Barghouti and his close friend Mahmoud Darwish, the Nigerian playwright Wole Soyinka, the Portuguese writer Jose Saramago, the Spanish poet Juan Goytisolo, the South African writer and painter Breyten Breytenbach, the Italian writer Vincenzo Consolo and Chinese American writer Bei Dao. All were crowded into one taxi and Mahmoud, the driver, tied their suitcases to the top of the car very tightly to make sure they stay put, and then he gave instructions to the crane to begin its mission of transferring the men to the other side of the trench. To their amazed horror, the men waited and then witnessed the large crane carry them upwards and suspend them 'between earth and sky':

> The suspended bubble of air in which we seven are swinging is now our place of exile from this earth. It is our disabled will and our attempt, in a mixture of courage and fear, to impose our will through wit and cunning. This bubble of air

is the unyielding Occupation itself. It is the rootless roaming of the Palestinians through the air of others' countries. In the world's air we seek refuge from our earth. We sink into the upper spaces. We sink upward.... This absurd bubble of air is Mahmoud's way of letting no obstacle defeat him and force him to take us back in failure.

(19)

This suspended bubble of air becomes laden with symbolism for the poet, simultaneously representing the artists' exile from this earth, the unyielding Occupation and the rootless roaming of the Palestinians through the skies of other peoples.

However, if one were to read even more deeply, this suspended bubble of air comes to represent the Palestinian condition itself, which has been suspended in both time and place. Time seems to have come to a stop for the placeless Palestinians. Their villages, towns and cities are intentionally not allowed to develop. This is something that Barghouti comments on in *I Saw Ramallah* and Edward Said also mentions in *After the Last Sky*. Palestine has been taken off the map and out of time to ensure that Palestine's villages, towns and cities would never change, prosper or grow as Barghouti writes in *I Saw Ramallah*:

The Occupation kept the Palestinian village static and turned our cities back into villages. We do not weep for the mill of the village but for the bookshop and the library. We do not want to regain the past but to regain the future and to push tomorrow into the day after. Palestine's progress in the natural paths of its future was deliberately impeded, as though Israel wished to make of the whole Palestinian community a countryside for the city of Israel. More than that, it plans to turn every Arab city into a rural hinterland for the Hebrew State.

(147)

I would add to Barghouti's words above that Israel does not only wish to make of the Palestinian community a hinterland, but also by not allowing for growth and development, the Occupation plans for the total extinction of the Palestinian population still living on the land of historic Palestine. In the natural process of life, whatever does not grow and develop dries up and withers away, and this is the hope of the occupying forces.

Said says this much in *After the Last Sky*: 'On the West Bank and Gaza, "development" (the systematic strengthening of Palestinian economic and social life) is forbidden, whereas "improvement" is tolerated so long as there isn't too much of it; so long as it doesn't become development' (20). The idea is not to allow for development in order to make life as hard as it possibly could be for the Palestinians and to continue Israel's practice of deportation, the demolition of Palestinian homes, the uprooting of olive trees with the aim of depopulating the land of its indigenous population and encouraging Jewish immigration from all over the world under conditions of the so-called Law of Return, designed to make Palestinians stateless again as the American critic Judith Butler argues in her article '"What Shall We Do without Exile?": Said and Darwish Address the Future' (2012: 35).

Despite this difficulty and what seems to be a hopeless situation, Barghouti presents Palestinian ingenuity as embodied in the character of Mahmoud, the driver. The harder that Israel tries to break the will of the Palestinian people, the more adept the Palestinians become at inventing new ways of overcoming the obstacles, the trenches, the walls and checkpoints. In fact, this difficulty gives birth to stoic resistance. As the title of Butler's article above suggests, exile and the future are connected. Exile, as Said writes in *After the Last Sky*, describes the general condition of Palestinians, whether on their land or in actual physical exile. Palestinians 'at home', like exiles abroad live exilic lives:

> Exiles at home as well as abroad, Palestinians also still inhabit the territory of former Palestine (Israel, the West Bank, Gaza), in sadly reduced circumstances. They are either 'the Arabs of Judea and Samaria', or, in Israel, 'non-Jews'. Some are referred to as 'present absentees'.
>
> (12)

It is this exilic existence that creates this feeling of non-belonging, restlessness, waiting, being suspended, a feeling of not having arrived, of being out of place and out of time that underscores the utter importance of return, the 'return of the millions' to the homeland (*I Saw Ramallah*, 38). Only after the return of the millions can Barghouti write the new chapter of his actual return to Ramallah, which sadly will remain unwritten after the poet's passing in early 2021. This is why Barghouti could only say I 'saw' Ramallah, not I 'returned' to Ramallah and 'I was born there' from abroad and 'I was born *here*' (my emphasis) in Deir Ghassanah only temporarily before he was exiled again.

It is in this sense then that the very tension and feeling of incompleteness created by exile that keeps all eyes on the homeland, which for Palestinians is their compass that keeps their focus on Palestine and everything Palestinian. I asked Barghouti in a 2016 interview for *Arab Studies Quarterly* if this focus on Palestine by Palestinians exiled abroad is just a sentimental remembering to which the poet poignantly responded:

> No, this is not sentimental; this is very realistic and very concrete. When you lose your country by force to your enemies, you are deprived of what can never be forgotten forever, which is your worth. You feel that your worth is in restoring this land that you have lost. Until it is restored, you are not normal. You don't lead a normal life wherever you go. And in Palestine, the Palestinian [is treated like he/she has] no history; it cuts across all strata of Palestinian society; it is not a class issue.
>
> (2016c: 663)

There is actually more truth to this than just one's psychological worth. Even in neighbouring Arab countries where Palestinians are allowed citizenship such as in

Jordan (in Lebanon and Syria, for example, Palestinians are not allowed citizenship), Palestinians do not really enjoy all the perks that come with citizenship, whether this is in governmental university education and scholarships, governmental positions, the army, the security apparatus or other similar jobs. This lack of 'normality' described by Barghouti above can be felt rippling through society. The Palestinian people's out of placeness is directly connected to that initial rupture in 1948, and until the people have been restored to the land, as Barghouti says, 'you are not normal'.

The title and concept behind 'I saw Ramallah', I feel has its roots in earlier Palestinian fiction, especially that of Barghouti's friend Kanafani. In fact, the idea of returning and seeing was also on Kanafani's mind when he wrote *Returning to Haifa* after 1967 when the 'West Bank', Gaza, the Sinai Peninsula and the Golan Heights became occupied territory after the Arabs lost more land to Israel in what Palestinians call the *Naksa* or setback. Although Kanafani does use the word 'return' in the title of his novella, his character in the story, Said makes it clear to his wife Saffiya that they are not actually seeing Haifa out of their own agency. The Zionist settler colony is showing it to them (151). In other words, the colonizer wants to show the colonized what they lost forever and how their loss can never be reversed.

Here, Kanafani warns against the enemy's attempt to defeat the colonized not only on the ground by dispossessing Palestinians of their land, but also by defeating them psychologically and imaginatively. Kanafani's fiction, then, is to be seen within the context of countering this pessimism and defeatism with a revolutionary ethics as put forward by Bashir Abu-Manneh in his chapter on Kanafani entitled 'Ghassan Kanafani's revolutionary ethics' in his book, *The Palestinian Novel: From 1948 to the Present* (2016). As mentioned above, the very idea of a homeland must first be enabled by the acceptance of a narrative that imagines this homeland and directly addresses the root of the problem and the moral justification of Palestinian resistance (Said, *The Politics of Dispossession*, 256). In fact, this is exactly what Kanafani endeavoured to do in his literature, which he did not distinguish from his activism or his Palestinianness. Abu-Manneh perceptively points out that 'Kanafani is the one Palestinian writer who had the makings of a Fanon' (71).

Kanafani dared to speak truth to power, not only as an artist, but also as a revolutionary activist. He spoke words that others simply could not articulate effectively to Western media as can be seen below in this interview with the Australian journalist Richard Carleton in Beirut in 1970 on the Palestinian liberation movement. The organization referred to below is the Popular Front for the Liberation of Palestine (PFLP). I quote this part of the interview at length:

RC: Why won't your organization engage in peace talks with the Israelis?
GK: You don't mean exactly 'peace talks.' You mean capitulation.
    Surrendering.
RC: Why not just talk?
GK: Talk to whom?

RC: Talk to the Israeli leaders.
GK: That is a kind of conversation between the sword and the neck, you mean?
RC: Well, if there are no swords and no guns in the room, you could still talk.
GK: No. I have never seen any talk between a colonialist [...] and a national liberation movement.
RC: But despite this, why not talk?
GK: Talk about what?
RC: Talk about the possibility of not fighting.
GK: Not fighting for what?
RC: No fighting at all. No matter what for.
GK: People usually fight for something. And they stop fighting for something. So you can't even tell me why we should speak about what. Why should we talk about stopping to fight? Why?
RC: Talk to stop fighting to stop the death and misery, the destruction and the pain.
GK: The misery and the destruction, the pain and the death of whom?
RC: Of Palestinians. Of Israelis. Of Arabs.
GK: Of the Palestinian people who are uprooted, thrown in the camps, living in starvation, killed for twenty years and forbidden to use even the name Palestinians?
RC: They're better that way than dead though.
GK: Maybe to you. But to us, it's not. To us, to liberate our country, to have dignity, to have respect, to have our [...] human rights is something as essential as life itself.
(PFLP Ghassan Kanafani, Richard Carleton Interview on YouTube)

The above interview, I think, reveals two very important points that need to be made, one may be rather obvious, but the other not as obvious and needs some unpacking. Kanafani's Fanonian attitude, of which Abu-Manneh speaks, the revolutionary ethnics, can be felt in Kanafani's defiant and sometimes sarcastic answers above: The interviewer asks, 'But despite this, why not talk?' to which Kanafani sarcastically answers 'Talk about what?' For Kanafani, there is only one solution, and that is to fight the colonizer, to resist colonization and occupation. There can be no other solution. Talk, discussions, so-called peace negotiations is like a conversation between the neck (the colonized) and the sword (the colonizer). What can the sword tell the neck? The line of questioning and answering continues with Kanafani's sarcastic answers to the interviewer: The interviewer pushes his point forward, 'Talk about the possibility of not fighting', and Kanafani ridicules the questioning with his 'Not fighting for what?' The interviewer's question about fighting seems to imply that the Palestinians are fighting for the sake of fighting or possibly for terroristic reasons, meaning that there is no cause or reason for this troublesome fighting of the Palestinians. The interviewer tells Kanafani to stop the fighting in order to stop the death of Palestinians, Israelis and Arabs to which Kanafani retorts that it is the Palestinians who are suffering, being an uprooted people, living in refugee camps in conditions of starvation and being killed for over twenty years (the interview was in 1970) to which the interviewer arrogantly responds, well it is better off than being dead.

This exchange is quite similar to one that appears earlier in this book between Said and Tim Sebastian on the programme, *Hardtalk*. Sebastian, like Carleton, tells Said that Palestinians under occupation do not need protection because all they have to do is stay inside and not protest to which Said sarcastically responds, 'Oh you mean eat grass and stones.' These conversations, the first between Kanafani and Carleton in 1970 and Said and Sebastian in 2003, reveal a certain consistency in the official Western strategy of dealing with the Palestinian cause. The attitude is clearly a dehumanizing, white supremacist/imperialist perspective that is founded on long-standing Western complicity with the Zionist project. These interviewers, representing the official Western stance, dehumanize Palestinians to the extent that Palestinians, in their minds, should be forced to accept living in refugee camps, being uprooted from their homes and starved in addition to being massacred every few years for the sake of keeping the peace for Israel. Palestinians do not have a right to live like other people in the safety and plenty of their homes as they do in the West or the Western-created Zionist state. Thus, Kanafani made it a point that his narrative tell the story of Palestinian resistance, dignity and defiance of the dehumanizing Western/Zionist gaze. In the face of Western/Zionist dehumanization of the Palestinians, the cultural production of the colonized for Kanafani, as it was for Fanon, is 'entangled in this broad struggle for humanist articulation' (Abu-Manneh, 71).

As Kanafani argues in *Palestinian Resistance Literature 1948–1968*, Palestinian literature was placed under cultural siege by Israel. This separated Palestinian literature in occupied Palestine from modern literary developments in Arab capitals, such as Beirut, Baghdad and Cairo. This meant that 1948 Palestinian literature under occupation took on a life of its own as it responded to the conditions of occupation and oppression (66). This literature developed into the theory of resistance literature itself. The literature of what Abu-Manneh calls the 'remnant', those Palestinians who remained after the 1948 dispossession, became a combative literature of resistance, and the writer or agent of this literature, Kanafani called '*al-adib al-maqatil*' or 'combatant writer'. Abu-Manneh quotes from Kanafani's *Palestinian Resistance Literature 1948–1968*:

> In the period between 1948 and 1968, Arab intellectuals in occupied Palestine presented, under the worst conditions of repression and cultural imprisonment, a historical model for resisting culture, with all its awareness, consciousness, steadfastness, and steeliness. More importantly, with all its continuity, upsurge, and depth.
>
> (qtd. in Abu-Manneh, 76)

For Kanafani then, the writer's cultural resistance can create a resistant consciousness in Palestinian society, equipped with the required 'steeliness' that is absolutely necessary for the armed struggle.

In her examination of anti-colonial violence, Neelam Srivastava underscores Fanon's concept of revolutionary violence and how it differs from colonial violence. In line with Fanon, and I would argue Kanafani, Srivastava contends that anti-colonial violence involves an 'ethical dimension' that is absent from the oppressive violence of the colonizer (307). In order to further support her argument, Srivastava employs Jacques Derrida's and Walter Benjamin's reasoning on the justice entailed in revolutionary violence and its 'cleansing' force. Drawing on Benjamin's ideas, Srivastava quotes Jean Amery: 'in contradiction to oppressive violence, [revolutionary violence] creates equality in negativity: in suffering. Repressive violence is denial of equality and thus of man. Revolutionary violence is eminently *humane*' (Amery qtd. in Srivastava, 307).

This is precisely what Abu-Manneh describes in his characterization of Kanafani's concept of humanist revolutionary nationalism, which differs from the anti-humanist nationalism practiced by the colonial power (77). Kanafani's humanist nationalism anticipates the outlines of a better world, a concept emphasized by Williams, and which I discussed earlier in the book. Abu-Manneh uses words that resemble Williams's terms in his description of Kanafani's resistance literature: 'This is the core value that resistance literature imbues in him and that he comes to recommend to others: a hope and anticipation that through struggle a better life can be had' (78). This is the moral advantage that both Kanafani and Said had over their interviewers (Carleton and Sebastian respectively) whose linguistic violence represents the anti-humanist stance of the colonizer.

Representing the Palestinian catastrophe and ensuing struggle has proved to be difficult, even for the brilliant Kanafani, especially before the second historical rupture, which is the 1967 Arab defeat or *Naksa*. In an illuminating discussion on the difficulty of representing the Palestinian struggle in literature, Cleary explains that this difficulty revolves around, not the idea of resistance itself, but rather the difficulty of imagining a future Palestine because of two important aspects. They are, according to Cleary, 'territorial division and geographical dispersal' (189). Historic Palestine has been territorially divided, making borders ambiguous, especially with the continuous compromises of the 'official' Palestinian side as represented by PLO leadership. Another point raised by Cleary has to do with the vast geographical dispersion of the Palestinians all over the world, making it difficult for them to construct a 'collective project of state formation' (186). Cleary also traces the changing Palestinian strategies that would lead to a Palestinian state/nation and the different decades of the Palestinian struggle, which he summarizes by examining various periods. From 1948 to 1967, the Palestinian cause was seen as part of a greater pan-Arab nationalism. After 1967, some Palestinian organizations promoted a '"secular democratic state" within the historic boundaries of Palestine'. Later, the two-state solution was touted in the Algiers Conference of 1988 (187–9) as the most 'realistic' solution (of course by the PLO). Cleary argues that the Palestinians, 'commended for their "realism" … would also continually be pressed to lower expectations even further … and the Israelis impelling them towards ever more drastic compromises' (189). Thus, for Cleary, '[i]t is in this exceptionally difficult national struggle that the development of the modern Palestinian novel needs to be assessed' (ibid.).

This difficulty is reflected in Kanafani's 1963 novella *Men in the Sun*, the most prominent Palestinian work that directly engages with borders, gateways, checkpoints, refugee camps, prisons, barbed wire fences – all enclosed spaces that have come to most accurately characterize Palestinian life in general. This particular novel revolves around the oppressive life of refugee camps, suffocating enclosed spaces and cruel and repressive borders. All of these represent spaces of oppression for Palestinians, especially those living under occupation and those living in exile in refugee camps in neighbouring Arab countries, the kind of life that the Western journalists interviewing both Kanafani and Said arrogantly believed that Palestinians should accept in order to be allowed to 'live'. Historical and journalistic accounts of Palestinian life simply cannot say what literature can represent, especially within the Palestinian context.

Cultural production, for Kanafani, must bear witness to the inhuman conditions of the Palestinians. Set ten years after the *Nakba* in 1958, the men in the sun, around which this novella revolves, are three characters, Abu Qais, Assad and Marwan, who are Palestinian refugees who want to be smuggled to Kuwait, in search of a better life, through the Iraqi desert by Abul Khaizuran, a Palestinian water tank driver who promises to smuggle the men in his empty water tanker for money. Tragically, the men never make it to their destination, dying of heat suffocation in Abul Khaizuran's closed water tanker as they move from one checkpoint to another at the Iraqi border under a ruthless, August sun in the Iraqi desert. Ironically, these men in the sun do not die under direct sunlight but in the oxygen-deprived, dark space of a water tank. The difficulty that envelopes Kanafani's novella is that it presents readers with more questions than answers, complicating any attempted interpretation of Kanafani's narrative. The recurring symbolism of suffocating enclosed spaces, borders and checkpoints, however, underscores the Palestinian condition of dispossession, a lack of ('legal') space(s) and placelessness, which as Kanafani narrates, are the result of the 1948 *Nakba* and the complicity, complacency and corruption of Arab regimes that left the displaced Palestinians suffocated in appalling conditions in scattered refugee camps.

Marwan, the youngest of the travellers, questions the dehumanizing conditions of their travel to Kuwait, where 'money comes first, and then morals' (42): 'Can you imagine it? In heat like this, who could sit in a closed water tank?' (49). Yet, this is the predicament of the Palestinians, especially the villagers who have lost their land and livelihood and have been forced into refugee camps that are similar to the closed, empty water tank in which the men have to wait at the borders of Arab countries and then get thrown away near a rubbish dump after they suffocate to death, stripped of their money and meagre valuables by the smuggler Abul Khaizuran. The theme of waiting, which has become a commonplace in Palestinian literature, is prominently featured in *Men in the Sun*. In fact, it is the characters' fateful waiting in the closed water tank that leads to their death – waiting at borders in a 'no-place' as Joe Cleary calls it: '... the tragedy that brings the narrative to conclusion occurs in a space which is quite literally a "no-place" since the men die in a juridical "no man's land" between states that defies representation' (198).

While as Abu-Manneh states that *Men in the Sun* is a 'classical depiction of the powerlessness of dispossession' (78), it is also an indictment of the role of the Arab regimes in the continuing Palestinian tragedy. *Men in the Sun* was published in 1963, before the founding of the Palestinian resistance organizations, such as the PLO (1964) and the Marxist PFLP (1967) of which Kanafani became a founding member. The novella shows how pan-Arab nationalism as propagated by the Arab nationalist Movement (ANM) was an ambitious, politically progressive idea that the deeply divided Arab world, the majority of which was and still is under the Western sphere of influence, would never contemplate. Instead of seeing in Palestine and Palestinians its main cause, the Arab regimes seemed to have disposed of the Palestinian cause as Abul Khaizuran does of the bodies of the three men at the end of this dark tale, an ending foreshadowed at the beginning of this narrative by the black bird, which keeps circling in the sky above Abu Qais (22, 25).

Like the Arab regimes, the Shatt al-Arab, a river formed by the meeting of the 'two great rivers, Tigris and Euphrates' (22), has nothing to offer these men, who die of suffocation and thirst in the parched Iraqi desert at the Iraqi/Kuwaiti border. In fact, these men never really reach any *place*. They literally die in between (divided) states, at the border as they wait for Abul Khaizuran who is kept by the border guards as they trivially and ironically tease the castrated smuggler about a supposed sexual relationship with a prostitute as the waiting men outside lay dying in an enclosed capsule. This scene underscores the stark irony of the silliness and corruption of the Arab border officials inside and the tragedy of the Palestinian men unfolding outside. If the men outside represent the Palestinian condition of dispossession, exile and ensuing suffering and the men inside represent the Arab response, the message is clear – not only have the Arab regimes turned their backs on the suffering of the Palestinians, but they are also completely oblivious to it altogether. The barbaric cruelty of the last scene of the novella may have seemed too harsh for many to digest at the time. The final scene of *Men in the Sun* remains one of the harshest and most haunting in Arabic literature, especially when the omniscient narrator describes how Abul Khaizuran threw the corpses of the three men in the space 'where the municipality's dustcarts usually stopped to dump their rubbish' (73).

Cleary's superb examination of Kanafani's novella is relevant to my discussion of Kanafani's work. Cleary titles his chapter on Kanafani's *Men in the Sun* 'The meaning of disaster: the novel and the stateless nation in Ghassan Kanafani's *Men in the Sun*.' The point here is that the 1948 *Nakba* marked a great rupture that 'castrated' the lives of Palestinians – this traumatic *separation* from the land is a metaphorical castration. As Cleary argues, Abul Khaizuran's castration in 1948 as a result of a bomb that explodes in front of him when he was a young freedom fighter is symbolic of the bigger historical castration of Palestine from its people. Abul Khaizuran is unable to confront his physical castration; he pushes it away. Similarly, the three refugees flee in search of 'delusory silver linings in Kuwait' (217). Kanafani's emphasis on the 'ideologeme of "flight"' (ibid.), whether it is Abul Khaizuran's escape from his physical reality or the three migrants' escape from their lived reality in the refugee camps, is, for Cleary, an unwillingness or an inability to come to terms with the meaning of the catastrophe:

> Faced with a catastrophic situation – the novel seems to suggest – there is a natural tendency to shrink in horror from the event, to seek for some sort of escape from an overwhelmingly hostile and seemingly hopeless environment when what is really called for is a lucid registration of the catastrophe. The meaning of the catastrophe, in short, needs to be diagnosed before it can be overcome.
>
> (216)

Cleary underscores Kanafani's contempt for flight and those who want to escape and leave behind the homeland, leave the lived political sphere, as Assad does in the novella, in order to escape to a 'safer' private sphere, which ends up being these men's journey to death.

The catastrophe must be confronted, understood and then overcome. Perhaps the most controversial part of Kanafani's narrative and the one that has produced the most discussion and disagreement comes at the end of the novella with Abul Khaizuran's questions, which he screams out and which echo through the desert after he disposes of the bodies (and strips them of their money and Marwan's watch):

> The thought slipped from his mind and ran onto his tongue: 'Why didn't they knock on the sides of the tank?' .... 'Why didn't you knock on the sides of the tank? Why didn't you say anything? Why?' The desert suddenly began to send back the echo: 'Why didn't you knock on the sides of the tank? Why didn't you bang the sides of the tank? Why? Why? Why?'
>
> (74)

So, why did these men not knock on the sides of the tank? Because they were mentally castrated. These men were already mentally castrated when they took the decision to flee. We do not expect them to knock on the sides of the tank. They had already surrendered before their fateful journey ever began. Thus, Kanafani's novella is about various forms of castration – historical, geographical, physical and mental. The historical castration of Palestine is also connected to the Arab world's endless geographical divisions into states and mini-states designed by Britain and France in the Sykes-Picot Agreement in 1916, separating occupied Palestine from Lebanon, Jordan, Iraq and Kuwait that Cleary calls a 'criss-crossed' 'dystopian world' (218).

Where do the Palestinians fit into all of these borders and checkpoints that are meant to keep out or exploit the poor and homeless? The stateless Palestinians are indeed suffocated in a no-place in the desert, in between borders and states, a catastrophic colonially imposed status quo that benefits only the bourgeois nationalism and corruption of these Western-backed regimes and their backers. Abul Khaizuran's questions are also Kanafani's questions to his own people – the Palestinians, why did you not stay and resist? Kanafani is clear – catastrophe must be confronted head on. Escaping into a private sphere is a selfish and dangerous endeavour. The Palestinian condition is a collective, national one, especially as a great number of Palestinians are still refugees to this day. Not only is Palestine a living cause, it is also a catastrophic one.

Mahatma Gandhi, known for his peaceful resistance, has a curiously similar stance to that of Kanafani concerning the ideologeme of flight, which Gandhi sees as 'mental violence':

> If the choice is set between cowardice and violence I would advise violence. I praise and extol the serene courage of dying without killing. Yet I desire that those who have not this courage should rather cultivate the art of killing and being killed, then basely to avoid the danger. This is because he who runs away commits mental violence; he has not the courage of facing death by killing. I would a thousand times prefer violence than the emasculation of a whole race. I prefer to use arms in defence of honour than remain the vile witness of dishonor.
> (Gandhi qtd. in Srivastava 317)

It is interesting to note that Gandhi sees flight as the 'emasculation of a whole race', which is in line with Kanafani's idea of castration – different forms of castration as mentioned above. Kanafani's men in the sun are victims of traumatic dispossession, but rather than confronting the catastrophe, they ran away, thus emasculating themselves, and it is ironically the physically castrated Abul Khaizuran who interrogates the corpses of the mentally castrated men in the sun. While as Cleary points out that the ending of *Men in the Sun* upset many people, the 'bleakness of its conclusion [striking] a raw nerve with [its] audience' (221), it fulfilled its purpose, and that is to make people uncomfortable. There is no glorious heroic act of resistance at the end, but a painful and necessary questioning, a national self-interrogation – why did you escape? Why did you run away? This is a questioning that forces people to think deeply about the meaning of the catastrophe as Cleary points out and what must be done to confront it. In fact, this interrogation, the idea of flight, amputation, castration and being cut out of place and time appear often in Kanafani's fiction.

Perhaps the most revealing questioning in Palestinian literature comes in another of Kanafani's novellas entitled *Returning to Haifa*. Since *Returning to Haifa* was published after the 1967 *Naksa* and the birth of Palestinian resistance movements, this novella, unlike the earlier *Men in the Sun*, seems to signal further development in Kanafani's thinking. While I agree with Abu-Manneh that Kanafani's revolutionary thinking is a 'whole project of social and political transformation, requiring deep self-emancipation' (85) and is premised on humanity, 'justice and mutuality' (86), I believe that Abu-Manneh may have overlooked the significance of the armed struggle, which is actually not just the 'standard advocacy of armed struggle' (86). The concept of armed struggle in *Returning to Haifa* involves growth, transformation and the 'deep self-emancipation' that the main character Said S gains within the context of this narrative. I tend to disagree that Kanafani seemed to be 'more inclined to favour a moral rather than a military confrontation' (Abu-Manneh, 88). Abu Manneh's statement raises an important question though. Is the violence of the oppressed immoral, as Abu-Manneh seems to imply?

For Fanon, the violence of the oppressed is *necessary* for the making of a new man and woman, for the colonized to move from the state of dehumanization to one of rehumanization: 'Decolonization is the veritable creation of new men ... the "thing" which has been colonized becomes man during the same process by which it frees itself' (36–7). In *The Wretched of the Earth*, Fanon argues that in order to overturn the colonizer/colonized relationship, where the 'last shall be first', the colonized must use 'all means' possible to achieve a state of decolonization:

> The naked truth of decolonization evokes for us the searing bullets and the bloodstained knives which emanate from it. For if the last shall be first, this will only come to pass after a murderous and decisive struggle between two protagonists. That affirmed intention to place the last at the head of things ... can only triumph if we use all means to turn the scale, including, of course, that of violence.
>
> (37)

Revolutionary violence, for Fanon and I would add Kanafani, cannot be equated with the violence of the colonizer. Drawing on the work of Jean Amery and Walter Benjamin, Srivastava distinguishes between the violence of the colonizer and that of the colonized. The violence of the colonizer is aimed at dehumanization and repression, but the violence of the colonized is meant to end that repression and to rehumanize the oppressed (307). In fact, for Fanon revolutionary violence is a 'cleansing force', which has the effect of creating a new individual who is free 'from his inferiority complex and from his despair and inaction; [violence] makes him fearless and restores his self-respect' (94).

To further illustrate his point, Fanon focuses on Aime Cesaire's poetry in an excerpt about a rebel and his mother whereby the rebel explains to his mother how striking and killing the colonizer also killed the slave inside of him, and the colonizer's spilled blood is the 'only baptism that I remember today'. Fanon uses Cesaire's fictional representation of the transformation of the rebel from a slave to a man *precisely through violence* to render the psychological importance of violence for the rehumanization of the colonized:

> It was an evening in November ...
> And suddenly shouts lit up the silence;
> We had attacked, we the slaves; we, the dung underfoot, we the animals with patient hooves,
> We were running like madmen; shots rang out ... We were striking. Blood and sweat cooled and refreshed us. We were striking

where the shouts came from, and the shouts became more strident
and a great clamour rose from the east: it was the outhouses burning
and the flames flickered sweetly on our cheeks.
> Then was the assault made on the master's house.
> They were firing from the windows.
> We broke in the doors.

The master's room was wide open. The master's room was brilliantly
lighted, and the master was there, very calm ... and our
people stopped dead ... it was the master ... I went in. 'It's you',
he said, very calm.
It was I, even I, and I told him so, the good slave, the faithful
slave, the slave of slaves, and suddenly his eyes were like two cock-
roaches, frightened in the rainy season ... I struck, and the blood spurted;
that is the only baptism that I remember today.

(Cesaire qtd. in Fanon 87–8)

This passage by Cesaire is a good example of Fanon's transforming violence of the oppressed that would kill the slave inside the colonized individual and enable the birth of a new man or woman. Here we see the gradual transformation of the colonized into an empowered being who is able to create the kind of fear in the colonizer that the colonizer created in the colonized. Thus, it was he the 'faithful slave, the slave of slaves' who became human again by baptizing himself in the blood of the colonizer, thus signalling the birth of a new man because '[f]or the native, life can only spring up again out of the rotting corpse of the settler' (88).

Thus, I would argue that for Kanafani, the armed struggle which he brings up at the end of *Returning to Haifa* is not as Abu Manneh describes, the 'standard advocacy of armed struggle' (86) – far from it. It actually represents a transformation in the character of Said S, who at the beginning of the narrative is 'returning', but only sentimentally, after the humiliating defeat of 1967 to see what happened to their home in Haifa, which they fled in blinding fear in 1948 along with waves of people who were all heading to the port. More importantly, they wanted to see what happened to their baby son, Khaldun, whom Said's wife, Safiyya, left in his crib when everyone in Haifa started running toward the sea, guided by the bullets and bombs of the British army and Zionist gangs. Kanafani describes the tumultuous scene:

> The sky was on fire, crackling with shots, bombs and explosions, near and far. It was as though the very sounds themselves were pushing everyone toward the port. Even though he could not concentrate on anything specific, he couldn't help but see how the throng of people thickened with every step. People were pouring from the side streets into the main street leading down to the port – men, women and children, empty-handed or carrying a few small possessions, crying or being floated along in a paralyzed silence in the midst of the clamor and confusion.
>
> (155)

As Kanafani describes above, the people who were pouring or were being floated along were moving in paralyzed silence, not knowing what was happening to their world – the sky above them was on fire with bombs and bullets flying from all directions, a kind of 'shock and awe' effect that forced people into a stupefying and unthinking silence. Still, the castrating idea of flight haunted Kanafani and became a recurrent theme in his work.

Returning to Haifa represents a transformation in the thinking of the main character Said S as he moves from a state of castration, dehumanization and fear to that of a liberated, rehumanized individual who understands the true meaning of Palestine, as he says of his son Khalid at the end of the novella. In fact, the other characters in this novella, as I believe, exist to enable the transformation in Said S's thinking. At the beginning of the novella, Said S tells his wife that they are not seeing Haifa, but rather the enemy, in order to humiliate and further dehumanize them, is showing it to them: 'You're not seeing it. They're showing it to you' (151). The lack of agency entailed in this statement is painfully true. Said S's words show that he acknowledges his own castration and dehumanization. It was only after his face-to-face confrontation with his 'son' Khaldun who was raised by Iphrat and Miriam, the Jewish couple who took over Said S's family home and child, that Said S's transformation began. It is indeed true that Kanafani, as Abu Manneh argues, humanizes Miriam who is a Holocaust survivor and the woman who brought up Khaldun as Dov, a soldier in the Israeli army.

However, the transformation that Kanafani is positing here is not necessarily one 'where adversaries are no longer in a state of negative dialectic, no longer opposites' (Abu Manneh, 89). In order for this kind of universal and mutual humanity to be realized, the dehumanized must first be rehumanized. Israel must first be dismantled and seen for what it really is, and Kanafani, ironically, uses Miriam for this revelation. The comparison between Nazi Germany and Israel is clear in the killing and disposing of the corpse of the Arab child and the killing of Miriam's brother in Nazi Germany. The narration of these two events appears on the same page in the novella, forcing the reader to make the connection:

She grabbed her husband's arm and, trembling, cried out:

'Look!' But her husband didn't see anything when he looked where she was pointing. The two men were wiping their palms on the sides of their khaki shirts. She said to her husband: 'That was a dead Arab child! I saw it! And it was covered with blood!' Her husband guided her across the street, then asked: 'How do you know it was an Arab child?' 'Didn't you see how they threw it onto the truck, like a piece of wood? If it had been a Jewish child they would never have done that.'

(169)

One line later, the events jump back eight years to Auschwitz where Miriam's father and brother were killed:

> Miriam had lost her father at Auschwitz eight years before .... The German
> soldiers didn't find anyone, but on their way back down the stairs they came upon
> her ten-year-old brother .... She saw it all through the narrow slit made by a short
> gap between the stairs. She also saw how they shot him down.
>
> (169)

Kanafani's juxtaposition of these two events, the killing of an Arab child in occupied Palestine and the killing of a Jewish child in Nazi Germany, underscores the necessity of the complete dismantlement of the racist and exclusivist Israeli state in the same way that Nazi Germany as an ideology and power structure was destroyed.

The most significant scene in this novella that brings about the complete transformation in Said S's character is his encounter with Dov, not Khaldun, but Dov, a soldier of the Occupation army who tells his birth father that his identity was shaped by his adoptive parents: 'From the time I was small I was a Jew .... Even when they told me – later on – that my parents were Arabs, it didn't change anything ... After all, in the final analysis, man is a cause' (181). It is at this moment that Said S comes to a realization, which enables his transformation that begins with the metaphorical death of Khaldun, who represents Palestinian shame, fear and flight. The Arab child 'thrown onto the death cart like a lump of worthless wood' (170) was Khaldun, says Said S (183). The psychological killing of Khaldun by Said S marks the beginning of the birth of a new man, Khalid, his son who was born after their flight from Haifa in 1948. It is now that Said S dearly wished that he had allowed Khalid to join the *fidayeen*, the Palestinian resistance fighters. Said S then tells Dov, 'Maybe your first battle will be with a *fida'i* named Khalid' (182). This is a Fanonian-type confrontation that would pit the colonizer against the colonized, a decisive battle that would entail a violent struggle. It is at this point in the cycle of events that Said S realizes that man is indeed a cause, regardless of his flesh and blood.

Kanafani continues the interrogation of Said S through the character of Dov who tells Said S 'You should not have left Haifa ... you should not have left an infant in its crib .... You're all weak! Weak! You're bound by heavy chains of backwardness and paralysis!' (185). Again, Kanafani dwells on the idea of castration and paralysis, but stops short of turning his narrative into a story of paralyzing self-blame and allows Said S some logical reasoning: 'Two wrongs do not make a right. If that were the case, then what happened to Iphrat and Miriam in Auschwitz was right' (185). The point that Kanafani is making here is that the Zionist colonizers and Jewish terrorist gangs, the Haganah and Irgun, did to the Palestinians what the Nazis did to the Jews, and Miriam herself, a trustworthy witness who saw what happened in Nazi Germany and Palestine, narrates this to us. As in my discussion on Barghouti who rejects the dangerous and crippling sentimentality of trying to retrieve an old, static image of an unchanging Palestine, Kanafani's Said S now sees Palestine with radically different eyes and his perspective is enabled by a new sense of agency, an empowerment that Said S now desires to see in his son Khalid, the *fida'i* who, to borrow from Cleary's argument, understands the meaning of the catastrophe, the 'true Palestine' (186) and what must be done.

Kanafani concludes with the inevitable violent confrontation, which entails the rehumanization of the dispossessed. For Khalid, reflects Kanafani:

> Palestine is something worthy of a man bearing arms for, dying for. For us, [Said S and Safiyya] for you and me, it's only a search for something buried beneath the dust of memories .... We were mistaken when we thought the homeland was only the past. For Khalid, the homeland is the future. That's how we differed and that's why Khalid wants to carry arms .... Men like Khalid are looking toward the future, so they can put right our mistakes and the mistakes of the whole world. Dov is our shame, but Khalid is our enduring honor. Didn't I tell you from the beginning that we shouldn't come – because that was something requiring a war? Let's go!
>
> (187)

Thus, for Kanafani, it is about a human being's shame and honour, about human worth. One human being cannot be the slave of another – the colonized must kill the slave inside of him through *sumud* (steadfastness), and this requires a war, says Kanafani – *fight, not flight*.

Earlier in this section on the novel and memoir, I mentioned that different Palestinian and Arab writers are in, what I believe to be, necessary dialogue. This is especially true in the work of Susan Abulhawa whose two novels revolve around Kanafani's creation of Dov, and using Kanafani's novel *Returning to Haifa* as a springboard for her own ideas, Abulhawa, living in her American exile, narrates from her particular place and time, sometimes reformulating and reworking Kanafani's narrative perspective. Abulhawa writes in the 'Author's Note' at the end of the 2010 edition of *Mornings in Jenin*: 'The seed for this book came from Ghassan Kanafani's short story [novella] about a Palestinian boy who was raised by the Jewish family that found him in the home they took over in 1948' (326). However, unlike Kanafani's *Returning to Haifa*, which focuses on events following the 1967 *Naksa*, Abulhawa's novel is more historically encompassing, beginning before the 1948 *Nakba* (precisely 'The [Olive] Harvest' in 1941 in Ein Hod, a village near Haifa), and is divided up into several parts: 'El Nakba', 'El Naksa', 'The Scar of David', 'El Ghurba (state of being a stranger)', 'Albi Fi Beirut (my heart in Beirut)', 'Elly Bayna (what there is between us)', 'Baladi (my country)' and 'Nihaya o Bidaya (an end and a beginning)' (vii–ix). In narrating Palestinian history, albeit by focusing on one family, the Abulheja's, Abulhawa is responding (rather powerfully and effectively) to Said's call for the institutionalization of Palestinian history in narrative form.

The novelist explains in her 'Author's Note': '... the late Dr. Edward Said influenced the making of this book in no small way. He lamented once that the Palestinian narrative was lacking in literature, and I incorporated his disappointment into my resolve' (327). *Mornings in Jenin* was originally published in the United States as *The Scar of David*, each title emphasizing a particular angle, one a reformulation and the other a continuation of previous literary work on Palestine. The more well-known title of *Mornings in Jenin* continues the tradition of writing on Palestine by using the names of towns and villages in the title of the work – Kanafani's *Haifa*, Barghouti's *Ramallah*, Abulhawa's *Jenin* and Ashour's *Tantoura*. This naming is also a necessary rewriting and reclaiming of Palestinian history. With the title *Scar of David*, Abulhawa spotlights her reformulation of Kanafani's Khaldun/Dov story by means of which Kanafani interrogates the Palestinian self, especially the idea of flight. Khaldun/Dov, in Kanafani's story, is abandoned as a baby who was still in his crib when his mother Safiyya flees in a daze to join the crowd outside.

However, the idea of abandonment is downplayed by Abulhawa, who prefers a less self-accusatory Palestinian narrative. In Abulhawa's narration, the child Ismael, the son of Dalia and Hasan and who later became David, was never abandoned or forgotten by his mother, but rather forcibly snatched and stolen from her by Moshe, a member of one of the Jewish terrorist gangs at the time. This is a version of events, in Abulhawa's mind, that perhaps more closely resembles the forcible dispossession of Palestinians from their ancestral land, which she describes at the end of the chapter wherein she very poignantly narrates the twin acts of the snatching of baby Ismael and the loss of the Palestinian village of Ein Hod:

> As the people of Ein Hod were marched into dispossession, Moshe and his comrades guarded and looted the newly emptied village. While Dalia lay heartbroken, delirious with the loss of Ismael, Jolanta rocked David to sleep. While Hasan tended to his family's survival, Moshe sang in drunken revelry with his fellow soldiers. And while Yehya and the others moved in anguished steps away from their land, the usurpers sang 'Hatikva' and shouted, 'Long live Israel!'
>
> (39)

Abulhawa's narration is perhaps more sympathetic and less interrogative of the Palestinian self/psyche than Kanafani's more psychologically confrontational narration. While Kanafani's Dov does not reconcile with his birth parents because 'man is a cause', not flesh and blood, Abulhawa's David, who as baby Ismael had been scarred by an injury on his face, later reunites with his sister, Amal who left the Jenin refugee camp for the United States, then Beirut, and the United States again. Unlike Kanafani's uncompromising twenty-year-old Israeli soldier Dov, Abulhawa's 53-year-old David is more mature and understanding of the depth of Palestinian loss and dispossession and the contrived nature of Israel. This, Abulhawa allows us to see, in the meeting between Amal and David.

Abulhawa seizes the opportunity of their meeting in Amal's apartment in Philadelphia to impart to her reader historical, documentary type information about the establishment of Israel through the eyes of David as he looks at old pictures that Amal has in her apartment: 'He looked on in silence at the proof of what Israelis already know, that their history is contrived from the bones and traditions of Palestinians' (263). Unlike Kanafani's Dov, who rejects the filiative ties of his biological Palestinian parents, Abulhawa's David accepts the fact that the 'heritage that ran through his blood was vintage' and that the 'improvised history of modern Israel was not really his' (264). Abulhawa masterfully performs a transformation in reverse. Whereas in Kanafani, it is Said S and not Dov who is transformed in his old Haifa home that now belongs to a Jewish family, in Abulhawa, it is David who is transformed in his exiled, Palestinian sister Amal's Philadelphia apartment.

Another point of departure between Kanafani's and Abulhawa's narratives revolves around the use of violence/armed struggle against the colonizer, which for Kanafani is necessary not only for the sake of liberation, but also for the rehumanization of the dehumanized and dispossessed. Abulhawa's representation of Amal's *fidayee* brother Yousef is perhaps less than convincing in *Mornings in Jenin*. Yousef's wife, Fatima and child, Falasteen, and the unborn child that Fatima was carrying in her womb were mutilated in the Sabra and Shatila massacres in Beirut in 1982. While Abulhawa describes the gruesome massacre and quotes from the British journalist Robert Fisk's *Pity the Nation* for factual supporting evidence, she refuses to allow Yousef to take his revenge against those who enabled these bestial massacres. After telling his sister Amal over the phone, 'They ripped my Fatima's belly with a knife ... They killed my babies!' (227), Yousef vows revenge. However, a letter from Yousef at the very end of the novel reveals that he does not take part in the 1983 bombing of American forces and intelligence personnel in Beirut in retaliation for the Sabra and Shatila massacres less than a year earlier because as Yousef says, 'I'll live this pain but I'll not cause it. I'll eat my fury and let it burn my entrails, but death shall not be my legacy' (321).

Why Abulhawa chooses to end *Mornings in Jenin*, which also powerfully documents the 2002 Jenin Camp massacre, in this way is difficult to understand and is possibly linked to the difficulty of (Palestinian) narration and representation in exile, especially in the West. Perhaps this is the most palatable ending within the context of Abulhawa's *American* exile and Western readership. From the Fanonian (and Kanafanian) perspective, however, this line of thinking cannot be empowering, transforming or re-humanizing for the oppressed and dispossessed, the massacred and mutilated. Is the response to the brutal and genocidal massacre of one's people, one's own family, to respond with love and humanity, as Abulhawa does in the final two lines of *Mornings in Jenin* in Yousef's voice? Yousef writes to Amal: *'For I'll keep my humanity, though I did not keep my promises .... and Love shall not be wrestled from my veins'* (322).

However, using Fanonian reasoning, haven't the dispossessed already been dehumanized? What about those whose children were mutilated in the massacres? Why did Abulhawa rationalize the massacres in this way? Here perhaps one needs to revisit Said's concept of the affiliations of the text. The text is worldly in the sense that it is affiliated to the world, to the context from which it springs. The text needs to be acceptable in its original context, which includes not only the reading public, but also the publisher. Under the silencing power of a contrived Western discursive mask of 'love and humanity', the voices of the dispossessed are forever silenced. The evidence used in Abulhawa's novel from Robert Fisk's *Pity the Nation*, albeit sympathetic to the dispossessed, is still the voice of a white, male Western journalist that here is called upon to speak on behalf of the mutilated women, children and embryos who were violently ripped out of their mothers' wombs and never had a chance to speak. If they had been able to speak, what would they have said and how would they have said it? It is this difficulty of representation – how to represent these voices that have been forever silenced and are lost in the telling in *Mornings in Jenin*.

However, it is important to point out here that Abulhawa seems to have been already clarifying her previous stance on the use of revolutionary violence or the armed struggle in her second novel *The Blue Between Sky and Water*. In very clear messaging in the 'Epilogue' to this novel, Abulhawa champions the 'Palestinian resistance fighters' in Gaza. In full support of these Palestinian fighters, Abulhawa writes:

> Through it all, Palestinian resistance fighters, holed up in tunnels with little more than bread, salt, and water, refused to surrender, and continued to fight a vastly superior military force. Despite the horrors and terror they suffered, Palestinians in Gaza supported the resistance because, in the words of one man, "We'd rather die fighting than continue living on our knees as nothing more than worthless lives Israel can use to test their weapons." I'd like to salute those Palestinian fighters. They willingly stepped into a realm where death was all but assured, for nothing less than the cause of freedom. Their courage was the stuff of legends.

This very pro-resistance stance on Abulhawa's part is not a transformation in her views as much as it is a clarification of her position on the moral right of the colonized to use all means possible to end their oppression, siege and colonization.

Also deeply influenced by Kanafani's work, which she studied in detail, is the Egyptian novelist and scholar, Radwa Ashour who was married to the Palestinian poet, Mourid Barghouti and the mother of the popular poet, Tamim Barghouti. Like Abulhawa's novel *Mornings in Jenin*, Ashour's novel *The Woman from Tantoura: A Novel of Palestine* (2014) traverses several important places, spaces and times in Palestinian history, beginning with the 1948 *Nakba* and ending with a rare Arab victory wherein Israel was expelled from Southern Lebanon in 2000, a remarkable victory led by the Lebanese resistance, Hezbollah. The whole novel is narrated from the perspective of the main character Ruqayya. The difficulty of representation is especially poignant in this novel, which opens with a twelve-year-old Ruqayya at the time of the *Nakba* in the Palestinian fishing village of Tantoura, near Haifa. The importance of the telling in this woman's own voice is not lost upon Ashour whose character Hasan, the son of Ruqayya, encourages his now elderly mother to tell her story:

> He said, 'Mother, what I'm asking for isn't a composition but testimony' .... I said, 'I wish I knew how. Besides, it's hard to tell, it's not something to tell. It branches out, and it's heavy. How many wars can a single story bear? How many

massacres?'.... Then one evening he surprised me with a large notebook, on the cover of which he had written 'al-Tantouriya'. The woman from Tantoura.

(162–3)

I [Hasan] say that I wanted others to hear your voice, the voice of Ruqayya the woman from Tantoura.

(185)

The character of Hasan understands that the experience of the *Nakba* and all the ensuing catastrophes need to be narrated in many voices that would all be included in this fabric of narration, and of course, this includes the voice of Ruqayya.

This perspective is rather similar to Ashour's comments on her own novel on Palestine when asked by a journalist if she considers *The Woman from Tantoura* to be parallel history to history that has already been told. Ashour answers:

It's an exaggeration to talk about parallel history; the novel follows a thread in this history, and this is a thread suspended among thousands or hundreds of thousands of threads in the fabric of history. I worked hard to weave it through story and characters and language and rhythms to make this fabric a visible, felt experience that readers are conscious of and that affects them.

(Ashour interviewed by Mayada ElDemerdash, 2010)

Ruqayya's is one of many voices that must be heard and that represents one thread in this fabric of Palestinian history. This thread is one of hundreds of thousands of threads, making a rich narrative fabric that would enable a mass telling, and collective memory against forgetfulness, to rephrase the title of Darwish's long prose poem *Memory for Forgetfulness* (2013).

For Ashour, it is essential to listen to this voice, which has been silenced on many levels – by dominant (Zionist) history, which continues to this day, by the male Arab voice that tells of male suffering, heroics and trauma and the Palestinian woman's voice itself, a voice that has learned to silence her own trauma as a kind of defence mechanism. This novel, then, represents a space for the Palestinian woman whose voice interweaves moments of silence with those of vocalization. However, there are moments when silence can turn into a mode of survival and resistance, not weakness because sometimes to think the unthinkable and speak the unspeakable would be to rationalize the irrational by imposing upon the story a discursive Western paradigm that either intentionally silences the tale and the storyteller or lacks the necessary repertoire and experience to tell such a story.

Perhaps the best example of this silence in the novel is Ruqayya's narration of what happened in Beirut in 1982, specifically in a chapter Ashour calls 'Flies', which is an interesting word choice to describe the Sabra and Shatila massacres. The reader, listening carefully to Ruqayya's story, which her son asks her to tell in her own voice, is confronted by a difficulty of narration and representation and by a memory that she wants to kill. Ruqayya, addressing the reader, struggles with the memory that her son wants her to express:

> Do I want to kill it so that I can live, or am I trying to revive it even if I die because … because why? I suddenly scream: Damn memory, damn its mother and father, damn the sky over it and the day it was and the day it will be. Damn the flies!
>
> I saw the flies with my own eyes.
> In a deep pit, that was yet big enough.
> Ambulance crews with gloves and protective masks
> Were scattering white powder,
> Bringing the bodies on stretchers,
> Placing one body next to the other.
> They were stretching a sheet over them all, a covering
> ….
> A smell
> And clouds
> Of flies.
> Let it escape, let it go. May it never return.
> Stretch out a sheet as you saw them doing, to cover what you saw throughout years, and the day of the smell and the flies.
> Leave the page blank, Ruqayya.
>
> (149–50)

The variation in Ruqayya's thought processes above is signalled by the difference in the length of the lines. The longer lines with which this excerpt starts represent Ruqayya's grappling with the idea of recalling this memory that she does not want to remember because it is unbearably painful, traumatic and torturous. Then the switch to the shorter lines represents the actual memory to which readers feel they are intruding because the memory is very painful as Ruqayya begins to recite … the gloves and protective masks, the white powder, the bodies on stretchers.

The image of the flies, clouds of flies and the smell is repeated, so it is an image that stays with the reader. One wonders if Ashour's emphasis on the flies and the smell at Sabra and Shatila is an allusion to an earlier narration of these events that influenced many Arab writers – that of Genet's 'Four Days at Shatila', a narrative discussed earlier in this book. In Genet's narration, the image of the flies is a recurrent one:

> But there were so many flies. If I lifted the handkerchief or the Arab newspaper placed over a head, I disturbed them. Infuriated by my action, they swarmed onto the back of my hand and tried to feed there.
>
> (4)

> A photograph doesn't show the flies nor the thick white smell of death.
>
> (5)

> He's as large as life and the only shape he will ever have is the one formed by the stances, positions, and grotesque gestures of the dead fermenting in the sun under clouds of flies.
>
> (6)

> Her black and swollen face, turned towards the sky, revealed an open mouth, black with flies ...
>
> (8)

Why are the flies such an important part of the memory of the Sabra and Shatila massacres for Genet, Ashour and other writers? The most obvious reason is that they were there, hundreds, perhaps thousands of them, feeding on the decaying flesh of the corpses. Another reason could be that the human mind psychologically rejects the idea of how human beings that were living just hours ago should be degraded and dehumanized in such a meaningless way as to become the fodder for flies before they are piled up into mass, unmarked graves to be buried and forgotten forever. The absurdity of the situation is beyond human comprehension.

However, it is what Ashour does next that is perhaps the most shocking, artistically speaking. Imitating the sheets, which the ambulance crews were spreading over the dead bodies, Ashour makes Ruqayya spread a sheet – here a blank page to cover what Ruqayya 'saw throughout years, and the day of the smell and the flies'. The blank page that Ashour leaves in the middle of her novel, in its commanding silence, signals to the reader the importance of stopping to remember and perhaps to read *Al-Fatiha*, a collective prayer or moment of silence for all those who were massacred at Deir Yassin, Tantoura and all the massacres of the past and the one of the 'day of the smell and the flies' at Sabra and Shatila in 1982. Silence, here, is Ruqayya's resistance, a way of speaking the unspeakable horrors of Palestine. In defiance of speech that would describe and rationalize the unimaginable, Ashour chooses silence in order to undermine the hegemonic discursive rationalizations that speech would impose upon the power of silence to speak the unspeakable. Here, Ashour, through Ruqayya, refuses to legitimate or make comprehensible these massacres with language. She stretches a blank sheet to cover the corpses of Palestine's massacred, spanning the decades, but this page carries with it the unspeakable and immeasurable anger and resistance of the living.

Silence is recalcitrant, argue Maggie MacLure et al. in their article aptly entitled, 'Silence as Resistance to Analysis: "Or, on Not Opening One's Mouth Properly."' The writers maintain that silence is the 'trace of something Other at the heart of utterance – something intractable, unspeakable, unreasonable, unanalyzable. Silence confounds interpretation [...] [;] it also incites the search for meaning and is therefore productive' (MacLure et al., 2010: 492). Ashour uses this resistant strategy of defying the rationalizations of the hegemonic imperialist/Zionist discourse of Western mainstream media. At the same time, however, Ashour allows for other threads to be added to the fabric of her narrative. After Ruqayya's resistant silence, we are presented with 'Abed's Testimony' (188). Abed is one of Ruqayya's sons who narrates in detail to Bayan Nuwayhid al-Hout (not a fictional character; she is a writer, activist and the wife of Shafiq al-Hout, a Palestinian politician, journalist and activist) the events of the 1982 Beirut massacres. We are told that according to the Lebanese Red Cross, '3,000 [were killed], not including those who remained under the rubble, nor those who were bulldozed, nor those who were kidnapped or lost', writes Ashour in the voice of Abed (200). Another 3,000 people are counted among the missing, according to Agence France, one of whom is Ruqayya's husband, writes Abed to his brothers, Sadiq and Hasan, who are living in exile (200). Ashour melds fact (numbers of the dead, important events and some characters, such as Bayan) with fiction, Ruqayya and her family.

The horrors that befall the Palestinian people in this novel, both personal and collective, are of a *Nakba* that continues. Ruqayya remembers all that came before 1982 when she was forced to leave her village of Tantoura along with 500 or 600 women, children and old men in 1948:

> At the cemetery two trucks were waiting. Threatening us with their weapons, they told us to get in .... They crammed us into the trucks, and they began to move. Suddenly I shouted and pulled my mother's arm, pointing with my hand to a pile of corpses. She looked where I was pointing and shouted, 'Jamil, my cousin Jamil!' But I pulled her arm again with my left hand and pointed with the right to where my father and brothers were: their corpses were next to Jamil's, piled one next to the other at a distance of a few meters from us.
>
> (47–8)

This novel is also a study of how different people deal with trauma. In this particular episode, Ruqayya sees and mentally processes the scene she witnesses – that of the corpses of her father and two brothers whereas her mother sees with her eyes, but erases with her mind and imagines that her husband and sons are somehow living in Egypt. The traumatized mind creates survival mechanisms to enable the continuation of life.

The repeated pain, repeated trauma, which Ashour narrates in this novel, is very much a collective one that unites a people in pain, especially when she allows her characters and readers to mourn not only the deaths of fictional figures, but also real public figures in whose lives her fictional characters participate, such as Kanafani who was assassinated by the Israeli Mossad along with his niece and the 'attempted assassination of Anis Sayegh', the founder of the Palestine Research Center in Beirut (113). The reader sees Ruqayya fully participating in the horror of believing that Dr. Anis, like Kanafani, had been assassinated, but is told by her son Abed at the hospital, 'He's still alive. The doctors are operating on him. He was hit in the face, in his eyes and ears and left hand. Go home, I'll call later to reassure you' (114). Dr. Anis of whom Ashour speaks is a real person whose Research Center in Beirut Israel destroyed in 1982 and transferred all of its valuable documents about Palestinian life and history to Israel in an effort to erase any form of documentation of Palestinian existence.

The continuous trauma of the *Nakba*, argues Ahlam Abukhoti, applying Gayatri Spivak's concept of strategic essentialism, can be said to unite Palestinians by constructing a unique cultural identity based on a collective trauma. Abukhoti states, '[u]sing the Nakba strategically as a constant component of Palestinian identity, transformed this cultural trauma to a powerful unifying tool in the face of social or political divisions caused by other variables composing this identity' (49). This unifying tool is evident in Ashour's novel, especially in the large, old key that all the older women wear around their necks, whether or not these women really believe that these keys will actually open the doors to the homes they left behind in Palestine. To underscore the urgency of a future return to Palestine as represented by the key 'hung on a cord around her neck, like my mother' (117), Ashour focuses on Lebanon's refugee camps, where most of the action of this novel takes place, especially in the Shatila refugee camp, which was populated by refugees who came from 'villages in Upper Galilee ... from Majd al-Kurum and Safsaf and al-Birwa and Deir al-Qasi and Saasaa and al-Khalisa' (116).

While the naming of these villages in the Upper Galilee is indeed important factual information that Ashour is providing here, I believe that another equally important aim is to keep these names a part of the living memory of these people, especially as these villages are all located in 1948 occupied Palestine – in a part of historic Palestine that has come to be accepted *fait accompli* by many in the Arab world as Israel. In an interview with Ashour entitled, 'Radwa Ashour's Tantoura: Palestinian nakba and resisting fait accompli', Ashour, in answer to the question why 'al-Tantoureyya now', states: 'Probably it is a novelistic response to the official position that pushes us to condone ... that the Palestinian coast (I mean Acre, Haifa, Jaffa, Lod) has become Israel, and that it is our duty to accept this reality as a *fait accompli*.' Thus, Ashour's novel can be read as a counter-discourse to the defeatism of those who have accepted the loss of 1948 occupied Palestine. The people of the refugee camps, the women of Shatila who still wear their old, rusty house keys and their descendants have not accepted this fate, and the conclusion of Ashour's 'al-Tantoureyya' enacts their resistance and defiance.

The traumatic pain of the *Nakba* and all the massacres that followed and that continue to this day have not broken the will of the Palestinian people. These continuous nakbas have enabled the construction of a unifying national identity in the Palestinian community's various cultures of exile. Despite or perhaps because of this communal pain, Palestinians have garnered a revolutionary strength, a strength that involves the will to fight, to refuse surrender, to document atrocities. It is documentation that Ashour is obsessed with in this novel. Said writes in *The Politics of Dispossession*, interestingly dedicated to 'Bayan and Shafiq al-Hout' who I mentioned above, and precisely in an essay called 'Permission to Narrate':

> I recall during the siege of Beirut obsessively telling friends and family there, over the phone, that they ought to record, write down their experiences; it seemed crucial as a starting point to furnish the world some narrative evidence, over and above atomized and reified TV clips, of what it was like to be at the receiving end of Israeli 'antiterrorism', also known as 'peace for Galilee' (258).

Ashour applies Said's urgent calls to this novel as represented in the character of Abed, Ruqayya's son, who is documenting Israeli war crimes, such as the bombing of the Jad building in 1982 where many women, children and old people took refuge, killing them all. Abed says, 'We have plenty of witnesses, we have documents, we have reports ... and we have books documenting what happened' (352). Ashour's characters record, document and like Ruqayya, write everything down in notebooks.

In the final chapter of this novel entitled 'Across Barbed Wire', Ashour addresses a recurrent Kanafani theme, the concept of confined space, such as refugee camps, borders and barbed wire fences. However, rather than the despair and loss we see at the end of *Men in the Sun*, Ashour portrays a joyous scene across the barbed wire fence, separating Southern Lebanon from occupied Palestine, precisely occupied Galilee from which many of Lebanon's Palestinian refugees originate. It is important to point out that Ashour's novel ends with the Lebanese resistance's victory over Israel in May, 2000, something that Said himself described as a victory: 'For the first time in my life, and in the lives of the people gathering at Fatma Gate, we won. We won one' (*Power, Politics and Culture*, 2004: 446). Thus, it is with this new-found optimism that Ashour defies all *fait accompli* discourses and treaties of surrender. Seven large buses take Palestinians from different refugee camps to the border to celebrate the expulsion of the Israelis from Southern Lebanon and to meet with their relatives in occupied Palestine across barbed wire fences.

Ashour's narration here is telling for two main reasons. Firstly, the novelist is clear about the great role of the Lebanese resistance, specifically Hezbollah. Ashour seems to be saying that there is no room for ambiguity and political equivocation. People must be clear about where they stand. The novelist chooses an elderly woman to make these genuine affiliative pronouncements in order to emphasize that this is the truth of the matter and not factional political positioning:

> 'God protect al-Sayyid Hasan, if it wasn't for him and for the resistance we wouldn't be able to set foot on any of this land. Twenty-three years of occupation, and they're gone for good.' Voices rose praying for al-Sayyid: 'God protect him, God keep him for us, he's brought us good luck, God grant the same for Palestine.'
>
> (354)

It is obvious that Ashour is presenting/constructing a revolutionary ethics, based not on allegiance to any particular religion, sect or ethnicity, but on a liberationist discourse that can imagine victory and a future Palestine.

Secondly, this clarity that Ashour is calling for is directly related to what she presents in the closing pages of her novel, a reclaiming by naming the villages of the Northern Palestinian coast from which so many of Lebanon's Palestinian refugees come. The following passage, which I here quote at length, represents a gathering of Palestinians at the border with occupied Palestine, separated from southern Lebanon by a barbed wire fence, about seventy four years of history, dispossession, refugee camps and exile:

> We saw them line up and the passengers get off, carrying signs and flags. In the flash of an eye it was as if the barbed wire had disappeared from view, covered by the bodies of the residents on both sides ... People were meeting each other:
>
> 'We are from Haifa ...'
> 'We came from Ain al-Helwa; originally we're from Suffurya.
> From al-Zeeb. From Amqa. From Safsaf. From al-Tira. From ...'
> 'We're from Umm al-Fahm ...'
> 'We're came from the Mieh Mieh Camp ...'

'We're from Shafa Amr ...'
'We came from the Rashidiya Camp ...'
'We are from Acre ...'
'We came from the Burj al-Shamali Camp ...'
'We're from Arraba ...'
'We came from al-Bass Camp ...'
'We're from Nazareth ...'
'We came from Sidon ...'
'We're from al-Bi'na ...'
'We came from Tyre ...'
'We're from Jaffa ...'
'We came from Jezzin ...'
'We're from Sekhnin ...'
'We came from Ghaziya ...'
'We're from Lid ...'
'We're from Deir al-Qasi ...'
'We came from al-Bazuriya ...'
'We're from al-Jdayda. We're from al-Rama. We're from ...'
'And the lady is ...?'
'From Tantoura.'

The naming of these Palestinian villages (a few are towns in southern Lebanon) and refugee camps is there for a purpose. Ashour details the villages and refugee camps in this manner to inform the reader where all these people gathering at the border are from. The reading of the names of these villages in this way represents a collective remembering that would enable a collective return. The oral exchange of the names of ethnically cleansed villages from 1948 Palestine with the names of refugee camps is to underscore the fact that, to quote Barghouti, 'that a people was expelled from its land and has to return .... Is the end that we have come to today other than that beginning?' (2011: 214)

As if to bring home this point, Ashour dramatizes a symbolic scene between the seventy-year-old Ruqayya and her four-month-old granddaughter, little Ruqayya, who the elderly Ruqayya is surprised to see across the barbed wire fence, having come from Canada. After Hasan raises his baby daughter over the fence and hands her to his mother, Ruqayya narrates:

> I touch the silver and feel it, and then I touch the key. I lift the cord from around my neck, and put it around the little one's neck. I kiss her forehead, and give her to the tall man to give back to Hasan across the wire .... I say in a loud voice, 'The key to our house, Hasan. It's my gift to little Ruqayya'.
>
> (358)

Ashour's emphasis on the new generation of Palestinians who will continue the struggle and keep the narrative alive is clear in this scene of passing down the key to the family home in Tantoura to little Ruqayya. If the elderly Ruqayya does not return, little Ruqayya will, and here Ashour's master stroke of mixing fact and fiction is felt as the reader is introduced not only to little Ruqayya, but also to little Naji from Ain al-Helwa, which is the same refugee camp from which the popular Palestinian cartoonist Naji al-Ali hails. On her way back home on the bus, Ruqayya sits next to little Naji who draws the old woman in charcoal. Ruqayya falls asleep and wonders 'Would Naji meet little Ruqayya, one day, across the wire, or without it?' (362) To quote one of Ashour's favourite novelists, Toni Morrison who writes at the end of her novel *Beloved*: 'This is not a story to *pass* on' (emphasis mine, 275).

4

WRITINGS ON THE WALL

Palestine writes on walls and in notebooks: Revolutionary imaginings

This chapter, as the title suggests, speaks to Palestinian protest, resourcefulness, ingenuity, inventiveness and creativity in resistance that is still in the making, a resistance that has not yet been absorbed into international mainstream media and academia and is not dominant or hegemonic in any sense. This is a resistance that is documented in notebooks, on refugee camp walls and on Israel's oppressive apartheid wall. Although there certainly seems to have been a significant shift in global public opinion on Palestine after the latest 2021–2 events with the continued ethnic cleansing policies of Israel in Jerusalem/Al Quds and other cities and towns, 'this shift has not as yet influenced [...] the politics from above and the mainstream media in the West', wrote Pappe to me in an email in 2021. In fact, the Palestinian cause still does not have the permission to narrate other than in offbeat conferences, such as *Palestine Writes* (2020) composed of Palestinian writers and activists and a select few from the international community who are known supporters of the Palestinian cause in academia and political activists from the African American community and human rights organizations.

The Palestinian cause has not yet entered the international political imaginary in the same way that South Africa's anti-apartheid struggle had before it.[1] This solidarity is, of course, necessary and urgent: to have Angela Davis's now decades old solidarity with the Palestinian cause is crucial. African American women writers have been at the forefront in their solidarity with Palestine. To name a few of them here is important: Toni Morrison, Alice Walker and June Jordan. One of the first African Americans to speak out about Palestine was James Baldwin who very perceptively stated in 1979:

> But the state of Israel was not created for the salvation of the Jews; it was created for the salvation of the Western interests. This is becoming clear (I must say that it was always clear to me). The Palestinians have been paying for the British colonial policy of 'divide and rule' and for Europe's guilty Christian conscience for more than thirty years.
>
> (qtd. in King, 2014)

Perhaps it was Baldwin's early stance with the oppressed that caught Said's eye and led to his declaration in *Representations of an Intellectual* that Baldwin and Malcolm X represent the kind of intellectual consciousness that has most deeply influenced his ideas on what it means to be an intellectual. It is a mind in opposition that defiantly challenges the centre of power and stands with the oppressed when it is not the fashion to do so, argues Said (xv). Said is not as keen on the stances of Martin Luther King who did not seem to possess the deep understanding of anti-colonial struggles and specifically the Palestinian struggle for liberation as Baldwin and Malcolm X did.

In a book of collected interviews with Said, entitled *Power, Politics and Culture*, edited by Gauri Viswanathan, Said states:

> With the emergence of the civil rights movement in the middle '60s – and particularly in '66-'67 – I was very soon turned off by Martin Luther King, who revealed himself to be a tremendous Zionist, and who always used to speak very warmly in support of Israel, particularly in '67, after the war.
>
> (209)

It seems that King was not able to connect Black American suffering with the suffering of other oppressed peoples in this world and adopted the imperialist/Zionist world vision without examining or critiquing it. Baldwin and Malcolm X, who were able to see Black American suffering as part of a greater global human suffering that resulted from the historical catastrophes of slavery and imperialism, however, possessed this world revolutionary vision and imagination. What for Martin Luther King was 'civil rights' was for Baldwin and Malcolm X human rights that could only be realized by a revolutionary imagination.

One of the boldest, revolutionary imaginations in the United States today is that of African American professor at Temple University Marc Lamont Hill who declared in a speech on 29 November 2018 at the UN's International Day of Solidarity with Palestine:

> So as we stand here on the 70th anniversary of the Universal Declaration of Human Rights and the tragic commemoration of the Nakba, we have an opportunity to not just offer solidarity in words but to commit to political action, grassroots action, local action, and international action that will give us what justice requires. And that is a free Palestine from the river to the sea.
>
> (jadaliyya.com)

Hill's words, especially a 'free Palestine from the river to the sea' sent shockwaves through mainstream American media and academia, leading to Hill's firing from the American broadcaster CNN. Even the idea of 'imagining' a free Palestine is criminal in the United States and other Western countries.

Another African American scholar, Robin D. G. Kelley has coined the term, 'imagining revolution', which is an empowering act. In an article entitled 'From the River to the Sea to Every Mountain Top: Solidarity as Worldmaking', Kelley argues that solidarity becomes a way of remaking the world by imagining revolution. Solidarity, then, should be geared towards having the imaginative power to not merely plot coalitions, or the traditional nationalist ideas of nation-building, but rather the more transformational idea of 'worldmaking' that can imagine revolution (2019: 73). Harping on the same theme, Bill Mullen calls his blog 'From the River to the Sea', a popular Palestinian slogan, which refers to the hope that Palestine will someday be free from the River Jordan to the Mediterranean Sea. In an article entitled 'Palestine and Our Emancipation', Mullen (2018) explains that the mantra 'from the river to the sea' is a dream that Palestinians have of being free, an 'audification of what Robin D. G. Kelley calls freedom dreams' (billvmullen. com). For Mullen, the Palestinian cry for freedom is a call for all our freedom, to be able to move and breathe. It is a cry for a 'world without walls', writes Mullen.

But the truth is our world is a world of walls and fences. This includes the wall that Donald Trump promised, but was not able to build, the wall he was supposed to model after the Israeli apartheid wall of which Trump was in awe (timesofisrael.com, 2018). Israel's apartheid wall of oppression is symbolic of what Israel is and represents – a militarized settler colonial state of checkpoints, sieges, baseless imprisonments, torture protocols, barbed wire fences, blockades, land theft and the dispossession of the Indigenous people of the land that is now seventy-four years old. It is in this sense, then, that Palestinian resistance can be seen as writings on the wall.

Perhaps, to drive my point home a little further, I here quote from a poem entitled, 'Songs: IV. History of a Poetic' by Salvadoran poet, Roque Dalton:

That was when he began writing on the walls
in his own handwriting
on fences and buildings
and on the giant billboards
The change was no small thing
quite the contrary
in the beginning
he fell into a deep creative slump.
It's just that sonnets don't look good on walls
and phrases he was mad about before, like
"oh abysmal sandalwood, honey of moss"
Looked like a big joke on peeling walls.

(qtd. in Harlow, 1987: 1)

Revolutionary discourse and art begin on walls – refugee camp walls, apartheid walls, walls that were constructed to keep the oppressed and dispossessed behind walls. If forced to write and draw within the oppressive restrictions of governmental institutions, as in the Arab world whose governments are obviously controlled by the biggest imperial power of our day, the United States, the revolutionary artist will indeed fall into a 'deep creative slump', as Dalton writes.

This is unfortunately the story for not only the revolutionary artist, but also the professor and the student who are not allowed to think outside the inane political and ideological restrictions of a regime that is controlled by the American or Zionist embassy. So naturally, the first parchment the child in a refugee camp has is the wall of imprisonment. This, ironically, marks the beginning of that child's creativity and ability to imagine revolution and victory. This is the environment that gave birth to the great Palestinian artist, Naji al-Ali in the Ain al-Hilweh refugee camp in Lebanon. Al-Ali's defiant art came to an end when he was mercilessly assassinated by a Palestinian who worked for the Israeli Mossad in London.[2] However, the case has not been closed, and investigations are still ongoing. Israel's apartheid wall has also served as canvas to much Palestinian and international art, one notable example being the anonymous English street artist, Banksy. The oppressed people's artists, poets, singers, dancers and scientists do not have the luxury of expressing their revolutionary cultural and scientific productions in fancy art exhibitions, large recital halls, theatres, dance halls, state of the art lecture halls and modern laboratories nor is their work supported by governments and prestigious institutions.

Olive trees: Uprooting and bitterness: Barghouti and Hamdi K. Hamdi, the intertwining of life, literature and science

It is not too much of an exaggeration to say that Palestinian life revolves around the olive tree. In his memoir *I Was Born There, I Was Born Here*, Mourid Barghouti writes a beautiful two-page ode to olive trees, which he mourns and describes as 'dishonored corpses', 'murdered' and uprooted by the notorious Israeli bulldozer. Barghouti focuses on the inseparability of the olive tree and the Palestinian family tree; therefore, the uprooting of the olive tree is literally the uprooting of Palestinian life:

> Everywhere you look, huge olive trees, uprooted and thrown over under the open sky like dishonored corpses. I think: these trees have been murdered, and this plain is their open collective grave. With each olive tree uprooted by the Israeli bulldozers, a family tree of Palestinian peasants falls from the wall .... The olive in Palestine is not just agricultural property. It is people's dignity, their news bulletin, ... the indispensable basis of their daily meals. If anyone falls ill, the oil is his medicine ....
>
> (10–11)

Barghouti's description of the murder of these olive trees is reminiscent of the many massacres that have befallen the Palestinian people, beginning in the 1940s with massacres in different Palestinian villages, such as Deir Yassin and Tantoura, 1950s such as Kafr Qasim, the 1980s with Sabra and Shatila and continuing into the new millennium with the Jenin Camp massacre and the sieges on Gaza.

No one knows more about the great significance of Palestine's olive trees than its poets and scientists. A brilliant Palestinian scientist, with a PhD in biochemistry from the United States, Hamdi Khalil Hamdi, my late brother who sadly passed from this life in July, 2020, researched and patented Oleuropein, a compound found in the leaves of the olive tree. In an important and highly cited scientific article entitled 'Oleuropein, a non-toxic olive iridoid, is an anti-tumour agent and cytoskeleton disruptor' (2005), Hamdi K. Hamdi and Raquel Castellon write:

> Oleuropein, a non-toxic secoiridoid derived from the olive tree, is a powerful antioxidant and anti angiogenic agent. Here, we show it to be a potent anti-cancer compound, directly disrupting actin filaments in cells ... in a cell free assay. Oleuropein inhibited the proliferation and migration of advanced grade human tumor cell lines in a dose responsive manner ....
>
> (Hamdi and Castellon, 769)

While Palestine's poets sang about the olive tree, Palestinian scientists, such as Hamdi, researched it scientifically and wondered about the power of this tree that dotted the Palestinian landscape. Amazed by its ability to grow so stubbornly over thousands of years, Hamdi spoke about and documented the powers of the olive tree's leaves, which he said remained unaffected by the elements and seemed to possess certain powerful compounds that kept them protected. This fact is what inspired Hamdi's thinking about the gift of life that the olive tree held within its very leaves. I recall very clearly Hamdi's scientific explanation to me about the olive tree's *bitter* leaves that he said is the key to their efficacy against many diseases, including cancer, which is the disease he investigated in the above-mentioned article. His desire was to cure all the sick people in Palestinian refugee camps for free. Before his premature and abrupt death at the age of fifty-six, Hamdi's mind was preoccupied with trying to unlock the genetic secrets of different human diseases. In fact, Hamdi had already been working on genetic codes to different diseases and had downloaded countless genetic codes from the most important genetic data bank in the world, something about which Hamdi was very excited. He was working on important scientific projects that would unlock the genetic codes to human diseases, such as cancer, heart disease, diabetes and others. His mind was always working overtime, coding and decoding the most complicated genetic codes even while having a normal conversation about the weather. In fact, very few understood the human genome in the way that Hamdi understood it.

Hamdi's scientific brilliance, however, was not seized upon or supported by any Arab government or research centre. This lack of sponsorship is inevitably part of what it means to be an exiled and uprooted Palestinian, not to *belong* to any nation per se. Said's words in 'Reflections on Exile' are quite fitting here: 'Exiles look at non-exiles with resentment. *They* belong in their surroundings, you feel, whereas an exile is always out of place. What is it like to be born in a place, to stay and live there, to know that you are of it, more or less forever?' (2000: 180–1). While Hamdi's restless mind could design and decipher the most complicated biochemical equations, his conscience was also completely possessed by the bitter trauma of Palestine and its tragic history. Palestine animated Hamdi's life and science.

In the final days, hours and even minutes of his life, still strong of mind, but weak of body, Hamdi listened to old speeches by Malcolm X and revolutionary Palestinian songs while he was being quarantined alone in a very small hotel room in Amman, Jordan due to the Covid-19 pandemic in July 2020. Hamdi loved the oppressed and stood in solidarity with them – African Americans, Native Americans and of course his own people, the Palestinians. I spoke to him over the phone on the very day he passed from this life on 14 July 2020. He very much wanted to live, but had been quite tired and ill with fever and chills for the previous two weeks in Saudi Arabia where he had been teaching at a university, and suggested that he may, in fact, die on the very day he sadly left this world. On this fateful day, Hamdi asked for bitter Arabic coffee and wanted to know about the progress I was making on my book, *Imagining Palestine*. What is most striking about the actual day he died was his indomitable will to live, his refusal to surrender and his late style defiance of the pain that he was feeling and as he revealed to me just hours before he passed, *hiding*.

To slightly alter bell hooks's words from her essay 'Choosing the Margin as a Space of Radical Openness', Hamdi literally *chose* to *live* on the *margin* with his pain, which seems to symbolically mirror Palestinian life in general. However, it is precisely in this marginal and bitter space that Hamdi created his Thirdspace resistance as Soja would say or what Palestinians call *sumud*. Hamdi's life is indeed a very good example of living in *sumud*. In bitter spaces, such as the olive leaf, Arabic coffee and the marginal spaces of the oppressed in this world, Hamdi found life, resistance and scientific creativity. And Hamdi was a storyteller, narrating stories about the ancient Sumerians, the bravery of the Indigenous peoples of the Americas, the genius of Malcolm X and the heroics of the Palestinian martyrs whose names Hamdi memorized by heart. Hamdi's children's names were carefully chosen, rich in historical, cultural and political significance and affiliations; each one tells a story. Hamdi, who literally passed from this world mid-sentence while speaking on the phone with us and ironically imprisoned in his hotel room, a metaphorical and physical exile and siege, faced his death like a true intellectual *fidayee* of the Palestine that he loved so much. Like so many of Palestine's exiled intellectuals, Hamdi's journey in his different places and cultures of exile in the Arab world and the United States was a bitter one. Being uprooted from his parents' native Palestine, no place in this world was home.

Is it only a coincidence that when the poet Mourid Barghouti came to my house for an interview for the journal *Arab Studies Quarterly* in June 2016, the first thing he asked for was bitter Arabic coffee? 'Make it *alqam*', Barghouti said in Arabic to me. *Alqam* is Arabic for bitter – it seems that bitterness is a quality of Palestinian life. About three months before the great Palestinian poet passed from this life in February 2021 and in response to my tweet to him that I was at the time working on his poetry and memoirs for this book, he wrote to me 'Looking forward. Bless.' Unfortunately, both the poet Mourid and the scientist Hamdi did not live to see the completion of this project, but their work lives on in their literature and science respectively. Both mourned the uprooting of their beloved olive trees. This melding of the olive tree with Palestinian life is a common theme in Palestinian literature.

Mahmoud Darwish once said of the olive tree: 'If the olive trees knew the hands that planted them, their oil would have become tears ...' (qtd. in Karkar, 2007).

Israel has uprooted hundreds of thousands of olive trees. In her article entitled 'The Olive Trees of Palestine Weep' (2007), Sonja Karkar states that Israel has destroyed more than one million olive trees since 1967, which amounts to an intentional and criminal destruction of Palestinian life and existence:

> For more than forty years, Israel has uprooted over 1 million olive trees and hundreds of thousands of fruit trees in Palestine with terrible economic and ecological consequences for the Palestinian people. Their willful destruction has so threatened Palestinian culture, heritage and identity that the olive tree has now become the symbol of Palestinian steadfastness because of its own rootedness and ability to survive in a land where water is perennially scarce.
>
> (51)

This deep connection between the Palestinian and the olive tree is historical, cultural, social, and economic all at once. Perhaps over the past several years, one of the most iconic images of Palestinian resistance against Israel's policy of the systematic uprooting of olive trees is that of the old woman Mahfoutha Shtaya from the village of Salem, near Nablus on the occupied West Bank, who was photographed defiantly embracing her olive tree, trying to stop Israeli settlers from uprooting it (Qumsiyeh, 2009).

The outsider may not quite absorb all the dynamics involved in the image of Mahfoutha and her olive tree. However, Soja's Thirdspace trialectics of historicality, spatiality and sociality can help put this image into sharper focus: the historical and spatial frameworks of the *Nakba*, *Naksa*, massacres, the constant land dispossessions and uprooting of Palestinian olive and fruit trees are defining factors in Mahfoutha's 'lived space' or sociality in the present (Soja, 1996: 10). Mahfoutha's response is one of Thirdspace resistance, a *sumud* based on this learned knowledge, her lived space reality. In his article entitled, 'The Olive Tree – Not Just an Ordinary Tree', Mazin Qumsiyeh, like Barghouti above, lists all the Palestinian uses of the olive tree over hundreds, even thousands of years: olives and olive oil are a necessary food source on Palestinian breakfast, lunch and dinner tables; olive pits have been used to make Christian and Muslim prayer beads over hundreds of years; olive wood has always been used to make souvenirs and artefacts to sell to travellers to the 'Holy Land', and these trees provide the Palestinian family with shelter and memorable moments. The olive tree represents a whole way of life for Palestinians (Qumsiyeh, 2009).

It seems Palestine's inhabitants hundreds and even thousands of years ago knew about the powerful medicinal effects of the oil of the olive leaf to fight disease (Melhem, 2018). It was a Palestinian scientist, Hamdi K. Hamdi, who proved this scientifically when he identified the specific compound (Oleuropein) found in abundance in the olive leaf and examined and documented its specific mechanism of action (2005) in our post-millennial era as discussed above. In her article entitled 'Uprooting the History and Future of Palestine', Jewish American activist, Anna

Baltzer, who witnessed first-hand the uprooting of hundreds of Palestinian olive trees in the village of Kifl Haris in 2003 describes how for Palestinian farmers, the olive tree equals their existence, detailing how Palestinians care for their olive trees like they care for their own family members.

Baltzer explains how these trees were described as *hamil* (حامل) or pregnant by their owners, meaning they were bearing fruit before they were violently ripped from the soil that was their home for thousands of years. Baltzer movingly writes:

> It is not an exaggeration to personify trees with the word '*hamil*'; to many families who have been with their trees for hundreds of years, generation after generation, the fruit-bearers are an integral part of the family. I felt sick watching the trees ripped from the earth with the American-made bulldozers .... By the time the Wall is completed, more than two million trees will have been uprooted since 2001 .... Some of them may have stood since the time of the Romans, and Jesus. They are irreplaceable. Stealing them is a rape of the land, and the destruction of both the history and future of the Palestinian people.
>
> (2003)

Indeed some of these trees are older than the Romans and Jesus. In fact, the oldest olive tree in the world is located in the Palestinian village of Walaja, near Bethlehem – *Al Badawi* tree, which is looked after by Salah Abu Ali whose family owns the orchard near it. It is said that *Al Badawi* tree was named after Ahmed Al-Badawi, a '13th-century Sufi imam who is said to have spent many hours sitting in the shade of the tree'. Some refer to it as 'the tree of our master Ahmad al-Badawi' (Melhem, 2018). Using the method of carbon dating, Italian and Japanese teams tested *Al Badawi* tree and estimated its age to be approximately 3,000–5,500 years old. If the older estimation holds true, this 'would make the Al Badawi tree the oldest olive tree in the world' (Ruffin, 2020).

For Palestinians, their sustenance and very existence depend on the existence of the olive tree. This continuous destruction of olive groves represents a systematic plan by Israel to force Palestinians into exile, a kind of ethnic cleansing. According to the United Nations Development Programme (UNDP), the World Food Programme (WFP) and the UN Office for the Coordination of Humanitarian Affairs (OCHA), 80 per cent of all the orchards in the occupied West Bank and Gaza Strip are made up of olive trees (Relief Web, 2006). Thus, uprooting olive trees that are thousands of years old habitats is at once the destruction of a whole way of life. This is a glaring example of environmental genocide, in addition to the uprooting of a culture and its people. This ecological violence amounts to a war crime against this land and its people.

Israel's geographical and ecological violence should be seen in tandem with its brutal psychological and physical violence against the Palestinian population. In Darwish's 'Earth Presses Against Us', the poet, in response to those who have massacred Palestinian innocents vows, 'our blood will plant olive trees' (2003: 9). Thus, planting olive trees has become an act of resistance and staying rooted in this land. In Darwish's last few words in this short poem ('our blood will plant olive trees'), the olive tree, a symbol of rootedness in Palestinian culture, will grow strong, watered by Palestinian blood. In her article entitled 'Bethlehem: "No matter how many olive trees they destroy, [we] will plant more!"' Megan Perry states that olive 'trees are being violently destroyed as a form of collective punishment, in an attempt to force Palestinians from their land. Despite this desecration many Palestinian farmers are using farming as a form of resistance ...' (theecologist.org, 2014).

In fact, several solidarity groups have been springing up to offer Palestinians support in planting olive trees. These organizations include: 'US Campaign for Palestinian Rights' whose website actively campaigns for the planting of olive trees in the occupied West Bank under the heading of 'Rooting Resistance' and the 'JAI Olive Tree Campaign'. According to this website, these activists distribute:

> olive saplings among farmers, sponsored by individuals, YMCAs, YWCAs, churches, church related organizations, human rights organizations, as well as solidarity and advocacy groups around the world, as an act of solidarity and support to help 'Keep Hope Alive' .... in the occupied West Bank and Gaza Strip areas where olive trees have been uprooted and destroyed by the Israelis, or where fields are threatened to be confiscated by the Israeli military Occupation, or where parts of the Israeli apartheid wall and settlements are constructed on part of the land.

These campaigns represent Thirdspace resistance, to use Soja's term, a type of resistance that takes into account the historicality, spatiality and sociality of the Palestinian context and roots resistance, defiance and hope against the inhumanity, brutality and despair of the Occupation. The olive tree with its olive fruit and bitter leaves remains a life-giving force, offering Palestinian society with food, medicine and sustenance for thousands of years.

Drawings on the wall: Naji al-Ali

Like Hamdi's and Barghouti's bitter olive leaves and coffee described above, which represent Palestinian experience in its difficulty, resilience, *sumud* and creativity, the bitter *al-hanthal* (الحنظل) plant inspired Naji al-Ali's cartoon character Hanthala, whose persona encompasses the characteristics of this plant, and who has been, ever since his creation by al-Ali in the year 1969 (Black, 'Drawing Defiance', theguardian.com), a powerful symbol of Palestinian resistance, creativity and *sumud*. Al-Ali's Hanthala possesses a powerful critical consciousness, sparing no one his biting, sarcastic and often bitter criticism as he observes the ongoing catastrophe of Palestine and the role of the Arab world and the rest of the world in it. In addition to wielding a powerful critical pen pointed at all who conspire and allow the Palestinian catastrophe to continue, al-Ali once said that he created Hanthala to be the conscience of the Palestinian people. However, al-Ali also feared that he might become a 'tanbal'[3] like his friends, especially when he left the

Ain al-Hilweh refugee camp in Lebanon (to which his family was forced to escape when al-Ali was only ten years old at the time of the 1948 *Nakba*) in order to work in Kuwait (kanan48.wordpress). In 'My Signature, Hanthala: The Symbol of the Child', al-Ali states: 'I had friends with whom I shared my work, protests, and prison days until one day they became "tanabel" running businesses and buying stocks. I was worried about myself from turning [in]to a "[tanbal]" too and being consumed' (ibid.).

Hanthala, then, was created to fight against the dying of the conscience, which can be equated with the dying of the Palestinian cause. Al-Ali/Hanthala is Said's intellectual, but his walls are not in Harvard or Columbia, but in refugee camps and prisons. In fact, it was on the walls of refugee camps and prisons that al-Ali began to draw:

> I started drawing on the walls of the refugee camps and the clubs when political awareness started finding its way among the people of the refugee camps .... I learnt to draw in prison when other prisoners learnt handcrafting, poetry ..., and there I drew on the walls of the prisons.
>
> (kanan48.wordpress)

It is from these drawings on the walls of Ain al-Hilweh that Ghassan Kanafani discovered Naji al-Ali. Al-Ali states that Kanafani published his drawings in the magazine called *al-Hurriyeh* (Freedom), in which Kanafani was an editor at the time. Al-Ali often spoke of giving birth to a 'new Arab human being' (kanan48.wordpress) in Hanthala, which is reminiscent of Fanon's idea of the 'veritable creation of new men' (36) ...; the '"thing" which has been colonized becomes man during the same process by which it frees itself' (1967: 37). Hanthala, then, represents the defiant Palestinian child of the refugee camps who cannot be tamed by any power – he speaks truth to power wherever and whenever this is necessary. Hanthala remains as al-Ali conceptualized him – ten years old, the age al-Ali was when he was forced to leave his home village of Shajara in Northern Palestine, along with his family, where they ended up in Lebanon in a refugee camp. Hanthala is an unkempt, barefoot child of the refugee camps with tattered clothes and 'hedgehock-like hair because the hedgehock uses its hair as a weapon' (kanan48.wordpress). Al-Ali's Hanthala speaks in the name of the poor and oppressed, the marginalized and refugees.

In an interview with the popular Egyptian novelist, academic and family friend, Radwa Ashour in 1984 in Budapest, al-Ali said of Hanthala, '[h]e was the arrow of the compass, pointing steadily towards Palestine. Not just Palestine in geographical terms, but Palestine in its humanitarian sense – the symbol of a just cause, whether it is located in Egypt, Vietnam or South Africa' (kanan48.wordpress). Time itself would have to wait upon this ten-year-old child that al-Ali refused to allow to age, an unnatural act in the same way that being uprooted, dispossessed and forced to live in refugee camps is an unnatural crime against humanity.

Hanthala appears to the audience with his back turned to them and his hands folded backwards. This is all the observer will ever see of Hanthala until he returns to his homeland. Only then will Hanthala face forward and be allowed to grow. In the meantime, Hanthala will wait, observe and record the atrocities committed against his people and the complicity of Arab regimes and the world in this crime. This is not only a betrayal of a just Palestinian cause, but also a betrayal of humanity itself. Betrayal is what al-Ali feared would become a matter of perspective, a point of view. In fact, as al-Ali's son Khalid al-Ali[4] told me in an email dated 21 April 2022, his father wrote and popularized the following statement about betrayal:

أخشى ما أخشاه أن تصبح الخيانة وجهة نظر
What I fear most is that betrayal will become a point of view

It is as if al-Ali predicted decades ago what has actually transpired in the post-millennial era – the betrayal of the Palestinian cause is now a point of view, a matter of one's perspective. Many Arab regimes have already disposed of the Palestinian cause, labelled Palestinian resistance as terrorism and signed humiliating treaties of surrender and defeat with the Zionist enemy without even mentioning the word Palestine or Palestinian.

Thus, for al-Ali, these defeatist Arab regimes have betrayed the Palestinian cause and humanity itself. In defiance of Arab defeatism and surrender, al-Ali counters with what he considered three main postulates or premises and then a conclusion regarding the Palestinian cause in figure one below. The man's shirt in the sketch reads: 'No reconciliation, No negotiations, No recognition, the refugees of 1948.' On the inside of the man's open shirt, al-Ali lists the names of Palestinian

Figure 4.1 No Reconciliation, No Negotiations, No Recognition – 1948 Refugees. Published on 6 November 1985 in Al Qabas newspaper (Kuwait)

refugee camps in different places, such as Sabra and Shatila, Ain al-Hilweh, Nahr al-Barid, al-Buss, Bourj al-Shamali, Bourj al-Barajneh, al-Badawi, al-Mieh Mieh, and al-Rashidiyyeh in Lebanon. Al-Yarmouk in Syria, Jabalya in Gaza, Dheisheh in the West Bank and Wihdaat and al-Baqaa in Jordan are other refugee camps mentioned by al-Ali outside Lebanon.

Thus, for al-Ali, the message is clear. No Arab regime or even the Palestinian leadership has a right to negotiate on behalf of the millions in the refugee camps who are awaiting their return to their homeland. These refugees are never going to reconcile, negotiate with or recognize Israel – to do so would mean their own extinction and the death of the Palestinian cause. These refugees, like Hanthala, live in the temporariness of exile with their hearts and minds focused on one conviction and one conviction alone – return.

Living in refugee camps can never be normal and cannot be normalized or accepted. There is nothing to negotiate or reconcile for Hanthala. This child of the refugee camps has a right to return to al-Shajara in 1948 Palestine and so do the refugees from the above mentioned refugee camps who await their return to Palestine, all of Palestine as suggested by the names of the different refugee camps mentioned in the sketch. The vast majority of the inhabitants of these refugee camps come from villages in 1948 Palestine. In fact, the very existence of refugee camps underscores the idea of temporariness and waiting, which is represented in Hanthala's own existence, being frozen in time (his age at the time of the *Nakba*) and space (the refugee camp).

Hania Nashef states, 'he [Hanthala] remains alive through his suspension through time and space' (2020: 38). Despite the Palestinian people's very different places and cultures of exile, Hanthala, the child symbol of the refugee camps, unites the Palestinian consciousness. He is a character that 'all Palestinians and Arabs could identify with even though they may have not experienced the refugee camp' (Nashef, 40). The Palestinians' different places/spaces of exile, their different cultures of exile, both inside and outside occupied Palestine, this perpetual waiting – all underscore the necessity of the return of the Palestinians to their ancestral lands. In *Palestinian Culture and the Nakba: Bearing Witness* (2020), Nashef, commenting on a Naji al-Ali cartoon (figure two below), which she translates as 'exiles' cemetery and the suitcase', argues that Hanthala is a witness to the 'diasporic death of all Palestinians', but at the same time, the suitcase on top of the grave can also mean the 'death of exile, a return to the place of birth' (Nashef, 40).

For Hanthala, as for Palestinians in their diverse cultures of exile, the death of exile does indeed signal the coveted return to the homeland. Exile, al-Ali is saying, can never be a permanent situation. Like the refugee camps set up for the Palestinians seventy-four years ago, exile is temporary, and the return of the refugees or their descendants as this cartoon seems to suggest is inevitable – even if the first generation of refugees have all but died. Similarly, for al-Ali's close friend, Mourid Barghouti, the death of exile means the inevitable return not only of the living, but also of the Palestinian dead to historic Palestine as he suggests in *I Saw*

Figure 4.2 The Cemetery of Exile. Published on 26 July 1986 in Al Qabas newspaper (Kuwait)

Ramallah, 'Our dead are still in the cemeteries of others. Our living are clinging to foreign borders' (38).

Naji al-Ali's critical consciousness represents the conscience of the Palestinian people and the Arab masses that, unlike Arab regimes, see in Palestine their compass. It is, in fact, al-Ali's popular critical cartoons, like Kanafani's fiction and activism before him, which led to his assassination as al-Ali himself predicted in an interview with Joan Mandell two years before he was assassinated in London. Al-Ali told Mandell, 'Don't be surprised if I'm killed a month from now', ... 'I'm a marked man, but I'm relaxed' (merip.org). Al-Ali's son Khalid al-Ali told me in an email dated 21 April 2022 that the 'assassin was never caught, and no one was charged. Investigation is ongoing. A Palestinian who was part of Force 17 is wanted for interrogation.' However, according to the *Electronic intifada*, Scotland Yard has questioned a Palestinian man who worked for the Israeli Mossad as a double agent (El Fassed, *The Electronic Intifada*, 2004).

The title of an article by Victoria Brittain may help explain the reason behind al-Ali's fateful prediction, 'They had to die: assassination against liberation' (2006). Although in her article Brittain concentrates on political leaders of liberation movements, I believe that her argument can be expanded to include consensus builders, artists, poets, novelists – popular cultural figures who have great impact on people. It can be argued that with the assassination of figures like Kanafani and al-Ali, the enemy hopes to stunt awareness, 'silence the witness and extinguish the flame of resistance' (Hamdi, 2011: 23). Thus by killing the storyteller, the enemy aims to silence the story. It is possible to read al-Ali's prediction of his own assassination in this particular sketch:

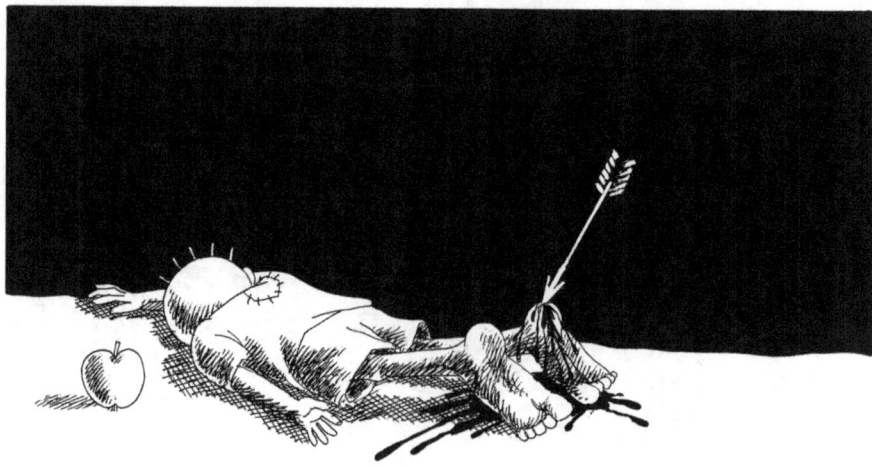

Figure 4.3 The Death of the Artist. Published on 29 April 1987 in Al Qabas newspaper (Kuwait)

Although Barbara Harlow points out that this cartoon was his last, 'drawn just before his assassination' (1996: 13), Khalid al-Ali told me in an email that this cartoon, which 'was published on 29 April 1987 in Al Qabas Newspaper, Kuwait, was not his last cartoon'. This wordless cartoon (Figure 3.3) shows Hanthala face down with blood under his feet, an arrow in his heel set against a black sky with an unbitten apple a few spaces away from him. The two objects (other than Hanthala himself) in this cartoon are allusions: one classical, referring to Achilles' heel with the arrow or artist's pencil that caused the death of the artist; the other biblical, except unlike Adam and Eve, Hanthala never bit into the apple. The child died, innocent and uncorrupted like his creator who refused the corruption of politicians, political parties and organizations.

The art of this formidable artist led to his martyrdom, and al-Ali joins a long list of the martyrs of Palestine before and after him. However, the killer does not understand that Hanthala is an idea that will survive the martyrdom of the artist, and will grow and indeed has grown even stronger as evidenced by the omnipresence of Hanthala everywhere in Palestinian life and culture – on refugee camp walls and most recently on Israel's Apartheid Wall, where international artists are now drawing Hanthala in many different contexts. One in particular is by the artist Matthew DeMaio whose sketch called 'Handala and the Statue of Liberty' shows Hanthala as a baby Jesus and Mary as a Statue of Liberty. Describing DeMaio's sketch, Rebecca Ruth Gould writes: 'The Statue of Liberty embraces her suffering son, who wears a crown of thorns … While these images are globally implicated through their Christian and American symbolism, they nonetheless succeed in powerfully evoking the Palestinian experience in occupation' (2014: 11–12). Hanthala has certainly outlived his creator, but as al-Ali predicted, he does indeed continue to live through this ten-year-old boy from the refugee camps who is still waiting to return to his home: 'Hanthala, who I created, will not end after my end. I hope that this is not an exaggeration when I say that I will continue to live with Hanthala, even after I die' (kanan48.wordpress).

Al-Ali's murals live and have effectively participated in keeping the Palestinian cause alive. Drawings on walls tell stories, stories from below, especially when these drawings are made by Palestinians themselves – artists from the inside and not progressive Western artists who come to draw on the wall and relay messages with which Palestinians do not necessarily agree. As Bahira Amin points out:

> Many Palestinian activists object to international artists who come to Palestine for a "spraycation" – using the wall as their canvas for easy points for progressiveness on social media …. Their art, some argue, also normalizes the appearance of the wall, mainstreaming instead of highlighting its injustice.
>
> (scenearabia.com)

The danger in the apartheid wall becoming a 'spraycation' stop for foreign artists has the effect of normalizing not just the apartheid wall, but also what it represents – the occupation, more specifically the settler colonialism of Israel. In order to fight against this kind of normalization effect, if I may term it as such, and also to better represent the Palestinian mindset, local Palestinian artists, such as an artist 'working under the pseudonym Vince Seven (VIN7)' who 'painted a revolutionary battle scene depicting a future storming of the separation wall and the triumphant exaltation of the Palestinian national flag on the wall in Bethlehem' (Larkin, 2014: 146).

Figure 4.4 Leila Khaled, a Palestinian Icon: Don't Forget the Struggle

This same artist also painted Leila Khaled on the apartheid wall in Bethlehem, immortalizing this iconic Palestinian fighter, carrying an AK-47, wearing army fatigues and the traditional Palestinian kuffeyeh on her head[5] and a very important message in English next to her image, 'Don't Forget the Struggle', says the artist.

The artist, in the painting above, is probably responding to artists who wish to convert the struggle into a purely peaceful one involving only the doves of peace and colourful balloons. Thus, the message here is clear – Western artists cannot dictate to the Palestinians the nature of their struggle, which came into existence in response to a very brutal form of dispossessive settler colonialism.

Thus, the artist makes an obvious reference to the importance of the armed struggle as here represented by the iconic image of Leila Khaled, who hijacked two airplanes, one in 1969 and 1970. The armed struggle is itself as Khaled says 'politics in practice' (qtd. in Irving, 94). This iconic image of Leila Khaled travelled the world as Sarah Irving states:

> This was the era of Che Guevara, killed in Bolivia just two years earlier, and of liberation struggles in South East Asia. The right of oppressed peoples to resist by armed means was discussed worldwide, and the heroes of these movements decorated the walls of student bedrooms and left-wing homes. The second wave of feminism was also breaking, adding another aspect to the environment in which news of this young female hijacker would be received.
>
> (2012: 5)

While some Western feminists and progressives found in Leila Khaled a theoretical symbol of female empowerment, for many working inside the Palestinian movement, people like Leila, despite all the hardships she faced as a woman, was theory in the making as the struggle did not have time to theorize. In the context of the Palestinian struggle, it is the reality that made the theory. Irving, responding to the comments of the feminist writer, Robin Morgan who argued that 'there are two well-fostered stereotypes of the Palestinian woman: she is a grenade-laden Leila Khaled or she is an illiterate refugee willingly producing sons for the revolution' (qtd. in Irving, 7) points out that this is a 'generalization [that] may say more about Western perceptions than Palestinian reality' (7).

In fact, during this era of anti-colonial struggles (1950s–70s) and especially within the Palestinian context, specifically the late sixties, there was no hard dividing line, separating women who took care of their families and did charity work on the one hand and those who actively participated in the national project on the other as Khaled explained to me in conversation. The woman in the refugee camp, 'producing sons for the revolution' could have easily become a Leila Khaled and Khaled did of course become a loving mother to her own children. For Khaled, a woman bearing arms at that time was actively taking part in, not only the national struggle, but also the social one (Irving, 94). Khaled tells a story of how once in Lebanon, as she was distributing 'illicit ANM leaflets during a military curfew', she very riskily told a Lebanese army soldier that she was seeking medical help for a pregnant neighbour of hers. Not only wasn't she arrested, as Leila narrated to the journalist Eileen McDonald, but the soldier even guarded her supposed search for a midwife (Irving, 20).

My own mother, Naziha Hamdi, or as she likes to be called 'Um Hamdi' (the mother of her firstborn son, Hamdi, which is the traditional naming pattern for Arab parents generally), confirms Khaled's description of events at that period of time. In fact, as Naziha, or Um Hamdi, has often narrated to me, women (including herself) took active part in the liberation struggle, such as hiding AK-47s underground, so they can eventually reach their destination to the *fidayeen* in occupied Palestine via secret routes and distributing ANM leaflets in Palestinian refugee camps in Jordan, such as Al Wihdaat and Al Baqaa, all in a day's work. These women were not only 'middle class' women, but also women from the refugee camps. In fact, the woman who would accompany Um Hamdi was Um Issa from the Wihdaat refugee camp in Amman, Jordan. This point about the widespread involvement of Palestinian women in the struggle is corroborated by Soraya Antonius who states, '[w]omen began to participate, publicly, in every crisis' (qtd. in Irving, 92). Khaled relayed to me this very idea in my conversation with her for the conclusion of this book. Khaled explained that Palestinian women were involved in political and social activism since 1917, and especially during the 1936 revolt. Khaled told me, 'Palestinian women bore arms. This, of course, was not widespread, but some women martyrs who bore arms from this era were Helweh Zidan and Fatmeh Ghazzal.'

Palestinian women, Khaled said, 'organized, mobilized, and were involved in fighting against the Zionist invasion and land confiscation', in addition to 'looking after orphans'. Palestinian women founded a 'United Palestinian Women's Organization' that 'established a hospital in Nablus and a kindergarten for the children of martyrs'. However, it was not until after 1967 that women's participation became more widespread, as reported to me by Khaled, who described how Palestinian women 'assisted fighters by supplying them with weapons or hiding fighters from the enemy'. For these women activists, revolutionaries and in some cases fighters, not only were they taking part in something dangerously exciting, but they were also doing something sacred, serving their people and the Palestinian cause. The sanctity of the 'Cause', as they called it, empowered them both physically and mentally. These Palestinian women represented women's empowerment in praxis even before their counterparts in the West could theorize about it.

Palestinian song, dance and revolution: From heritage to resistance

The difficulty of representing the Palestinian experience does not only apply to literature, but also to popular culture, such as song and dance. Who is the Palestinian and how is the Palestinian identity and experience to be represented in song and dance? What constitutes a revolutionary song or dance is also in need of reassessment and re-examination, especially as many folk songs and dances from past eras have been undergoing a constant process of repurposing. Palestinian song and dance is grounded in the inseparable dynamics of Palestinian heritage and resistance and is deeply entwined in imagining and constructing a future Palestinian nation. Hall's astute formulation of the concept of cultural identity in which he recognizes the 'importance of the act of imaginative rediscovery which [the] conception of a rediscovered, essential identity entails' (393) is essential in understanding the role of Palestinian heritage and folk culture in resistance. Palestinian heritage songs are not only unearthed but are also re-conceptualized in the context of an ongoing Palestinian revolution. Songs of resistance are born out of the reality of the Palestinian struggle and daily life. They are also subject to change and to various influences, including Arab, Islamic and even Western.

Both the essential and the dynamic aspects of Palestinian national identity are necessary in mobilizing Palestinians living under occupation, and in exile, to imagine a future Palestine. Traditional Palestinian heritage song and dance, such as *ahazij*, *ataaba* songs, the *dabke*, the wedding *zafe* and organized dance troupes, such as *El-Funoun* and *Hanouneh* serve to unify the Palestinian community by enabling an affiliative relationship to an imagined Palestine. For national identities placed under erasure by the kind of settler colonialism that Palestinian identity has been confronting for over seventy years now, 'music, art, dance, literature, poetry … become spaces in which the Self is imagined and performed into being and thus become sites of contestation themselves' (Alajaji, 2013: 98).

It is essential to clarify here that as an endangered cultural and national identity, the filiative 'imaginative rediscovery' of a Palestinian identity is a crucial part of constructing a collective Palestinian community composed of diverse cultures of exile. This is an idea similar to the one discussed earlier in this book, specifically Moore's poignant argument that Palestinian narratives 'privilege ways of remembering towards the future' (2018: 252). Both Fanon and Hall understand this impulse and address this need. Fanon writes in *The Wretched of the Earth*, 'Colonisation is not satisfied merely with holding a people in its grip and emptying the native's brain [...] [but] [b]y a kind of perverted logic, it turns to the past of the oppressed people, and distorts, disfigures, and destroys it' (210). It is a necessary pride in oneself, one's culture and one's history that the oppressed must first explore on their journey to constructing a collective national identity. Hall writes that this kind of shared experience and 'conception of cultural identity [...] continues to be a very powerful and creative force in emergent forms of representation amongst hitherto marginalized peoples' (223). For peoples that have undergone both cultural and ethnic cleansing, this kind of initial return to an authentic self is an important first step, which obviously progresses into a more dynamic and reconstructed form of cultural identity.

This is true of Palestinian song and dance, whereby old heritage songs and dances are reconfigured, recontextualized and repurposed to serve present and future contexts of the Palestinian resistance and liberation struggle. The importance of centring a return to the Self within the Palestinian context as argued by Ted Swedenburg (1990: 21) and Sylvia Alajaji (2013: 98–9) is rooted in Palestinian dispossession and erasure. Thus, there is a definite urgency in mobilizing the worldwide Palestinian community around a shared Palestinian culture and heritage. So much of Palestinian literature, music, song and dance 'rests not only on defining the Self but also in proving that the Self once existed – not just exists, but *existed*' (Alajaji, 99). In fact, this is what Said spends the whole first part of *The Question of Palestine* (1992 [1979]) doing – proving that Palestinians both exist and have existed in historic Palestine for thousands of years, deconstructing the Zionist lie articulated by Golda Meir who claimed 'that the Palestinians did not exist' (1992 [1979]: 5).

Thus, it is in going back to a point of origin, the place where it all began, the urgent need for being rooted and grounded in the land that a Palestinian national identity based on the figure of the *fellah* or peasant has been able to mobilize and unite Palestinians in their diverse cultures of exile. Darwish's early poem 'Identity Card' emphasized the *fellahi* origins of the Palestinian Arab identity, which represents the very essence of the poet's resistance as he proudly and defiantly announces that he is an Arab who 'descends from the family of the plough' (Darwish – Bitaqat Hawiyyah (ID Card) (barghouti.com). In an article entitled 'The Palestinian Peasant as National Signifier', Ted Swedenburg argues that:

> [f]or Palestinian nationalism ... the peasant carries an unusually heavy symbolic weight ... the overwhelming cultural presence of the *fallah* flows from the endangered status of the Palestinian nation. It is a nation imagined but unrealized, a people whose relation to their territory has been severed again and again, whose identity is tenuous and constantly under threat. The figure of the peasant serves as a crucial ideological weapon in the Palestinian confrontation with Israeli colonial policies.
>
> (1990: 19)

The concept of the *fellah* comes with a whole symbology of Palestinian village life, such as the olive tree, the Palestinian *thobe* or traditional village dress, the *dabkeh* dance and songs about Palestinian nature and martyrs. Although not all Palestinians are *fellahin*, the life of the village, its trees, hills, songs, dances and even the *fellahi* dialect have become a part of the Palestinian imaginary. Because, as Swedenburg argues above, the Palestinian has been repeatedly severed from his ancestral land, the *fellah* represents a powerful symbol of rootedness and defiance.

Perhaps the *dabkeh* dance is the most prominent in this repertoire of Palestinian culture, both inside and outside occupied Palestine. This is a dance that is traditionally performed at weddings, social gatherings and celebrations. According to Sarah Amawi, the *dabkeh* has two possible origins: the first is connected to ancient Canaanite fertility rites whereby peasants take part in vigorous foot stomping rituals in order to scare away evil spirits and allow their seedlings to grow. A more likely origin, however, is related to a Levantine style of house construction whereby roofs were made of wood, straw and dirt/mud and were in need of being compacted. This brought together friends and neighbours who all took part in this foot stomping activity that soon became a gathering that combined work, cooperation and celebration (patrimoinedorient.org).

European Zionist colonizers appropriated the *dabkeh* in order to establish for themselves an 'authentic Israeli' culture before and after the 1948 *Nakba* according to dance historian Nicholas Rowe who states:

> [T]he actual Zionist salvage and appropriation of indigenous peasant dances can be seen as both methodical and politically orchestrated. During the 1930s and 1940s, Zionist dancers researched the local peasant dabkeh. The steps were re-choreographed into stage presentations of folk dance by Zionist youth .... Zionist immigrant Lea Bergstein began creating new dances based on the indigenous peasant dances of Palestine that she observed.
>
> (2010: 85)

Rowe accurately conveys the above idea in a section of his book entitled 'Indigenous Dances Become Zionist Dances'. Not only did the Zionist movement conduct the most systematic, notorious and barbaric land theft crimes of the twentieth century in broad daylight, but also followed up this form of settler colonial dispossession of Indigenous Palestinians with cultural theft and genocide. Zionists hoped to erase the memory of Palestine.

This Zionist appropriation or theft of Indigenous Palestinian culture does not, of course, end with the *dabkeh* dance, it also includes other forms of cultural theft ranging from dress, dance and song to food. As Roger Sheety (2015) explains, Zionist militias, from 1947 to 1949, looted and destroyed 'tens of thousands of books, paintings, musical recordings, furniture, and other artifacts ... from Palestinian homes, libraries, and government offices'. During its invasion of Lebanon in 1982, Israel again stole thousands of Palestinian historical documents and books with the aim of continuing its crime of cultural memoricide.

In addition to the physical expulsion of the Palestinians, this cultural memoricide, as pointed out by the historians Pappe and Masalha, is a necessary part of the total annihilation of Palestinian history and memory. Masalha writes:

> The founding myths of Israel have dictated the conceptual removal of Palestinians before, during and after their physical removal in 1948 .... The de-Arabisation of Palestine, the erasure of Palestinian history and elimination of the Palestinians' collective memory by the Israeli state are no less violent than the ethnic cleansing of the Palestinians in 1948 and the destruction of historic Palestine: this elimination is central to the construction of a hegemonic collective Israeli-Zionist-Jewish identity in the State of Israel.
>
> (2012: 89)

In addition to Masalha's statement above about the conceptual removal of Palestinians even before the establishment of Israel, the settler colony constructed a discourse to convince the world that the fabricated 'Israeli-Zionist-Jewish identity' is 'genuine'. This endeavour involved stealing certain aspects of the culture of the Indigenous Palestinians, then propagating the myth of the non-existence of the Palestinians.

Thus, after the 1948 ethnic cleansing, Israel de-Arabized the names of towns and villages in historic Palestine while at the same time appropriating/stealing certain aspects of Palestinian heritage and culture, then claiming that Palestinians never existed on this 'empty' land. It is within this context of physical and cultural genocide that Palestinians have been repurposing Palestinian heritage and culture as forms of resistance – to say not only do Palestinians exist, but have always *existed* in time and place, on *this* land (historic Palestine), and here's Palestinian heritage to prove it. It is for this reason that the *dabkeh* is much more than just a peasant dance performed on special occasions. It has become a vigorous dance of resistance, and the more vigorously danced, the greater the resistance and defiance symbolized by the foot stomping of the dancers. Even the *dabkehs* performed at wedding ceremonies become an affirmation and celebration of *Palestinianness*.

Nicholas Rowe provides a very succinct presentation on a new realization among Palestinians that there would have to be a necessary reconstruction of Palestinian national identity after the 1967 defeat or *Naksa*, which for Palestinians living on the 'West Bank' meant occupation and the loss of land to hundreds of new Zionist settler colonies. The imminent danger meant that Palestinians needed to rethink, refocus and restructure a collective Palestinian national identity (111–13). This new and urgent need to construct 'unifying symbols of collective identity through folkloric heritage' led to the establishment of the Centre for Popular Palestinian Heritage in Al-Bireh, Ramallah in 1972. The Centre publishes the journal *Heritage and Society* (Rowe, 113). However, as Rowe argues, the Palestinian nationalist folklore revival movement, in its aim to counter the ongoing ethnic and cultural cleansing of Palestine, tended to homogenize and essentialize Palestinian culture into a kind of static peasant culture and symbology. This meant that the Palestinian urban dances, which were heavily influenced by the kind of modernization that the rest of the Arab world was undergoing along with rural women's dances, were sidelined or overlooked in order to enable the construction of a collective and unifying Palestinian nationalist identity (115).

The Director of the Centre for Popular Palestinian Heritage, Abdel-Aziz Abu Hadba, defending the Centre's project of promoting a collective Palestinian identity based on peasant symbology, states that 'Palestinian folklore is a necessity for Palestinian national identity. Through my folklore I struggle against my enemy' (qtd. in Rowe, 115). This atmosphere laid the framework for the *dabkeh* to take centre stage as the symbol of Palestinian national identity that all Palestinians could embrace, and not only in villages where the *dabkeh* has always been a part of celebratory culture, but also in urban centres where the *dabkeh* was previously seen as a peasant dance. After the 1967 *Naksa* and the urgency for a reimagined or repurposed heritage, the *dabkeh* became a classless symbol of Palestinian national identity (Rowe, 116–17).

In this sense, the figure of the *fellah* and the *dabkeh* are mobilizing and unifying symbols that preserve the Palestinian Self from cultural erasure by merging the past and the present as argued by Sylvia Alajaji: 'Thus, the Self that is being saved from erasure – the "authentic" Self, the Self that embodies and validates the counter-narrative – is and must be … ever *present*. Inscribing the past onto the present not only negotiates the two into simultaneity, but it also binds them together: the past dependent on the present, the present on the past' (101). The performance of the *dabkeh* has become an act of defiance and resistance. Dance troupes in the occupied 'West Bank', such as the Sharaf al-Tibi and El-Funoun were harassed and arrested by the Israeli army because the Occupation saw these *dabkeh* dance troupes as symbols of defiance and cultural resistance. Rowe points out that these *dabkeh* performances often became targets for raids by the Israeli army, thus elevating these dancers to the stature of Palestinian national heroes (151).

El-Funoun's performances of Palestinian heritage and culture, particularly their storytelling through the *dabkeh*, are dangerous for the Occupation. In 1988, during the First Palestinian Intifada, the Occupation arrested three members of El-Funoun, the 'writer, Wasim Al-Kurdi, [the] musician, Suheil Khoury, and [the] dabkeh dancer, Muhammad Ata'. Although the three men were being held at three different detention centres, they were able to compose one of their most well-known shows, 'Marj Ibn Amer'. Al-Kurdi wrote the lyrics, which were then smuggled to Khoury who wrote the musical score to which Ata was able to mentally choreograph the actual *dabkeh*, according to the Palestinian museum website (2016). A production such as Marj Ibn Amer is dangerous for the Occupation because it counters precisely what Israel fears most, the imagined return of the Palestinians to their Indigenous land, these Palestinians who were not supposed to have ever existed according to Zionist propaganda, probably best represented in Golda Meir's words previously quoted.

These imagined returns are '"returns" to the past' (Alajaji, 107) that speak to the Palestinian present. One of the young *dabkeh* dancers that Alajaji talked to says 'I dance with the group about my grandparents and my grand-grandparents. How was their life and how was their work? How was the land there?' (106–7). The idea of returning to the past in these dances is not for the purpose of reliving it, but rather to signal a return, not to the past, but to the land in the present, anticipating the outlines of a better world as discussed earlier in this book. The actual performance of the *dabkeh* becomes a defiant declaration of one's *Palestinianness* wherever the *dabkeh* may be taking place – in a performance hall, at a wedding, a protest or more dangerously at the Gaza border with occupied Palestine under the bombing and sniper fire of the Zionist occupation army. In fact, this is what happened during the 'Great March of Return' in the year 2018 when a group of young men and women from Gaza performed the 'Great Dance of Return'. It is in the very performance of the *dabkeh* under sniper fire that these young people dressed in the traditional Palestinian kuffiyeh expressed their national identity, a very real Palestinian identity embedded in the past and extending into the present ('The Great Dance of Return' – Gaza border, YouTube). However, the important difference between the performance of the *dabkeh*, past and present, revolves around its purpose whereby in the past it was more of a communal celebratory dance, nowadays, the emphasis is on the performativity of identity, defiance and resistance.

This repurposing of Palestinian song and dance holds true for Palestinians living under occupation as well as those living in exile. In their article entitled 'The Ghosts of Resistance: Dispatches from Palestinian Art and Music', Yara El-Ghadban and Kiven Strohm write that Palestinian youth in Montreal, Canada gathered to perform Palestinian song and dance, 'wear Palestinian traditional clothes, play recordings of Palestinian songs like *dal'una*, and choreograph dabke dances alternating with poetry' (184). However, they were not performing for a foreign audience or to bring attention to their cause; rather these young people were doing it for themselves, a kind of performing into being, into agency – they would affirm their *Palestinianness* in their performance: 'In many ways they were dancing for themselves, talking to themselves, dreaming collectively' (184). In exile, the *dabkeh* can be seen as an affirmation of Palestinian identity. In occupied Palestine, however, it is not only an affirmation of identity, but also an act of resistance. As of this writing (March, 2022), for example, Israel is continuing to expel Palestinian families in the Sheikh Jarrah neighbourhood of Jerusalem/Al Quds from the homes they have inhabited for hundreds (perhaps thousands) of years and stop Muslims from praying at Al Aqsa Mosque during the last days of the holy month of Ramadan. Thus, the act of praying at Al Aqsa Mosque has become not only a religious act, but even more significantly, an act of resistance in the same way that the *dabkeh* at the Gaza border and in the streets of Hebron, Nablus, Ramallah and elsewhere is an act of cultural resistance.

Songs are also strongly connected to resistance and revolution, both secular and Islamic. For example, one of the earliest poems of Palestinian resistance penned in 1930 by the popular poet Nuh Ibrahim during the time of the British mandate in Palestine, 'From Akka Prison', was in the early 1980s turned into song in praise of the martyrs and armed resistance of the Palestinian revolutionaries of the 1970s–80s. In fact, this kind of repurposing of heritage song/dance spans decades of Palestinian struggle and resistance. Nuh Ibrahim originally wrote this poem, which was very popular in Palestine's rural areas, in tribute to the three Palestinian revolutionaries, Muhammed Jamjoum, Atta al-Zeer and Fouad Hijazi, who took part in the Buraq Uprising in 1929 during the British Mandate period. With these executions, known as 'Red Tuesday', the British hoped to terrorize the Palestinian population and thereby crush their resistance to British rule, but as the historian Rena Barakat argues on the Palestinian Journeys website, 'these executions gave Palestine its first recognized martyrs, memorialized in poetry, song, and in public gatherings' (paljourneys.org).

Although this poem was written in 1930 during the British Mandate of Palestine, it was repurposed in the early 1980s by the Palestinian singing group *Al Ashiqeen*, who sang it with a new sense of purpose, not only to commemorate the martyrs of the Buraq Uprising, but also sang in praise of contemporary martyrs and freedom fighters after the 1982 Israeli invasion of Lebanon and the Sabra and Shatila massacres. *Al Ashiqeen*'s adaptation of Ibrahim's poem had the effect of linking Palestine's martyrs of the early twentieth century to those of the latter part of the century. In a strong, sombre voice and tone, the lead singer of *Al Ashiqeen* sings of the bravery of the now celebrated three martyrs of Palestine who took part in the Buraq Uprising against the British colonizer and Zionist Jews during the period of the British Mandate of Palestine and were executed by the British as a result.

In addition to transforming this poem from 1930 into a song, *Al Ashiqeen* also repurposed the melody of a very popular traditional Arabic *mawwal*,[6] known widely in the Levant region as *ala dal una* for the song, 'From Akka Prison' (McDonald, 2013: 101). Here, the lead singer of *Al Ashiqeen*, Hussein Munther (54), sings in a slow and solemn way (my translation):

Church bells are heard

They were three men, racing towards their death
Their feet upon the necks of the executioners
They have become legends, *ya khal*[7], they have become legends ...
Throughout the land
Ya Ein, Ya Ein, Ya Ein, Ya Ein[8] *(mawwal to express pain)*
We love the oppression of prison – oh for you our land, for your sake
When you call, our land, your heroes heed the call ...
On Tuesday ... the three
Await ... who will sacrifice his life for you
Ya Ein, Ya Ein, Ya Ein, Ya Ein (mawwal to express pain)

From Akka Prison, a funeral procession – Mohammed Jamjoum and Foaud Hijazi
Oh punish, my people, punish the (British) High Commissioner and his helpers

Chorus sings: From Akka Prison, a funeral procession – Mohammed Jamjoum and Foaud Hijazi/ Oh punish, my people, punish the (British) High Commissioner and his helpers

Church bells heard

Mohammed Jamjoum with Atta Zeer, Fouad Hijazi – our pride and joy
Our fate and destiny
At the hands of the oppressor's law that has come to execute us.

Chorus sings: Mohammed Jamjoum with Atta Zeer, Fouad Hijazi – our pride and joy/Our fate and destiny/At the hands of the oppressor's law that has come to execute us

Mohammed says I'll be first
I fear Atta that I will grieve too painfully for you
Hijazi says I'll be first
We do not fear death ...

This theme of martyrs and martyrdom has perhaps been the most prominent one in Palestinian songs for over ninety years[9] now with martyrdom being celebrated as it is above in terms of it being the epitome of bravery, courage and loyalty to the cause.

This, however, is not to say that there is no deep sorrow and grief over the loss of life. It goes without saying that all these martyrs are very dear to their families, but the reality of the Palestinian experience has also meant that this sorrow and grief is by necessity shaped and moulded by a steely endurance, which is indeed displayed by these three martyrs who, according to the popular poet Ibrahim, raced to their death, all of them wanting to be the first to be executed by the British colonizer because they feared the pain of grieving for their comrades even if for a few minutes before their turn came. In order to be able to endure the ongoing tragic sorrow of losing a loved one in this way, the Palestinian community has had to create ways of dealing with this kind of tragic loss. Since young, unmarried men have been martyred at a disproportionately higher number than other age groups and genders, songs about martyred young men usually portray their martyrdom as a celebration of their wedding day where the young man is referred to as a bridegroom and traditional Palestinian ululations, called *zaghareet*, are heard in celebration of his martyrdom. People come to offer their condolences to the parents of the martyr while at the same time congratulating them on his martyrdom. It is an act of *sumud* and endurance, a living in *sumud*, that turns a deeply painful experience into one of pride in a mother's son or daughter who has joined the long line of Palestine's martyrs both inside and outside occupied Palestine.

In another song sung in a sad and solemn tone by the same group, *Al Ashiqeen*, the martyr is envisioned as a bridegroom who closes his eyes and holds out his hand, so his friends and relatives can put the traditional henna on his hands. Although this song was traditionally sung on the night before the wedding called 'henna night' in preparation for the wedding next day, it has been repurposed in Palestinian culture and is now sung to celebrate the martyrdom of the young, unmarried man or woman. In traditional Palestinian culture, the highest point of happiness and achievement for the Palestinian mother is when she can celebrate the marriage of her children. Thus, the death of her child robs her of her greatest joy. In order to be able to endure such great loss, the repurposing of these traditional wedding songs into songs celebrating the martyr/bride(groom) is not only an act of resistance and defiance, but also a coping mechanism that allows the grieving mother to endure a kind of extreme *sumud* or steadfastness.

In a video uploaded to YouTube by the Palestinian Media Observatory group, a woman is shown grieving for her martyred son, singing and placing henna on his hands: 'He put *kohl*[10] in his eyes and held out his hand to receive the henna', she cries through her tears and makes a traditional trilling sound or *zaghroota*, simultaneously celebrating and grieving for her martyred son. This grieving mother is heard saying to her dead son, 'Diya just got engaged and married, Oh Diya, my love.' Then singing and crying, she says, 'he wore his kohl and held out his hand to receive his henna. A small gazelle wrapped in his death shroud.'

Diya's father is then heard saying, 'we'll join you soon, Diya. Don't be afraid, we're coming too.' Then the traditional zaghareet are heard from the mother of the martyr as well as from the other women there. The scene shown in this video has become a very common one in occupied Palestine. The grieving mother becomes a tower of strength who defies the agony of losing her son or daughter and rather celebrates his/her martyrdom for the sake of Palestine. The mothers and fathers of martyrs in Palestinian culture are loved and respected for their great *sumud* and endurance.

Al Ashiqeen have popularized another song about martyrdom and the bridegroom, a very prominent theme in Palestinian culture and such songs are sung by the closest relatives of the martyred young people, especially if they are still unmarried. This song entitled 'They brought in the martyr, they brought in the bridegroom' was posted on YouTube by the Palestinian National Self-Representation Campaign (my translation):

> They brought in the martyr ... they brought him
> They brought in the bridegroom ... they brought him
> In the flag of revolution,[11] ... they wrapped him
> Oh the joy of his mother and father
> I am his mother, oh the joy of his mother
> On his wedding day, the night his blood was shed
> Oh soil of freedom embrace him
> Oh his brothers, join the revolution
> With the *zaghroota*, come let's celebrate
> They brought in the martyr ... they brought him
> They brought in the bridegroom ... they brought him
> In the flag of the revolution, ... they wrapped him
> Oh the joy of his mother and father.
> (Palestinian National Self-Representation Campaign, YouTube)

The song above represents the occurrence of actual everyday events within the context of Palestinian culture and life. When the martyr is brought in to his/her parents wrapped in the Palestinian flag, his parents are congratulated on this highest form of sacrifice. The deep pain of the martyr's parents is described as great joy, again, as a necessary coping mechanism. Because martyrdom is a very common occurrence, a whole repertoire of endurance rituals, if I may term them as such, are practiced. These endurance rituals include condolence visits that are intentionally turned into celebratory gatherings and songs and *zaghareet* to defy death and the enemy that aims to break the will of the Palestinian people.

The village of al-Shajara, which was ethnically cleansed on 7 May 1948 by Zionist terrorist gangs (Pappe, 88), is also remembered in Palestinian culture for being the home village of the great artist and critic Naji al-Ali and his cousin, who is arguably the most popular singer of Palestinian revolutionary songs, known to the Arab masses as 'Abu Arab', which literally means 'the father of Arabs' in Arabic. Abu Arab was born Ibrahim Mohammed Saleh and was seventeen years old when his family was forced out of their home village of al-Shajara in 1948 (middleeastmonitor. com). Abu Arab's songs revolve around the concept of return, resistance and an imagined reclamation of the land. In his important article on Palestinian music entitled 'Liberating Songs: Palestine Put to Music', Joseph Massad points out that in the mid to late seventies, Abu Arab, like 'Al-Firqah al-Markaziyyah (the Central Band), associated with Fatah' (2003: 31), sang unapologetically revolutionary songs about resistance, *sumud*, return and the Palestinian freedom fighters – the *fidayeen*. Abu Arab, 'associated with the guerrillas [...] produced tens of songs about the struggle. His music also used [...] Palestinian [folk] tunes, including popular *mawwals* and *mijana* sung to revolutionary lyrics accompanied by *oud*, *qanun*, violin, and *riqq*' (Massad, 2003: 31).

Often singing in a rural Palestinian accent, Abu Arab's music became tremendously popular in the refugee camps inside and outside occupied Palestine (ibid.) and is still popular today. Abu Arab is a master of the *mawwal*, which the singer uses to his great advantage because of his strong, baritone vocals. In his song 'Ya Yuma lou jani al eid', which translates into 'Oh Mother, if the Eid (holiday) comes', Abu Arab sings a deeply emotional, traditional *mawwal* about the impossibility of experiencing the joy of Eid when one is separated from his loved ones and his homeland (my translation):

Oh Mother, Oh Mother, Oh Mother
They said the Eid has come
I told them the Eid is for those who can enjoy it.
What good is the Eid to those who are separated from their loved ones?
Oh Mother, *Aaakh ya Yuma*[12]
The Eid, Oh Mother, is when our homeland returns, and I return to my homeland
And kiss its earth, Oh mother – *Aaakh ya Yuma.*
Ooooooooooooofff[13]

Abu Arab's style speaks to the Palestinian people's psyche and uses their language and their dialect to express emotions and ideas that the vast majority of Palestinians in exile and under occupation experience. This is a collective feeling of deep separation, rupture, of being unnaturally cut, truncated from one's own land, history, experiences and everyday life.

This kind of amputation has often been expressed in Palestinian literary productions, especially the work of Kanafani, Barghouti, Darwish and many others. The theme of waiting, as in al-Ali's Hanthala who awaits his return, is also present in Abu Arab's song. Although the Eid holiday comes every year, it does not come psychologically, emotionally and *metaphorically* for the Palestinian exile (here exile in the sense of being both real and metaphorical). Thus, the truncated and amputated Palestinian waits, suspended like Barghouti's crane that suspends the poets in the air between earth and sky as discussed earlier. This suspension, tension and waiting is the very experience of exile – the exile of

Palestinian farmers living on their occupied lands, the exile of Palestinian exiles living in refugee camps, the exile of Palestinian poets and intellectuals, the exile of Palestinians from their past and present, the exile of Palestinians from their Eid as in Abu Arab's song. The Palestinian Eid can only return when Palestinians return to their homeland.

Return is also the main theme at the centre of Abu Arab's song 'Hadi ya bahar hadi', which translates into 'Calm down sea, be patient' in which Abu Arab implores the sea to calm its waves and allow Palestinians to return to their homeland. Like most of Abu Arab's songs, this one also begins with the slowly and emotionally sung *mawwal*, which makes up the first two lines below (addressing his family home's mulberry tree). After this, the song picks up pace with line 3 when the singer exhorts the sea to be calm, be patient and to even physically lower its tide to allow for the return of the Palestinians (my translation):

O' mulberry of our home, be patient despite time's oppression.
We shall return despite the length of our journey ... *ya, yaaa, ya yaba*.[14]
O' mulberry, I swear by God, we shall return,
no matter how long our journey is ... *yaba, yaba, yaba, yabaaa ooooooooooooooooooofffff*

(*sung in a faster pace*)

O' sea be calm, we've been away for far too long.
Send my greetings to the land that nurtured us.
O' sea be calm, we've been away for far too long.
Send my greetings to the land that nurtured us.
Send my greetings to the olive tree and to the family that nurtured me ...
And to my loving mother who still sniffs our pillows.

Send my greetings to my land, the soil of my father and grandfathers.
The songbird is still singing for our return.

O' stars send my greetings to the fields and orchards of my homeland.
And the butterflies are flying around awaiting our return.

In this song, Abu Arab sketches a real Palestinian existence as represented by his family's mulberry and olive trees and their orchards that await their return. Abu Arab is saying 'I am from there', as the Palestinian poet Darwish says loud and clear in his poem 'I am from there', which was translated as 'I belong there' in the book *Unfortunately, It Was Paradise* (2003).

What all these artists are saying is that their existence in Palestine is real, not contrived. The evidence is there on the ground. There is no need to consult Biblical records and try to contrive an existence and appropriate or rather *steal* the Indigenous people's culture, ranging from their food to their dress, songs and dances in the way that Zionist settlers have done in Palestine. The mulberry and olive trees that Abu Arab's forebears planted are still there, and they await the Palestinian family's return. These mulberry and olive trees are part of a whole symbology of Palestinian identity and existence of which Abu Arab sings in his rural accent. It is to Palestinian nature and Palestinian life that Abu Arab wishes to return and from which the Palestinian people have been unnaturally separated. His fingerprints, footprints and odour are still on the land that longs for the return of the Palestinian. Similarly, Darwish, in 'I am from there' (انا من هناك), begins his poem with these facts on the ground, so to speak:

> [I am from there]. I have many memories. I was born as everyone is born.
> I have a mother, a house with many windows, brothers, friends, and a prison cell with a chilly window! (2003: 7)

Thus, it is with these actual facts on the ground that Darwish's poem begins. There is the fact of his birth, his mother, brothers and friends who *existed* on this land. It was on his own land that the poet was imprisoned for refusing his own dispossession.

The poet ends with the inevitable return of the Palestinians who have been unnaturally uprooted and separated from their homeland:

> [I am from there]. When heaven mourns for her mother, I return heaven to her mother.
> And I cry so that a returning cloud might carry my tears.
> To break the rules, I have learned all the words needed for a trial by blood.
> I have learned and dismantled all the words in order to draw from them a single word: *Home*.
>
> (2003: 7)

In this poem, as in Abu Arab's song, return is the controlling idea. To return is to make whole again. Separation is dehumanizing and returning to one's homeland is an act of rehumanization because the true 'return' entails a reconstruction and reconstitution of what was so wrongly and inhumanely cut and ruptured. This reconstruction entails a reimagining of Palestine, a Palestine that indeed *existed* in the past and continues to exist in the imaginings of the Indigenous people of the land generation after generation. This return will end the waiting of all the Palestinian Hanthalas, the feeling of being suspended in time and place, of being cut out of time and space. Abu Arab sings, 'O' sea be calm, we've been away for far too long', and the poet answers with 'When heaven mourns for her mother, I return heaven to her mother.' But before the poet and singer can return, there needs to be a complete dismantling of the oppressive Zionist structure in order to be able to 'draw from [its demise] a single word: *Home*.'

In a clear nod to the Palestinian armed resistance, Abu Arab sings the praises of the *fidayeen*, who in his song 'Ya yuma, fi daga 'ala babna', which translates into 'Oh Mother, there's a knock at our door' are portrayed as the fearless heroes of the Palestinian revolution. In a YouTube video, Abu Arab is heard telling the story behind the song. He narrates this story about a *fidai* called Bilal (my translation):

A young man entered [occupied] Palestine, but then the Occupation closed the borders, and the young man and his comrades couldn't go back to Syria or Lebanon. They had to live in caves for six or seven months. In Bilal's home village [in Palestine], his mother was told that he had been martyred in the Battle of Shqeef Castle in Southern Lebanon. His mother accepted condolences from people from the village who came to pay their respects. After a period of a few months, Bilal travelled to his home village and knocked on his mother's door at twelve midnight. She asked who it was, and he answered, 'I'm Bilal'. She said 'You're a liar! You're an Israeli who has come to see if we cooperate with the *fidayeen*, go away!' Bilal went to the neighbours' house and knocked on their door. They opened the door and went to his mother. She opened the door. Instead of kissing her son, she kissed his Kalashnikov rifle.

After a long, soulful *mawwal*, Abu Arab sings these words with the help of his backup singers (my translation):

Oh Mother, there's a knock at our door
Oh Mother, this is the knock of our loved ones.
Oh Mother, this is a strong knock
Oh Mother, this is the knock of *fidaiyeh*.[15]
Oh Mother, the lovers of freedom
are knocking on our door.
Oh Mother, these are the *nashamah*[16]
Oh Mother, the seekers of dignity.
Oh Mother, we are not orphans
Oh Mother, with the presence of our comrades.
Oh Mother, these are the precious ones
Oh Mother, those who seek the heights.
Oh Mother, the ones who stay up all night
to liberate our soil.
Oh Mother, these are my brothers
Oh Mother, the saviours of our homeland.
Oh Mother, they sacrifice for us
Oh Mother, the liberators of our homeland.
Oh Mother, if they amputate my legs
I'd fight them with my hands.
Oh Mother, nuclear bombs do not frighten us.
Oh Mother, this is a strong knock
Oh Mother, the knock of *fidaiyeh*.
Oh Mother, there's a knock at our door
Oh Mother, these are the lovers of freedom.

In this repetitious song, Abu Arab not only sings in praise of the revolutionaries, the *fidayeen*, but importantly takes part in creating the image of the fearless *fidai* who does not fear the Zionist death machine. *Fidai* in Arabic means one who sacrifices himself/herself for a cause. Thus, the idea of sacrifice and martyrdom is inscribed in the very word. Abu Arab sang this song about a fearless *fidai* code named 'Bilal'.[17] This song has recently been repurposed and refocused and sung by the young revolutionaries, the *nashamah* of the 2021 'Save Sheikh Jarrah' and 'Save Silwan' protest movements that have united, for the first time possibly, Palestinians all over the globe under the now popular slogan of 'Palestine will be free, from the river to the sea' – Palestinians under occupation in 1967 Palestine with those in Gaza and 1948 occupied Palestine with those in exile.

The supposed 'Israelization' of Palestinians in 1948 occupied Palestine proved to be false, considering the latest events mentioned above. Palestinians from 1948 occupied Palestine, who were intentionally called 'Arab Israelis' by Israel, rather than Palestinians in order to separate them from Palestinians elsewhere, protested in support of their comrades in Jerusalem/Al Quds. Young Palestinians from Jerusalem/Al Quds fought back against Israel's continuous policies of ethnic cleansing. One of these young Palestinians is 23-year-old Muna El-Kurd, who can be said to have ignited the 'Save Sheikh Jarrah' movement that attracted millions from around the world with her unapologetic, hard-hitting style on social media. El Kurd, along with her twin brother Mohammed El-Kurd, documented Israel's continuous ethnic cleansing of Palestine in their own neighbourhood of Sheikh Jarrah where Israel has forcefully placed settlers from New York in her family home. It is this generation of young people, of revolutionaries, the *nashamah fidayeen* of whom Abu Arab sings that are now facing down Israel's barbaric ethnic cleansing policies inside their very homes and the government supported settler chants of 'death to Arabs' with their *sumud*, documentation, protest, song, thunderous voices and exquisite articulation. It is these young people who could be heard singing Abu Arab's 'Oh Mother, there's a knock at our door' in answer to the 'death to Arabs' chanting of the settlers who are supported by the Israeli Occupation Forces (IOF). These unarmed young Palestinians see themselves as *fidayeen* who fight back with whatever means are available to them. As of this writing (February, 2022), the Zionist occupation forces continue their ethnic cleansing campaign in Sheikh Jarrah and Silwan, a town near the Sheikh Jarrah neighbourhood in Jerusalem/Al Quds by taking over homes of Palestinians and replacing them with Zionist settlers.

Mohammed El-Kurd was able to exquisitely express his experiences in a book of poetry which he called *Rifqa* (2021), the name of his grandmother. El-Kurd perfected the art of answering, commenting on and critiquing Western media coverage of Palestine. In his poem 'Fifteen-Year-Old Girl Killed for Attempting to Kill a Soldier (with a Nail File)', El-Kurd intelligently chooses a line by Fanon as an epigraph to his poem: 'In its bare reality, decolonization reeks of red-hot cannonballs and bloody knives' (29). The main idea of this poem revolves around the Western media's coverage of Palestinian acts of resistance. The poem describes the killing of a fifteen-year-old Palestinian girl who attacked an Israeli soldier with a nail file:

> I held my arsenal.
> People who give excuses for executions
> fear the rifle more than they fear the reason.
> I put her in tulle – girl to their gaze,
> angel to their accusations. Otherwise
>
> nail file becomes the villain, despite
> context. Context: they want cats
> declawed, they want knocked doors
> unanswered, they want the other cheek.
>
> *Terrorist Avenges.* Headlines delusional.
> Are all heads equal? Is a soldier's heart
> Equal to her brother's? I'll hold my arsenal.
> When they ask me next time,
> I'll say God held her hand.
>
> (30)

El-Kurd here criticizes those who 'give excuses for [the] executions' of young Palestinians without providing historical context. The young girl in her death 'tulle' (shroud) ironically becomes the villain and the terrorist in Western 'Headlines delusional'. However, in the next line, El-Kurd alludes to the Egyptian poet Amal Dunqal's poem 'Do not reconcile' in which Dunqul asks 'Are all heads equal?' In line with Dunqul's and Fanon's ideas, El-Kurd postulates that revolutionary violence, unlike colonial violence, is *just* because its aim is the end of oppression. If asked again by Western media what he thinks about Palestinian acts of resistance, which the West calls 'terrorism', El-Kurd writes, 'I'll say God held her hand.'

In fact, it is this Palestinian defiance and resilience in 1967 occupied Palestine, especially in the Sheikh Jarrah neighbourhood that resonated with Palestinians in 1948 occupied Palestine and the resistance in Gaza. Israel's ruthless pounding of Gaza killed hundreds of Palestinians and wiped out whole Palestinian families in addition to flattening several high-rise buildings, including the residence of foreign media. It was from the ruins of these devastated areas in Gaza that a music band of young Gazans chose to perform. Surrounded by the rubble of what used to be a residential high-rise building, the Al-Shuruq tower, a Palestinian band performed popular revolutionary songs originally sung by Al-Firqah al-Markaziyyah (the Central Band) in the 1970s. One of these songs performed by the Gaza band was 'We promise God, we will never leave.' The new band of young Gazans sang these words of defiance and resilience from the site of the devastated Bourj Al Shurouq building, which was totally obliterated by Israeli warplanes in the latest Israeli offensive against Gaza in May-June 2021 (euronews.com).

Palestinian culture is *living*. It need not be excavated. It is not a museum culture that needs to be contrived and taught to settlers coming from different parts of the world. The living heritage of Palestine has been refocused and repurposed for the aim of creating a culture of resistance. To imagine Palestine does not mean to contrive something that was not there, but rather to make possible the very idea of resistance, victory and liberation. Imagining Palestine is an *enabling* idea; this leads us to the last part of this book, which deals with how leading intellectuals, who have long written about the Palestinian cause, imagine a future Palestine as we continue the conversation started by Said in his essay 'On Lost Causes'.

Conclusion

CONTINUING THE CONVERSATION: PALESTINE, A LIVING CAUSE

Said begins his essay entitled 'On Lost Causes', reflecting on how some causes are thought to be 'lost' because these causes are:

> associated in the mind and in practice with a hopeless cause: that is, something you support or believe in that can no longer be believed in except as something without hope of achievement. The time for conviction and belief has passed, the cause no longer seems to contain any validity or promise, although it may once have possessed both.
>
> (527)

Said's definition of what makes a cause lost or living revolves around the idea of belief, conviction – a kind of thinking into being. This indeed is the controlling idea of this book – the power of imagining and refusing defeat. In his essay, Said questions how a people who have been struggling against British colonization and Zionism for over a century can simply surrender in the way that the Palestinian leadership did in Oslo in 1993 with the signing of the Oslo Accords. Said levels a scathing attack against the Palestinian leadership and focuses on the very idea of capitulation and defeatism, which he fiercely rejects and interrogates:

> Let me skip directly to Oslo and after. The mystery there – indeed, from my viewpoint, […] is how a people that had struggled against the British and the Zionists for over a century […] were persuaded […] to declare in effect that their hope of real national reconstruction and real self-determination was in effect a lost cause.
>
> (549)

For Said, defeatism, to be defeated, to surrender is a matter of choice. This is not to say that there are not actual defeats on the ground or the fact that the Palestinian cause was isolated and attacked by the most powerful nations in the world, especially the United States. Moreover, Palestinians did not have the support of surrounding Arab states. All this is true, but to pronounce the death of the

Palestinian cause in the way that the Palestinian leadership has done is, for Said, unforgivable and unconscionable.

Said lashes out at Yasser Arafat for becoming Israel's 'local enforcer' (550) and considers the Palestinian Authority's role as a betrayal of the Palestinian cause. Arafat (and Mahmoud Abbas after him) is a 'symbol of defeat, the very embodiment of a lost cause, now compelled to speak not of Palestinian self-determination but of Israeli security as his top priority' (551). Said, then, uses the power of the intellectual imagination to reject the humiliation, dehumanization and 'dishonor of grinning or bowing survivors who opportunistically fawn on their conquerors' (552). Against this kind of broken will defeatism, Said, using Adorno's ideas, posits the 'intransigence of the individual thinker' (552) who can act, imagine victory, create the very *possibility of resistance* with an intellectual rigor that simply does not, cannot surrender to defeat. It is through thinking, imagining, beginning again that the intransigent individual thinker can 'express the momentum of the general, thereby blunting the anguish and despondency of the lost cause, which its enemies have tried to induce' (553).

In line with the conversation that Said started in 'On Lost Causes', I would argue that the kind of revolutionary intellectual that Said had in mind is the 31-year-old martyr Bassel al-Araj who was killed by Israeli Occupation Forces on 6 March 2017. Al-Araj, now an icon of resistance, was both Said's intransigent intellectual and Kanafani's Khaled in *Returning to Haifa*, one who understood what Palestine means and what it takes to liberate it. Al-Araj, who read and taught revolutionary theory and practice and learned by heart the details of the more than 100-year-old Palestinian struggle against colonialism and the travails of all its heroes, died fighting to the last bullet. After his assassination, pictures were circulated online by Palestinian activists that 'show stains of blood, Bassel's trademark blue show, his *kuffiyeh*, a gun and a pile of books' (*The Electronic Intifada*, Hassan, 2017). A pharmacist by training, he quit his job because he opposed any form of cooperation with the Occupation and started teaching at the 'Popular University, an informal education project' that goes against the mainstream of what is taught at formal Palestinian universities. There, al-Araj taught a 'course called "Palestinian resistance since the inception of settler-colonialism"' (*The Electronic Intifada*, Ashly, 2020). What al-Araj rejected most fiercely is precisely what Said utterly despised before him – and that is the ideology of defeatism.

Because al-Araj was such a revolutionary intellectual, he was feared not only by Israel but also by the Palestinian Authority (PA), the 'local enforcer[s]' of the Occupation, to use Said's term. Before al-Araj was killed by Israel, he was arrested and tortured by the PA along with five of his comrades. One of al-Araj's comrades told *The Electronic Intifada*, 'al-Araj represented the "rejection of defeat" – and was willing to give his life for it …. [he] attempted to help those around him realize that "resistance is possible"' (ibid.). Al-Araj rightly believed that a revolution cannot become a state, an authority or government because the 'obligations and duties of the state became a burden on the back of the revolution, at the expense of liberation' (al-Araj trans. by Nassar, *The Electronic Intifada*, 2020).

These 'states' and 'authorities', such as the PA, do the Occupation's job of silencing revolutionary thought and figures and not allowing for liberation, and for this reason, writes al-Araj about the PA in a book posthumously published under the title *I Have Found My Answers*, 'Let us dismantle it and let them fall'. The title of this book *I Have Found My Answers* (2018) is actually a line taken from his will, which was discovered after al-Araj's assassination:
If you are reading this, then I have died, and my soul has ascended to its Creator.
...

It is hard to write one's own will. I have read for many years the wills of martyrs and have always been puzzled by them: quick, brief, short on eloquence and without satisfying our search for answers to our questions about martyrdom. I am now on the path to my fate satisfied and convinced that I have found my answers. How foolish I was. Is there anything more eloquent than the martyr's act? I was supposed to write this months ago, but what kept me from doing so was your questions, you, the living. Why should I answer you, look for yourselves.
(al-Araj trans. by Nassar, *The Electronic Intifada*, 2020)

The answers that al-Araj found revolve around what life is worth and what Palestine means for the hundreds of thousands who still live in refugee camps, for those who are still suffering in squalid conditions and at military checkpoints.

It is for them that al-Araj not only theorized and taught about resistance, but also acted on it and refused the defeatism of the PA and their cooperation with the colonizers by means of security arrangements to keep Palestinians enslaved and dispossessed after the Oslo Accords turned the *Nakba* into a party, according to Somdeep Sen:

But it was a hastily scribbled proclamation, 'It's a Nakba, Not a Party, Idiots', on a door in Ramallah's Arafat Square that truly grasped the realities of Palestinian politics today [...]. The Oslo accords effectively bureaucratized a guerrilla movement and ensured [...] that the Palestinian fighter took off 'the fatigues and put on a suit'. But in doing so, it instilled all the ostensible symbols of 'normalcy' into the Palestinian every day.
(170)

However, living in refugee camps for over seventy years is not normal; being subjected to continuous ethnic cleansing as we are witnessing today as of this writing in many areas of Jerusalem/Al Quds is not normal; living with military checkpoints is not normal; Palestinian women giving birth and newborn babies dying at military checkpoints is not normal; having several generations of whole families wiped out by Israeli warplanes as witnessed every couple of years in Gaza is not normal; living in the open-air prison of Gaza is not normal; administrative arrests of activists and children and their subjection to the most vicious forms of torture are not normal and the list is endless. It is indeed a continuous *Nakba* and no guise of normalcy can be forced upon this situation. Palestinians everywhere are indeed united in pain, a shared experience of 'historical pain' that is repeated, to use Barghouti's term and concept of repeated historical pain (2011: 144). This can never and will never be normalized. To quote al-Araj's comments on the PA and Israel and all their enabling machinery, 'dismantle it and let them fall.'

What Said was able to foresee in the 1990s – the fact that the Palestinian people can be seen as a unified community has perhaps now become all the more real in 2021–2. This became apparent after the latest protest movements in 1948 occupied Palestine, especially in Lydd and Ramla and the 'Save Sheikh Jarrah', 'Save Silwan' and other Palestinian town protests in 1967 occupied Palestine against continued ethnic cleansing in occupied Jerusalem/Al Quds and the latest response by the Palestinian resistance in Gaza. Said's words in the 1990s about a united Palestinian consciousness ring even more true today, especially when this consciousness has become reinvigorated with Palestinians from 1948 occupied Palestine coming to the defence of their brethren in the 1967 occupied territories along with Palestinians in Gaza and in exile who are all forming a united movement of Palestinian resistance against the Zionist colonization of Palestine. All are, in unison, calling for one free, democratic Palestinian nation from the river to the sea, as the popular slogan has it.

In 'On Lost Causes', Said argues that at the time of the first *intifada* (uprising of Palestinians in occupied Palestine) in late 1987 and which lasted for four years, the tide started turning in favour of Palestinians, and these events certainly had a positive effect on a collective Palestinian consciousness:

> There was certainly an advance in Palestinian consciousness; there was a sense that although we were separated into three entirely discontinuous groups – Israeli Palestinians, inhabitants of the West Bank and Gaza, diaspora Palestinians who made up more than half the total number of our people – we were unified as a people, and regarded as such by an appreciable number of nations; we had now gained the status of a people with a real claim to a homeland.
>
> (547)

This advance in Palestinian consciousness is now more pronounced than it was at the time of Said's writing of the words above. Despite all efforts to separate and divide the Palestinian people into different groupings, give them different namings and provide critical and theoretical discussions on how Palestinians do not constitute a particular national identity, a Palestinian consciousness has indeed remained intact in the Palestinian people's different cultures of exile whether in London, New York or in the Palestinian refugee camps of Syria, Lebanon and Jordan.

The most recent protests in May 2021 have shown the world that Palestinian voices in Al Quds are heard loud and clear in Ramla, Lydd, Gaza and all the places of Palestinian exile in this world. Layla Hallaq, a young Palestinian activist from Haifa told *Al Jazeera* 'What is remarkable is that within '48 [...], Palestinians who have long been ignored or deemed as "Israeli Arabs" are once again restating powerfully that they are Palestinians.' Further commenting on

Palestinian protests in 1948 Palestine, 1967 Palestine, Gaza and of Palestinians in exile, Hallaq states that these protests are indeed 'unprecedented' in the sense that they 'are not only of solidarity, but one of a shared cause and mutual pain experienced by every Palestinian' (*Al Jazeera*.com, Alsaafin, 16 May 2021). In fact, this degree of Palestinian unity had not been experienced before, especially inside 1948 Palestine. Now a new narrative is being constructed for Palestinians everywhere, especially those living inside Zionist controlled lands. Palestinians form a national community with a 'shared cause' and 'mutual pain', a pain that can only be healed by the return of the Palestinians to a liberated Palestine. This new generation of Palestinian activists/revolutionaries, such as Hallaq and Muna and Mohammed El-Kurd, is reformulating and effectively transforming the discourse on Palestine. These young people's invigorating, unabashed and unapologetic style and their very effective use of social media have indeed won the Palestinian cause international solidarity.

In order to continue this conversation started by Said about the vitality of the Palestinian cause and the fact that no cause can ever be lost, I asked several intellectuals who have written extensively about Palestine and the Palestinian cause some questions on how they envision, imagine a future Palestinian nation – in other words to *think* it into being. Participating in this conversation are the following intellectuals, most of whom are themselves Palestinian exiles: Ibrahim Aoude, Nur Masalha, Ilan Pappe, Ramzy Baroud, Rami Siklawi, Terri Ginsberg, Steven Salaita, Jamal Nassar and from inside Gaza, the young professor Refaat Alareer. I am also very happy to include in this conversation the legendary Leila Khaled, a true icon of Palestine who I had the honour of meeting recently. My questions essentially revolved around resistance strategies, envisioning a future Palestine, the right of return and the vitality of the Palestinian cause.

Ibrahim Aoude is a political scientist, the editor of *Arab Studies Quarterly* and a Palestinian refugee/exile who has never returned to his homeland because his 'US passport' allows him 'to visit [occupied Palestine] as a US tourist. And so he will not come until he may return as a Palestinian, alongside all Palestinians who hold the right of return' (Cooper, 2014: xxiii). As Aoude told me in conversation, resistance and liberation strategies must by necessity be multipronged; however, Aoude very clearly spells out that the armed struggle must always be front and centre and integrated with other forms of resistance:

> It is significant to note that civil disobedience and otherwise non-violent struggle undertaken against land seizures, detentions, executions and incarcerations of Palestinian children, men and women have largely been unsuccessful in checking the advances of Zionism in all of Palestine. Those forms of struggle are important and would yield tangible results, if and only if, they are integrated with armed struggle.

As Aoude points out, '[t]he period from 1958 (if not before) until 1 January 1965, had been years of preparation for the beginning of the contemporary armed struggle', a statement which can be corroborated by similar statements made earlier in the book by Khalil Hamdi, one of the founding members of the Arab Nationalist Movement (ANM) in Jordan. Aoude clarifies that a liberation movement must use all 'forms of struggle', but the armed struggle can never be disavowed as the PA has done. It is for this reason that Aoude strongly believes that the PA is a real obstacle to liberation as it is literally the security arm for Israel. Aoude argues '[t]he Palestinian bourgeoisie's betrayal of liberation, had catastrophic consequences culminating in a Palestinian National Authority working as a security force, trained by the US, for the Zionist enemy in exchange for "a fistful of dollars" and privileges stripped of dignity ….' Aoude explains that Israel's strategic goals as a settler colony and the United States' unconditional support for this aggressive form of settler colonialism necessitate *all* forms of resistance against Israel, and this entails replacing the bourgeoisie Palestinian Oslo class and their beneficiaries with 'political forces that go for the jugular of Zionism to liberate all of Palestine'.

Leila Khaled, the iconic Palestinian fighter whose image holding her AK 47 in the late 1960s and early 1970s conquered the world, especially among Palestinians, other Arabs and young people all over the world on the political left, is the epitome of the Palestinian armed struggle for the liberation of Palestine. Khaled's name became the subject of song even for people who did not understand the Palestinian cause.[1] In answer to my question about resistance strategies, Khaled, now in her seventies, is as resolute now as she was in her twenties (my translation from Arabic):

> All forms and means of resistance must be used because we are resisting a brutal and merciless colonizer that must be uprooted from Palestinian land. That's why the armed struggle is our main course of action. Alongside the armed struggle, political and popular means must also be employed; for example, BDS is an excellent way to put pressure on this brutal colonization – all these means of resistance strengthen and vitalize the armed struggle – they all work in unison. The most important point to understand is that this Zionist colonization is enabled by military and economic power. This is why the resistance must be up to this level of challenge. However, the armed struggle is in need of time to make the colonizers feel that they will ultimately lose. The colonized have a moral and legal right to resist by *all means possible*, including armed resistance, and this is based on United Nations' resolutions, which state that all colonized people have a right to armed struggle. All these political attacks against the Palestinian resistance, calling it 'terrorism', are invalid. The worst kind of terrorism is colonization. What have we seen from this settler colonization other than the dispossession of our people, land theft, massacres and the construction of illegal settlements? Organized armed resistance can bring about a change in the balance of power, which in turn will eventually lead to deterrence and the defeat of the colonizer.

Listening to Leila Khaled, one feels that resistance is an embodiment of what it means to be Palestinian. This woman, who in her twenties was involved in physical forms of resistance, is now still, if not more, unwavering in her mental resistance.

Echoing these sentiments is Rami Siklawi, a scholar who has studied Palestinian refugee camps in Lebanon. Siklawi agrees with both Aoude and Khaled, arguing that the 'Palestinian national struggle' [...] represents a continuous 'history of resistance' for over a hundred years, and the Palestinian national identity itself has come to be defined as an 'identity of resistance' on the world stage. In line with thinkers such as Kanafani, Fanon, Cabral and Said, Siklawi argues that Palestinians have every right to use 'all means necessary to resist Zionist colonization'. In total agreement with these thinkers is Terri Ginsberg, an American film studies' scholar, who argues that the 'only way forward' is to:

> push by any means necessary for the overthrow and cessation of Zionist control of the Arab and Middle East region and, in that framework, for the transformation of the global political-economic structures and their cultural entailments which continue to foster capitalist imperialism and/as Zionist hegemony.

One of the fiercest critics of Israel and the author of the groundbreaking book, *The Ethnic Cleansing of Palestine*, the defiant and oppositional historian Ilan Pappe argues that in terms of resistance strategies, 'there is no need to re-invent the wheel and one can base a strategy on past successful struggles of decolonization and liberation. They consist of several elements: a liberation movement struggling on the ground – the Palestinians have been at it since 1920 .... The second element is international solidarity.' This liberation movement on the ground of which Pappe speaks inevitably means that a revolution in progress cannot become a state – that would indeed be a 'betrayal of liberation', as Aoude argues.

Nur Masalha, a well-known Palestinian historian, the editor of *The Journal of Holy Land and Palestine Studies* and the author of several important books on Palestine, including his seminal book entitled *Expulsion of the Palestinians* (1992), believes that there can be no successful resistance strategy 'without creating representative Palestinian leadership, with wide support and legitimacy among the Palestinians'. It is only through this kind of strong unity, states Masalha, that Zionist settler colonialism can be successfully resisted. Moreover, Masalha continues, Palestinian resistance must integrate popular and cultural resistance with strong international solidarity. Ramzy Baroud concurs – a successful resistance strategy must be popular, decentralized and diverse. Such a popular, decentralized, grassroots, collective struggle, argues Baroud, cannot be defeated:

> The power of popular resistance lies in the fact that it is decentralized, diverse, and engages numerous communities. It cannot be easily, if at all, defeated. It follows that any form of resistance that emanates from collective engagement is a legitimate form of resistance, be it civil disobedience ... or armed resistance. Only the people on the ground, whose action is directed by grassroots leaderships are capable of articulating their political discourse and aspirations, and are fully aware of what works and what doesn't in terms of their resistance strategy at any given time and place.

Baroud, like all the intellectuals participating in this conversation, opposes any form of centralized authority (the PA specifically) during the struggle for liberation or a revolution in progress. This authority by its very nature does not and cannot represent the Palestinian people or their aspirations for a liberated Palestine precisely because it (the PA) exists to facilitate the occupation and preserve the security of Israel.

Providing an added strand to the discussions above is an important voice belonging to a young Palestinian professor from the besieged, open-air prison of Gaza, Refaat Alareer, who edited an impressive collection of short stories called, *Gaza Writes Back: Short Stories from Young Writers in Gaza, Palestine* (2014). Alareer's brother, Mohammed Alareer, a young father of two, was brutally killed in 2014 by 'an Israeli airstrike while at home. While he was at home' in a neighbourhood of Gaza called Shijaiya, 'whose name means the "land of the brave"' (Alareer, 2014). In answer to my question about resistance strategies, Alareer's answer is quick, direct and unequivocal – 'ALL means of resistance are legitimate and even moral.' Alareer's words perhaps unintentionally invoke the ideas of Walter Benjamin's divine or revolutionary violence in his essay called 'Critique of violence' and Fanon's ideas on the transformational violence of the oppressed.

For Alareer, as he told me in conversation, such brutal settler colonialism must be countered by using *all means possible*. He explains that Israel's continuous ethnic cleansing and genocide of the Palestinian people 'proves that it is not only armed Palestinian resistance that Israel is after. Israel is after the very existence of Palestinians'. Alareer is accurate here – Israel does not only want to destroy the armed resistance. Israel's exaggerated use of violence, using the most destructive weapons known to man against civilians in Gaza, is aimed at terrorizing people, breaking their will by means of Israel's false and baseless hope that Palestinian people will eventually surrender, just get up and leave. Alareer argues that 'Israel' has massacred Palestinians even during peaceful protests, such as the 'Great March of Return' in Gaza where hundreds of unarmed Palestinians, including young medics and people in wheelchairs, were mercilessly killed by Israeli snipers. It was hunting season for the brutal occupier. In the occupied 'West Bank', where there is no organized armed resistance, says Alareer, Palestinians are slaughtered on a daily basis, their homes demolished and their lands stolen from them.

Steven Salaita, whose criticism of Israel on social media cost him his position at the University of Illinois at Urbana-Champaign, insists that in addition to diverse resistance strategies (the Boycott, Divest, Sanctions movement, armed struggle, peaceful protests and stone throwing), voices from across the ideological spectrum must by necessity be represented – both secular and religious (Islamic). Salaita's important point on the mobilization of all sectors of society is, in fact, emphasized by the anti-colonial thinker Fanon who states in his book *The Wretched of the Earth*, '[a] struggle which mobilizes all classes of the people and which expresses their aims and their impatience, which is not afraid to count almost exclusively on the people's support, will of necessity triumph' (246). In fact, this is a point that all who participated in this conversation agreed upon. The mobilization of the masses, cutting across all sectors, social classes, religions, sects and ethnicities, is foundational and a key to the success of the Palestinian struggle. An interesting point to mention here is that everyone either directly or indirectly mentioned the great significance of the Boycott, Divest and Sanctions (BDS) movement, which according to the social scientist Jamal Nassar is a very effective resistance strategy: 'Given the state of apartheid that exists, the most effective strategy is the boycott, divestment and sanctions [movement] to make apartheid too expensive to maintain.'

In answer to the question on how he envisions a future Palestinian nation, Pappe's response is worth quoting in full:

> My own preferred vision is a one democratic state solution. It is a very good question to ask what nation it would be. The basis, in my mind, has to be the Palestinian nation, and it would decide how to integrate, what is by now a third generation of Jewish settlers, who over the years became a separate ethnic group. Its collective cultural rights can be recognized within the building of a future Palestine. It will be an incremental process that would include the dismantling of the colonialist Zionist institutions, the introduction of a restitutive justice mechanism for Palestinian repatriation and compensation and finally redistribution of the natural resources, such as land. Like the rest of the Mashreq, its version of democracy will also engage with the Islamic civilization and the collective identities still cherished by some communities.

Pappe's response speaks to the historical and moral injustice inflicted upon the Palestinian people, and I think that his vision of a one democratic state in a future *Palestinian* nation that would entail the total dismantlement of all 'colonialist Zionist institutions' addresses the very core of the historical injustice of the *Nakba* or what Pappe has called the 'ethnic cleansing of Palestine'. It is quite significant that Pappe's use of terms such as 'restitutive justice', 'repatriation' 'compensation' and a 'redistribution of natural resources', namely land allows for the healing of deep, historical pain and also allows for the necessary 'building of a future Palestine', a democratic state that could then indeed integrate what Pappe calls a 'third generation of Jewish settlers' as a 'separate ethnic group' with full rights within a future Palestine. This kind of integration is, of course, 'incremental', and this is not only an integral part of the building or constructing process, but is also significantly and essentially part of the healing process. The last part of Pappe's response very effectively addresses a democratic Palestine that would at the same time allow for the return of Palestine to itself, its history and culture, so to speak. Palestine belongs to the Mashreq, *Bilad al-Sham*, which existed within the context of an Islamic civilization that has always been open to the diverse, collective identities of this region.

Aoude's imagining of Palestine, like Pappe's above, draws out the contours of a Palestinian nation that most effectively and justly addresses the past, present and future of *Bilad al-Sham* and the greater Arab region, with a tortured Palestine at its heart. Aoude sees Palestine as the core, the centre of a much larger anti-Zionist and anti-global capitalist project. Aoude argues that an all-encompassing, multi-pronged resistance strategy would have to work in unison in order:

> to achieve the strategic goals of the Palestinian revolution – A Palestinian State for all those who envision living in a democratic, multiethnic, multiracial society. Only the defeat of the Zionist-global capitalist project in West Asia and North Africa and the upholding of the national rights of the Palestinian people, especially UN Security Council Resolution 194 that calls for the return of the Palestinian refugees to Palestine can bring peace with justice to the region.

In fact, Aoude's vision of a 'democratic, multiethnic, multiracial society' in a future Palestine is one with which all the intellectuals taking part in this conversation wholeheartedly agree. There was no mention of a 'two state solution' or even a 'bi-national state solution' by any of the intellectuals with whom I engaged in conversation.

On how she imagines a future Palestinian nation, Khaled combined this imagining of Palestine with the Palestinian right of return. This woman warrior took her time with this question, bringing up facts and detailing who has the right to return according to UN resolution 194 to romanticizing about what she imagines this return would look like. All the interviewer could do in this situation is to sit back and *listen*, and let this great woman speak her truth:

> I imagine a democratic state where everyone can live equally – this is a human and ethical aim. For Jews who now live in occupied Palestine, I say our problem is not with Jews. Our problem is that we are colonized, and we were expelled from our lands [Khaled was born in Haifa, Palestine and her family was expelled from their home in 1948 and fled to Lebanon]. How do I imagine Palestine? Well, first, Palestinians must return – yes, this is the beginning of my imagining of Palestine. Of course, this will not happen easily because we must reach a point, where by means of the *continuation* of our struggle, there would be a dismantling of this Zionist state and enemy losses under colonization are greater than their winnings ... I can only imagine a democratic state with the return of the Palestinian refugees to their lands, according to UN resolution 194. For Israelis who have already settled on our land, they will have two options: 1.) they agree to live in a free, democratic Palestine as equal citizens with Palestinians or 2.) they leave to the countries of their origins. Palestinians really have no option but to return to Palestine, and this is a right protected not only by UN resolutions, but is also a moral and just right because the Palestinian cause is a just cause ... I imagine that Palestine will welcome its people who were expelled 73 years ago ... I imagine that the trees will welcome us back, the rocks of Palestine will welcome us back. I know my words here are romantic and imaginary, but the pain is deep and our longing to return is very strong .... And Palestine must return to its Arab roots ... Palestine is an integral part of this region, this Mashreq.

For Khaled, we cannot speak of the liberation of Palestine and Palestinians without the liberation of all of historic Palestine from the grasp of the colonizer and the return of the Palestinian refugees. Khaled even questioned the listing of a two-state solution or binational state as options alongside the one state solution in the question itself.

Similarly, for Masalha, the two-state solution was never a viable option because it was always 'a cover for Israeli apartheid and annexation processes in the West Bank'. According to Masalha, there is really only 'one rational and progressive solution: a "democratic state" in historic Palestine in which everyone will be an equal citizen. Cultural, religious and linguistic rights will be guaranteed to all social groups.' Similarly, Baroud believes that the 'so-called "Two State Solution"' could never 'deliver the most basic justice to the Palestinian people. First, it will accentuate their [Palestinians in different areas] political and geographic fragmentation [and] break down their sense of nationhood.' Baroud continues that since the Palestinian right of return is a central issue for any future 'solution', the only real prospect is the one state solution 'as it will end Palestinian fragmentation'.

Like Khaled and Baroud, the three intellectuals – Pappe, Aoude and Siklawi – underscore the absolute necessity of the Palestinian right of return, which they argue is a legal and moral right. On '11 December 1948, the United Nations General Assembly issued [...] UN resolution 194, during its third session, which stipulated that Palestinians have the right of return to their homes in Palestine' (Siklawi), and this essential right 'has to be an integral part of such a solution. It is a prerequisite without which there is no hope for any solution' (Pappe). It is with the return of the Palestinian refugees to Palestine as stipulated by 'UN Security Council Resolution 194' that 'peace with *justice* [can be brought] to the region' (My emphasis, Aoude). All the intellectuals with whom I spoke declared the resounding death of the two-state solution. Nassar says that a few years back the so-called two state solution was on life support, but now it has completely died 'with no chance of resurrection'.

Similarly, for Ginsberg, the two-state solution simply does not exist in her dictionary since she does not even mention it in her response to my question on how she envisions a future Palestine. Emphasizing the absolute need to dismantle Zionism, Ginsberg reiterates:

> the classic Palestine liberationist position that a genuine solution will only be reached if Zionism is completely removed as a structural foundation of any ensuing state formation, which means Zionists must relinquish their wrongheaded belief, borne of false consciousness, that Jewish safety may only be achieved through the establishment and maintenance of a Jewish-supremacist national entity in historic Palestine or anywhere else, for that matter.

Ginsberg believes that the biggest remaining obstacle in the necessary dismantlement of Zionist structures is what she calls the 'prevailing cynicism' of official Palestinian bodies, such as the Palestinian Authority and Arab regimes that believe that the Zionist entity cannot be defeated. This defeatist attitude, argues,

Ginsberg, is a form of 'complicity' that sees the current status quo as unchangeable; these defeated parties 'refus[e] to challenge [Zionism] explicitly and thickly' because they believe that nothing can ever exist outside the global capitalist order.

In her excellent book *Visualizing the Palestinian Struggle: Towards a Critical Analytic of Palestine Solidarity Film* (2016), Ginsberg underscores the significance of Palestine solidarity films, such as *The Palestinian*, which features the British actress Vanessa Redgrave 'holding a Kalashnikov AK rifle above her head [...] dancing against only a blue sky in the background, marking a moment of *jouissance* that is [... an] expression of a real need "to liberate Palestine"' (73). Agreeing with Ginsberg and the other intellectuals taking part in this conversation, Alareer also imagines 'one democratic state for all regardless of religion, or colour, or race' in a 'free Palestine from the river to the sea'; however, after the total dismantlement of Israel, Alareer underscores, all '[r]acist Zionists who have blood on their hands must be tried for war crimes' and crimes against humanity.

In answer to my question on whether or not the Palestinian cause is a living one, there was complete consensus – a resounding yes. As Baroud explains, '[a] cause is living or dead, won or lost, based largely, if not entirely, on the will of those who are fighting for it'. For Ginsberg, the very justice and inclusivity of the Palestinian cause are indeed what keeps it *living* – this is a 'single Palestinian state for all of its inhabitants, from the river to the sea, regardless of their religious affiliation, [which] plays itself out in a dialectical relationship with Zionist efforts to quash it'. For Khaled, Palestine is an open wound, and as long as this 'historical injustice is not addressed ... and because [the Nakba continues], and the Palestinian people continue to resist, this cause will remain alive'. The most recent events that are still taking place in Sheikh Jarrah, Silwan, Beita, Lifta and other Palestinian towns where the continuous ethnic cleansing of Palestine is countered with Palestinian *sumud*, defiance and resilience, have proved to the world that Palestine is indeed a very living cause. This is not only because of the intransigence of Palestinian intellectuals, but more importantly the intransigence and *sumud* of the Palestinian people inside and outside occupied Palestine – those who struggle on the ground and those in exile, whether in refugee camps or in the world's largest cities. The Palestinian community in every corner of this earth has indeed united under the umbrella of a distinct Palestinian national identity, an identity which, despite or perhaps precisely because of the many cultures of exile in which Palestinians live, refuses to die. It is this kind of intransigence that has won the Palestinians and their cause, not mere sympathy, but international solidarity (Masalha).

As Pappe points out, however, while there is a 'dramatic shift in western, and global public opinion about Palestine', this solidarity has not in any way impacted 'politics from above and the mainstream media in the West'. And as if to further illustrate Pappe's point about 'politics from above', Pappe wrote in a Facebook post on 27 July 2021 about his own silencing by Facebook and YouTube:

> Today Facebook and Youtube went one step further in succumbing to Zionist pressure. Early today I was supposed to converse with John Pilger on Palestine

[... but we] were blocked on Youtube [...]; half an hour ago I was supposed to speak through a chat room on FB with Paul Salvator[i] [...] and we were not allowed to go on air.

Pappe ended the above post with the words, 'We will not be silenced and will tell the truth about the oppression of Palestine.' The continuous effort to silence the Palestinian narrative underscores the fact that Palestine still does not have the permission to narrate its story, as Said would say.

However, the narrators of Palestine have grown in number, and as this conclusion shows their voices have also grown louder and more defiant of the colonial, racist Zionist regime and their enablers. All the intellectuals participating in this conversation emphasized the dismantlement of Israel and its institutions. Siklawi argues that Zionism is an imperialist and racist ideology, which does not have roots in the Arab region or in historic Palestine. There was never a historical Israel prior to 1948: 'Once the British completed their colonial duties, the Zionist occupation of Palestine began in 1948. One should be mindful that the British colonial occupation of Palestine played the key role in facilitating Zionist settlements and reinforcing Zionist power inside Palestine prior to 1948.' It is now becoming clearer to the international community, especially at the level of the masses, that Zionism is indeed an extreme form of apartheid[2] and any just solution would have to include at its very heart the complete dismantlement of Israel – to quote Bassel al-Araj, 'Let us dismantle it and let them fall.'

If there is one word that perhaps best encapsulates the Palestinian experience and the very *act* of imagining Palestine, it would have to be return, in Arabic *awda*. عودة Palestinian intellectuals, poets, refugees, exiles, even those living under occupation have all imagined and reimagined their return home to Palestine. The living speak of returning, the dying speak of being returned to Palestine. In fact, as Khaled explained, return is a deeply entrenched idea in the Palestinian imaginary: the 'Palestinian right of return has become historical and cultural knowledge ... that is handed down from one generation to the next.' The concept of return has come to take on different shades of meaning in the Palestinian vocabulary. Because the Palestinian experience is very much about rupture, being cut out of time and place, being separated from one's geography, home and family and being exiled, return is not only about returning to a physical place – home. It is also about returning to one's history, culture, to one's space and self, to enable the healing and construction process to begin. When a people are forced to live and die in refugee camps for all their lives, they dream of return, a return to life, to end the waiting and allow Palestinian time to continue or after the rupture, to begin again. Sometimes, the words 'refugee camps' become just words to scholars writing about the Palestinian cause, but for the people of the camps, it is a way of life – a very difficult life that has its roots in catastrophe, and for the millions of these refugees, the catastrophe continues.

In an article entitled 'The Palestinian Refugee Camps in Lebanon Post 1990: Dilemmas of Survival and Return to Palestine', Siklawi argues that these refugees have been 'forgotten by the international community and the Arab regimes', and all sides in this equation are 'partners in this crime', which has prolonged 'Palestinian suffering' (2019: 80). Siklawi points out that these Palestinian refugees in Lebanon live in the most difficult and inhumane conditions:

> these refugee camps are actually *ghettos* with inhuman living conditions. Adding to the Palestinians' hellish existence are several factors, such as deprivation from work permits and the lack of civil rights. This has led to the emergence of many social diseases, such as drugs, crime, and the shift toward extremism.
>
> (81)

Siklawi goes on to explain that these refugee ghettos become almost like inescapable prisons. Once you are born in a refugee camp, you are condemned to it, unable to leave due to the security situation in Lebanon. Siklawi quotes Sheikh Maher Hammoud from Lebanon in this conversation about Palestinians who live in very inhumane and unhealthy living conditions in Lebanon's refugee camps and are unable to leave:

> [They] are unable to leave the camps for various reasons and due to the lack of opportunities. Even to leave Lebanon and obtain a visa is very difficult except by means of illegal immigration through the sea towards Europe. However, inside the camps, the living conditions are unhealthy: no roads, no infrastructure, too many people and too little income. Entering and leaving the camps is very complicated and usually controlled by the security situation.
>
> (81)

Despite the seeming hopelessness of Palestinian life in the refugee camps, Palestinians have been able to survive – against all odds.

As Khaled explained to me in conversation, the main role of the 'Palestinian woman after the1948 Nakba … was in protecting her family. And the Palestinian woman [in the refugee camps] did indeed protect her family when the man was either imprisoned, martyred or fighting.' These Palestinian refugees in Lebanon, but also in Jordan, Syria and occupied Palestine – all Palestinian exiles have a legal and moral right to return to Palestine. Return is indeed the dream of every Palestinian, a dream that has deep roots in a reality in the making. Perhaps then it is not difficult to understand why in 2001 on Said's last trip to South Africa where he visited the 'District Six Museum', 'Said signed his name and wrote a simple yet profound one-word message on the museum's memorial cloth in Arabic: "Return"' (Vally, 2017: 4). This collective Palestinian return will enable al-Ali's refugee child, Hanthala, to finally face forward and make his way home. Darwish can finally declare the 'return of the wandering soul as if nothing had happened' (2003: 161), and Barghouti can announce the 'return of the millions, that is the true return' because '[o]ur dead are still in the cemeteries of others. Our living are clinging to foreign borders' (2005: 38).

During the writing of this book, many Palestinians (in blood and heart) who are an integral part of the Palestinian narrative and revolution, which is still being written, passed from this life before fulfilling their dream of return. I name some of them here, to quote the Irish poet William Bulter Yeats, 'To murmur name upon name/As a mother names her child' – my father, Khalil Ismail Hamdi, one of the founders of the Arab Nationalist Movement and the armed struggle for the liberation of Palestine, my brother, Hamdi Khalil Hamdi, the scientist who rooted his science in the very nature of Palestine, the two great Palestinian poets, Mourid Barghouti who sang of Palestine's repeated historical pain and Izzidin al-Manasra, whose only wish was 'not to sleep in a grave in exile', the fearless professor and oppositional intellectual who spoke truth to power, Abdelsattar Qasem, and who wanted to take part in this conversation, but left us before he could and Anis al-Naqash, the great Lebanese revolutionary who was every bit a Palestinian, and who when he knew of the imminence of his own death, wrote, 'My life is done, but the [Palestinian] narrative has not ended.' To all the martyrs of Palestine – we promise you to continue the struggle until there is a collective return to Palestine that would truly enable the Palestinian people to finally realize their genuine liberation, *TAHRIR*.

NOTES

Figures

1   Illustrations 4.1–4.3 are published with the permission of the Naji al-Ali family.

Introduction

1   Ethnic cleansing is a term used by the historian Ilan Pappe in his book entitled *The Ethnic Cleansing of Palestine* (2006). Pappe asserts that the term Nakba is 'an elusive term as it refers more to the disaster itself rather than to who or what caused it' (xvii). This is why Pappe prefers the term ethnic cleansing as it suggests that there is an agent that caused this catastrophe.
2   The Palestinian poet Mourid Barghouti maintains that the term 'West Bank' represents verbicide or the genocide of language, and Palestinians should avoid falling into the trap of using such terminology. The poet writes in *New Internationalist* (2003): 'When the Israeli army occupied Deir Ghassaneh [Barghouti's home village] and the whole eastern part of Palestine in 1967, the news bulletins began to speak of … [Israel's] occupation of the West Bank. The pollution of language can get no more blatant than in the term West Bank. West of what? Bank of what? The reference here is the west bank of the River Jordan, not to eastern Palestine. The west bank of a river is a geographical location – not a country, not a homeland.'
3   Haram al-Sharif refers to the Masjid Al Aqsa compound, which includes Masjid Al Aqsa and the Dome of the Rock.
4   The resistance that is discussed here describes the armed resistance that started forming after the ethnic cleansing of Palestine in 1948. However, Palestinian resistance against the British mandate of Palestine was already in place before 1948. Rosemary Sayigh (2007) points out that the 'roots of the [Palestinian] Revolution can be traced back' to the 'Great Revolt of 1936–39, and the uprising of Sheikh Izzideen al-Qassam that exploded it' (152).
5   The 'I' in the word Indigenous is used in its capitalized form for good reason. According to Christine Weeber, this was first used by the University of British Columbia's Indigenous Foundations. This capitalization of the 'I' was 'later adopted by the United Nations'. According to the UN, Indigenous is 'used to refer broadly to peoples of long settlement and connection to specific lands who have been adversely affected by incursions by industrial economies, displacement, and settlement of their traditional territories by others' (Weeber, 19 May 2020). While the UN uses the capitalized version to refer to some Indigenous populations, such as Native Americans or American Indians, the First Nations of Canada and other peoples around the world, it does not do so within the context of the Palestinian people. However, the definition of Indigenous communities provided by the UN

applies to the Palestinian context, and thus this term is capitalized in this book when referring to the Indigeneity of the Palestinians and all other Indigenous communities.

6 'Shock and Awe' is a terroristic military strategy used by the United States at the time of the invasion of Iraq in 2003. The aim of this strategy is to achieve 'rapid dominance over an adversary by the initial imposition of overwhelming force and firepower'. See https://www.oxfordreference.com/view/10.1093/oi/authority.20110803100502693.

7 See 'From Sheikh Jarrah to Silwan, Israel's ethnic cleansing goes [on] with impunity', *The Jordan Times* (7 July 2021) https://www.jordantimes.com/opinion/osama-al-sharif/sheikh-jarrah-silwan-israels-ethnic-cleansing-goes-impunity and 'The draconian law used by Israel to steal Palestinian land' *Al Jazeera* (8 July 2021) https://www.aljazeera.com/news/2021/7/8/how-israel-backs-settlers-to-confiscate-palestinian-lands

8 See 'US ends aid to Palestinian refugee agency Unrwa', *BBC News* (31 August 2018) https://www.bbc.com/news/world-us-canada–45377336

9 The original years of publication of Kanafani's books, as shown here, were taken from Bashir Abu-Manneh's book entitled *The Palestinian Novel: From 1948 to the Present* (2016).

Chapter 1

1 'Israel has a right to self-defense' is a long-standing refrain to every atrocity committed by Israel, the most recent aggressions include the total flattening of high-rise residential buildings and the killing of whole families in Gaza in May 2021. See an example of this here: https://www.nytimes.com/2021/05/12/world/middleeast/biden-netanyahu-israel.html

2 For example, the US invasion of Iraq in 2003 was called by the American aggressors 'Operation Iraqi Freedom'. Thus, the Americans were supposedly bringing Iraqis 'freedom' by literally killing hundreds of thousands of Iraqis. For the naming of the American invasion of Iraq, see: https://www.history.navy.mil/browse-by-topic/wars-conflicts-and-operations/middle-east/operation-iraqi-freedom.html

3 Louis Althusser's description of ideological state apparatuses (ISAs) are especially helpful in understanding how the state can manipulate several state apparatuses, especially the media in order to create the kind of hegemonic thinking or mind control necessary, enabling the state to gain the 'consent' of the public.

4 Tareq Ismail's and Max Fuller's essay entitled 'The disintegration of Iraq: The manufacturing and politicization of sectarianism' (2008) is a good example. Also, Raymond Baker's, Shireen Ismail's and Tareq Ismail's excellent book entitled *Cultural Cleansing in Iraq: Why Museums Were Looted, Libraries Burned and Academics Murdered*, expands on the West's role in repurposing and inciting this divide to enable the desired 'state ending' and refashioning of a New Middle East.

5 For more information on the numbers of Palestinians martyred and injured in the 'Great March of Return', see this document prepared by the United Nations in 2020: https://www.un.org/unispal/document/two-years-on-people-injured-and-traumatized-during-the-great-march-of-return-are-still-struggling/

Chapter 2

1. See Sinan Antoon's 'In the Presence of Darwish' in *The Nation* (2008).
2. See Leila Shahid's article entitled 'Testimonies: The Sabra and Shatila Massacres: Eye Witness Reports' (2002).
3. The United States' destructive role in the Arab World certainly cannot be summarized in a footnote. US intervention whether in Iraq, Libya, Syria, Yemen, Lebanon or occupied Palestine, to which all other interventions are ultimately tied, has caused mass destruction and fragmentation, not only in the infrastructure of these nations, but also in their social fabric. The US government calls this 'creative chaos', a 'strategy envisioned by the Bush administration to create havoc in the Arab world in order to restructure a "new Middle East" whose necessary pain has been catastrophic for key Arab states, especially Iraq and Syria' (Hamdi, 2016a: 36).
4. This senseless killing introduced the 'I can't breathe' slogan, which were the last words that George Floyd uttered before his death under the 'knee-to-neck maneuver' of the white police officer.
5. Ferguson refers to the shooting death of a young black man named Michael Brown in Ferguson, Missouri by a white policeman in 2014. This incident resulted in mass protests and unrest in Ferguson. In the same year, half way across the world, Israel heavily bombarded the Gaza Strip, killing over 2,251 Palestinians and wounding more than 11,000. For more on this solidarity movement, see Kristian Davis Bailey's 'Black-Palestinian Solidarity in the Ferguson-Gaza Era' (2015).
6. The Jim Crow laws were a 'collection of state and local statutes that legalized racial segregation' and 'existed for about 100 years, from the post-Civil War era until 1968' (history.com).
7. I am using the term 'Trumpism' here to refer to the white nationalist fervour that came to the fore during the Trump administration (2016–20).
8. This poem has also been translated by Fady Joudah as 'The "Red Indian's" Penultimate Speech to the White Man' (*Harvard Review*, 2009). However, here I am using the translation by Sargon Boulos from the book *Mahmoud Darwish: The Adam of Two Edens* (2000).
9. Steven Salaita provides an interesting reading of Darwish's poem, 'The "Red Indian's" Penultimate Speech to the White Man' in his excellent book entitled *Inter/Nationalism: Decolonizing Native American and Palestine* (2016). Salaita uses Fady Joudah's translation in *Harvard Review* (2009). Ramzy Baroud's online article entitled 'Palestinian-Native American Link Is Slowly Merging' (2016) offers some insights into Darwish's 'Speech of the Red Indian', using Sargon Boulos's translation in *The Adam of Two Edens* (2000). Ben White's online article 'Dispossession, Soil, and Identity in Palestinian and Native American Literature' (2005) briefly discusses 'The Speech of the Red Indian'.
10. Anti-Semitism is a curious accusation levelled against Arabs who are, in fact, a Semitic people who speak a Semitic language. Thus, technically, to be accused of being anti-Semitic for an Arab individual means to be accused of self-hatred.
11. Although Ibn Khaldoun is a renowned and well-respected fourteenth-century Arab scholar and historian who is said to be one of, if not, the most important figure in the fields of historiography and sociology ('Ibn Khaldun': *New World Encyclopedia*), Darwish attacks the thinker for surrendering his nation/people to the Mongols.
12. For more information on BDS, see their website at https://bdsmovement.net/what-is-bds
13. See Surat Al-'Ankabut in the *Holy Quran*, Chapter 29:41.

Chapter 3

1. See Salman Rushdie's interview with Edward Said (1986) on YouTube: https://www.youtube.com/watch?v=vAmLNc_4VtE. This interview was published in the *New Left Review*.
2. For more information on this kind of Israeli-Arab alliance, see two articles: '"Decorating the cage": How UAE Plans to Modernize Israeli Checkpoints Could Entrench Israel's Occupation' (english.alaraby.co.uk) and 'UAE Investment in Upgrading Israeli Checkpoint Only Entrenches Occupation' (english.wafa.ps).
3. These are words taken from Barghouti's memoir (*ISR*). Commenting on the real physical quality of the 'Occupied Territory', Barghouti states, 'Who would dare make it into an abstraction now that it has declared its physical self to the senses?' (6).

Chapter 4

1. Although mainstream media and academia have not yet latched on to the Palestinian cause (and perhaps never will because they represent the very power that enables them), the Palestinian cause has gained in popularity and international solidarity recently (May–June 2021) with the 'Save Sheikh Jarrah', 'Save Silwan', 'Save Beita' and 'Save Lifta' protest movements and Israel's massacres of whole Palestinian families in Gaza and the total destruction of residential buildings and infrastructure. This will be discussed in more detail in the conclusion.
2. It has been reported that a Palestinian student by the name of Ismail Suwan who worked for the Israeli Mossad assassinated Naji al-Ali in London: 'Ten months after Naji al-Ali was shot, Scotland Yard arrested a Palestinian student who turned out to be a Mossad agent. Under interrogation, the Jerusalem-born man, Ismail Suwan, said that his superiors in Tel Aviv had been briefed well in advance of the plot to kill the cartoonist' (El Fassed, *The Electronic Intifada*, 2004).
3. In colloquial Arabic, a 'tanbal' means one who is very lazy; as used by al-Ali, however, 'tanbal' means one who has a lazy (im)moral conscience or no conscience at all.
4. I would like to acknowledge the advice of Naji al-Ali's son, Khalid al-Ali for his gracious help and permission to use the cartoons that appear in this section.
5. Actually, the painting on the wall is a very close representation of the picture of Leila Khaled in her youth at the time she (along with her PFLP comrades) hijacked airplanes, one in 1969 and another in 1970. See Sarah Irving's important book on Leila Khaled entitled, *Leila Khaled: Icon of Palestinian Liberation* (2012), published by Pluto Press.
6. A *mawwal* is a part in a song where the singer expresses his or her vocal virtuosity by repeating a certain word or phrase, not necessarily meaning anything in particular, but expressing a kind of reflective sorrow or joy.
7. A direct translation of *ya Khal* is 'Oh uncle'; however, here no one in particular is being addressed. This is a general expression of communion.
8. A direct translation of *Ya Ein* is 'Oh (my) eye'.
9. The theme of martyrdom in poems and songs has been popular in Palestine for more than ninety years, which began with the Palestinian resistance against the British colonizers. The poem above written by the popular Palestinian poet Nuh Ibrahim commemorates the execution of the three martyrs, Mohammed Jamjoum, Fouad

Hijazi and Atta Al Zeer, in 1929. This theme of martyrdom continued, of course, into the 1930s with the Palestinian Revolt against the British colonizers from 1936 to 1939.
10. *Kohl* is a black eye make-up that Palestinians and Arabs, in general, wear. While wearing this eye make-up is very common among women, men, especially bridegrooms in traditional Palestinian society, also wear this eye make-up. It is also common for mothers to use this eye make-up on their babies in traditional Palestinian culture.
11. The flag of the revolution is the Palestinian flag.
12. *Aaakh* here is an expression of pain or painful longing. Ya Yuma means oh mother.
13. *Ooof* here does not have a specific meaning, but is a traditional sound made in the *mawwal* and can be understood as an expression of sorrow.
14. *ya, yaaa, ya yaba translates into* oh, oooh, oh father.
15. *Fidaiyeh* refers to the Palestinian *fidayeen*, the armed fighters of the Palestinian revolution.
16. *Nashamah* is a word used in Levantine culture to describe young men and women who are respectful, hospitable, brave, dignified, proud and loyal to their homeland.
17. Bilal's real name is Basheer Taqatqa. He fought against Israel's occupation of Southern Lebanon in the early 1970s (heritagepalestinian.blogspot.com).

Conclusion

1. The British band The Tear Drop Explodes sang a song in honour of Leila Khaled entitled 'Like Leila Khaled Said'; however, as the lyrics of this song seem to show, this song, ironically, has nothing to do with the Palestinian cause.
2. Some important human rights organizations, such as Amnesty International, have declared that Israel is an apartheid state. Agnes Callamard, Amnesty International's Secretary General, states 'Our report reveals the true extent of Israel's apartheid regime. Whether they live in Gaza, East Jerusalem and the rest of the West Bank, or Israel itself, Palestinians are treated as an inferior racial group and systematically deprived of their rights' (amnesty.org).

BIBLIOGRAPHY

Books

Abu-Fakhr, Saqr. (2003) *The Palestinian National Movement: From the Armed Struggle to a Disarmed State*. Beirut: Arab Institute for Research and Publishing.
Abulhawa, Susan. (2011) *Mornings in Jenin*. London: Bloomsbury.
Abulhawa, Susan. (2015) *The Blue between Sky and Water*. New York and London: Bloomsbury.
Abu-Lughod, Lila. (2007) 'Return to Half-Ruins: Memory, Postmemory, and Living History in Palestine'. In Sa'di, Ahmad and Abu-Lughod, Lila, (eds). *Nakba: Palestine, 1948 and the Claims of Memory*. New York: Columbia University Press, 77–104.
Abu-Lughod, Lila and Sa'di, Ahmad. (2007) 'Introduction: The Claims of Memory'. In Sa'di, Ahmad and Abu-Lughod, Lila, (eds). *Nakba: Palestine, 1948 and the Claims of Memory*. New York: Columbia University Press, 1–24.
Abu-Manneh, Bashir. (2016) *The Palestinian Novel: From 1948 to the Present*. Cambridge, UK: Cambridge University Press.
Akash, Munir. (2000) 'Introduction'. In Darwish, Mahmoud. *The Adam of Two Edens*. Akash, Munir and Moore, Daniel (trans.). Syracuse, NY: Syracuse University Press, 19–46.
Alajaji, Sylvia. (2013) 'Performing Self: Between Tradition and Modernity in the West Bank'. In Kanaaneh, Moslih, Thorsen, Stig-Magnus, Bursheh, Heather and McDonald, David A. (eds). *Palestinian Music and Song: Expression and Resistance since 1900*. Bloomington and Indianapolis: Indiana University Press, 97–113.
Ali, Kazim. (2010) 'Afterword'. In Hammad, Suheir (ed), *Born Palestinian, Born Black & The Gaza Suite*. Brooklyn, NY: UpSet Press, 93–5.
Anderson, Benedict. (2006 [1983]) *Imagined Communities*. London and New York: Verso.
Antoon, Sinan. (2011) 'Translator's Preface'. In Darwish, Mahmoud, *In the Presence of Absence*, Antoon, Sinan (trans.). Brooklyn, NY: Archipelago Books, 5–9.
Ashcroft, Bill and Ahluwalia, Pal. (1999) *Edward Said*. London: Routledge.
Ashour, Radwa. (2014) *The Woman from Tantoura*. Heikkinen, Kay (trans.). Cairo and New York: The American University in Cairo Press.
Ball, Anna. (2012) *Palestinian Literature and Film in Postcolonial Feminist Perspective*. New York and London: Routledge.
Baker, Raymond W., Ismael, Shereen T. and Ismael, Tareq Y. (2010) 'Ending the Iraqi State', In R. W. Baker, S. T. Ismael and T. Y. Ismael (eds). *Cultural Cleansing in Iraq: Why Museums Were Looted, Libraries Burned and Academics Murdered*. London and New York: Pluto Press, 3–48.
Barghouti, Mourid. (2005) *I Saw Ramallah*. Soueif, Ahdaf (trans.). London: Bloomsbury.
Barghouti, Mourid. (2008) *Midnight and other Poems*. Ashour, Radwa (trans.). Todmorden, Lancs: Arc Publications.
Barghouti, Mourid. (2011) *I Was Born There, I Was Born Here*. Davies, Humphrey (trans.). London: Bloomsbury.
Bernard, Anna. (2013) *Rhetorics of Belonging: Nation, Narration, and Israel/Palestine*. Liverpool: Liverpool University Press.

Cabral, Amilcar. (1994) 'National Liberation and Culture'. In Williams, Patrick and Chrisman, Laura (eds). *Colonial Discourse and Post-Colonial Theory: A Reader*. Essex: Pearson, 53–65.

Cleary, Joe. (2002) *Literature, Partition and the Nation State: Culture and Conflict in Ireland, Israel and Palestine*. Cambridge, UK: Cambridge University Press.

Dabashi, Hamid. (2020) *On Edward Said: Remembrance of Things Past*. Chicago: Haymarket Books.

Darwish, Mahmoud. (2000) *The Adam of Two Edens*. Akash, Munir and Moore, Daniel (eds). Haddawi, Husain et al. (trans.). Syracuse, NY: Syracuse University Press.

Darwish, Mahmoud. (2003) *Unfortunately, It Was Paradise*. Antoon, Sinan and El-Zein, Amira (eds). Akash, Munir and Forche, Carolyn (trans.). Berkeley, CA: University of California.

Darwish, Mahmoud. (2007) *The Butterfly's Burden*. Joudah, Fady (trans.). Tarset: Bloodaxe.

Darwish, Mahmoud. (2009a) *A River Dies of Thirst*. Cobham, Catherine (trans.). Brooklyn, NY: Archipelago Books.

Darwish, Mahmoud. (2009b) *Almond Blossoms and beyond*. Shaheen, Mohammad (trans.). Northampton, MA: Interlink.

Darwish, Mahmoud. (2011) *In the Presence of Absence*. Antoon, Sinan (trans.). Brooklyn, NY: Archipelago Books.

Darwish, Mahmoud. (2013) *Memory for Forgetfulness: August, Beirut, 1982*. Muhawi, Ibrahim (trans.). Berkeley: University of California Press.

Eagleton, Terry, Jameson, Frederic and Said, Edward. (1990) *Nationalism, Colonialism and Literature*. Minneapolis, MN: University of Minnesota Press.

El-Ghadban, Yara and Strohm, Kiven. (2013) 'The Ghosts of Resistance: Dispatches from Palestinian Art and Music'. In Kanaaneh, Moslih, Thorsen, Stig-Magnus, Bursheh, Heather and McDonald, David A. (eds). *Palestinian Music and Song: Expression and Resistance since 1900*. Bloomington and Indianapolis: Indiana University Press, 175–200.

El-Kurd, Mohammed. (2021) *Rifqa*. Chicago: Haymarket Books.

Fanon, Frantz. (1963) *The Wretched of the Earth*. Farrington, Constance (trans.). New York: Grove Press.

Fisk, Robert. (2001) *Pity the Nation: Lebanon at War*. Oxford: Oxford University Press.

Ginsberg, Terri. (2016) *Visualizing the Palestinian Struggle: Towards a Critical Analytic of Palestine Solidarity Film*. London: Palgrave Macmillan.

Hall, Stuart. (1994) 'Cultural Identity and Diaspora'. In Williams, Patrick and Chrisman, Laura (eds). *Colonial Discourse and Post-Colonial Theory: A Reader*. Essex: Pearson, 392–403.

Hammad, Suheir. (2010) *Born Palestinian, Born Black & The Gaza Suite*. Brooklyn, NY: UpSet Press.

Harlow, Barbara. (1987) *Resistance Literature*. New York and London: Methuen.

Harlow, Barbara. (1996) *After Lives: Legacies of Revolutionary Writing*. London: Verso.

Herman, Edward and Chomsky, Noam. (1988) *Manufacturing Consent: The Political Economy of the Mass Media*. New York: Pantheon.

Hirsch, Marianne. (2012) *The Generation of Postmemory: Writing and Visual Culture after the Holocaust*. New York: Columbia University Press.

Hirst, David. (2010) *Beware of Small States: Lebanon, Battleground of the Middle East*. London: Faber and Faber.

hooks, bell. (1990) *Yearning: Race, Gender, and Cultural Politics*. Boston, MA: South End Press.
Hughes, Langston. (1990) *Selected Poems of Langston Hughes*. New York: Vintage.
Irving, Sarah. (2012) *Leila Khaled: Icon of Palestinian Revolution*. London: Pluto Press.
Kanafani, Ghassan. (2013 [1966]) *Resistance Literature in Occupied Palestine*. Beirut: Dar al-Adab.
Kanafani, Ghassan. (2013 [1968]) *Resistance Literature in Occupied Palestine*. Beirut: Dar al-Adab.
Kanafani, Ghassan. (1999) *Men in the Sun and Other Palestinian Stories*. Kilpatrick, Hilary (trans.). Boulder, CO: Lynne Rienner.
Kanafani, Ghassan. (2000) *Palestine's Children: Returning to Haifa and Other Stories*. Harlow, Barbara and Riley, Karen E. (trans.). Boulder, CO: Lynne Rienner.
Karkar, Sonja. (2007) 'The Olive Trees of Palestine Weep'. In Cook, W. A. (ed), *The Plight of the Palestinians*. New York: Palgrave MacMillan, 51–3.
Khalidi, Rashid. (2010) *Palestinian Identity: The Construction of Modern National Consciousness*. New York: Columbia University Press.
Mannes-Abbott, Guy. (2008) 'Introduction'. In Barghouti, Mourid, *Midnight and Other Poems*. Ashour, Radwa (trans.). Todmorden, Lancs: Arc Publications, 9–28.
Maracle, Lee. (2000). *Bent Box*. Penticon, BC: Theytus Books.
Masalha, Nur. (1992) *Expulsion of the Palestinians: The Concept of 'Transfer' in Zionist Political Thought, 1882–1948*. Washington DC: Institute for Palestine Studies.
Masalha, Nur. (2012) *The Palestine Nakba: Decolonising History, Narrating the Subaltern, Reclaiming Memory*. London: Zed Books.
Masalha, Nur. (2018) *Palestine: A Four Thousand Year History*. London: Zed Books.
Massad, Joseph. (2003) 'Liberating Songs: Palestine Put to Music'. *Journal of Palestine Studies*, 32 (3), 21–38.
Mattar, Karim. (2013) 'Mourid Barghouti's "multiple displacements": Exile and the national Checkpoint in Palestinian literature'. *Journal of Postcolonial Writing*, 50 (1), 103–15.
Mattawa, Khaled. (2014) *Mahmoud Darwish: The Poet's Art and His Nation*. Syracuse: Syracuse University Press.
McDonald, David A. (2013) *My Voice Is My Weapon: Music, Nationalism, and the Poetics of Palestinian Resistance*. Durham and London: Duke University Press.
Moore, Lindsey. (2018) *Narrating Postcolonial Arab Nations: Egypt, Algeria, Lebanon, Palestine*. London: Routledge.
Nashef, Hania. (2019) *Palestinian Culture and the Nakba: Bearing Witness*. Oxfordshire, UK: Routledge.
'Operation Iraqi Freedom: Definition'. (2020) *Naval History and Heritage Command*. Available at: https://www.history.navy.mil/browse-by-topic/wars-conflicts-and-operations/middle-east/operation-iraqi-freedom.html [Accessed: 20 July 2021].
Pappe, Ilan. (2006) *The Ethnic Cleansing of Palestine*. London: Oneworld.
Qabaha, Ahmad. (2018) *Exile and Expatriation in Modern American and Palestinian Writing*. London: Palgrave Macmillan.
Rowe, Nicholas. (2010) *Raising Dust: A Cultural History of Dance in Palestine*. London and New York: I.B. Tauris.
Said, Edward. (1975) *Beginnings: Intention and Method*. New York: Basic Books, Inc., Publishers.
Said, Edward. (1995 [1978]) *Orientalism: Western Conceptions of the Orient*. London: Penguin.
Said, Edward. (1992 [1979]) *The Question of Palestine*. New York: Vintage.

Said, Edward. (1997 [1981]) *Covering Islam: How the Media and the Experts Determine How We See the Rest of the World*. New York: Vintage.
Said, Edward. (1993 [1986]) *After the Last Sky: Palestinian Lives*. London: Vintage.
Said, Edward. (1991) *The World, the Text and the Critic*. London: Vintage.
Said, Edward. (1994a) *Culture and Imperialism*. London: Vintage.
Said, Edward. (1994b) *Representations of the Intellectual*. London: Vintage.
Said, Edward. (1994c) *The Pen and the Sword: Conversations with David Barsamian*. Monroe, Maine: Common Courage Press.
Said, Edward. (1995) *The Politics of Dispossession*. New York: Vintage.
Said, Edward. (2000) *Out of Place: A Memoir*. New York: Vintage.
Said, Edward. (2001) *Reflections on Exile and Other Literary and Cultural Essays*. London: Granta.
Said, Edward. (2004a) *Humanism and Democratic Criticism*. New York: Columbia University Press.
Said, Edward. (2004b) *Power, Politics and Culture: Interviews with Edward W. Said*. Viswanathan, Gauri (eds). London, Berlin and New York: Bloomsbury.
Said, Edward. (2005) 'Foreword'. In Barghouti, Mourid, *I Saw Ramallah*. Soueif, Ahdaf (trans.). London: Bloomsbury, vii–xi.
Said, Edward. (2006) *Conversations with Edward Said and Tariq Ali*. London, New York and Calcutta: Seagull Books.
Said, Edward. (2007) *On Late Style: Music and Literature against the Grain*. New York: Vintage.
Salaita, Steven. (2016) *Inter/Nationalism: Decolonizing Native America and Palestine*. Minneapolis, MN: University of Minnesota Press.
Sayigh, Rosemary. (2007) *The Palestinians: From Peasants to Revolutionaries*. London and New York: Zed Books.
Sazzad, Rehnuma. (2017) *Edward Said's Concept of Exile*. London and New York: I.B. Tauris.
Soja, Edward. (1996) *Thirdspace: Journeys to Los Angeles and Other Real-and-Imagined Places*. Oxford: Blackwell Publishing.
Viswanathan, Gauri. (1989) *Masks of Conquest: Literary Study and British Rule in India*. New York: Columbia University Press.
Williams, Patrick. (2009) '"Naturally, I reject the term "diaspora"": Said and Palestinian Dispossession'. In Keown, Michelle, Murphy, David and Procter, James (eds). *Comparing Postcolonial Diasporas*. London: Palgrave Macmillan, 83–103.
Williams, Patrick. (2010) '"Outlines of a better world": Rerouting postcolonialism'. In Wilson, Janet, Sandru, Cristina and Welsh, Sarah Lawson (eds). *Rerouting the Postcolonial: New Directions for the New Millennium*. London and New York: Routledge, 86–97.
Wood, Michael. (2007) 'Introduction'. In Said, Edward (ed.), *On Late Style: Music and Literature against the Grain*. New York: Vintage, xi–xix.

Journals

AbuKhoti, Ahlam Mustafa. (2018) 'Calling the Phoenix: Integrating the Trauma of the Nakba into Palestinian Identity'. *Limina: A Journal of Historical & Cultural Studies*, 24 (1), 48–61.

Alduraidi, Hamza and Waters, Catherine M. (2017) 'Health-related Quality of Life of Palestinian Refugees Inside and Outside Camps in Jordan'. *Nursing Outlook*, 65, 436–43.

Bailey, Kristian Davis. (2015) 'Black-Palestinian Solidarity in the Ferguson-Gaza Era'. *American Quarterly*, 67 (4), 1017–26.

Brittain, Victoria. (2006) 'They Had to Die: Assassination against Liberation'. *Race & Class*, 48 (1), 60–74.

Butler, Judith. (2012) '"What Shall We Do without Exile": Said and Darwish Address the Future'. *Alif: Journal of Comparative Poetics*, 32, 30–54.

Darwish, Mahmoud. (2007) 'Edward Said: A Contrapuntal Reading'. Anis, Mona (trans.). *Cultural Critique*, 67, 175–82.

Darwish, Mahmoud. (2009) 'The "Red Indian's" Penultimate Speech to the White Man'. Joudah, Fady (trans.). *Harvard Review*, 36, 152–9.

El Hajj, Hind and Harb, Serene. (2015) 'Space, Mobility and Agency in Palestinian American Poetry'. *Arab Studies Quarterly*, 37 (3), 224–43.

Falk, Richard. (2013) 'Rethinking the Palestinian Future'. *Journal of Palestine Studies*, 42 (4), 73–86.

Genet, Jean. (1983) 'Four Hours in Shatila'. *Journal of Palestine Studies*, 12 (3), 3–22.

Gould, Rebecca Ruth. (2014) 'The Materiality of Resistance: Israel's Apartheid Wall in an Age of Globalization'. *Social Text*, 32, 1–21.

Hagopian, Elaine C. (2004) 'Ibrahim and Edward'. *Arab Studies Quarterly*, 26 (4), 3–22.

Hamdi, Hamdi K. and Castellon, Raquel. (2005) 'Oleuropein, a Non-toxic Olive Iridoid, Is an Anti-tumor Agent and Cytoskeleton Disruptor'. *Biochemical and Biophysical Research Communications*, 334 (3), 737–970.

Hamdi, Tahrir. (2011) 'Bearing Witness in Palestinian Resistance Literature'. *Race & Class*, 52 (3), 21–42.

Hamdi, Tahrir. (2016a) 'Reading, Imagining and Constructing Iraq'. *International Journal of Contemporary Iraqi Studies*, 10 (1–2), 35–51.

Hamdi, Tahrir. (2016b) 'Darwish's Geography: Space, Place and Identity under Construction'. *Interventions*, 19 (2), 238–57.

Hamdi, Tahrir. (2016c) 'The Power of Poetry to Travel: An Interview with Mourid Barghouti'. *Arab Studies Quarterly*, 38 (4), 656–75.

Hamdi, Tahrir. (2019) 'The Arab Intellectual and the Present Moment'. *Arab Studies Quarterly*, 41 (1), 59–77.

Hammad, Suheir. (2008) 'A Prayer Band'. *The National Women's Studies Association Journal NWSA Journal*, 20 (3), 1–4.

Harlow, Barbara. (1986) 'Return to Haifa: "Opening the Borders" in Palestinian Literature'. *Social Text*, 13/14, 3–23.

Ihmoud, Sarah. (2019) 'Murabata: The Politics of Staying in Place'. *Feminist Studies*, 45 (2–3), 512–40.

Ismael, Tareq and Fuller, Max. (2008) 'The Disintegration of Iraq: The Manufacturing and Politicization of Sectarianism'. *International Journal of Contemporary Iraqi Studies*, 2 (3), 443–73.

Kanafani, Ghassan. (1968) 'Resistance Literature in Occupied Palestine'. *Afro-Asian Writings*, 65–79.

Kanafani, Ghassan. (1990) 'Thoughts on Change and the 'Blind Language''. Harlow, Barbara and Yaziji, Nejd (trans.). *Alif: Journal of Comparative Poetics*, 10, 137–57.

Kelley, Robin D.G. (2019) 'From the River to the Sea to Every Mountain Top: Solidarity as Worldmaking'. *Journal of Palestine Studies*, 48 (4), 69–91.

Larkin, Craig. (2014) 'Jerusalem's Separation Wall and Global Message Board: Graffiti, and the Art of Sumud'. *The Arab Studies Journal*, 22 (1), 134–69.
MacLure, Maggie, Holmes, Rachel, Jones, Liz and MacRae, Christina. (2010) 'Silence as Resistance to Analysis: Or, on Not Opening One's Mouth Properly'. *Qualitative Inquiry*, 16 (6), 492–500.
Maracle, Lee. (2012) 'Remembering Mahmoud 1986'. *Decolonization: Indigeneity, Education & Society*, 1 (1), 181–5.
Mattar, Karim. (2012) 'Mourid Barghouti's "multiple displacements": Exile and the National Checkpoint in Palestinian Literature'. *Journal of Postcolonial Writing*, 50 (1), 103–15.
Meari, Lena. (2014) '*Sumud*: A Palestinian Philosophy of Confrontation in Colonial Prisons'. *The South Atlantic Quarterly*, 113 (3), 547–78.
Rashed, Haifa, Short, Damien and Docker, John. (2014) 'Nakba Memoricide: Genocide Studies and the Zionist/Israeli Genocide of Palestine'. *Journal of Holy Land and Palestine Studies*, 18 (1), 1–23.
Schwarz, Ori. (2013) 'Arab Sounds in a Contested Space: Life Quality, Cultural Hierarchies and National Silencing'. *Ethnic & Racial Studies*, 37 (11), 2034–54.
Sen, Somdeep. (2015) 'It's Nakba, Not a Party: Re-Stating the (Continued) Legacy of the Oslo Accords'. *Arab Studies Quarterly*, 37 (2), 161–76.
Shahid, Leila. (2002) 'Testimonies: The Sabra and Shatila Massacres: Eye-witness Reports'. *Journal of Palestine Studies*, 32 (1), 36–58.
Siklawi, Rami. (2019) 'The Palestinian Refugee Camps in Lebanon Post 1990: Dilemmas of Survival and Return to Palestine'. *Arab Studies Quarterly*, 41 (1), 78–94.
Spivak, Gayatri. (2005) 'Thinking about Edward Said: Pages from a Memoir'. *Critical Inquiry*, 31 (2), 519–25.
Srivastava, Neelam. (2010) 'Towards a Critique of Colonial Violence: Fanon, Gandhi and the Restoration of Agency'. *Journal of Postcolonial Writing*, 46 (3–4), 303–19.
Swedenburg, Ted. (1990) 'The Palestinian Peasant as National Signifier'. *Anthropological Quarterly*, 63 (1), 18–30.
Vally, Salim. (2017) 'Introduction to the Special Issue in Memory of Edward W. Said'. *Journal of Holy Land and Palestine Studies*, 16 (1), 1–5.
Williams, Patrick. (2012) 'No Aesthetics Outside My Freedom'. *Interventions: International Journal of Postcolonial Studies*, 14 (1), 24–36.

Websites

Abou Jalal, Rasha. (2014) 'Israel accused of using illegal weapons in Gaza War'. *Al-Monitor*, Available at: https://www.al-monitor.com/originals/2014/08/israel-use-banned-weapons-dime-gaza-war.html [Accessed: 5 September 2020].
Abu Arab. (ND) 'Calm down sea, be patient (Hadi ya bahar hadi)'. Available at: https://www.youtube.com/watch?v=2sg4akWHHxk&ab_channel [Accessed: 19 August 2021].
Abu Arab. (ND) 'Oh Mother, there's a knock at our door (Ya Yuma fi daga "ala babna")'. Available at: https://www.youtube.com/watch?v=inOnE2RGgCk&ab_channel
Abu Arab. (2019) 'Oh Mother, if the Eid (holiday) comes (Ya Yuma lou jani al eid)'. Available at: https://www.youtube.com/watch?v=AAgJmwvGxwM&ab_channel=EhabObaidat [Accessed: 18 August 2021].

Abu Arab. (2014) 'Abu Arab, poet of the Palestinian revolution, dies'. *Middle East Monitor*, https://www.middleeastmonitor.com/20140409-abu-arab-poet-of-the-palestinian-revolution-dies/ [Accessed: 18 August 2021].
Adonis. (2017) 'Afflictions'. Mattawa, Khaled (trans.). *Kenyon Review*, Available at: https://kenyonreview.org/kr-online-issue/2017-septoct/selections/adonis-763879/ [Accessed: 12 August 2021].
Al-Ali, Naji. (1998) 'My signature, Hanthala: The symbol of the child'. *Kanan 48*, Available at: https://kanan48.wordpress.com/naji-al-ali/ [Accessed: 17 August 2021].
Al-Araj, Bassel. (2020) 'Dismantle it and let them fall'. Nassar, Tamara (trans.). *The Electronic Intifada*, Available at: https://electronicintifada.net/content/dismantle-it-and-let-them-fall/31281 [Accessed: 19 August 2021].
Alareer, Refaat. (2014) 'The story of my brother, martyr Mohammed Alareer'. *The Electronic Intifada*, Available at: https://electronicintifada.net/content/story-my-brother-martyr-mohammed-alareer/13653 [Accessed: 19 August 2021].
Al Ashiqeen. (2016) 'From Akka prison'. Palestine channel, Available at: https://www.youtube.com/watch?v=BMzm-gex6iI&ab_channel=Palestine [Accessed: 18 August 2021].
Al-Awda, The Palestine Right of Return Coalition. (ND). 'FAQs about Palestinian refugees'. Available at: https://al-awda.org/learn-more/faqs-about-palestinian-refugees/ [Accessed: 6 October 2020].
Alsaafin, Linah. (2021) 'Palestinian protests in Israel showcase "unprecedented" unity'. *Al Jazeera*, Available at: https://www.aljazeera.com/news/2021/5/16/palestinian-protests-in-israel-showcase-unprecedented-unity [Accessed: 19 August 2021].
Al Sharif, Osama. (2021) 'From Sheikh Jarrah to Silwan, Israel's ethnic cleansing goes [on] with impunity'. *The Jordan Times*, Available at: https://www.jordantimes.com/opinion/osama-al-sharif/sheikh-jarrah-silwan-israels-ethnic-cleansing-goes-impunity [Accessed: 20 July 2021].
Althusser, Louis. (1971) 'Ideology and ideological state apparatuses'. In Lenin and Philosophy and Other Essays, trans. B. Brewster. *New York: Monthly Review Press*, Available at: http://www.marxists.org/reference/archive/althusser/1970/ideology.htm [Accessed: 15 August 2015].
Amawi, Sarah. (2020) 'Dabke: From social dance to political stance'. Available at: https://patrimoinedorient.org/index.php/en/2020/06/09/dabke-from-social-dance-to-political-stance/ [Accessed: 17 August 2021].
American Jewish Committee: Global Jewish Advocacy. (ND) 'The working definition of anti-Semitism', Available at: https://www.ajc.org/the-working-definition-of-antisemitism [Accessed: 12 August 2021].
Amnesty International. (2022) 'Israel's apartheid against Palestinians: A cruel system of domination and a crime against humanity', Available at: https://www.amnesty.org/en/latest/news/2022/02/israels-apartheid-against-palestinians-a-cruel-system-of-domination-and-a-crime-against-humanity/ [Accessed: 29 March 2022].
Antoon, Sinan. (2008) 'In the presence of Darwish: A tribute to the premier Arab poet of the past half-century'. *The Nation*, Available at: https://www.thenation.com/article/archive/presence-darwish/ [Accessed: 18 September 2020].
Ashly, Jaclynn. (2020) 'Bassel al-Araj: An icon for a lost generation'. *The Electronic Intifada*, Available at: https://electronicintifada.net/content/bassel-al-araj-icon-lost-generation/31051 [Accessed: 19 August 2021].

Ashour, Radwa. (2010) 'Mayada ElDemerdash interviews Radwa Ashour: 'Radwa Ashour's Tantoura: Palestinian nakba and resisting fait accompli'. *Egypt Independent*, Available at https://egyptindependent.com/radwa-ashours-tantoura-palestinian-nakba-and-resisting-fait-accompli/ [Accessed: 16 August 2021].

Bajec, Alessandra. (2020) '"Decorating the Cage": How UAE plans to modernise Israeli checkpoints could entrench the occupation'. *The New Arab*, Available at: https://english.alaraby.co.uk/analysis/uae-plan-modernise-checkpoints-could-entrench-israels-occupation [Accessed: 14 August 2021].

Baltzer, Anna. (2003) 'Anna's eyewitness reports from Palestine: Uprooting the history & future of Palestine'. Available at: http://annainpalestine.blogspot.com/2003/12/wall-trees.html [Accessed: 17 August 2021].

Barakat, Rena. (2007) 'From Acre prison with love: The life and times of Nuh Ibrahim, poet of the 1936 Revolt'. *Palestinian Journeys* Website, Available at: https://www.paljourneys.org/en/story/9562/acre-prison-love [Accessed: 18 August 2021].

Barghouti, Mourid. (2003) 'Verbicide'. *New Internationalist*, Available at: https://newint.org/columns/essays/2003/08/01 [Accessed: 5 February 2020].

Baroud, Ramzy. (2016) 'Palestinian Native-American story link is slowly merging'. *Gulf News*, Available at: https://gulfnews.com/opinion/op-eds/palestinian-native-american-story-link-is-slowly-merging-1.1929883 [Accessed: 12 August 2021].

'Birthpangs of a new Middle East'. (2006) *International Socialist Review*, 49 (September–October), Available at: https://isreview.org/issues/49/birthpangs.shtml [Accessed: 8 August 2021].

Black, Ian. (2008) 'Drawing defiance'. *The Guardian*, Available at: https://www.theguardian.com/world/2008/mar/10/israelandthepalestinians1 [Accessed: 17 August 2021].

Britannica.com (ND) 'Ezekiel'. *Britannica.com*, Available at: https://www.britannica.com/topic/religion [Accessed: 12 August 2021].

Cockburn, Patrick. (2016) 'We finally know what Hillary Clinton knew all along…'. *Independent*, Available at: https://www.independent.co.uk/voices/hillary-clinton-wikileaks-email-isis-saudi-arabia-qatar-us-allies-funding-barack-obama-knew-all-along-a7362071.html [Accessed: 3 March 2021].

Darwish, Mahmoud. (1964) 'Identity card'. Available at: http://www.barghouti.com/poets/darwish/bitaqa.asp [Accessed: 17 August 2021].

Darwish, Mahmoud. (2007) 'You, from now on, are not yourself'. *HebaAlbeity* Blog, Available at: https://hebaalbeity.wordpress.com/2013/06/19/you-from-now-on-are-not-yourself-mahmoud-darwish/ [Accessed: 30 July 2021].

Darwish, Mahmoud. (ND) 'Introduction' to "The Speech of the Red Indian", Available at: https://www.youtube.com/watch?v=V5a5cREU0SQ [Accessed: 12 August 2021].

Darwish, Mahmoud. (2017) 'Sabra and Shatila'. El Kurdi, Saad (trans.). *The Palestine Project*. Available at: https://thepalestineproject.medium.com/sabra-and-shatila-4ce9c3d4a7e7 [Accessed: 2 February 2021].

El Fassed, Arjan. (2004) 'Naji al-Ali: The timeless conscience of Palestine'. *The Electronic Intifada*, Available at: https://electronicintifada.net/content/naji-al-ali-timeless-conscience-palestine/5166 [Accessed: 25 March 2022].

'Gazans watch music concert amidst rubble'. (2021) *Euronews*, Available at: https://www.euronews.com/2021/06/28/gazans-watch-music-concert-amidst-rubble [Accessed: 19 August 2021].

'Great dance of return—Gaza border'. (2018) *Arab Way*, Available at: https://www.youtube.com/watch?v=l7xYIiNLTUY&ab_channel=ArabWay [Accessed: 18 August 2021].

Goldstein, Alexis. (2014) 'Palestinians and Ferguson protesters link arms via social media'. *Yes Magazine*, Available at: https://www.yesmagazine.org/social-justice/2014/08/16/palestinians-and-ferguson-protesters-link-arms-via-social-media [Accessed: 13 September 2020].

Hassan, Budour Youssef. (2017) 'Never obey the occupation: The legacy of Bassel al-Araj'. *The Electronic Intifada*, Available at: https://electronicintifada.net/content/never-obey-occupation-legacy-bassel-al-araj/19851 [Accessed: 19 August 2021].

Heritagepalestinian.blogspot. (2018) 'The story behind the song of the Fidayee Bilal: Oh Mother, there's a knock at our door'. Available at: https://heritagepalestinian.blogspot.com/2018/10/ [Accessed: 19 August 2021].

History.com Editors. (2018 [2021]) 'Jim Crow Laws'. *History.com*, Available at: https://www.history.com/topics/early-20th-century-us/jim-crow-laws [Accessed: 9 August 2021].

International Holocaust Remembrance Alliance. (2016) 'Working definition of antisemitism'. IHRA website, Available at: https://www.holocaustremembrance.com/resources/working-definitions-charters/working-definition-antisemitism [Accessed: 10 November 2020].

Jadaliyya Reports. (2018) 'Marc Lamont Hill at United Nation's International Day of Solidarity with Palestine'. *Jadaliyya.com*, Available at: https://www.jadaliyya.com/Details/38202 [Accessed: 17 August 2021].

Jaggi, Maya. (2002) 'Poet of the Arab world: Interview with Mahmoud Darwish'. *The Guardian*, Available at: https://www.theguardian.com/books/2002/jun/08/featuresreviews.guardianreview19[Accessed: 11 March 2020].

Jordan, June. (2007) 'Moving towards home'. *Al Awda: The Palestine Right to Return Coalition*, Available at: http://www.al-awda.org/until-return/june.html [Accessed: 18 November 2020].

Jordan, June. (2020) *Solidarity for Palestinian Human Rights—McMaster*, Available at: https://www.facebook.com/sphr.mac/videos/june-jordan-names-palestine-and-queer-liberation-as-the-two-issues-that-are-a-li/302147084319841/ [Accessed: 19 November 2020].

Joubran, Trio Le, Waters, Roger and Darwish, Mahmoud. (2018) 'Supremacy'. Available at: https://www.youtube.com/watch?v=8i-TMG7k_QM [Accessed: 12 August 2021].

JTA and TOI Staff. (2018) 'Trump invokes "Israel's Wall" in tense exchange over border Security'. *The Times of Israel*, Available at: https://www.timesofisrael.com/trump-invokes-israels-wall-in-tense-exchange-over-border-security/ [Accessed: 17 August 2021].

Kanafani, Ghassan and Carleton, Richard. (1970) 'PFLP Ghassan Kanafani, Richard Carleton interview'. Available at: https://www.youtube.com/watch?v=3h_drCmG2iM&ab_channel=JamesCarleton [Accessed: 16 August 2021].

Kanan48.wordpress. (ND) 'Naji al-Ali'. *Kanʿan 48: Palestine Diary*, Available at: https://kanan48.wordpress.com/naji-al-ali/ [Accessed: 17 August 2021].

King, Jamilah. (2014) 'This is what James Baldwin wrote about Israel and Palestine in 1979'. *Colorlines*, Available at: https://www.colorlines.com/articles/what-james-baldwin-wrote-about-israel-and-palestine-1979 [Accessed: 17 August 2021].

Kul Al Arab. (2022) 'Raed Nasrallah of Nazareth, a Christian Murabit in Masjid Al Aqsa: This mosque concerns me regardless of my religion.' *Kul Al Arab*, Available at: https://www.alarab.com/amp/article/1029487 [Accessed: 17 April 2022].

Lis, Jonathan, Ashkenazi, Yair, Khoury, Jack and Pulwer, Sharon. (2016) 'Israel's Nationalistic "Loyalty in Culture" Bill passes legal test.' *Haaretz*, Available at:

https://www.haaretz.com/israel-news/.premium-culture-loyalty-bill-gets-ags-qualified-okay-1.5409115.

Lynch, Colum. (2018) 'Trump and allies seek end to refugee status for millions of Palestinians'. *Foreign Policy*, Available at: https://foreignpolicy.com/2018/08/03/trump-palestinians-israel-refuwaand-allies-seek-end-to-refugee-status-for-millions-of-palestinians-united-nations-relief-and-works-agency-unrwa-israel-palestine-peace-plan-jared-kushner-greenb/ [Accessed: 14 April 2022].

Macias, Amanda. (2019) 'American firms rule the $398 billion global arms industry: Here's a roundup of the world's top 10 defense contractors, by sale'. *CNBC*, Available at: https://www.cnbc.com/2019/01/10/top-10-defense-contractors-in-the-world.html [Accessed: 12 August 2021].

Mahmoud Darwish Foundation. (ND) 'Mahmoud Darwish's biography'. Available at: http://mahmouddarwish.ps/en/article/80000160/Mahmoud-Darwish---Biography [Accessed: 20 February 2020].

Mandell, Joan. (1987) 'Naji al-'Ali remembered'. *Middle East Report*, 149 November/December, Available at: https://merip.org/1987/11/naji-al-ali-remembered/ [Accessed: 17 August 2021].

Maqusi, Samar. (2016) 'Photo gallery: Baqa'a camp'. *Refugee Hosts*, Available at: https://refugeehosts.org/2016/11/10/photogallery-refugees-in-baqaa-camp-jordan/ [Accessed: 14 August 2021].

Mattawa, Khaled. (2017) 'On Adonis's "Concerto Al-Quds"'. *Kenyon Review*, Available at: https://kenyonreview.org/kr-online-issue/2017-septoct/selections/khaled-mattawa-656342/ [Accessed: 25 July 2021].

Melhem, Ahmad. (2018) 'Palestine's oldest olive tree symbol of cultural heritage'. *Al-Monitor*, Available at: https://www.al-monitor.com/originals/2018/11/palestines-oldest-olive-tree-searches-its-birth-date.html [Accessed: 17 August 2017].

MK. (2020) 'UAE investment in upgrading Israeli checkpoint only entrenches occupation'. *Palestine News & Info Agency*, Available at: https://english.wafa.ps/Pages/Details/120675 [Accessed: 14 August 2021].

Mullen, Bill. (2018) 'Copy of "Palestine and Our Emancipation"'. From the River to the Sea Blog (Bill Mullen), Available at: https://www.billvmullen.com/from-the-river-to-the-sea [Accessed: 17 August 2021].

Naddaff, AJ. (2020) 'Nizar Qabbani's 1967 letter to Gamal Abdel Nasser'. *Arablit.org*, Available at: https://arablit.org/2020/09/28/nizar-qabbanis-1967-letter-to-gamal-abdel-nasser/ [Accessed: 13 August 2021].

Nasrallah, Hassan. (2000) 'Nasrallah's victory speech, Bint Jbeil, Lebanon'. Available at: https://www.youtube.com/watch?v=0YnH7qhENDQ [Accessed: 13 August 2021].

New World Encyclopedia (ND) 'Ibn Khaldun'. *New World Encyclopedia*, Available at: https://www.newworldencyclopedia.org/entry/Ibn_Khaldun [Accessed: 12 August 2021].

Oxford Reference, Shock and Awe (Definition). Available at: https://www.oxfordreference.com/view/10.1093/oi/authority.20110803100502693 [Accessed: 15 January 2021].

Palestine Chronicle. (2021) 'Atallah Hanna calls on Muslims, Christians to defend Jerusalem together'. *The Palestine Chronicle*, Available at: https://www.palestinechronicle.com/atallah-hanna-calls-on-muslims-christians-to-defend-jerusalem-together/ [Accessed: 17 April 2022].

Palestinian and Arab academics. (2020) 'Palestinian rights and the IHRA definition of antisemitism'. *The Guardian*, Available at: https://www.theguardian.com/news/2020/nov/29/palestinian-rights-and-the-ihra-definition-of-antisemitism [Accessed: 20 December 2020].

Palestinian Media Observatory Group. (2018) 'Palestinian mother puts Henna on her martyred son'. Available at: https://www.youtube.com/watch?reload=9&app=desktop& v=uB8bRxTIZGM&feature=youtu.be [Accessed: 18 August 2021].

Palestinian Museum. (2016) 'Palestinian journeys'. Available at: https://palmuseum. wordpress.com/2016/08/14/ [Accessed: 18 August 2021].

Palestinian National Self-Representation Campaign. (ND) 'They brought in the martyr, they brought in the bridegroom'. Available at: https://www.youtube.com/watch?app=de sktop&v=FvCdbjnUr4I&ab_channel [Accessed: 18 August 2021].

Pappe, Ilan. (2014) 'Ilan Pappe's interview on *HARDtalk*'. *BBC*, Available at: https://www. youtube.com/watch?v=4lsmFS75ed4 [Accessed: 15 November 2021].

Parry, William. (2018) 'How poet Mahmoud Darwish inspired a rock collaboration of a lifetime'. *The National*, Available at: https://www.thenationalnews.com/arts-culture/music/how-poet-mahmoud-darwish-inspired-a-rock-collaboration-of-a-lifetime-1.778935 [Accessed: 12 August 2021].

Perry, Megan. (2014) 'Bethlehem: "No matter how many olive trees they destroy, [we] will plant More"'. *Ecologist: Informed by Nature*, Available at: https://theecologist.org/2014/ jul/18/bethlehem-no-matter-how-many-olive-trees-they-destroy-will-will-plant-more [Accessed: 17 August 2021].

Qumsiyeh, Mazin. (2009) 'The olive tree—Not just an ordinary tree'. *Desertpeace*, Available at: https://desertpeace.wordpress.com/2009/10/21/the-olive-tree-not-just-an-ordinary-tree/ [Accessed: 17 August 2021].

Relief Web. (2006) 'OPT: The olive harvest in the West Bank and Gaza—Oct. 2006'. Relief Web, Available at: https://reliefweb.int/report/occupied-palestinian-territory/opt-olive-harvest-west-bank-and-gaza-oct-2006 [Accessed: 17 August 2021].

Ruffin, Jason. (2020) 'In Palestine, protecting one of the world's oldest olive trees Is a 24/7 job'. *Atlas Obscura*, Available at: https://www.atlasobscura.com/articles/world-oldest-olive-trees [Accessed: 17 August 2021].

Said, Edward. (1986). 'Salman Rushdie interviews Edward Said'. *Institute of Contemporary Arts In London*, Available at: https://www.youtube.com/watch?v=vAmLNc_4VtE [Accessed: 13 August 2021].

Said, Edward. (1990) 'On Jean Genet's Late Works'. *Grand Street Magazine*, Available at: http://www.grandstreet.com/gsissues/gs36/gs36c.html [Accessed: 22 February 2020].

Said, Edward. (1998 [2014]) 'In search of Palestine: Edward Said's Return Home'. *BBC*, Available at: https://www.youtube.com/watch?v=R09FjpTf_3Q [Accessed: 8 October 2020].

Said, Edward. (2001) 'My guru: Elegy for Ibrahim Abu-Lughod'. *London Review of Books*, Available at: https://www.lrb.co.uk/the-paper/v23/n24/edward-said/my-guru [Accessed: 13 August 2021].

Said, Edward. (2002) Edward Said's interview on *HARDtalk/Part 2*'. *BBC*, Available at: https://www.youtube.com/watch?v=r5ULAYd8heY [Accessed: 5 September 2020].

Saliba, Therese. (2016) 'June Jordan's songs of Palestine and Lebanon'. *The Feminist Wire*, Available at: https://thefeministwire.com/2016/03/june-jordans-songs-of-palestine/ [Accessed: 3 March 2021].

Sheety, Roger. (2015) 'Stealing Palestine: A study of historical and cultural theft'. *Middle East Eye*, https://www.middleeasteye.net/big-story/stealing-palestine-study-historical-and-cultural-theft [Accessed: 17 August 2021].

Shoaibi, Halla. (2011) 'Childbirth at checkpoints in the occupied Palestinian territory'. *The Lancet*, Available at: http://www.thelancet.com/pb/assets/raw/Lancet/abstracts/ palestine/palestine2011-4.pdf [Accessed: 13 August 2021].

Stewart, Heather and Elgot, Jessica. (2018) 'Labour antisemitism row: Unite boss accuses Jewish leaders of "truculent hostility"'. *The Guardian*, Available at: https://www.theguardian.com/politics/2018/aug/16/labour-antisemitism-row-unite-boss-accuses-jewish-leaders-of-truculent-hostility [Accessed: 10 November 2020].

Trudell, John. (1986). 'Rich Man's War' Lyrics. *AKA Graffiti Man*, Available at: https://www.antiwarsongs.org/canzone.php?id=50625&lang=en [Accessed: 12 August 2021].

US Campaign For Palestinian Rights. (ND) 'Rooting Resistance'. Available at: https://uscpr.org/rooting-resistance [Accessed: 17 August 2021].

'US ends aid to Palestinian refugee agency Unrwa'. (2018) *BBC News*, Available at: https://www.bbc.com/news/world-us-canada-45377336 [Accessed: 18 September 2020].

Warrior, Robert Allen. (1989) 'Canaanites, cowboys, and Indians: Deliverance, conquest, and liberation theology today'. Available at: https://www.rmselca.org/sites/rmselca.org/files/media/canaanites_cowboys_and_indians.pdf [Accessed: 12 August 2021].

Weeber, Christine. (2020) 'Why capitalize "Indigenous"?' Available at: https://www.sapiens.org/language/capitalize-indigenous/ [Accessed: 14 April 2022].

Wootlif, Raoul. (2018a) 'Final text of Jewish nation-state law, approved by the Knesset early on July 19'. *The Times of Israel*, Available at: https://www.timesofisrael.com/final-text-of-jewish-nation-state-bill-set-to-become-law/ [Accessed: 10 November 2020].

Wootlif, Raoul. (2018b) 'Israel passes Jewish state law, enshrining "national home of the Jewish people"'. *The Times of Israel*, Available at: https://www.timesofisrael.com/knesset-votes-contentious-jewish-nation-state-bill-into-law/ [Accessed: 10 November 2020].

Young, Robert (2014) 'Dar al-Ma'mun conversations: Robert J.C. Young'. Available at: https://www.youtube.com/watch?v=0-mYkMUHh3c&ab_channel=Daral-Ma%27m%C3%BBn [Accessed: 8 October 2016].

INDEX

Abu Arab 188–93
   'Ya yuma lou jani al eid' 189
   'Hadi ya bahar hadi' 190
   'Ya yuma, fi daga 'ala babna' 191–3
Abu-Fakhr, Saqr *The Palestinian National Movement: from the Armed Struggle to a Disarmed State* 11
Abulhawa, Susan 21, 24, 116, 127, 129, 150–3
   Mornings in Jenin 116, 129, 150–3
   The Blue Between Sky and Water 115, 116, 153
Abu-Lughod, Ibrahim 13, 117, 123
Abu-Lughod, Lila (*Nakba: Palestine, 1948 and the Claims of Memory*) 11–13
Abu-Manneh, Bashir (*The Palestinian Novel: From 1948 to the Present*) 138–41, 143, 145–6
Adonis 23, 75, 88–90, 133
   Concerto Al-Quds 88–90
Adorno, Theodor 4, 40–1, 71, 113, 198
affiliations 8, 27–8, 33, 52, 82, 100, 119–21, 124, 126, 152, 168, 208
Ahluwalia, Pal 27–8
Akash, Munir 87, 91
Alajaji, Sylvia 180–1, 183–4
Al-Ali, Naji 24, 161, 166, 171–7, 188–9, 210
Al Aqsa Mosque 6–7, 95, 185
Al-Araj, Bassel 198–200, 209
   I Have Found My Answers 199
Alareer, Refaat 204, 208
Al Ashiqeen 24, 79, 185–8
Al Jazeera 200–1
al murabitat 7 see also murabata
Al Qassim, Samih 51
Al Quds 7, 21, 185, 193, 199–200
   see also Jerusalem
Althusser, Louis 48
Al-Zeer, Atta 185

American Indian 85, 87, 88, 92, 96, 97, 98, 99, 212
Anderson, Benedict (*Imagined Communities*) 5–6, 8–10, 22, 44, 116, 130
anticipatory discourse '"Outlines of a better world": rerouting postcolonialism' 4
   see also Williams, Patrick
anti-colonial discourse 43
anti-Semitism 3, 16–17, 91
Antoon, Sinan 67–8, 91
Aoude, Ibrahim 24, 117, 201–3, 205–7
apartheid wall 163, 165–6, 171, 176–8
Arab Nationalist Movement 11, 50, 143, 211
Arab Studies Quarterly 117, 137, 168, 201
Arafat, Yasser 41, 123, 198–9
Ashcroft, Bill 27–8
Ashour, Radwa 21, 24, 116, 127, 129, 151, 153–61, 172
   'Radwa Ashour's Tantoura: Palestinian nakba and resisting fait accompli': An Interview 158–9
   The Woman from Tantoura 115, 129 153–61
Association of Arab-American University Graduates (AAUG) 117

Bailey, Kristian Davis 80, 82–3
   'Black-Palestinian Solidarity in the Ferguson-Gaza Era' 80–1
   see also Black-Palestinian Solidarity
Balfour, Arthur 38–9
Ball, Anna 3, 31, 79
   Palestinian Literature and Film in Postcolonial Feminist Perspective 3
Baqa'a camp 125–6, 130, 174, 179
barbed wire fences 142, 158–60
Barghouti, Mourid 1–2, 10, 14, 23–4, 29, 64, 103–13

I Saw Ramallah 23–4, 116, 129, 131–2, 137–8, 174–5
I Was Born There, I Was Born Here 24, 77, 106–7, 111, 113, 116, 129, 133–5
'Midnight' 103–13
Midnight and other poems 105
'Verbicide' 2
Barghouti, Omar 98
Baroud, Ramzy 24, 84, 86, 201, 203–4, 207–8
Basic Law (Israel) 15–16, 90
beginnings 2, 17, 21–3, 27–8, 35, 37–9, 43–4, 52, 61, 76, 103, 117–19, 123– 4, 134, 150, 160, 198
Bernard, Anna 3, 29, 31, 120, 129, 130–2
Rhetorics of Belonging, Nation, Narration, and Israel/Palestine 3
betrayal 62, 173, 198, 202, 203
bitterness 63, 166, 167, 168, 171
Black Lives Matter (BLM) 30, 80, 81
Black-Palestinian solidarity 80, 81, 221
borders 6, 8, 9, 13, 15, 19, 20, 23, 45, 46, 62, 63, 66, 69, 85, 98, 130, 131, 132, 141–4, 158, 159, 160, 175, 184, 185, 192, 210
Boycott, Divest, and Sanctions (BDS) 98, 204, 205
British mandate 20, 71, 185, 186, 212
Brittain, Victoria ('They had to die: assassination against liberation') 175
Buraq Uprising 185, 186
Butler, Judith 13, 136
'"What Shall We Do Without Exile": Said and Darwish Address the Future' 13, 137

Cabral, Amilcar ('National Liberation and Culture') 45, 49, 203
Camp David Accords 123
Canaan/Canaanite 86, 87, 88, 92, 93, 181
Carleton, Richard 138–41
catastrophe 150, 154, 164, 171, 209, 212
Cesaire, Aime 45, 146–7
checkpoints 8, 23, 65, 106, 108, 123, 135, 137, 142, 144, 165, 199, 215, 224
Chomsky, Noam 39, 43, 47, 48
Manufacturing Consent: the Political Economy of the Mass Media 47

Church of the Holy Sepulchre 7
Cleary, Joe (*Literature, Partition and the Nation State: Culture and Conflict in Ireland, Israel and Palestine*) 141, 143–5, 150
combatant writer 140
consummate negativity 4, 113
creative resistance 31, 48, 54, 126
critical consciousness 22, 27, 28, 33, 40, 171, 175

Dabashi, Hamid (*On Edward Said: Remembrance of Things Past*) 43
dabkeh 24, 181–5
Dalton, Roque 166
dal'una 185
dance 24, 127, 166, 179–85, 190
Darwish, Mahmoud 1, 4, 10, 13–14, 22–4, 41, 50–1, 55–75, 83–8, 91–6, 101–4, 106–7, 109, 115–16, 125–7, 129, 131–3, 135, 137, 154, 169–70, 189–91, 210
The Adam of Two Edens 86–7
Almond Blossoms and Beyond 55
The Butterfly's Burden 72
'Earth Presses Against Us' 62, 66, 116, 170
'Edward Said: A Contrapuntal Reading' 55–6, 59
In the Presence of Absence 61–2, 67, 85, 116
Memory for Forgetfulness: August, Beirut, 1982 62, 116, 154
'Mural' 24, 42, 115
'The "Red Indian's" Penultimate Speech to the White Man' 84, 214
'Sabra and Shatila' 65
'A State of Siege' 42, 62, 70, 72–3
Unfortunately, It Was Paradise 190
decolonial studies 4, 16, 43, 44
decolonization 15, 52, 106, 146, 193, 203
defeatism 103, 112, 138, 158, 173, 197, 198, 199
dehumanization 124, 125, 140, 146, 148, 198
detachment 120, 131
deterritorialization 101
diaspora 14–16, 70, 84, 127–30, 133, 200

difficulty of representation 24, 121, 127, 129, 132–5, 141, 153, 179
dispersion 14, 41, 125–7, 141
displacement 14, 23, 82–3, 98, 117, 120, 126, 129–32, 134–5
disposession 5, 11, 21, 27, 33, 37–8, 41, 43, 50, 55, 63, 65–6, 68, 81, 87, 97–8, 102, 125–9, 132–4, 138, 140, 142–3, 145, 151, 158–9, 165, 169, 180, 182, 191, 202, 214

Eagleton, Terry *Nationalism, Colonialism and Literature* 3, 5
El-Funoun 180, 184
El-Kurd, Mohammed 184, 193, 201
  Rifqa 193
El-Kurd, Muna 184
envision(ing) a future Palestine 15, 201, 205, 206, 207
  see also imagining Palestine
ethnic cleansing 1, 5, 8, 10–11, 13, 15, 17, 19–22, 25, 27, 37, 66, 90–1, 93, 115, 133–4, 163, 170, 180, 183, 193, 199–200, 203–5, 208, 212–13
  The Ethnic Cleansing of Palestine 11, 19, 21, 115, 134, 203
  see also Pappe, Ilan
exclusivist ideology 6–7, 9–10, 15, 90, 149
  ISIS (Daesh) 9
exile 2, 4, 6, 8, 10, 12–16, 18, 20, 22–5, 27–8, 30, 32–4, 36, 38, 40–4, 46, 48, 50–2, 54–67, 69, 73–4, 79, 82, 90–1, 107, 116, 118–21, 123–7, 129–37, 142, 150, 152, 156, 158–9, 167–8, 170, 174–5, 180–1, 185, 189–90, 193, 200–1, 208, 210–11
expulsion 10, 12, 13, 18, 19, 20, 21, 34, 159, 182, 203

Falk, Richard 'Rethinking the Palestinian Future' ('Moral imagination') 126
Fanon, Frantz 29, 30, 45, 48–9, 51–2, 83, 103, 106, 112, 128, 138–41, 146–7, 149, 152, 172, 180, 193, 194, 203–4
  The Wretched of the Earth 52, 146, 180
fellah(in) 181, 183
Ferguson 81, 214
Ferguson-Gaza 80–1, 214

fidayee, fidayeen 12, 106, 149, 152, 168, 179, 191–3, 216
fighting writer 51–2
filiation 27, 33, 52, 119–21, 124, 126
Fisk, Robert (*Pity the Nation: Lebanon at War*) 152
'From Akka Prison' 185–6
Floyd, George 30, 80, 93, 214

Gandhi, Mahatma 145
Gaza 2, 7, 14, 25, 30, 53, 62, 69, 75, 78, 80–1, 87, 91, 100–2, 116, 121–2, 129, 136–8, 153, 166, 170–1, 174, 184–5, 193, 195, 199–201, 204, 213–16
Genet, Jean 67–8, 75, 80, 155–6
  'Four Hours in Shatila' 68
genocide 2, 79–80, 96, 115, 170, 182–3, 204, 212
ghurba 127, 130, 150
Ginsberg, Terri 24, 201, 203, 207–8
  Visualizing the Palestinian Struggle: Towards a Critical Analytic of Palestine Solidarity Film 208
Gramsci, Antonio 10, 48, 74
Great Dance of Return 184
Great March of Return 53, 184, 213
Gulf, the 7, 10, 24, 86

Haganah 19, 128
Hagopian, Elaine 117
Hall, Stuart ('Cultural Identity and Diaspora' 16–17, 70, 85, 91, 98, 133, 180, 184)
Hamas 6, 24
Hamdi, Hamdi K. 24, 169, 171, 211
  'Oleuropein, a non-toxic olive iridoid, is an anti-tumor agent and cytoskeleton disruptor' 167
Hamdi, Khalil 11, 12, 202, 211
Hamdi, Tahrir 22, 47–8, 130, 175, 214
  'The Arab Intellectual and the Present Moment' 47
  'Bearing Witness in Palestinian Resistance Literature' 175
  'Darwish's Geography: Space, Place and Identity under Construction' 22

'The Power of Poetry to Travel: An Interview with Mourid Barghouti' 130
'Reading, Imagining and Constructing Iraq' 48
Hammad, Suheir 23, 75, 78–80, 82–3
  Born Palestinian, Born Black & The Gaza Suite 78
  'a prayer band' 82
  'silence' 79–80
Hammoud, Sheikh Maher 210
Hanna, Atallah 7
Hanthala 24, 171–7, 189, 191, 210
Haram al-Sharif 7, 212
Harlow, Barbara 48, 52, 165, 176
  After lives: Legacies of Revolutionary Writing 176
  Resistance Literature 48, 165
  'Return to Haifa: "Opening the Borders" in Palestinian Literature' 48
Hebrew
  archives 18, 19
  God 37, 38, 39
  language 13, 19
  state 136
  world 38
henna 187
heritage 24, 60, 128, 152, 169, 179–80, 183–5, 195, 216
Herman, Edward (*Manufacturing Consent: the Political Economy of the Mass Media*) 47
Hezbollah 10, 45–6, 48, 110, 112, 153, 159
Hijazi, Fouad 185–6, 216
Hill, Marc Lamont 164
Hirsch, Marianne (*The Generation of Postmemory: Writing and Visual Culture After the Holocaust*) 10, 12
  see also postmemory
historical pain 200, 205, 211
  see also Barghouti, Mourid
hooks, bell (*Yearning: Race, Gender, and Cultural Politics*) 27–32, 39, 44, 54, 69, 75, 77, 79, 168
Hughes, Langston ('The Negro Speaks of Rives') 83

Ibrahim, Nuh 185, 215
identity politics 35
ideological state apparatuses 10, 47, 213
Ihmoud, Sarah 7
imagining
  Palestine 1–2, 4–5, 8, 10, 14–15, 22, 25, 44, 61, 74, 97, 128, 168, 195, 209
  see also envisioning a future Palestine
  victory 103, 108–9
indigeneity 84–7, 96–8
indigenous people 17, 84–5, 87–8, 91, 96, 98–103, 144, 165, 168, 190–1
intellectual 14–15, 17, 22–5, 28–35, 39–44, 46, 48–57, 62, 70, 72, 74–5, 77, 98–100, 103, 106, 112–13, 115, 117–20, 122–3, 126, 131–2, 135, 140, 164, 168, 172, 190, 195, 198, 201, 204, 206–9, 211
  oppositional 28, 31, 33–4, 43, 203, 211
International Holocaust Remembrance Alliance (IHRA) 16, 17, 90, 91
Intifada 83, 108, 75, 84, 198, 199, 200, 215
intransigence 25, 40, 41, 44, 198, 208
Iraq 6, 9, 10, 19, 20, 47, 48, 49, 59, 122, 142, 143, 144, 213, 214
Irving, Sarah 178, 179, 215, 216
  Leila Khaled: Icon of Palestinian Revolution 215
Islamic umma 6, 9
Israeli apartheid 60, 165, 171, 207
Israeli Occupation Forces 45, 65, 193, 198

Jahaleen Bedouin 33, 34
Jamjoum, Muhammed 185, 186, 215
Jerusalem 7, 11, 20, 21, 34, 36, 37, 88, 89, 95, 122, 128, 133, 134, 160, 185, 193, 199, 200, 215, 216
Jim Crow era 82, 214
Jordan 11, 12, 20, 63, 77, 118, 122, 126, 180, 138, 144, 165, 168, 174, 179, 200, 202, 210, 212, 213, 221, 223
Jordan, June 23, 75, 76, 77, 78, 79, 80, 103, 163
  'Moving Towards Home' 75, 77, 78
Joudah, Fady 72, 93, 94, 214

Kanafani, Ghassan 12, 22, 24, 42, 45, 48–54, 116, 122, 127, 129, 138–53, 157–8, 172, 175, 189, 198, 203, 213

Men in the Sun and Other Palestinian Stories 22, 116, 129, 142, 143, 145, 159
Palestine's Children: Returning to Haifa and Other Stories 22, 52, 53, 116, 122, 129, 145–8, 150, 198
Resistance Literature in Occupied Palestine (1966) 22
Resistance Literature in Occupied Palestine (1968) 51
'Thoughts on Change and the "Blind Language"' 52
Khaled, Leila 24, 178, 202, 215, 216
Khalidi, Rashid 5, 6, 8
Palestinian Identity: The Construction of Modern Consciousness 5
Kelley, Robin D. G. 164, 165
keys 8, 124, 157, 158
King, Martin Luther 164

late style 23, 28, 29, 40–6, 52, 57, 58, 71, 88, 104, 105, 108, 123, 168
lateness 22, 27, 40, 44, 71, 113
Lebanon 3, 10, 12, 45, 46, 48, 63, 75, 110, 118, 126, 129, 130, 138, 144, 153, 158, 159, 160, 166, 172, 174, 178, 182, 185, 192, 200, 203, 206, 209, 210, 214, 216

Malcolm X 164, 168
Manifest Destiny 97, 98, 99
Maqusi, Samar 126
Maracle, Lee 23, 75, 95–103
'Remembering Mahmoud, 1986' 100–1
'Song to a Palestinian Child' 99
margin 28–33, 43, 44, 50, 54, 56, 59, 69, 75, 77, 79, 80, 83, 122
marginal spaces 29, 30, 31, 33, 44, 95, 119, 168
marginality 30, 31
Marj Ibn Amer 184
martyr 42, 53, 56, 69, 71, 72–74, 75, 105, 106, 107, 168, 176, 179, 181, 185–188, 192, 193, 198, 199, 210, 211, 213, 215–216
Masalha, Nur 2, 18, 19, 24, 38, 182, 201, 203, 207, 208
Expulsion of the Palestinians: The Concept of 'Transfer' in Zionist Political Thought, 1882–1948 18–19, 203
Palestine: A Four Thousand Year History 1–2
The Palestine Nakba: Decolonising History, Narrating the Subaltern, Reclaiming Memory 182
Masjid Al Aqsa 6, 7, 212
Masri, Bassem 81
massacres 12, 13, 19, 20, 21, 45, 62, 63, 64, 65, 68, 69, 75, 80, 83, 93, 101, 115, 152, 154, 156, 158, 166, 169, 185, 202, 214, 215
Mattar, Karim 127, 129, 131, 132
'Mourid Barghouti's "multiple displacements": exile and the national checkpoint in Palestinian literature' 132
Mattawa, Khaled 41, 42, 88
mawwal 186, 189, 190, 192, 215, 216
media 7, 10, 17, 24, 35, 37, 46, 47, 77, 81, 111, 112, 138, 156, 163, 164, 177, 187, 193, 194, 201, 204, 208, 213, 215
Meir, Golda 35, 128, 181, 184
memoricide 93, 115, 182
memory 9–14, 29, 53, 62, 64, 67–9, 85, 102–3, 108, 115–16, 123, 154–6, 158, 182
Moore, Lindsey 3, 31, 118, 119, 124, 180
Narrating Postcolonial Arab Nations: Egypt, Algeria, Lebanon, Palestine 3, 116
remembering... towards the future 116, 180
Mossad 48, 157, 166, 175, 215
Mullen, Bill 165
multiple displacements 23, 132, 134–5
Musallam, Basim 35
murabata/ al murabitat 7

Nakba 10, 12–14, 17, 19–20, 25, 27, 32, 37, 51, 61, 63, 68, 71, 83–4, 91, 102, 116, 127–8, 133–4, 142–3, 150, 153–4, 157–8, 164, 169, 172, 174, 182, 199, 205, 208, 210, 212
nakbas 10, 13–14, 25, 71, 158
Naksa 28, 34, 37, 50, 63, 116–18, 122, 126, 132, 138, 141, 145, 150, 169, 183
Nashef, Hania (*Palestinian Culture and the Nakba: Bearing Witness*) 174
Nasrallah, Hassan 45, 110–11
Nassar, Jamal 24, 198–9, 201, 205, 207
national culture 49

national discourse 6, 7
national identity 4–5, 8, 25, 35, 60–1, 115, 118, 120–1, 130, 158, 180, 183–4, 200, 203, 208
national liberation 3, 49, 61
nationalism 6, 35, 42, 60, 80, 82, 96–7, 141, 143, 145, 181, 214
nativist/nativism 35, 49
new generation (of Palestinians) 52, 81, 160

occupation 7, 10, 13–14, 22, 25, 30, 34, 45–6, 51, 56, 60–2, 65, 73, 82, 89, 103–8, 113, 116, 121, 123, 129–36, 139–40, 142, 149, 159, 171, 176–7, 180, 183–5, 189, 192–3, 198–9, 204, 209, 212, 215–16
olive trees 13, 64, 71–2, 99, 136, 166, 168–71, 190–1
one state solution 207
Oslo Accords 41, 123, 134, 197, 199

Palestine Liberation Organnization (PLO) 63, 64, 67, 80, 81, 141, 143
Palestine Research Centre 128
Palestinian Authority 92, 111, 134, 198, 207
Palestinian experience 8, 10, 24, 28, 61, 73, 127, 129, 130, 131, 132, 133, 134, 135, 171, 176, 179, 187, 209
Palestinian national identity 5, 8, 35, 121, 180, 183, 203, 208
Palestinianness 28, 42, 78, 123, 138, 183–5
Pappe, Ilan 11, 13, 17, 19–21, 24, 115, 134, 163, 182, 188, 201, 203, 205, 207–9, 212
  The Ethnic Cleansing of Palestine 11, 19, 21, 115, 134, 203
  'Ilan Pappe's Interview on *HARDtalk* 19, 45, 140
permission to narrate 18, 36, 158, 163, 209
placelessness 118–19, 142
Plan D or Dalet 19
Popular Front for the Liberation of Palestine (PFLP) 12, 50, 138–9, 143, 215
population transfer 18

(post) catastrophe 56
postcolonialism 3–4, 28–9, 74, 98, 127
postmemory 9–10, 12–14, 29
postmillennial era 3, 169, 173
postmodernism 42
post-nationalism 42
prisons 12, 30, 135, 142, 172, 210
Promised Land 1–2, 38, 84–5, 88, 99, 133

Qabaha, Ahmed 119–20, 124
Qabbani, Nizar 122

radical openness 29, 31–2, 54, 77, 168
Ramallah 11–12, 23–4, 69, 73, 116, 129–38, 151, 175, 183, 185, 199
Red Tuesday 185
refugees 12, 21, 22, 66, 77, 118, 126, 129, 142, 143, 145, 158, 159, 172, 173, 174, 206, 207, 209, 210
refugee camps 22–5, 29–30, 32, 61–5, 67, 69, 91, 121, 126, 130, 132, 140, 142, 144, 158–60, 167, 172, 174, 176, 179, 189–90, 199–200, 203, 208–10
rehumanization 146, 150, 152, 191
repeated pain 157
repetition 13, 14, 68, 72, 93, 103
resistance literature 22, 48–52, 140–1
resistance strategies 24, 201, 202, 203, 204
restlessness 22–3, 32–3, 43, 54, 62, 70, 130, 132, 137
return 1–2, 9, 14, 16–17, 21–4, 33, 40, 52–3, 59–61, 66–7, 70, 76–7, 82, 84–6, 90–1, 97, 100, 102–3, 110, 116, 122–4, 126–7, 130–2, 134, 136–8, 145, 155, 157, 160–1, 172, 174, 176, 180, 184, 189–91, 201, 204–7, 209–11, 213
revolutionary violence 141, 146, 153, 204
Rice, Condoleeza 48
right of return 2, 14, 24, 61, 76, 102–3, 124, 201, 206–7, 209
Rowe, Nicholas 182–3

Sabra and Shatila massacres 75, 154, 214
Sadat, Anwar 123
Said, Edward 2–3, 6–8, 10, 13–14, 18, 21–5, 27–49, 52, 54–63, 67–71, 77, 83, 85, 88–9, 91, 94, 99–101,

103, 105, 108, 113, 115–33, 136–8, 140–2, 146–50, 152–3, 157–9, 164, 167–72, 179, 181, 189, 192–3, 195, 197–8, 200–1, 203, 209–10, 215
After the Last Sky: Palestinian Lives 8, 23, 40, 62, 116–18, 121–5, 127, 136–7
Beginnings: Intention and Method 23, 37, 52, 124
Conversations with Edward Said and Tariq Ali 34, 123
Covering Islam: How the Media and the Experts Determine How We see the
Culture and Imperialism 44, 49
Edward Said's interview on *HARDtalk/Part 2* 45, 140
Humanism and Democratic Criticism 39
'On Lost Causes' 24–5, 41, 195, 197–8, 200
'My Guru: Elegy for Ibrahim Abu-Lughod' 117
'On Jean Genet's Late Works' 67
On Late Style: Music and Literature Against the Grain 40
Orientalism: Western Conceptions of the Orient 3, 23, 35–6, 46, 117
Out of Place: A Memoir 23, 49, 116, 118, 120–2, 124–5, 127
The Question of Palestine 23, 35–6, 39, 129
The Pen and the Sword: Conversations with David Barsamian 118
The Politics of Dispossession 68, 128, 138, 158
Power, Politics and Culture: Interviews with Edward W. Said 45–6, 159, 164
'Reflections on Exile' 41, 59–60, 120, 167
Reflections on Exile and Other Literary and Cultural Essays 41, 59–60, 120, 16
Representations of the Intellectual 23, 32
Rest of the World 36, 46
'Salman Rushdie interviews Edward Said' 127, 215
'In Search of Palestine: Edward Said's Return Home' 40
The World, the Text and the Critic 22–3, 28, 52, 124, 7

Salaita, Steven 24, 84, 92, 95, 96, 97–201, 204, 214
  Inter/Nationalism: Decolonizing Native America and Palestine 214
Sayigh, Rosemary (*The Palestinians: From Peasants to Revolutionaries*) 212
Sazzad, Rehnuma (*Edward Said's Concepts of Exile*) 33–4
sectarianism 49, 213
secular criticism 28, 43, 52
Sen, Somdeep 199
  'It's Nakba, Not a Party: ReStating the (Continued) Legacy of the Oslo Accords' 199
settler colonialism 5, 7, 15, 29, 61, 88, 127, 177–8, 180, 202, 204
Shahid, Leila 64, 214
  'The Sabra and Shatila Massacres: Eyewitness Reports' 64
Sheikh Jarrah 21, 185, 193–4, 200, 208, 213, 215
shock and awe 20–1, 47, 148, 213
Shtaya, Mahfoutha 169
siege 2, 14, 23, 28, 30, 42, 55, 61–4, 69–75, 80, 89, 93, 96, 105, 107, 116, 121, 132, 140, 153, 158, 165–6, 168
Siklawi, Rami 24, 117, 201, 203, 207, 209–10
  'The Palestinian Refugee Camps in Lebanon Post 1990: Dilemmas of Survival and Return to Palestine' 209
Soja, Edward 14, 24, 29, 31, 63, 69, 133, 168–9, 171
  Thirdspace: Journeys to Los Angeles and Other Real-and-Imagined Places 14
solidarity 4, 17, 23–4, 31–3, 50–1, 56, 67, 75, 77–83, 91, 95, 97–101, 103, 123, 126, 163–5, 168, 171, 201, 203, 208, 214–15
song 9, 24, 36, 59, 66, 79–80, 94–6, 99, 115, 127, 165, 168, 179–82, 185–91, 193–4, 202, 215–16
speaking truth to power 28, 33, 79
Spivak, Gayatri 28, 157
  'Thinking about Edward Said: Pages from a Memoir'

Srivastava, Neelam 141, 145–6
    'Towards a critique of colonial violence: Fanon, Gandhi 141
strategic essentialism 157
sumud 6–7, 24, 118, 123, 150, 168–9, 171, 187–9, 193, 208
Swedenburg, Ted 180–1
    'The Palestinian Peasant as National Signifier' 181 Sykes-Picot Agreement 10, 145
Syria 6–7, 9–10, 48–9, 88, 122, 129, 138, 174, 192, 200, 210, 214

trauma 10, 13, 18, 29, 44, 127, 143, 154–5, 157–8, 167, 213
trauma studies 10, 127
trialectics 14, 29, 63–4, 69, 133, 170
    spatiality, historicality and sociality 14, 29, 63–4, 69, 133, 170
triangular time 133
Trio Joubran 75, 93–5
troublemaking 118
Trudell, John 23, 75, 95–6
two state solution 206, 207

Umma (of Islam) 6–7, 9
United Nations Relief and Works Agency (UNRWA) 21–2, 213
uprooting 33–4, 60, 136, 166, 168–70

Vico, Giambattista 37–8
Viswanathan, Gauri 33, 164
    Masks of Conquest: Literary Study and British Rule in India 33

Warrior, Robert Allen 87
Waters, Roger 23, 39, 75, 83, 93–5
West Bank 2, 14, 20, 34, 52, 62, 69, 75, 82, 108, 122, 129, 132, 136–8, 169–71, 174, 183–4, 200, 204, 213, 216
White, Ben 214
Williams, Patrick 3–4, 10, 28–9, 31, 33, 39, 74, 98, 104–5, 113, 125, 127–9,132,141
    '"Outlines of a better world": rerouting postcolonialism' 4, 75, 98, 104, 141, 182
    '"Naturally, I reject the term 'diaspora'": Said and Palestinian Dispossession" 127–8
worldmaking 164–5
worldliness 28, 43, 72, 89, 131
Wounded Knee 87, 91, 100–3

Young, Robert 28

zaghroota/zaghareet 187–8
Zangwill, Israel 18, 38
Zionist settler colonialism 5, 7, 203

www.ingramcontent.com/pod-product-compliance
Lightning Source LLC
Chambersburg PA
CBHW062140300426
44115CB00012BA/1991